Statistics and Computing

Series Editors
J. Chambers
D. Hand
W. Härdle

Robert A. Muenchen · Joseph M. Hilbe

R for Stata Users

 Springer

Robert A. Muenchen
University of Tennessee
Office of Information Technology
Statistical Consulting Center
916 Volunteer Blvd.
Knoxville TN 37996-0520
Stokeley Management Center
USA
muenchen.bob@gmail.com

Joseph M. Hilbe
7242 W. Heritage Way
Florence Arizona 85132
USA
hilbe@asu.edu

ISBN 978-1-4614-2596-0   ISBN 978-1-4419-1318-0(eBook)
DOI 10.1007/978-1-4419-1318-0
Springer New York Dordrecht Heidelberg London

Printed on acid-free paper

Springer is part of Springer Science+Business Media (www.springer.com)

Preface

While R and Stata have many features in common, their languages are quite different. Our goal in writing this book is to help you translate what you know about Stata into a working knowledge of R as quickly and easily as possible. We point out how they differ using terminology with which you are familiar and we include many Stata terms in the table of contents and index. You can find any R function by looking up its counterpart in Stata and vice versa. We provide many example programs done in R and Stata so that you can see how they compare topic by topic.

When finished, you should be able to use R to:

- Read data from various types of text files and Stata data sets.
- Manage your data through transformations, recodes, and combining data sets from both the add-cases and add-variables approaches and restructuring data from wide to long formats and vice versa.
- Create publication quality graphs including bar, histogram, pie, line, scatter, regression, box, error bar, and interaction plots.
- Perform the basic types of analyses to measure strength of association and group differences and be able to know where to turn to cover much more complex methods.

Who This Book Is For

This book is, of course, for people who already know Stata. It may also be useful to R users wishing to learn Stata. However, we explain none of the Stata programs, only the R ones and how the packages differ, so it is not ideal for that purpose.

This book is based on *R for SAS and SPSS Users* [34]. However, there is quite a bit of additional material covered here, and, of course, the comparative coverage is completely different.

Who This Book Is Not For

We make no effort to teach statistics or graphics. Although we briefly state the goal and assumptions of each analysis, we do not cover their formulas or derivations. We have more than enough to discuss without tackling those topics too. This is also not a book about writing R functions, it is about using the thousands that already exist. We will write only a few very short functions. If you want to learn more about writing functions, we recommend John Chamber's *Software for Data Analysis: Programming with R* [5]. However, if you know Stata, reading this book should ease your transition to more complex books like that.

Practice Data Sets and Programs

All of the programs, data sets, and files that we use in this book are available for download at `http://r4stats.com`. A file containing corrections and clarifications is also available there.

Acknowledgments

We are very grateful for the many people who have helped make this book possible, including the developers of the S language on which R is based, Rick Becker, John Chambers, and Allan Wilks; the people who started R itself, Ross Ihaka and Robert Gentleman; the many other R developers for providing such wonderful tools for free and all the R-help participants who have kindly answered so many questions. Virtually all of the examples we present here are modestly tweaked versions of countless posts to the R-help discussion list, as well as a few Statalist posts. All we add is the selection, organization, explanation, and comparison.

We are especially grateful to the people who provided advice, caught typos, and suggested improvements, including Raymond R. Balise, Patrick Burns, Peter Flom, Chun Huang, Martin Gregory, Warren Lambert, Mathew Marler, Ralph O'Brien, Wayne Richter, Charilaos Skiadas, Andreas Stefik, Phil Spector, Michael Wexler, Graham Williams, Andrew Yee, and several anonymous reviewers.

A special thanks goes to Hadley Wickham, who provided much guidance on his `ggplot2` graphics package. Thanks to Gabor Grothendieck, Lauri Nikkinen, and Marc Schwarz and for the R-Help help discussion that led to Section 10.14: "Selecting First or Last Observations per Group." Thanks to Gabor Grothendieck also for a detailed discussion that lead to Section 10.4: "Multiple Conditional Transformations." Thanks to Michael A. McGuire for his assistance with all things Macintosh.

The first author is grateful to his wife, Carla Foust, and sons Alexander and Conor, who put up with many lost weekends as he wrote this book.

The second author wishes to thank Springer editor John Kimmel for suggesting his participation in this project and his wife, Cheryl, children Heather, Michael and Mitchell, and Sirr for their patience while he spent time away from them working on this book.

Robert A. Muenchen

muenchen.bob@gmail.com

Knoxville, Tennessee

January 2010

Joseph M. Hilbe

hilbe@asu.edu

Florence, Arizona

January 2010

About the Authors

Robert A. Muenchen is a consulting statistician and author of the book, *R for SAS and SPSS Users* [34]. He is currently the manager of Research Computing Support (formerly the Statistical Consulting Center) at the University of Tennessee. Bob has conducted research for a variety of public and private organizations and has co-authored over 50 articles in scientific journals and conference proceedings.

Bob has served on the advisory boards of the SAS Institute, SPSS Inc., the Statistical Graphics Corporation, and *PC Week Magazine*. His suggested improvements have been incorporated into SAS, SPSS, JMP, STATGRAPHICS, and several R packages.

His research interests include statistical computing, data graphics and visualization, text analysis, data mining, psychometrics, and resampling.

Joseph M. Hilbe is Solar System Ambassador with NASA/Jet Propulsion Laboratory, California Institute of Technology, an adjunct professor of statistics at Arizona State, and emeritus professor at the University of Hawaii. He is an elected Fellow of the American Statistical Association and of the Royal Statistical Society and is an elected member of the International Statistical Institute.

Professor Hilbe was the first editor of the *Stata Technical Bulletin*, later to become the *Stata Journal*, and was one of Stata Corporation's first senior statisticians (1991–1993). Hilbe is also the author of a number of textbooks, including *Logistic Regression Models* [21], *Negative Binomial Regression* [23], and with J. Hardin, *Generalized Linear Models and Extensions*, 2nd ed. [18] and *Generalized Estimating Equations* [19].

Contents

List of Tables

List of Figures

1

Introduction

1.1 Overview

R [38] is a powerful and flexible environment for research computing. Written by Ross Ihaka, Robert Gentleman (hence the name "R"), the R Core Development Team, and an army of volunteers, R provides a wider range of analytical and graphical commands than any other software. The fact that this level of power is available free of charge has dramatically changed the landscape of research software.

R is a variation of the S language, developed by John Chambers, Rick Becker, and others at Bell Labs[1]. The Association of Computing Machinery presented John Chambers with a Software System Award and said that the S language "... *will forever alter the way people analyze, visualize, and manipulate data...*" and went on to say that it is "... *an elegant, widely accepted, and enduring software system, with conceptual integrity....*" The original S language is still commercially available as Tibco Spotfire S+. Most programs written in the S language will run in R.

Stata, a product of Stata Corporation, has not yet incorporated an interface to R in its software, but users have already posted programs to use R within the Stata environment. It is expected that more facilities of this sort will be developed in the near future.

For each aspect of R we discuss, we will compare and contrast it with Stata. Many of the topics end with example programs that do almost identical things in both software applications. R programs are often longer than similar Stata code, but this is typically the case because R functions are more specific than Stata commands.

Many R functions will appear familiar to Stata users; that is, R functions such as lm or glm will appear somewhat similar to Stata's regress and glm commands. There are other aspects of the two languages, however, that may

---

[1] For a fascinating history of S and R, see Appendix A of *Software for Data Analysis: Programming with R* [5].

R.A. Muenchen, J.M. Hilbe, *R for Stata Users*, Statistics and Computing, DOI 10.1007/978-1-4419-1318-0_1,

appear more confusing at first. We hope to ease that confusion by focusing on both the similarities and differences between R and Stata in this text. When we examine a particular analysis (e.g., comparing two groups with a t-test) someone who knows Stata will have very little trouble figuring out what R is doing. However, the basics of the R language are very different, so that is where we will spend the majority of our time.

We introduce topics in a carefully chosen order, so it is best to read from beginning to end the first time through, even if you think you do not need to know a particular topic. Later you can skip directly to the section you need. We include a fair amount of redundancy on key topics to help teach those topics and to make it easier to read just one section as a future reference. The glossary in Appendix A defines R concepts in terms that Stata users will understand and provides parallel definitions using R terminology.

1.2 Similarities Between R and Stata

Stata is an excellent statistics package. One of the authors has used Stata for over 20 years and has authored many Stata commands.

Perhaps more than any other two research computing environments, R and Stata share many of the features that make them outstanding:

- Both include rich programming languages designed for writing new analytic methods, not just a set of prewritten commands.
- Both contain extensive sets of analytic commands written in their own languages.
- The pre-written commands in R, and most in Stata, are visible and open for you to change as you please.
- Both save command or function output in a form you can easily use as input to further analysis.
- Both do modeling in a way that allows you to readily apply your models for tasks such as making predictions on new data sets. Stata calls these *postestimation commands* and R calls them *extractor functions*.
- In both, when you write a new command, it is on an equal footing with commands written by the developers. There are no additional "Developer's Kits" to purchase.
- Both have legions of devoted users who have written numerous extensions and who continue to add the latest methods many years before their competitors.
- Both can search the Internet for user-written commands and download them automatically to extend their capabilities quickly and easily.
- Both hold their data in the computer's main memory, offering speed but limiting the amount of data they can handle.

1.3 Why Learn R?

With so many similarities, if you already know Stata, why should you bother to learn R?

- To augment Stata; i.e. to be able to perform statistical analyses that are not available in Stata, but which are available in R. R offers a *vast* number of analytical methods. There are now over 3,000 add-on packages available for R and this number is growing at an exponential rate. Therefore, knowing both gives you a much greater range of tools for analyzing data.
- To stay current with new analytic methods. The majority of statistics textbooks, and journal articles, now being published use either Stata or R for examples. R appears to be used more in many journals. Stata users not understanding R are therefore not able to learn as much from texts or articles using R for examples than they would be if they understood the language.
- If you continue to do all of your data management in Stata, you can learn just enough R to import your data and run the procedures you need.
- R is directly accessible from inside many statistics packages. SAS, SPSS, and STATISTICA offer the ability to run R programs from within their software. This means that when developers write programs in R, they are assured a very wide audience. Roger Newson has written an interface [36] between Stata and R that provides some of this ability. We expect to see more done on this topic in the near future.
- R has been object-oriented since its first version. Many of its commands sense the types of data structures you have and do the best thing for each. For example, once you tell it that gender is a categorical variable, it will take statistically proper actions if you use it as a linear regression predictor. At the time of publication, Stata Corporation had just announced its future move toward object orientation.
- Both languages consist of a core set of functions that are written in the C language. However, only developers at Stata Corporation can modify its most fundamental commands. Every aspect of R is open for anyone to modify in any way they like. This complete flexibility attracts many developers.
- Both R and Stata offer graphics that are flexible, easy to use, and of high quality. However, R also offers the very flexible and powerful Grammar of Graphics approach. As we will see, developers have even gone so far as replacing R's core graphical system.
- R is free. This means, of course, that you can use it for free, but it also means developers know that their work is available to everyone. That helps attract developers and is a major reason that there are so many add-on packages for it.

1.4 Is R Accurate?

When people first learn of R, one of their first questions is "Can a package written by volunteers be as accurate as one written by a large corporation?" People envision a lone programmer competing against a large corporate team. Having worked closely with several software companies over the years, we can assure you that this is not the case. A particular procedure is usually written by one programmer, even at Stata Corporation. A thorough testing process is then carried out by a few people within the company and then more thoroughly by Stata users on publication of the new command or function.

The R Development Core Team runs each release of R through validation suites that have known correct answers to ensure accurate results. They also go through "Alpha," "Beta," and "Release Candidate" testing phases, which are open to the public. Each phase has tighter restrictions on modifications of R. Finally, the production version is released. The details of this process are provided in R: Regulatory Compliance and Validation Issues, A Guidance Document for the Use of R in Regulated Clinical Trial Environments, available at http://www.r-project.org/doc/R-FDA.pdf [11].

When bugs are found in Stata, the developers typically make a fix within days. Users are in continual communication with other users and developers through the Statalist. An average of 100 communications are posted daily. Questions are answered by other users or by Stata staff.

R also has open discussions of its known bugs and R's developers fix them quickly too. However, software of the complexity of Stata and R will never be completely free of errors, regardless of its source.

1.5 What About Tech Support?

If a package is free, who supports it?

Stata users may call toll-free or e-mail technical support for problems they experience with the software or for advice on how to run various software commands. The response is near immediate, with a day delay in response being on the high side. Even experienced Stata users sometimes require technical advice for new commands or functions or have difficulties learning new areas of statistics or new methodologies (e.g. the matrix programming). We have always found support to he helpful and friendly.

You can also get support through the Stata Listserver, where it is normal to get assistance from someone the very day you post your request.

R's main source of support is the R-help mailing list. Other users and often developers themselves will often provide immediate help. Sometimes you may obtain different answers from various responders, but that is part of the nature of statistics. For details on the various R e-mail support lists, see Chapter 4, "Help and Documentation."

There are several commercial versions of R available, and the companies that sell them do provide phone support. Here are some of these companies and their web sites:

XL-Solutions Corp., `http://www.experience-rplus.com/`

Revolution Computing, Inc., `http://www.revolution-computing.com/`

Random Technologies, LLC, `http://random-technologies-llc.com/`

1.6 Getting Started Quickly

If you wish to start using R quickly, you can do so by reading fewer than 50 pages of this book. Since you have Stata to do your basic descriptive statistics, you are likely to need R's modeling functions. Here are the steps you can follow to use them.

1. Read the remainder of this chapter and Chapter 2, "Installing and Updating R." Download and install R on your computer.
2. Read the part of Chapter 3, "Running R," that covers your operating system.
3. In Chapter 5, "Programming Language Basics," read Section 5.3.2 about factors, and Section 5.3.3 about data frames.
4. Also in Chapter 5, read Section 5.6.1, "Controlling Functions with Arguments," and Section 5.6.2, "Controlling Functions with Formulas," including Table 5.1, "Example formulas in Stata and R."
5. Read Section 6.6, "Importing Data from Stata."

After reading the pages above, do all your data management in Stata, stripping out observations containing any missing values. Then write out only the variables and observations you need to a comma separated values file, mydata.csv. Assuming your variables are named y, x1, x2,..., your entire R program will look something like this:

```
library("Hmisc")  # Contains stata.get function.
library("OtherLibrariesYouNeed")  # If you need any.
mydata <- stata.get("mydata.dta") # imports your Stata file
mymodel <- TheFunctionYouNeed( y ~ x1+x2, data=mydata )
summary(mymodel)
plot(mymodel) # if your function does plots.
```

1.7 Programming Conventions

Although R has many ways to generate practice data and has a variety of example data sets, we will use a tiny practice data set that is easy to enter. We can then manipulate and print it repeatedly so that you can clearly see the changes.

You can download the practice data sets and program files from `http://r4stats.com`. The example programs are set to look for their matching data files in the directory (folder) named *myRfolder*, but that is easy to change to whatever location you prefer. Each program begins by loading the data as if it were a new session. That is not required if you already have the data loaded, but it makes it easier to ensure that previous programming does not interfere with the example. It also allows each program to run on its own.

Each example program in this book begins with a comment stating its purpose and the name of the file in which it is stored. For example, the programs for selecting variables each begin with a comment like the one below.

```
# R Program for Selecting Variables.
# Filename: SelectingVars.R
```

When displaying the programs within the book, we dispense with first line since it appears as the title of the section.

R's "#" symbol is like Stata's "*" symbol. Words after it are regarded as comments, until the end of the line. The filename in the practice files will always match, so the two files for this topic are *SelectingVars.do*, and *SelectingVars.R*. The R data objects and Stata data sets used in this book are also available. Their names are the same as that used in the book, with the extensions ".dta" and ".RData" for the Stata and R files, respectively. For example, our most widely used data object, mydata, is stored in both *mydata.dta* and *mydata.RData*. Also, all of the R objects we create, data and functions, are stored in *myAll.RData*.

1.8 Typographic Conventions

We write all programming code and the names of all commands, functions, and packages in `this Courier font`.

The names of other documents and menus are in *this italic font*.

Menus appear in the form *File>Save as...*, which means "choose *Save as...* from the *File* menu."

When learning a new language, it can be hard to tell the commands from the names you can choose (e.g., variable or data set names). To help differentiate, we use the common prefix "my" in names like *mydata* or *mySubset*.

R uses ">" to prompt you to input a new line and "+" to prompt you to enter a continued line. When there is no output to see, we delete the prompt characters to achieve a less cluttered look. However, when examples include both input and output, we leave the input prompts in place. That helps you identify which is which. So the first three lines below are the input we submitted and the last line is the mean that R wrote out.

```
> q1 <- c(1, 2, 2, 3,
+          4, 5, 5, 5, 4)
```

```
> mean(q1)
```

```
[1] 3.4444
```

R tends to pack its input and different sections of output tightly together. This makes it harder to read when you are learning it. Therefore, we also add spacing in some places to improve legibility. In the example above, we added a blank line on either side of the line containing "> `mean(q1)`."

2

Installing and Updating R

Stata and R are somewhat similar in that both are modular. Each comes with a single "binary" executable file and a large number of individual functions or commands. These are text files that users can modify in a text editor. Both applications come with their own built-in text editors, and both allow the use of outside text editors as well.

The binary executable files that come with R and Stata have been compiled from the "source code" version that was written using C. When you install R, you download the executable together with a set of add-on modules called *packages.*

These are different from Stata's *ado* files, which are single-purpose commands or functions. R packages contain a number of related functions that can be used for data management, graphics, or statistical analysis.

After the installation of the group of main R packages, a user may install other packages later when they are needed. There are over 3,000 packages to choose from. It is highly unlikely that someone would need them all.

The Comprehensive R Archive Networks (CRAN), located at http:// cran.r-project.org/, is R's equivalent to Stata's Statistical Software Components (SSC) Archive. The most important difference between the two archives is that CRAN is where you obtain R itself. The SSC contains only add-ons to Stata, of course.

To download R, go to the CRAN link above, choose your operating system under the web page heading *Download and Install R*. The binary versions install quickly and easily. Binary versions exist for many operating systems, including Windows, Mac OS X, and popular versions of Linux such as Ubuntu, RedHat, Suse, and others that use either the RPM or APT installers.

Since R is an Open Source project, there are also source code versions of R for experienced programmers who prefer to compile their own copy. Using that version, you can modify R in any way you like. Although R's developers write most of the analytic commands using the R language, they use other languages such as C and FORTRAN to write the most fundamental R functions.

R.A. Muenchen, J.M. Hilbe, *R for Stata Users*, Statistics and Computing, DOI 10.1007/978-1-4419-1318-0_2, © Springer Science+Business Media, LLC 2010

Each version of R installs into its own directory (folder), so there is no problem having multiple versions installed on your computer. You can then install your favorite packages for the new release.

2.1 Installing Add-on Packages

While the main installation of R contains many useful functions, many additional packages, written by R users, are available on the Internet. The main site for additional packages is at the CRAN web site under *Packages*. The equivalent to Stata's *Statistical Software Components (SSC)* Archive, CRAN is the best place to read about and choose packages to install. You usually do not need to download them from there yourself. R automates the download and installation process.

Before installing packages, your computer account should have administrative privileges and you must start R in a manner that allows administrative control. If you do not have administrative privileges on your computer, you can install packages to a directory to which you have write access. For instructions, see the FAQ (Frequently Asked Questions) at http://www.r-project.org/.

To start R with administrative control on Windows Vista and Windows 7, right-click its menu choice and then choose *Run as administrator*. Window's User Account Control will then ask for your permission to allow R to modify your computer.

On the R version for Microsoft Windows, you can choose *Packages>Install package(s)* from the menus. It will ask you to choose a CRAN site or "mirror" that is close to you; see Fig. 2.1, left. Then it will ask which package you wish to install (right). Choose one of each and click OK.

If you prefer to use a function instead of the menus, you can use the `install.packages` function. This is just like Stata's `ssc install` command. For example, to download and install Frank Harrell's `Hmisc` package [14], start R and enter this function call:

```
install.packages("Hmisc", dependencies=TRUE)
```

The argument `dependencies=TRUE` tells R to install any packages that this package "depends" on and those that its author "suggests" as useful. R will then prompt you to choose the closest mirror site and the package you need.

2.2 Loading an Add-on Package

Once installed, a package is on your computer's hard drive but not quite ready to use. Each time you start R, you also have to load the package from the library before you can use it. You can see what packages are installed and ready to load with the `library` function.

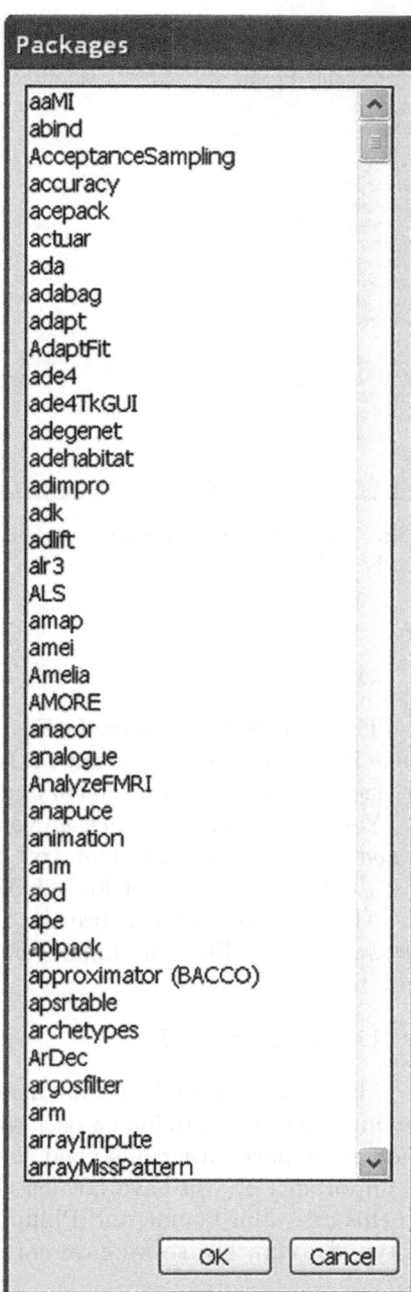

Fig. 2.1. When installing software, you first choose a mirror site (left). Then the next window appears, from which you choose the package you need (right).

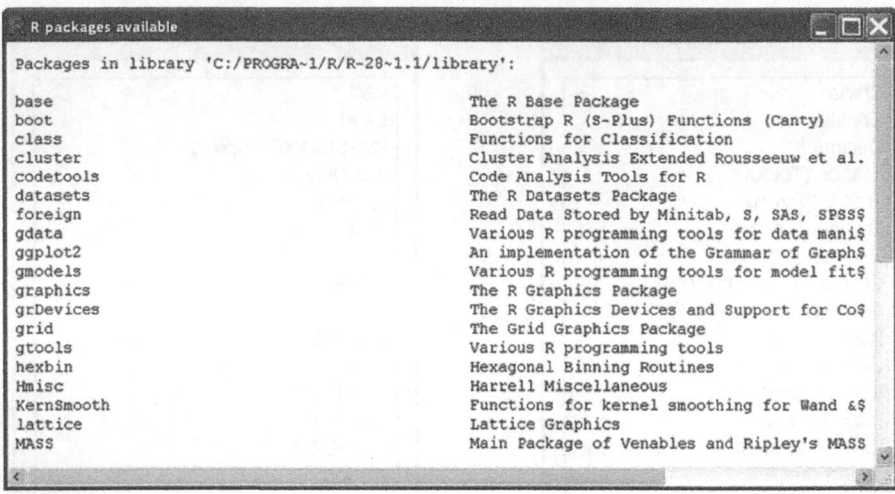

Fig. 2.2. The library function shows you the packages that are installed and are ready to load.

```
library()
```

That causes the window in Fig. 2.2 to appear, showing the packages you have installed. The similar `installed.packages` function lists your installed packages along with the version and location of each.

You can then load a package you need with the menu selection, *Packages >Load packages*. It will show you the names of all packages that you have installed but have not yet loaded. You can then choose one from the list.

Alternatively, you can use the `library` function. Here I am loading the `Hmisc` package. Since the Linux version lacks menus, this function is the only way to load packages.

```
library("Hmisc")
```

Many packages load without any messages; you will just see the ">" prompt again. When trying to load a package, you may see the error message below. It means you have either mistyped the package name (remember capitalization is important) or you have not installed the package before trying to load it. In this case, Jim Lemon and Philippe Grosjean's `prettyR` package [30] name is typed accurately, so we have not yet installed it.

```
> library("prettyR")

Error in library(prettyR) :
  there is no package called 'prettyR'
```

To see what packages you have loaded, use the `search` function.

```
> search()
```

```
[1] ".GlobalEnv"        "package:Hmisc"
[3] "package:stats"     "package:graphics"
[5] "package:grDevices" "package:utils"
[7] "package:datasets"  "package:methods"
[9] "Autoloads"         "package:base"
```

We will discuss this function in detail in Chapter 13, "Managing Your Files and Workspace."

Since there are so many packages written by users, two packages will occasionally have functions with the same name. That can be very confusing until you realize what is happening. For example, the `Hmisc` and `prettyR` packages both have a `describe` function that does similar things. In such a case, the package you load last will *mask* the function(s) in the package you loaded earlier. For example, we loaded the `Hmisc` package first, and now we am loading the `prettyR` package (having installed it in the meantime). The following message results:

```
> library("prettyR")
```

```
Attaching package: 'prettyR'
   The following object(s) are masked from package:Hmisc :
      describe
```

You can avoid such conflicts by detaching each package as soon as you are done using it by using the `detach` function. For example, the following function call will detach the `prettyR` package:

```
detach("package:prettyR")
```

One approach that avoids conflicts is to load a package from the library right before using it and then detach it immediately as in the following example:

```
> library("Hmisc")
> describe(mydata)
    ---output would appear here---
> detach("package:Hmisc")
```

If your favorite packages do not conflict with one anther, you can have R load them each time you start R by putting the function calls in a file named *".Rprofile."* That file can automate your settings just like the *profile.do* file for Stata. For details, see Appendix C.

2.3 Updating Your Installation

While Stata is configured to check for updates over the Internet every 7 days, in R you must tell it to check using the update.packages function.

```
> update.packages()

graph :
 Version 1.15.6 installed in C:/PROGRA~1/R/R-26~1.1/library
 Version 1.16.1 available at
   http://rh-mirror.linux.iastate.edu/CRAN
Update (y/N/c)?  y
```

R will ask you if you want to update each package. If you enter "y," it will do it and show you the following. This message, repeated for each package, tells you what file it is getting from the mirror you requested (Iowa State) and where it placed the file.

```
trying URL 'http://rh-mirror.linux.iastate.edu
  /CRAN/bin/windows/contrib/2.6/graph_1.16.1.zip'
Content type 'application/zip' length 870777 bytes (850 Kb)
opened URL
downloaded 850 Kb
```

This next message tells you that the file was checked for errors (its sums were checked) and it says where it stored the file. As long as you see no error messages, the update is complete.

```
package 'graph' successfully unpacked and MD5 sums checked

The downloaded packages are in
         C:/Documents and Settings/muenchen/Local Settings/
              Temp/Rtmpgf4C4B/downloaded_packages
updating HTML package descriptions
```

Moving to a whole new version of R is not as easy. First, you download and install the new version just like you did the first one. Multiple versions can coexist on the same computer. You can even run them at the same time if you wanted to compare results across versions. When you install a new version of R, you also have to install any add-on packages again. You can do that in a step-by-step fashion as we discussed above. An easier way is to define a character variable like "myPackages" that contains the names of the packages you use. The following is an example that uses this approach to install all of the packages we use in this book.

```
myPackages <- c("car","foreign","hexbin",
  "ggplot2","gmodels","gplots", "Hmisc",
  "lattice", "reshape","ggplot2","prettyR","Rcmdr")

install.packages(myPackages, dependencies=TRUE)
```

We will discuss the details of the c function used above later. We will also discuss how to store programs like this so you can open and execute them again in the future.

You can automate the creation of myPackages (or whatever name you choose to store your package names) by placing the code that defines it in your .Rprofile. Putting it there will ensure that myPackages is defined every time you start R. As you find new packages to install, you can add to the definition of myPackages. Then installing all of them when a new version of R comes out is easy. Of course, you do not want to place the `install.packages` function into your .Rprofile. There is no point in installing package every time you start R! For details, see Appendix C.

2.4 Uninstalling R

When you get a new version of any software package, it is good to keep the old one around for a while in case any bugs show up in the new one. Once you are confident that you will no longer need an older version of R, you can remove it.

On Microsoft Windows, R does not have an uninstaller accessible from the usual Windows *Add or Remove Programs* control panel. Instead, you can choose *Start>Programs>R, Uninstall R x.x.x*, where x.xx.x is the version of R you are using. That menu choice runs the uninstall program, unins000.exe. That program will remove R and any packages you have installed. That file is located in the folder c:/program files/R/R x.x.x/.

To uninstall R on the Macintosh, simply drag the application to the trash. Linux users can uninstall R by deleting /usr/local/lib/R.

Although it is rarely necessary to uninstall a single package, you can do so with the `uninstall.packages` function. First though, you must make sure it is not in use by detaching it. For example, to remove just the Hmisc package, use the following:

```
detach("package:Hmisc") #If it is loaded.
```

```
remove.packages("Hmisc")
```

Recall that R uses "#" to begin comments, so "#If it is loaded." is just a comment to document the program.

2.5 Choosing Repositories

While most R packages are stored at the CRAN site, there are other repositories. If the Packages window does not list the one you need, you may need to choose another repository. Several repositories are associated with the *BioConductor project*. As they say at their main web site, "BioConductor is an open source and open development software project for the analysis and comprehension of genomic data [16]." Another repository is at the *Omegahat Project for Statistical Computing* [48],

To choose your repositories, choose *Packages>Select repositories...* or enter the following function call and the *Repositories selection* window will appear (Fig. 2.3). Note that two CRAN repositories are selected by default. Your operating system's usual mouse commands work as usual to make contiguous or noncontiguous selections. On Microsoft Windows, that is Shift-click and Ctrl-click, respectively.

```
> setRepositories()
```

If you are working without a windowing system, R will prompt you to enter the number(s) of the repositories you need.

```
--- Please select repositories for use in this session ---
1: + CRAN
2: + CRAN (extras)
3:   Omegahat
4:   BioC software
5:   BioC annotation
6:   BioC experiment
7:   BioC extra

Enter one or more numbers separated by spaces
1: 1,2,4
```

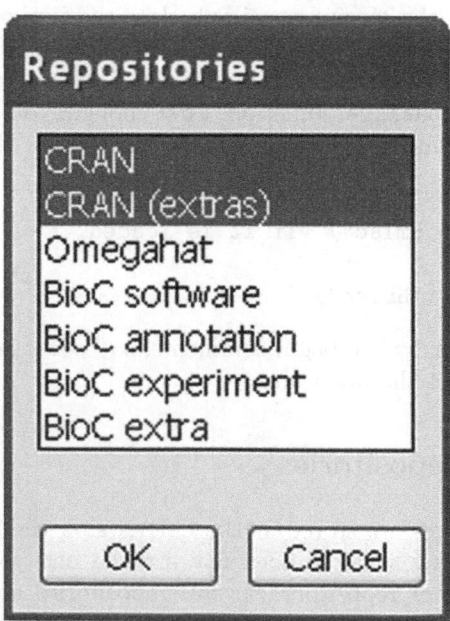

Fig. 2.3. Selecting repositories will determine which add-on packages R will offer to install.

2.6 Accessing Data in Packages

You can get a list of data sets available in each loaded package with the **data** function. A window listing the default data sets will appear (Fig. 2.4).

```
> data()
```

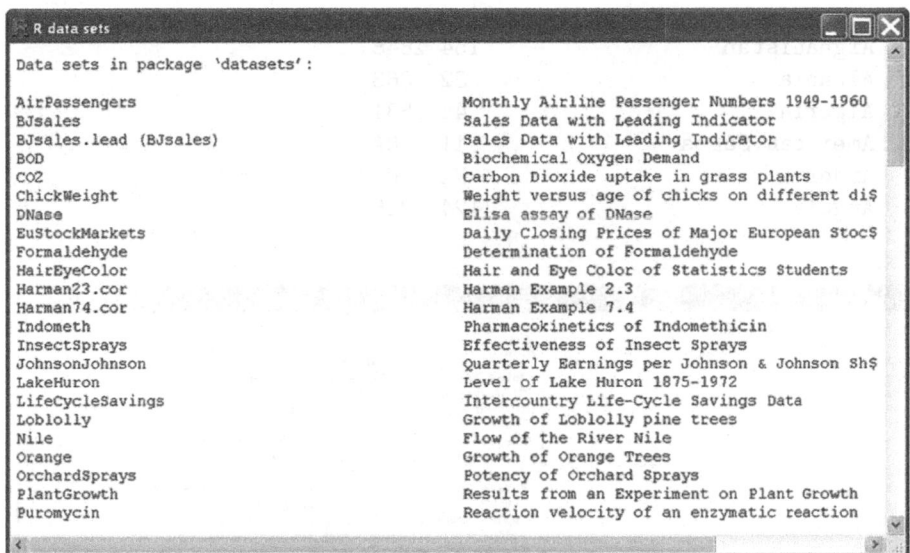

Fig. 2.4. The **data** function displays all of the practice data sets for the packages you have loaded.

You can use these practice data sets directly. For example, to look at the top of the CO2 file (capital letters C and O, not zero!), you can use the **head** function.

```
> head(CO2)
```

```
   Plant   Type  Treatment conc uptake
1    Qn1 Quebec nonchilled   95   16.0
2    Qn1 Quebec nonchilled  175   30.4
3    Qn1 Quebec nonchilled  250   34.8
4    Qn1 Quebec nonchilled  350   37.2
5    Qn1 Quebec nonchilled  500   35.3
6    Qn1 Quebec nonchilled  675   39.2
```

The similar **tail** function shows you the bottom few observations.

If you only want a list of data sets in a particular package, you can use the **package** argument. For example, if you have installed the **car** package [12] (from John Fox's *C*ompanion to *A*pplied *R*egression book), you can load it from the library and see the data sets only it has (Fig. 2.5) with the following statements. Recall that R is case sensitive, so using a lowercase "un" would not work.

```
> library("car")
> data(package="car")
> head(UN)
                 infant.mortality  gdp
Afghanistan                   154 2848
Albania                        32  863
Algeria                        44 1531
American.Samoa                 11   NA
Andorra                        NA   NA
Angola                        124  355
```

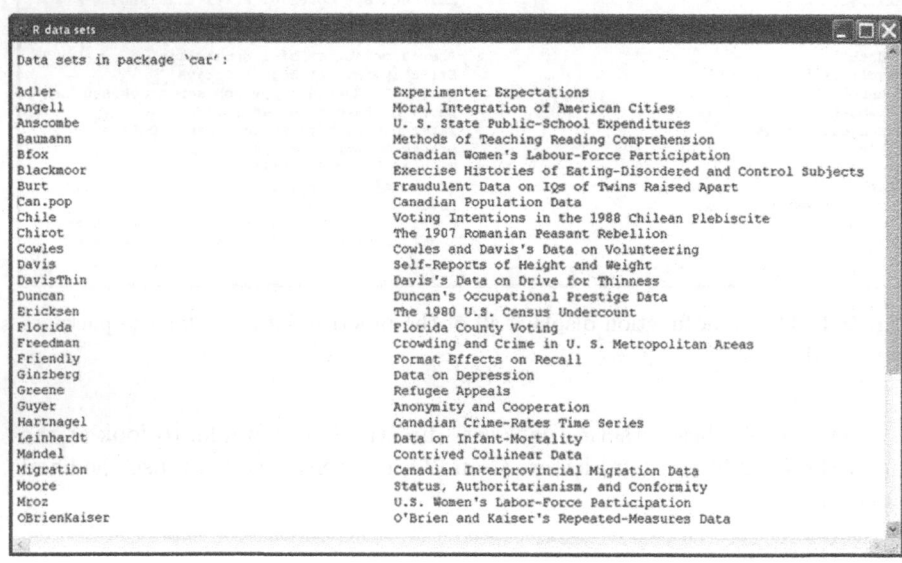

Fig. 2.5. Display of data sets in the car package.

To see all of the data sets available in all installed packages, even those not loaded from the library, enter the following function call:

```
data( package=.packages( all.available=TRUE ) )
```

3

Running R

There are several ways you can run R:

- Interactively using its programming language. You can see the result of each function call immediately after you submit it.
- Interactively using one of several graphical user interfaces (GUIs) that you can add on to R. Some of these use programming and some use menus much like Stata.
- Noninteractively in batch mode using its programming language. You enter your program into a file and run it all at once.

You can ease your way into R by continuing to use Stata or your favorite spreadsheet program to enter and manage your data and then use one of the methods below to import and analyze it. As you find errors in your data (and you know you will), you can go back to your other software, correct them, and then import it again. It is not an ideal way to work, but it does get you into R quickly.

3.1 Running R Interactively on Windows

You can run R programs interactively in several steps:

1. Start R by choosing *Start>All Programs>R>R x.x.x* (where x.x.x is the version of R you are using). The main R Console window will appear looking like the left window in Fig. 3.1. Then enter your program choosing one of the methods described in steps 2 and 3 below.
2. Enter R functions into the R console. You can enter function calls into the console one line at a time at the ">" prompt. R will execute each line when you press the Enter key. If you enter them into the console, you can retrieve them with the up arrow key and edit them to run again. We find it much easier to use the program editor described in the next step.

R.A. Muenchen, J.M. Hilbe, *R for Stata Users*, Statistics
and Computing, DOI 10.1007/978-1-4419-1318-0_3,
© Springer Science+Business Media, LLC 2010

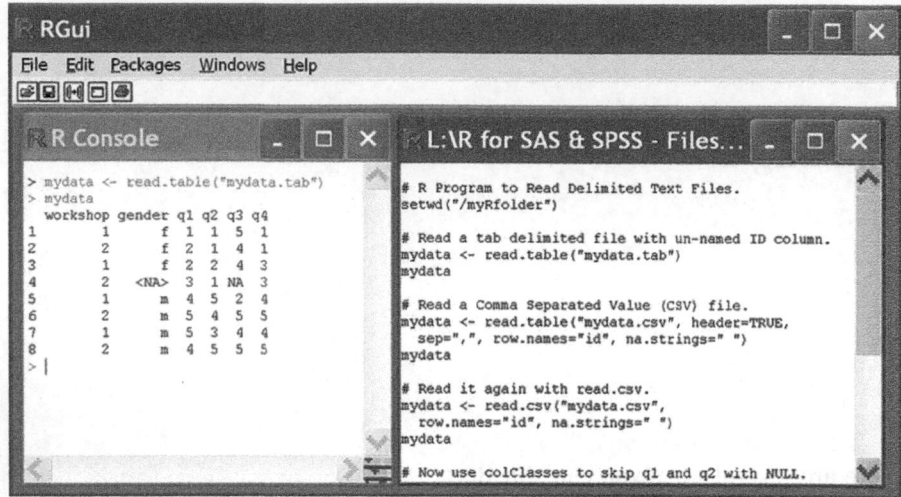

Fig. 3.1. R graphical user interface on Microsoft Windows.

If you type the beginning of an R function, such as "me" and press Tab, R will show you all of the R functions that begin with those letters, such as mean or median. If you enter the name of a function and an open parenthesis, such as "mean(," R will show you the arguments that you can use with that function.

3. Enter R functions into the R Editor. Open the R Editor by choosing *File>New Script.* You can see it in the bottom right corner of Fig. 6.1. You can enter programs as you would in the Stata commandline.

4. Submit your program from the R Editor. To submit just the current line, you can hold the Ctrl key down and press "r," for *r*un, or choose *Edit>Run line or selection.* To run a block of lines, select them first and then submit them the same way. To run the whole program, choose *Edit>Run All.*

5. As you submit program statements, they will appear in the R Console along with results and/or error messages. Make any changes you need and submit the program again until finished. You can clear the console results by choosing *Edit>Clear console* or by holding the Ctrl key down and pressing "l" (i.e. CTRL-l). See *Help>Console* for more keyboard shortcuts.

6. Save your program and output. Click on either the console window or the R Editor window to make it active and choose *File>Save to file.* Unlike in Stata, the console output will contain the commands and their output blended together.

7. Save your data and any functions you may have written. The data and/or function(s) you created are stored in an area called your workspace. You can save that with the menu selection, *File>Save Workspace....* In a later R session you can retrieve it with *File>Load Workspace....* You can also save your workspace using the save.image function:

```
save.image(file="myWorkspace.RData")
```

Later, you can read the workspace back in with the function call:

```
load("myWorkspace.RData")
```

For details, see Chapter 13, "Managing Your Files and Workspace."

8. Optionally save your history. R has a history file that saves all of the function calls you submit in a given session. This is just like the Stata log menu. Unlike Stata, however, the history of the past function calls is not cumulative on Windows computers. You can save the session history to a file using *File>Save History...* and you can load it into future session with *File>Load History....* There are also various R functions to do these tasks.

```
savehistory(file="myHistory.Rhistory")
loadhistory(file="myHistory.Rhistory")
```

Note that the filename can be anything you like, but the extension should be ".Rhistory." In fact the entire filename will be simply ".Rhistory" if you do not provide one. We prefer to always save a cumulative history file automatically. For details, see Appendix C.

9. To quit R, choose *File>Exit* or submit the function quit() or just q(). R offers to save your workspace automatically on exit. If you are using the save.image and load functions to tell R where to save and retrieve your workspace in step 4 above, you can answer *No*. If you answer *Yes*, it will save your work in the file ".RData" in your default working directory. Next time you start R, it will load the contents of the .RData file automatically. Creating a .RData file this way is a convenient way to work. However, we prefer naming each project ourselves as described in step 4 above.

3.2 Running R Interactively on Macintosh

Like Stata, R programs run interactively on the Macintosh. R does so in several steps.

1. Start R by choosing R in the Applications folder. The R console window will appear (see left window in Fig. 3.2). Then enter your program choosing one of the methods described in steps 2 and 3 below.

2. Enter R functions in the console window. You can enter function calls into the console one line at a time at the ">" prompt. R will execute each line when you press the Enter key. If you enter them into the console, you can retrieve them with the up arrow key and edit them to run again. We find it much easier to use the program editor described in the next step. If you type "me" at the command prompt and press Tab or hold the Command key down and press "." (i.e., CTRL-period), R will show you all of the R functions that begin with those letters, such as mean or median. When you type a whole function name, the functions arguments will appear below it in the console window.

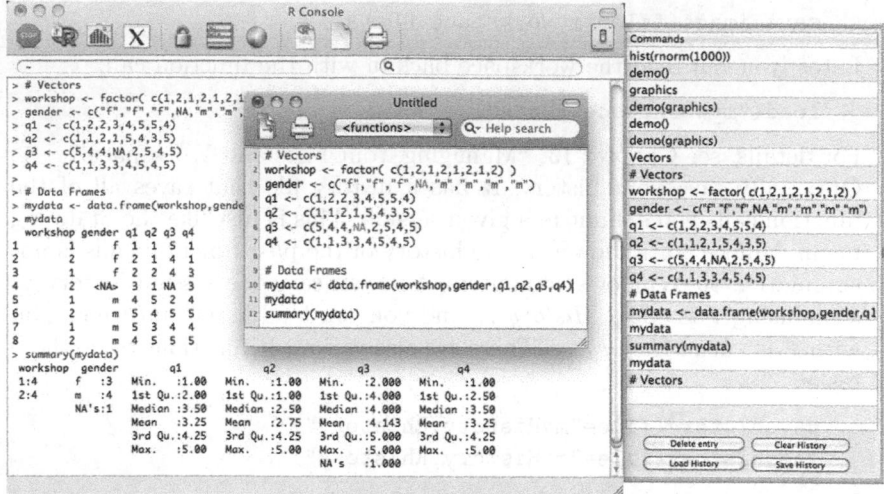

Fig. 3.2. R graphical user interface on Macintosh.

3. Enter R functions into the R Editor. Open the R Editor by choosing *File>New Document*. The R Editor will start with an empty window. You can see it in the center of Fig. 3.2. You can enter R programs as you would on the Stata command line or write *do* or *ado* files in the Stata editor.

4. Submit your program from the R Editor. To submit one or more lines, highlight them, then hold the Command key, and press Return, or choose *Edit>Execute*. To run the whole program, select it by holding down the Command key and pressing "a," and then choose *Edit>Execute*.

5. As your submit program statements, they will appear in the R Console along with results and/or error messages. Make any changes you need and submit the program again until finished.

6. Save your program and output. Click on a window to make it the active window and choose *File>Save to file*. The function calls and their output are blended together, unlike Stata.

7. Save your data and any functions you may have written. The data and/or function(s) you created are stored in an area called your *workspace*. You can save your workspace with *Workspace>Save Workspace File....* In a later R session you can retrieve it with *Workspace>Load Workspace File....* You can also perform these functions using the R functions save.image and load.

```
save.image(file="myWorkspace.RData")
```

```
load("myWorkspace.RData")
```

For details, see Chapter 13, "Managing Your Files and Workspace."

8. Optionally save your history. R has a history file that saves all of the functions you submit in a given session (and not the output). This is just like the Stata log menu. The history file is not cumulative on Macintosh computers. You can view your history by clicking on the *Show/Hide R command history* icon in the console window (to the right of the lock icon). You can see the command history window on the right side of Fig. 3.2. Notice that it has alternating stripes, matching its icon. Clicking the icon once makes the history window slide out to the right of the console. Clicking it again causes it to slide back and disappear. You can see the various buttons at the bottom of the history, such as *Save History* or *Load History*. You can use them to save your history or load it from a previous session. You can also use R functions to do these tasks.

```
savehistory(file="myHistory.Rhistory")
```

```
loadhistory(file="myHistory.Rhistory")
```

The filename can be anything you like, but the extension should be ".Rhistory." In fact the entire filename will be simply ".Rhistory" if you do not provide one. We prefer to always save a cumulative history file automatically. For details, see Appendix C.

9. Exit R by choosing *R>Quit R*. Users of any operating system can quit by submitting the function `quit()` or just `q()`. R will offer to save your workspace automatically on exit. If you are using the `save.image` and `load` functions to tell R where to save/retrieve your workspace in step 4 above, you can answer *No*. If you answer *Yes*, it will save your work in the file ".RData" in your default working directory. Next time when you start R, it will load the contents of the .RData file automatically. Creating a .RData file this way is a convenient way to work. However, we recommend naming each project yourself, as described in step 4 above.

3.3 Running R Interactively on Linux or UNIX

You can run R programs interactively in several steps.

1. Start R by entering the command "R," which will bring up the ">" prompt, where you enter commands. For a wide range of options, refer to Appendix B , An Introduction to R [52], available at http://www.r-project.org/ under *Manuals*, or in your R *Help* menu. You can enter R functions using either of the methods described in steps 2 and 3 below.

2. Enter R functions into the console one line at a time at the ">" prompt. R will execute each line when you press the Enter key. You can retrieve a function call with the up arrow key and edit it, and then press Enter to run again. You can include whole R programs from files with the `source` function. For details, see Section 3.4, "Running Programs That Include Other Programs." If you type the beginning of an R function name like "me" and press the Tab key, R will show you all of the R functions that

begin with those letters, such as mean or median. If you type the function name and an open parenthesis like "mean(" and press Tab, R will show you the arguments you can use to control that function.

3. Enter R functions into a text editor. Although R for Linux or UNIX does not come with its own GUI or program editor, a popular alternative is to use the Emacs editor in ESS mode. It color-codes your programs to help find syntax errors. You can submit your programs directly from Emacs to R. See the R FAQ at http://www.r-project.org/ under R for Emacs for details.

4. Save your program and output. Linux or UNIX users can route input and output to a file with the sink function. You must specify it in advance of any output you wish to save.

```
sink("myTranscript.txt", split=TRUE)
```

The argument split=TRUE tells R to display the text on the screen as well as route it to the file. The file will contain a transcript of your work. The function calls and their output are blended together, unlike Stata.

5. Save your data and any functions you may have written. The data and/or function(s) you created are stored in an area called your workspace. Users of any operating system can save it by calling the save.image function.

```
save.image(file="myWorkspace.RData")
```

Later, you can read the workspace back in with the function call

```
load("myWorkspace.RData")
```

For details, see Chapter 13, "Managing Your Files and Workspace."

6. R has a history file that saves all of the functions you submit in a given session. This is just like the Stata log menu. The Linux/UNIX version of R saves a cumulative set of function calls across sessions. You can also save or load your history at any time with the savehistory and loadhistory functions.

```
savehistory(file="myHistory.Rhistory")
```

```
loadhistory(file="myHistory.Rhistory")
```

Note that the filename can be anything you like, but the extension should be ".Rhistory." In fact the entire filename will be simply ".Rhistory" if you do not provide one.

7. Quit R by submitting the function quit() or just q(). R offers to save your workspace automatically on exit. If you are using the save.image and load functions to tell R where to save/retrieve your workspace in step 4 above, you can answer *No*. If you answer *Yes*, it will save your work in the file ".RData" in your default working directory. Next time you start R, it will load the contents of the .RData file automatically. Creating an .RData file this way is a convenient way to work. However, we prefer naming each project ourselves as described in step 4 above.

3.4 Running Programs That Include Other Programs

When you find yourself using the same block of code repeatedly in different programs, it makes sense to save it to a file and include it into the other programs where it is needed. Stata does this using a global constant, where the program code is assigned a unique name and recalled into the program code by giving the constant with a leading dollar sign. To include a program in R, use the source function

```
source("myprog.R")
```

One catch to keep in mind is that by default R will not display any results that sourced files may have created. Of course, any objects they create — data, functions, and so forth — will be available to the program code that follows. If the program you source creates actual output that you want to see, you can source the program in the following manner:

```
source("myprog.R", echo=TRUE)
```

This will show you all of the output created by the program. If you prefer to see only some results, you can wrap the print function around only those functions whose output you do want displayed. For example, if you sourced the following R program, it would display the standard deviation, but not the mean:

```
x <- c(1, 2, 3, 4, 5)
mean(x)          # This result will not display.
print( sd(x) )   # This one will.
```

An alternative to using the source function is to create your own R package. However, that is beyond the scope of this book.

3.5 Running R in Batch Mode

You can write a program to a file and run it all at once, routing its results to another file (or files). This is called batch processing. If you had a program named myprog.do, you would run it with the following command:

```
"C:\Program Files\Stata10\wstata" /b do myprog.do
```

Stata would run the program and place the results into a log file called myprog.log.

In R, you can find the details of running batch on your operating system by starting R and entering the following command. Note that the letters of BATCH must be all uppercase.

```
help(BATCH)
```

The following operating system command is an example of running an R batch job on Microsoft Windows. You will need to change the path of Rterm.exe to reflect its location on your computer and fill in your version in place of x.x.x.

```
"C:\Program Files\R\R-x.x.x\bin\Rterm.exe"
--no-restore --no-save < myprog.r  > myprog.out
```

The command wraps to two lines in this book, but enter it as a single line. It is too long to fit in a standard cmd.exe window, so you will need to change its default width from 80 to something wider, like 132. R will execute myprog.r and write the results to myprog.out.

It is easier to write a small batch file like myR.bat.

```
"G:\Program Files\R\R-x.x.x\bin\Rterm.exe"
--no-restore --no-save < %1 > %1.Rout 2>&1
```

Once you have saved that in the file myR.bat, you can then submit batch programs with the following command. It will route your results to myprog.Rout. You can also download this batch file with this book's example programs and data sets at http://r4stats.com.

```
myR myprog.R
```

UNIX users can run a batch program with the following command. It, too, will write your output to myprog.Rout.

```
R CMD BATCH myprog.R
```

There are, of course, many options to give you more control over how your batch programs run. See the help file for details.

3.6 Graphical User Interfaces

The main R installation provides an interface to help you enter programs. It does not include a point-and-click graphical user interface (GUI) for running analyses. There are, however, several GUIs written by R users. You can learn about several at the main R web site, http://www.r-project.org/ under *Related Projects* and then *R GUIs*.

3.6.1 R Commander

Our favorite GUI for general statistical analysis is John Fox's R Commander [13], which is similar to the Stata GUI. It provides menus for many analytic and graphical methods and shows you the R function calls that it enters, making it easy to learn to program in R as you use it. Since it does not come with the main R installation, you have to install it one time with the install.packages function.

```
install.packages("Rcmdr", dependencies=TRUE)
```

R Commander uses *many* other packages, and R will download and install them for you if you use the `dependencies=TRUE` argument.

Let us review the steps of a basic R Commander session. Below are the steps we followed to create the screen image you see in Fig. 3.3 .

1. We started R. For details see the section "Running R Interactively on Windows," or similarly named sections for other operating systems previously covered in this chapter.
2. Then, from within R itself we started R Commander by loading its package from the library. That brought up the window that looks something like Fig. 3.3.

    ```
    library("Rcmdr")
    ```

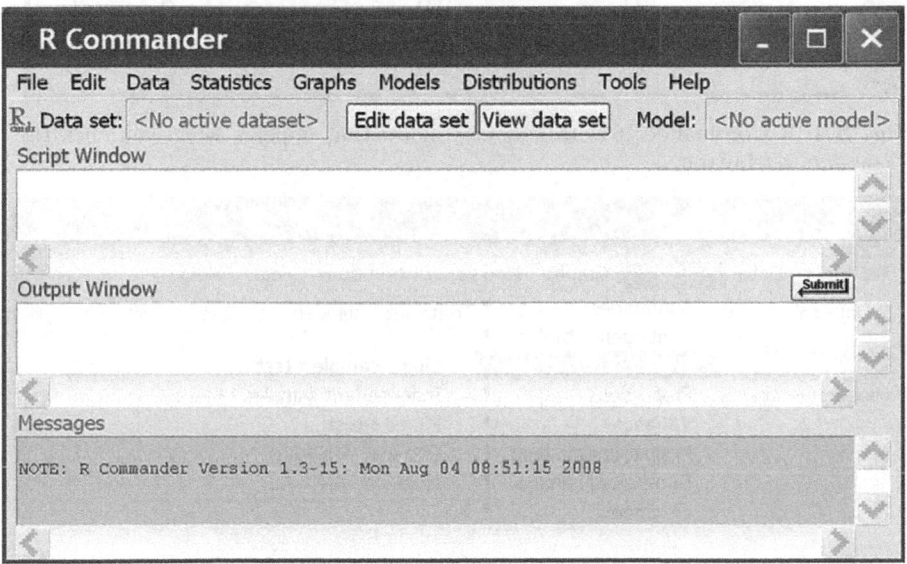

Fig. 3.3. The R Commander GUI, before any work is done.

3. We then chose *Data>Load a data set* and browsed to myRfolder, where our practice data sets are stored. We had to tell it to look for *All Files* because by default it looks for .RDA file types and ours are .RData. We then chose the file mydata.RData. R Commander uses a different file extension because it is unable to deal with more than one data set at a time. Since mydata.RData contains only one data set, it works fine.
4. We next click on the *View data set* button in order to view the data. Then the data appeared, as shown in Fig. 3.4.
5. We then chose *Statistics>Summaries>Active Data Set*. The output you see on the bottom of the screen in Fig. 3.5.

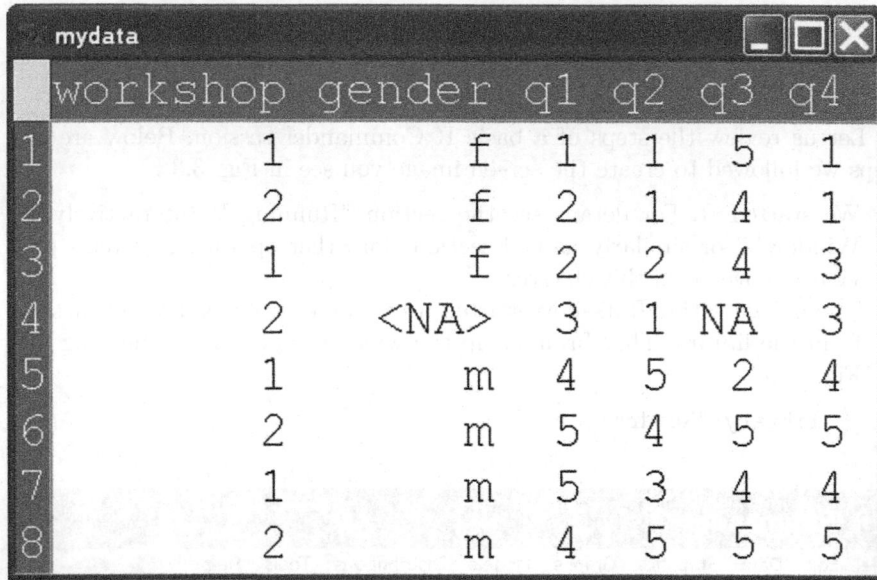

Fig. 3.4. R Commander's Data Viewer window that appears when you click the *View data set* button.

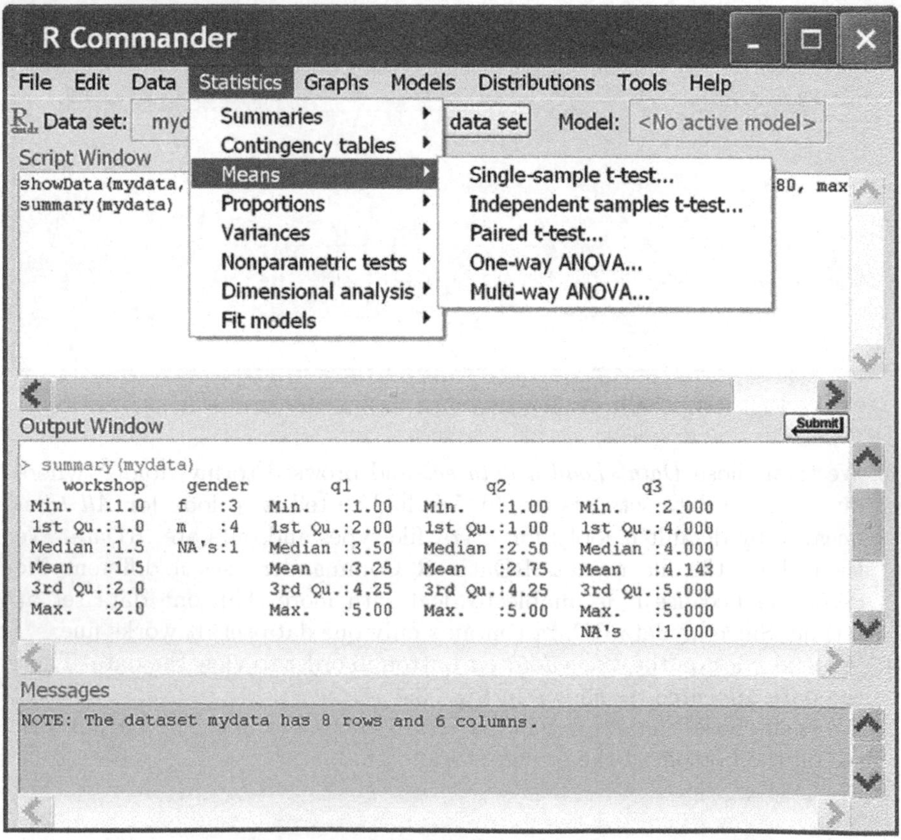

Fig. 3.5. The R Commander GUI with work in progress.

6. Finally, we chose *Statistics>Means....* You see that the menu is still open, showing that we can choose various t-tests and analysis of variance (ANOVA) procedures.

You can learn more about R Commander at `http://cran.r-project.org`, under *Packages.*

3.6.2 Rattle for Data Mining

Graham William's Rattle package [57] provides a tabbed-dialog box style of user interface. Although its emphasis is on data mining, the interface is useful for standard statistical analyses as well. Its name stands for the *R analytical tool to learn easily.* That name fits it well, as it is very easy to learn. Its point-and-click interface writes and executes R programs for you.

Before you install the **rattle** package, you must install some other tools. See the web site for directions `http://rattle.togaware.com`. Once it is installed, you load it from your library in the usual way.

```
> library("rattle")

Rattle, Graphical interface for data mining
   using R, Version 2.2.64.

Copyright (C) 2007 Graham.Williams@togaware.com, GPL

Type "rattle()" to shake, rattle, and roll your data.
```

As the instructions tell you, simply enter the call to the **rattle** function to bring up its interface.

```
> rattle()
```

The main Rattle interface shown in Fig. 3.6 will then appear. It shows the steps it uses to do an analysis on the tabs at the top of its window. You move from left to right, clicking on each tab to do the following steps:

1. Data. Choose your data type from a Comma Separated Value (CSV) file, Attribute Relation File Format (ARFF), Open DataBase Connectivity (ODBC), .RData file, R data object already loaded or created before starting Rattle, or even manual data entry.
2. Select. Choose your variables and the roles they play in the analysis. In Fig. 3.6 we have chosen gender as the target variable (dependent variable) and the other variables as inputs (independent variables or predictors).
3. Explore. Examine the variables using summary statistics, distributions, interactive visualization via GGobi [47], correlation, hierarchical cluster analysis of variables, and principal components. A very interesting feature in distribution analysis is the application of Benford's law, an examination of the initial digits of data values that people use to detect fraudulent data (e.g., faked expense account values)

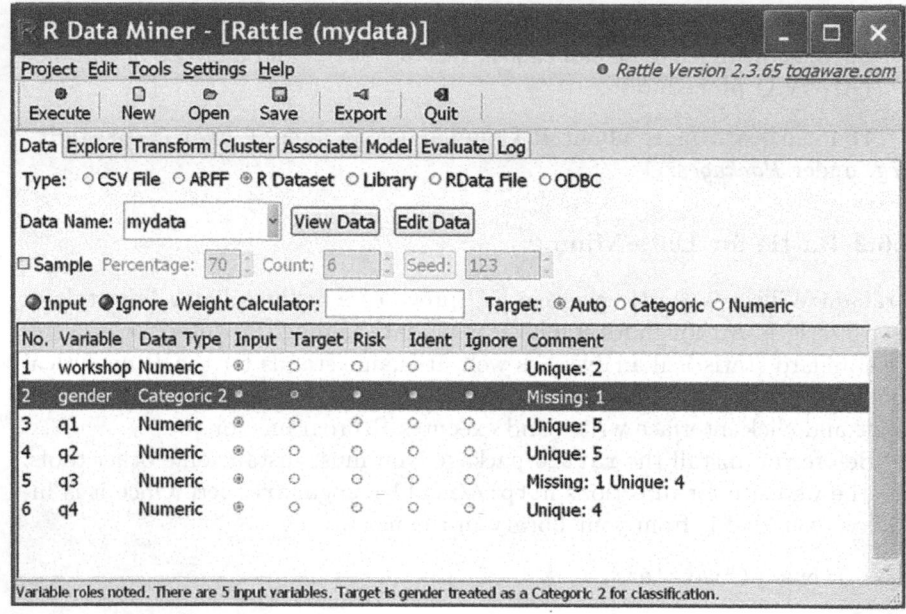

Fig. 3.6. Rattle GUI for data mining.

4. Transform. Replace missing values with reasonable estimates (imputation), convert variables to factors, or look for outliers.
5. Model. Apply models from tree, boost, forest, SVM, regression, or all.
6. Evaluate. Assess model quality and compare different models using confusion tables, lift charts, ROC curves, and so forth.
7. Log. See the R program that Rattle wrote for you to do all of the steps.

Figure 3.7 shows an R program that Rattle wrote when asked for box plots of my data (box plots not shown).

3.6.3 JGR Java GUI for R

The Java GUI for R, JGR [20] (pronounced "jaguar"), is very similar to R's own simple interface, making it very easy to learn. Written by Markus Helbig, Simon Urbanek, and Martin Theus, JGR provides some very helpful additions to R, like syntax checking in its program editor. It also provides the help files in a way that lets you execute any part of an example you select. That is very helpful when trying to understand a complicated example.

JGR is installed differently than most R packages. On Microsoft Windows or Apple Macintosh, you download two programs: an installer and a launcher. Running the installer installs JGR and double-clicking the launcher starts it up. The JGR web site that contains both programs is http://rosuda.org/JGR/.

Linux users follow slightly different steps that are described at the site.

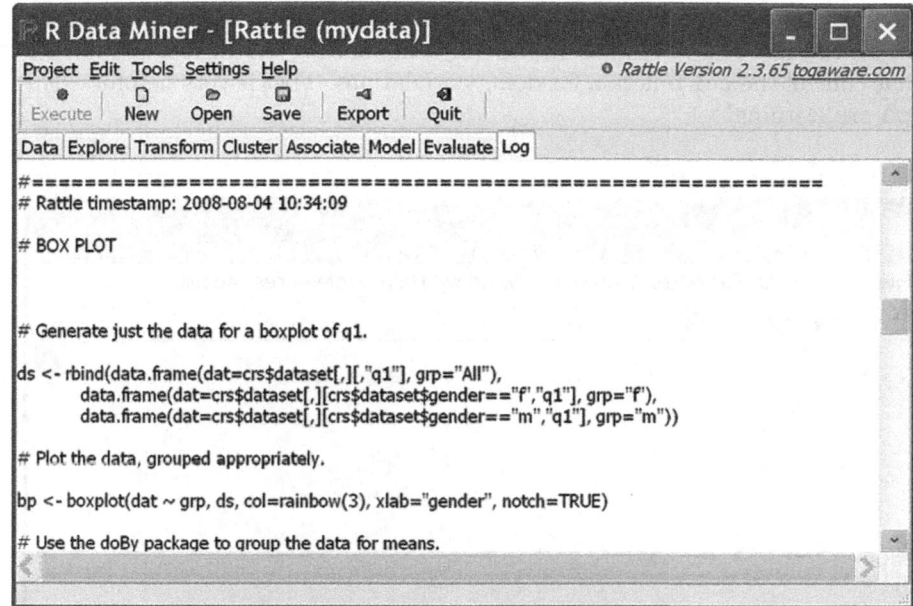

Fig. 3.7. An R program written by Rattle to do a box plot.

We started JGR by double-clicking on its launcher and opened an R program using *File>Open Document.* You can see the program in Fig. 3.8. Note that the JGR program editor has automatically color-coded my comments, function names, and arguments, making it much easier to spot errors. In the printed version of this book those colors are displayed as shades of gray.

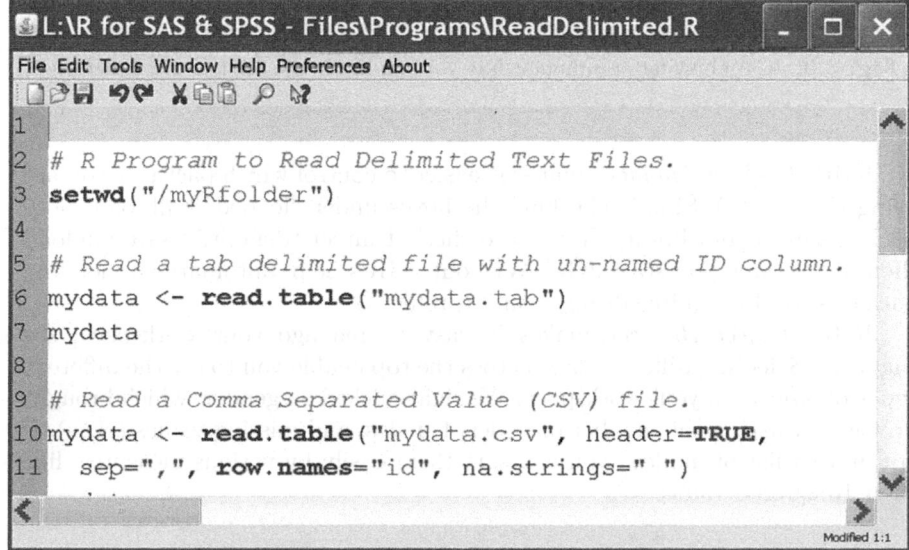

Fig. 3.8. Color-coded editor in JGR helps prevent typing errors.

In the next example, we typed "cor(" into the bottom of the console area shown in Fig. 3.9. JGR then displayed a box showing the various arguments that control the cor function for doing correlations. That is very helpful when you are learning!

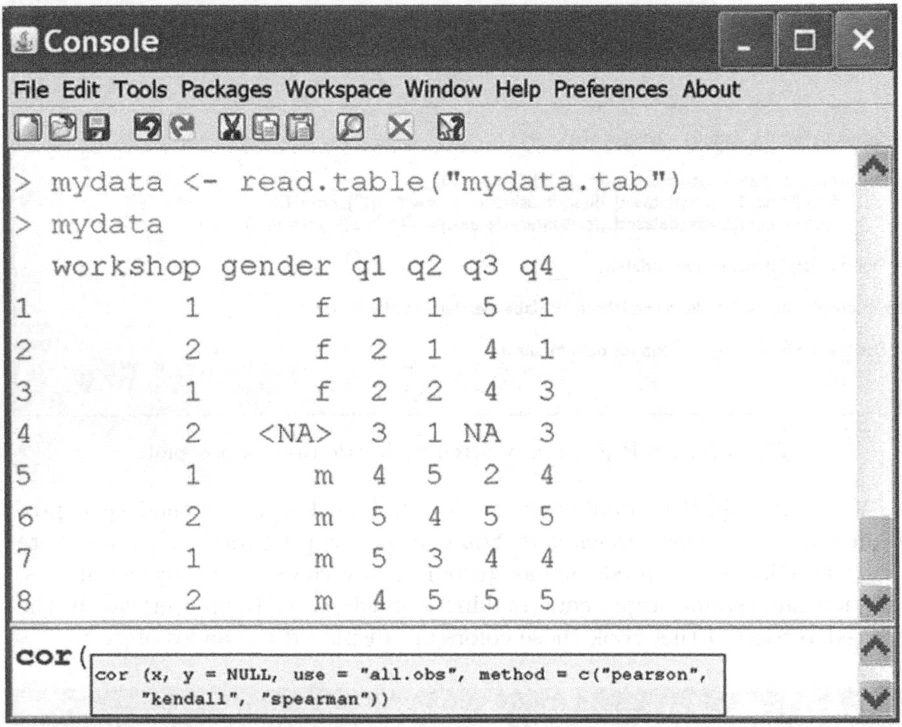

Fig. 3.9. JGR showing arguments that you might choose for the cor function.

JGR's *Package Manager* makes it easier to control which packages you are using (Fig. 3.10). Simply checking the boxes under "loaded" will load those packages from your library. If you also check it under "default," JGR will load them every time you start JGR. Without JGR's help, automatically loading packages would require editing your .Rprofile.

JGR's *Object Browser* makes it easy to manage your workspace; see Fig. 3.11. Selecting different tabs across the top enable you to see the different types of objects in your workspace. We right-clicked on gender, which brought up the box listing the number of males, females, and missing values (NAs). If you have a list of models, you can sort them easily by various measures, like their R-squared values.

Fig. 3.10. JGR's Package Manager, which allows you to load packages from the library on demand or at startup.

Double-clicking on a data frame in the Object Browser starts the *Data Table* editor (Fig. 3.12), which is much nicer than the one built into R. It lets you rename variables, search for values, sort by clicking on variable names, cut and paste values, and add or delete rows or columns.

There are many more useful features in JGR that are described on its web site.

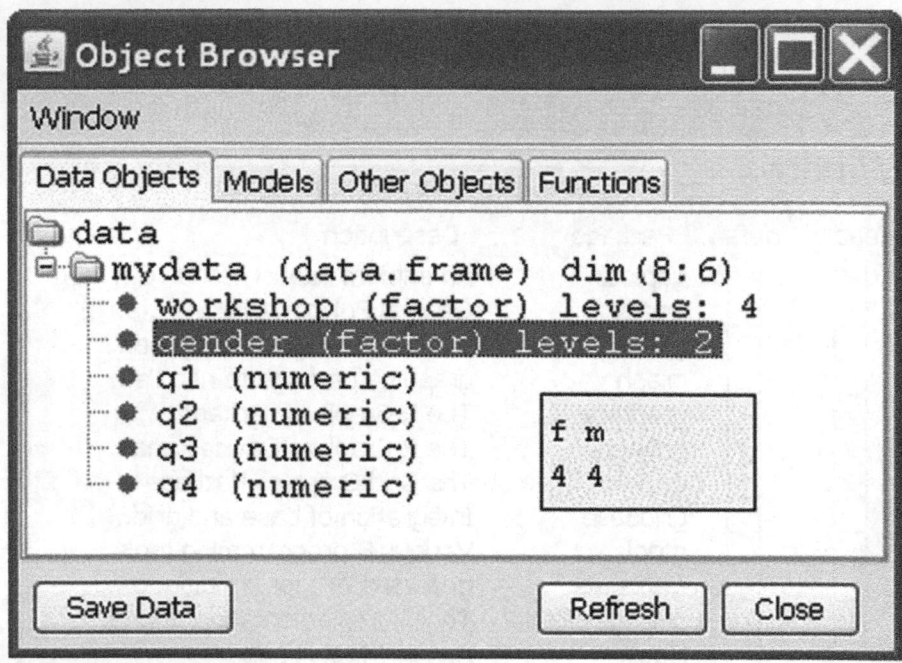

Fig. 3.11. JGR's Object Browser shows information about each object in your workspace.

row.names	workshop	gender	q1	q2	q3	q4
1	1	f	1.0	1.0	5.0	1.0
2	2	f	2.0	1.0	4.0	1.0
3	1	f	2.0	2.0	4.0	3.0
4	2	NA	3.0	1.0	NA	3.0
5	1	m	4.0	5.0	2.0	4.0
6	2	m	5.0	4.0	5.0	5.0
7	1	m	5.0	3.0	4.0	4.0
8	2	m	4.0	5.0	5.0	5.0

Fig. 3.12. JGR's Data Table editor, an improvement over R's primitive one.

4

Help and Documentation

4.1 Introduction

The full Stata package comes with 17 volumes of reference manuals. Both these manuals and the Stata help files are well written and authoritative and their style is consistent. They are of great help to beginners through advanced users.

R has an extensive array of help files and documentation. However, they can be somewhat intimidating at first, since many of them assume you already know a lot about R.

4.2 Help Files

To see how R's help files differ in style from those of Stata, let us examine the help file for the `print` function, which is similar to Stata's `list` command. The help file in R says you can use the `print` function to "Print Values," which is clear enough. However, it then goes on to say that "`print` prints its argument and returns it invisibly (via `invisible(x)`). It is a generic function which means that new printing methods can be easily added for new classes." That requires a much higher level of knowledge than does the Stata description of its similar command: "LIST displays case values for variables in the active data set." However, when you are done with this book, you should have no problem understanding most help files.

4.3 Starting Help

You can start the help system by choosing *Help>HTML Help* on Windows or *Help>R Help* on Macintosh. On any operating system you can submit the `help.start` function in the R Console. That is the way Linux/UNIX users start it since they lack menus.

R.A. Muenchen, J.M. Hilbe, *R for Stata Users*, Statistics
and Computing, DOI 10.1007/978-1-4419-1318-0_4,
© Springer Science+Business Media, LLC 2010

```
help.start()
```

Regardless of how you start it, you will get a help window that looks something like Fig. 4.1

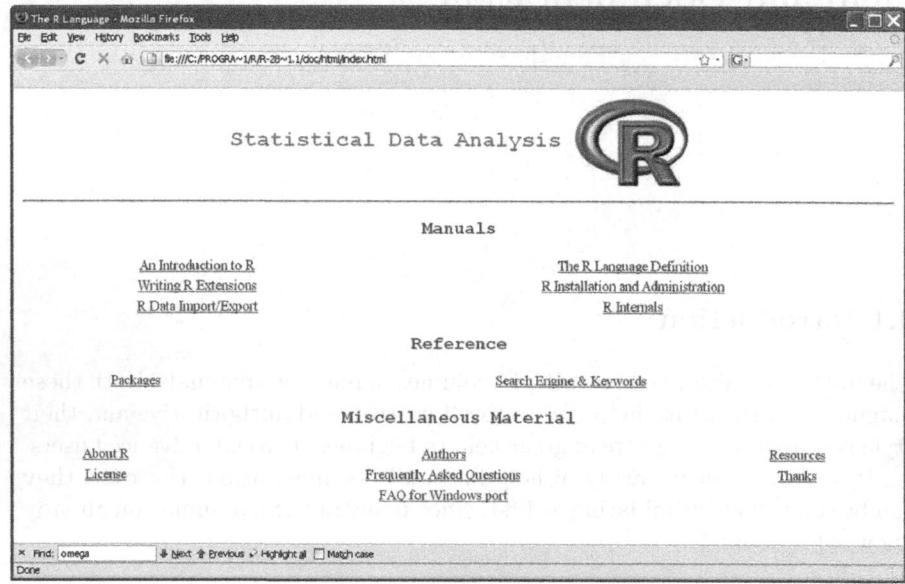

Fig. 4.1. R's main help window.

Similar to using Stata's command, to get help for a certain function such as **summary**, use the form

```
help(summary)
```

or prefix the topic with a question mark:

```
?summary
```

To get help on an operator, enclose it in quotes. For example, to get help on the assignment operator (equivalent to the equal sign in Stata), enter

```
help( "<-" )
```

If you do not know the name of a function or operator, use the **help.search** function to search the help files. This is similar to Stata's **findit** command.

```
help.search("your search string")
```

A shortcut to the **help.search** function is to prefix the term with two question marks, "??." For a single word search, use this form:

```
??yourstring
```

For a string with more than one term in it, enclose it in quotes:

```
??"your multi-word string"
```

A particularly useful help file is the one on extracting and replacing parts of an object. That help file is opened with the following function call. The capital letter in Extract is necessary.

```
help(Extract)
```

It is best to read that one after you have read Chapter 9, "Selecting Variables and Observations."

4.4 Help Examples

Most of R's help files include examples that will execute. You can cut and paste them into a script window to submit in easily understood pieces. You can also have R execute all of the examples at once with the example function. Here are the examples for the mean function, but do not try to understand them now. We will cover the mean function later.

```
> example(mean)

mean> x <- c(0:10, 50)

mean> xm <- mean(x)

mean> c(xm, mean(x, trim = 0.10))

[1] 8.75 5.50

mean> mean(USArrests, trim = 0.2)

  Murder  Assault UrbanPop     Rape
    7.42   167.60    66.20    20.16
```

R changes the prompt of each example function call from ">" to "mean>" to let you know that it is still submitting examples from the mean function's help files. Note that when an example is labeled "Not run," it means that while it is good to study, it will not run unless you adapt it to your needs.

A very nice feature of the JGR graphical user interface is that you can execute most help file example programs by submitting them directly from the help window. You simply select the part you wish to run, right-click on the selection, and then choose "run line or selection." See Section 3.6.3, "JGR Java GUI for R," for details.

Like Stata user-authorized commands, in R you must first install a package and then load it from your library before you can get help. So you cannot use help to find things that you do not already know something about.

A popular addition to R is Frank Harrell's `Hmisc` package [14]. It has many useful functions that add SAS-like capabilities to R. One of these is the `contents` function. Let us try to get help on it before loading the `Hmisc` package.

```
> help("contents")
```

```
No documentation for 'contents' in specified packages
and libraries: you could try '??contents'
```

The help system does not find it, but it does remind you how you might search the help files. However, that search would find the `contents` function only if the `Hmisc` package were already installed. If you did not already know that `Hmisc` had such a function, you might search the Internet (or read a good book!) to find it. Let us now load the `Hmisc` package from our library (after having installed it in the the meantime).

```
> library("Hmisc")
```

R responds with a warning. We will discuss what this means later, but it does not cause a problem now.

```
Attaching package: 'Hmisc'

  The following object(s) are masked from package:base :
      format.pval,
      round.POSIXt,
      trunc.POSIXt,
      units
```

Now that the `Hmisc` package is loaded, we can get help on the `contents` function with the function call `help(contents)`. We do not need to look at the actual help file at the moment. We will cover that function much later.

Now that `Hmisc` is loaded from the library, the `help.search` function can find the `contents` function (see Fig. 4.2)

```
> help.search("contents")
```

4.5 Help for Functions That Call Other Functions

R has functions that exist to call other functions. These are called *generic functions*. In many cases, the help file for the generic function will refer you to those other functions, providing all of the help you need. However, in some

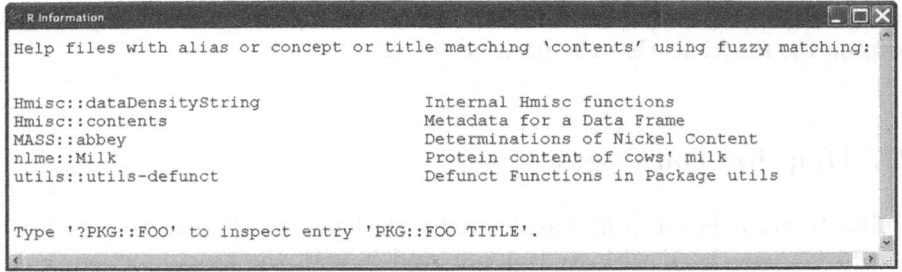

Fig. 4.2. Help search results on the string "contents."

cases you need to dig for such help in other ways. We will discuss this topic in Chapter 5 *Programming Language Basics*, section 5.6.3, *Controlling Functions with an Object's Class*. We will also examine an example of this in Chapter 15, "Traditional Graphics," section 15.9.9, "Scatter Plot Matrices."

4.6 Help for Packages

Thus far we have examined ways to get help about a specific function. You can also get help on an entire package by using the `help` argument in the `library` function. For example, the `foreign` package [7] helps you import data from other software. You can get help on the packages itself with

```
> library(help=foreign)
```

The window in Fig. 4.3 is only a partial view of the information R provides. To get help on a package, you must first install it, but you need not load it.

```
Documentation for package 'foreign'                                    _□×

                    Information on package 'foreign'

Description:

Package:      foreign
Priority:     recommended
Version:      0.8-29
Date:         2008-08-07
Title:        Read Data Stored by Minitab, S, SAS, SPSS, Stata, Systat,$
Depends:      R (>= 2.6.0), stats
Imports:      methods, utils
Maintainer:   R-core <R-core@r-project.org>
Author:       R-core members, Saikat DebRoy <saikat@stat.wisc.edu>, Rog$
              COPYRIGHTS file in the sources.
Description:  Functions for reading and writing data stored by statisti$
              Stata, Systat, ..., and for reading and writing .dbf (dBa$
LazyLoad:     yes
License:      GPL (>= 2)
Packaged:     Thu Aug 7 16:41:12 2008; ripley
Built:        R 2.8.1; i386-pc-mingw32; 2008-12-22 09:25:51; windows
```

Fig. 4.3. Help window for the `foreign` package.

However, not all packages provide help for the whole package. Most do provide help on the functions that the package contains.

4.7 Help for Data Sets

Unlike Stata, R has help files associated with data sets. If an R data set has a help file associated with it, you can read it with the `help` function. For example,

```
help(esoph)
```

will tell you that this is a data set is "Data from a case-control study of (o)esophageal cancer in Ile-et-Vilaine, France."

The rough equivalent to this in Stata is to place a label in a data set using the `label data` command. This allows a short one-line description of the data set.

4.8 Books and Manuals

Other books on R are available free at `http://cran.r-project.org/` under documentation. We will use a number of functions from the `Hmisc` package. Its manual is *An Introduction to S and the Hmisc and Design Libraries* [1] by Alzola and Harrell. It is available at `http://biostat.mc.vanderbilt.edu/twiki/pub/Main/RS/sintro.pdf`. The most widely recommended advanced statistics book on R is *Modern Applied Statistics with S* (abbreviated MASS) by Venables and Ripley [51]. Note that R is almost identical to the S language and books on S usually point out what the differences are. An excellent book on managing data in R is Phil Spector's *Data Manipulation with R* [44]. We will discuss books on graphics in the chapters on that topic.

4.9 E-mail Lists

There are several different e-mail discussion lists regarding R that you can read about and sign up for at `http://www.r-project.org/` under *mailing lists*. We recommend signing up for the one named *R-help*. There you can learn a lot by reading answers to the myriad of questions people post there.

If you post your own questions on the list, you are likely to get an answer in an hour or two. However, please read the posting guide, `http://www.R-project.org/posting-guide.html`, before sending your first question. Taking the time to write a clear and concise question and providing a descriptive subject line will encourage others to take the time to respond. Sending a small example that demonstrates your problem clearly is particularly helpful. See Chapter 12, "Generating Data" for ways to make up a small data set for that purpose. Also include the version of R you are using and your operating system. You can generate all of the relevant details using the `sessionInfo` function:

```
> sessionInfo()
R version 2.8.1 (2008-12-22)
i386-pc-mingw32

locale:
LC_COLLATE=English_United States.1252;LC_CTYPE=English_United...

attached base packages:
[1] stats  graphics  grDevices utils  datasets  methods base

loaded via a namespace (and not attached):
[1] tools_2.8.1
```

4.10 Searching the Web

Searching the Web for information on R using generic search engines such as Google can be frustrating, since the letter R refers to many different things. However, if you add the letter R to other keywords, it is surprisingly effective. Adding the word "package" to your search will also narrow it down.

An excellent site that searches just for R topics is Jonathon Barron's *R Site Search* at `http://finzi.psych.upenn.edu/search.html`. You can search just the R site while in R itself by entering the `RSiteSearch` function

```
RSiteSearch("your search string")
```

or go to `http://www.r-project.org/` and click *search*. If you use the Firefox web browser, there is a free plug-in called *RsiteSearch* you can use. Download it from `http://addictedtor.free.fr/rsitesearch/`.

4.11 Vignettes

Another kind of help is a vignette, a short description. People who write packages can put anything into its vignette. The function call

```
vignette(all=TRUE)
```

will show you vignettes for all of the packages you have installed. To see the vignette for a particular package, enter it in the **vignette** function with its name in quotes:

```
vignette("mypackage")
```

Unfortunately, many packages do not have vignettes.

5

Programming Language Basics

5.1 Introduction

R is an object-oriented language. Everything that exists in it — variables, data sets, functions (commands) — are all objects.

Stata has limitations on command and variable name lengths, based on the version of the software being used. The limits are large, though, and rarely result in a problem for Stata users. In Stata, leading periods in names are not allowed and data set names cannot have periods at all.

Object names in R can be any length consisting of letters, numbers, underscores "_," or the period "." and should begin with a letter.

However, in R if you always put quotes around a variable or data set name (actually any object name), it can then contain any characters, including spaces.

Case matters in both R and Stata, so you can have two variables—one named *myvar* and another named *MyVar*—in the same data set, although that is not a good idea! Some add-on packages tweak function names like the capitalized "**Save**" to represent a compatible, but enhanced, version of a built-in function like the lowercased "**save**."

As in any statistics package, it is best to avoid names that match function names like "**mean**" or that match logical conditions like "TRUE."

Commands can begin and end anywhere on a line and R will ignore any additional spaces. R will try to execute a function when it reaches the end of a line. Therefore, to continue a function call on a new line, you must ensure that the fragment you leave behind is not already a complete function call by itself. Continuing a function call on a new line after a comma is usually a safe bet. As you will see, R functions frequently use commas, making them a convenient stopping point. The R console will tell you that it is continuing a line when it changes the prompt from ">" to "+." If you see "+" unexpectedly, you may have simply forgotten to add the final close parenthesis, ")." Submitting only that character will then finish your function call. If you are getting the "+" and cannot figure out why, you can cancel the pending function call

R.A. Muenchen, J.M. Hilbe, *R for Stata Users*, Statistics and Computing, DOI 10.1007/978-1-4419-1318-0_5, © Springer Science+Business Media, LLC 2010

with the Escape key on Windows or CTRL-C on Macintosh or Linux/UNIX. For CTRL-C, hold the CTRL key down (Linux/UNIX) or the control key (Macintosh) while pressing the letter C. You may end any R function call with a semicolon. That is not required though, except when entering multiple function calls on a single line.

5.2 Simple Calculations

As with Stata's `display` command, you can use R as a calculator. You simply enter commands like

```
> 2+3
```

```
[1] 5
```

The "[1]" tells you the resulting value is the first result. It is only useful when your results run across several lines. We can tell R to generate some data for us to see how the numbering depends on the width of the output. The form 1:50 will generate the integers from 1 to 50.

```
> 1:50
```

```
[1]  1  2  3  4  5  6  7  8  9 10 11 12 13 14 15 16 17 18
[19] 19 20 21 22 23 24 25 26 27 28 29 30 31 32 33 34 35 36
[37] 37 38 39 40 41 42 43 44 45 46 47 48 49 50
```

Now, it is obvious that the numbers in square brackets are counting or indexing the values. We have set our line width to 64 characters to help things fit in this book. We can use the options function to change the width to 40 and see how the bracketed numbers change.

```
> options(width=40)
```

```
> 1:50
```

```
[1]  1  2  3  4  5  6  7  8  9 10 11 12
[13] 13 14 15 16 17 18 19 20 21 22 23 24
[25] 25 26 27 28 29 30 31 32 33 34 35 36
[37] 37 38 39 40 41 42 43 44 45 46 47 48
[49] 49 50
```

```
> options(width=64) #Set it wider again.
```

In Stata, this setting is replicated by "list, linesize(64)."

You can assign the values to symbolic variables like x and y using the assignment operator, a two-character sequence "<-." You can use the equal sign as Stata does, but there are some rather esoteric advantages to using "<-." Here we use it to assign values to x and y and then do some simple math.

```
> x <- 2

> y <- 3

> x+y
  [1] 5

> x*y
  [1] 6
```

We have added extra spaces in the above commands and extra lines in the output for legibility. Additional spaces do not affect the commands.

5.3 Data Structures

R has several different data structures, including *vectors, factors, data frames, matrices, arrays,* and *lists.* The *data frame* is most like a data set in Stata. Stata and R also have data structures specifically for time series, but those are beyond the scope of this book. Mata, the imbedded matrix language in Stata, supports matrices, arrays, vectors, and other similar R-like functions.

5.3.1 Vectors

A *vector* is an object that contains a set of values called *elements.* You can think of it as a Stata variable but that would imply that it is a column in a data set. It is not. It exists by itself and is neither a column nor a row. In Stata, a column is normally stored as a column. For R, it is usually one of two things: a variable or a set of parameter settings called *arguments* that you use to control a function.

Creating Vectors

To keep things simple, all of our examples will use the same data set, a pretend survey about how people liked various training workshops on statistics packages. Let us enter the responses to the first question, "Which workshop did you take?"

```
workshop <- c( 1,2,1,2,1,2,1,2 )
```

All of the values of workshop are numeric, so the vector's *mode* is *numeric*. Stata refers to that as a variable's *type*. As in Stata, if even if one value were alphabetic (character or string), then the mode would be *coerced*, or forced, to be *character*. R does all its work with *functions*, which are similar to Stata *commands* and *functions*.

Functions have a name followed by its parameters, called *arguments*, in parentheses. The c function's job is to combine multiple values into a single vector. Remember it as c=combine. Its arguments are just the values to combine—in this case 1,2,1,2....

To print our vector, we can use the `print` function. This is R's equivalent to the Stata `list` command. However, this function is used so often; it is the default function used when you *type the name* of any object! So when working interactively, these two function calls do exactly the same thing:

```
> print(workshop)

[1] 1 2 1 2 1 2 1 2

> workshop

[1] 1 2 1 2 1 2 1 2
```

We run all of the examples in this book *interactively*; that is, we submit function calls and see the results immediately. You can also run R in *batch mode*, where you would put all your function calls into a file and tell R to run them at once, routing the results to a file. In batch mode you must write out the `print` function. We will point out a few other instances when you must write out the `print` function name in later chapters. Although typing out the `print` function for most of our examples is not necessary, we will do it occasionally when showing how the R code looks in a typical analysis.

Let us create a character variable. Using R jargon, we would say we are going to create a *character vector*, or a vector whose *mode* is *character*. These are the genders of our hypothetical students:

```
> gender <- c( "f","f","f",NA,"m","m","m","m" )

> gender

[1] "f" "f" "f" NA "m" "m" "m" "m"
```

NA stands for Not Available, which R uses to represent missing values. Later we will read data from files whose values are separated by commas. In that case, R would recognize two commas in a row as having a missing value in between them. However, the values in the c function are its arguments. R does not allow its functions to have missing arguments. Entering NA gets around that limitation.

Even when entering character values for gender, never enclose the NA in quotes. If you did, it would be just those letters rather than a missing value. Now let us enter the rest of our data:

```
q1 <- c( 1,2,2,3,4,5,5,4  )
q2 <- c( 1,1,2,1,5,4,3,5  )
q3 <- c( 5,4,4,NA,2,5,4,5 )
q4 <- c( 1,1,3,3,4,5,4,5  )
```

Analyzing Vectors

To get a simple table of frequencies, we can use the **table** function, which is similar to Stata's **tabulate** command.

```
> table(workshop)

workshop
1 2
4 4

> table(gender)

gender
f m
3 4
```

The first thing you will notice about the output is how plain it is. No percents are calculated and no lines drawn to form a table. When you first see a table like the one for workshop, its complete lack of labels may leave you wondering what it means. There are four people who took workshop 1, and four people who took workshop 2. It is not hard to understand—just a shock when you come from a package that labels its output better.

This is a difference in perspective between R and Stata. R creates output that other functions can use immediately. Other functions exist that provide more output, like percents. Still others format output into publication-quality form. Stata allows use of statistical output via saved return codes.

Let us get the mean of the responses to question 3:

```
> mean(q3)

[1] NA
```

The result is NA or Not Available! Many R functions handle missing values differently from Stata. R will usually provide output that is NA when performing an operation on data that contains any missing values. It will typically provide the answer you seek only when you tell it to override that perspective.

There are several ways to do this in R. For the `mean` function, you set the NA remove argument, `na.rm`, equal to TRUE.

```
> mean(q3, na.rm=TRUE)

[1] 4.142857
```

Selecting Vector Elements

So far we have performed a few simple analyses on the entire vector. You can easily select subsets using a method called *indexing* or *subscripting*. You specify which of the vector's elements you want in square brackets following the vector's name. For example, to see the fifth element of q1, you enter

```
> q1[5]

[1] 4
```

When you want to specify multiple elements, you must first combine them into a vector using the c function. Therefore, to see elements 5 through 8, you can use

```
> q1[ c(5,6,7,8) ]

[1] 4 5 5 4
```

The colon operator, ":," can generate vectors directly, so an alternate way of selecting elements 5 through 8 is

```
> q1[ 5:8 ]

[1] 4 5 5 4
```

You can also insert logical selections. They generate logical vectors to perform your selection. Here we use "==" for logical equivalence, just as in Stata:

```
> q1[ gender=="m" ]

[1] NA  4  5  5  4
```

Usually the goal of any of these selection methods is to perform some analysis on a subset. For example, to get the mean response to item q1 for the males, we can use

```
> mean( q1[ gender=="m"], na.rm=TRUE )

[1] 4.5
```

R's ability to select elements of vectors is very flexible. We will demonstrate how to apply these techniques toward selecting parts of other data structures in the sections that immediately follow. Later we will devote three entire chapters showing how to apply these techniques to data sets in Chapter 7, "Selecting Variables" through Chapter 9, "Selecting Variables and Observations."

5.3.2 Factors

Two of the variables we entered above, workshop and gender, are clearly categorical. R has a special data structure called a *factor* for such variables. Regardless of whether the original data is numeric or character, when it becomes a factor, its mode is *numeric*. This is also true for Stata.

Creating Factors from Numeric Vectors

Before we create a factor, let us enter workshop again as a numeric vector and display its values.

```
> workshop <- c(1,2,1,2,1,2,1,2)

> workshop

[1] 1 2 1 2 1 2 1 2
```

Now let us perform two simple analyses.

```
> table(workshop)

workshop

1 2
4 4

> mean(workshop)

[1] 1.5
```

We see that four people took each workshop. We also see that the mean function happily provided the mean of the workshops, which is a fairly nonsensical measure for a categorical variable. R usually tries to do correct things statistically, but we have not yet told it that workshop is categorical.

You can select elements of factors the same way you select elements of vectors. For example, to choose the third element of gender, you can use

```
> gender[3]

[1] f

Levels: f m
```

To see the first two and the last two elements, you can put those index values into a vector using the c function like this:

```
> gender[ c(1,2,7,8) ]

[1] f f m m

Levels: f m
```

Let us now see the genders of the people who took the Stata workshop, which has a value of 2.

```
> gender[ workshop==2 ]

[1] "f" NA  "m" "m"
```

Now let us enter the variable again, convert it to a factor using the **factor** function, and display its values.

```
> workshop <- c(1,2,1,2,1,2,1,2)

> workshop <- factor( workshop )

> workshop

[1] 1 2 1 2 1 2 1 2

Levels: 1 2
```

After using the **factor** function, we see the display of workshop values has an additional feature, the levels. Let us repeat our two analytic functions:

```
> table(workshop)

workshop

1 2
4 4

> mean(workshop)

[1] NA
```

```
Warning message:
In argument is not numeric or logical: returning NA
```

The output from the `table` function is identical, but now the `mean` function warns us that this is not a reasonable request and it results in, or returns, a missing value of NA.

Now that workshop is a factor, we can check the genders of the people who took the Stata workshop (workshop 2) in two ways:

```
> gender[ workshop==2 ]

[1] "f" NA  "m" "m"

> gender[ workshop=="2" ]

[1] "f" NA  "m" "m"
```

The second example uses quotes around the 2 and it still works. This is due to the fact that the original numeric values are now also stored as value labels.

Let us enter workshop again and use additional arguments in the call to the `factor` function so we can assign more useful value labels.

```
workshop <- c(1,2,1,2,1,2,1,2)
workshop <- factor(
  workshop,
  levels=c(1,2,3,4),
  labels=c("R","Stata","SPSS","SAS")
)
```

The `factor` function call above has three arguments:

1. The name of a vector to convert to a factor.
2. The levels or values that the data can have. This allows you to specify values that are not yet in the data. In our case, workshop is limited to the values 1 and 2, but we can include the values 3 and 4 for future expansion. You cannot do that in Stata.
3. Optionally, the labels for the levels. The `factor` function will match the labels to the levels in the order they both appear here. The order of the values in the data set is irrelevant. If you do not provide the labels argument, R will use the values themselves as the labels.

Now when we print the data, it shows us that the people in our practice data set have only taken workshops in R and Stata. It also lists the levels so you can see what labels are possible:

```
> workshop

[1] R    Stata R    Stata R    Stata R    Stata

Levels: R Stata SPSS SAS
```

The `table` function now displays the workshop labels and how many people took each.

```
> table(workshop)

workshop

  R    Stata  SPSS SAS
  4      4      0    0
```

The labels have now replaced the original values. So to check the genders of the people who took the workshop on Stata, we can no longer use the value 2.

```
> gender[ workshop==2 ]

factor(0)

Levels: Male Female
```

When we select based on the value label, it works.

```
> gender[ workshop=="Stata" ]

[1] Female <NA>   Male    Male

Levels: Male Female
```

Creating Factors from Character Vectors

You can convert character vectors to factors in a similar manner. Let us again enter gender as a character vector and print its values.

```
> gender <- c( "f","f","f",NA,"m","m","m","m" )

> gender

[1] "f" "f" "f" NA "m" "m" "m" "m"
```

Notice that the missing value, NA, does not have quotes around it. R leaves out the quotes to let you know that it is not a valid character string that might stand for something like North America.

If we are happy with those labels, we can convert gender to a factor by using the simplest form of the `factor` function:

```
> gender <- factor(gender)

> gender

 [1] f f f NA m m m m

Levels: f m
```

If, instead, we want nicer labels, we can use the longer form. It uses the same approach we used for workshop, but the values on the levels argument need to be in quotes:

```
> gender <- factor(
+    gender,
+    levels=c("m","f"),
+    labels=c("Male","Female")
+ )

> gender

 [1] Female Female Female NA Male   Male   Male   Male

Levels: Male Female

> table(gender)

gender

  Male Female
     4      3
```

You now need to use the new labels when performing selections on gender. For example, to see which workshops the males took, this returns a value of NA because gender never has a value of "m" at this point.

```
> workshop[ gender=="m" ]

[1] <NA>

Levels: R SAS SPSS STATA
```

Instead, specifying the new label of "Male" find the workshops they took:

```
> workshop[ gender=="Male" ]
```

```
[1] <NA> R      Stata  R      Stata
```

```
Levels: R Stata SPSS SAS
```

Note that the last line of output conveniently tells you all of the levels of the factor even though the males did not take all of the workshops.

We will examine factors in more detail, and compare them to Stata value labels in Section 11.1, "Value Labels or Formats (and Measurement Level)."

For the remainder of the book we will use the shorter gender value labels, "m" and "f."

5.3.3 Data Frames

The data structure in R that is most like a Stata data set is the *data frame*. Stata data sets are always rectangular, with *variables* in the columns and *observations* in the rows. A data frame is also rectangular. In R terminology, the columns are called *vectors, variables,* or just *columns.* R calls the rows *observations, cases,* or just *rows.*

A data frame is a generalized *matrix*, one that can contain both character and numeric columns. A data frame is also a special type of *list*, one which requires each *component* to have the same *length.* We will discuss matrices and lists in the next two sections.

We have already seen that R can store variables in vectors and factors. Why does it need another data structure? R can generate almost any type of analysis or graph from data stored in vectors or factors. For example, getting a scatter plot of the responses to q1 versus q4 is easy. R will pair the first number from each vector as the first (x,y) pair to plot and so on down the line. However, it is up to you to make sure that this pairing makes sense. If you sort one vector independent of the others, or remove the missing values from vectors independently, the critical information of how the pairs should form is lost. A plot will still appear, but it will contain a completely misleading view of the data. Sorting almost any two variables in ascending order independently will create the appearance of a very strong relationship. The data frame helps maintain this critical pairing information.

Creating a Data Frame

The most common way to create a data frame is to read it from another source such as a text file, spreadsheet, or database. You can usually do that with a single function call. We will do that later in Chapter 6, "Data Acquisition". For the moment, we will create one by combining our vectors and factors. The following is our program so far:

```
workshop <- c(1,2,1,2,1,2,1,2)
```

```
workshop <- factor(workshop,
    levels = c(1,2,3,4),
    labels = c("R","Stata","SPSS","SAS") )

gender <- c("f","f","f",NA,"m","m","m","m")

gender <- factor(gender)

q1 <- c(1,2,2,3,4,5,5,4)
q2 <- c(1,1,2,1,5,4,3,5)
q3 <- c(5,4,4,NA,2,5,4,5)
q4 <- c(1,1,3,3,4,5,4,5)
```

Now we will use the **data.frame** function to combine our variables (vectors and factors) into a data frame. Its arguments are simply the names of the objects we wish to combine.

```
> mydata <- data.frame(workshop,gender,q1,q2,q3,q4)

> mydata
```

	workshop	gender	q1	q2	q3	q4
1	R	f	1	1	5	1
2	Stata	f	2	1	4	1
3	R	f	2	2	4	3
4	Stata	\<NA\>	3	1	NA	3
5	R	m	4	5	2	4
6	Stata	m	5	4	5	5
7	R	m	5	3	4	4
8	Stata	m	4	5	5	5

Notice that the missing value for gender is now shown as "<NA>." When R prints data frames, it drops the quotes around character values and so must differentiate missing value NAs from valid character strings that happen to be the letters "NA." If we wanted to rename the vectors as we created the data frame, we could do so with the following form. Here the vector "gender" will be stored in mydata with the name "sex" and the others will keep their original names. Of course, we could have renamed every variable using this approach.

```
mydata <- data.frame(workshop, sex=gender, q1, q2, q3, q4)
```

Although we had already made gender into a factor, the **data.frame** function will coerce all character variables to become factors when the data frame is created. You do not always want that to happen (for example when you have vectors that store people's names and addresses.) To prevent that from occurring, you can add the `stringsAsFactors=FALSE` argument in the call to the `data.frame` function.

R data frames have a formal place for an ID variable it calls *row names*. These can be informative text labels like subject names, but, by default, they are sequential numbers stored as character values. The `row.names` function will display them:

```
> row.names(mydata)
```

```
[1] "1" "2" "3" "4" "5" "6" "7" "8"
```

Stata displays sequential numbers like this in its data editor. However, those numbers are reassigned to new observations when you sort your data. Row names in R are more useful since sorting never changes their values. You can always use them to return your data to its original state by sorting on the row names. See Section 10.16, "Sorting Data Frames," for details.

Stata users typically enter an ID variable based on the built-in Stata constant "_n," which contains the observation/case number of data stored in memory. However, this variable is like any other unless you manually supply it to a procedure that identifies observations. In R, procedures that identify observations will do so automatically using row names. If you set an ID variable to be row names while reading a text file, the variable's original name (id, subject, SSN,...) vanishes. Since functions that do things—like identify outliers—will use the information automatically, you usually do not need the name. We will discuss row names further when we read text files and in Section 10.6, "Renaming Variables (...and Observations)."

Selecting Components of Data Frames

There are several ways to select the components of a data frame. For now, we will focus on just two: selecting by index numbers and by a method called $ notation. We will save the other methods for later chapters.

Selecting Data Frame Components by Index Numbers

While vectors and factors have only one-dimensional index values with which to select their elements, data frames have two. These are in the form

```
mydataframe[rows,columns]
```

For example, can choose the eighth observation's value of the sixth variable, q4, using

```
> mydata[ 8, 6 ]
```

```
[1] 5
```

If we leave out a row or column specification, R will assume we want them all. So to select all of the observations for the sixth variable, we can use

```
> mydata[ , 6 ]
```

```
[1] 1 1 3 3 4 5 4 5
```

It so happens that the above example is selecting a vector. We saw before that we could add index values to the end of a vector to select a subset of it. So for variable q4, we could choose its fifth through eighth elements using

```
> q4[ 5:8 ]
```

```
[1] 4 5 4 5
```

In our data frame, mydata[,6] is the same vector as variable q4. There-fore, we can make this same selection by appending the [5:8] to it to make the same selection:

```
> mydata[ , 6 ][ 5:8 ]
```

```
[1] 4 5 4 5
```

Selecting Data Frame Components Using $ Notation

Since the components of our data frame have names, we can also select them by those names using the form

```
myDataFrameName$myComponentName
```

Therefore, to select q1 from mydata, we can use

```
> mydata$q1
```

```
[1] 1 2 2 3 4 5 5 4
```

The variable q1 is still a vector, so we can append index values to it to make further selections. To select the fifth through eighth value (the males), we can use

```
> mydata$q1[ 5:8 ]
```

```
[1] 4 5 5 4
```

As we will soon see, there are many other ways to select subsets of data frames. We will save the other methods for Chapter 7, "Selecting Variables" through Chapter 9, "Selecting Variables and Observations."

5.3.4 Matrices

A *matrix* is a two-dimensional data object that looks like a Stata data set, but it is actually one long vector wrapped into rows and columns. Because of this, its values must be of the same mode, [i.e., all numeric, all character, or all logical (more on logical vectors later)]. This constraint makes matrices more efficient than data frames for some types of analyses.

Creating a Matrix

The cbind function takes *columns* and *binds* them together into a matrix:

```
> mymatrix <- cbind(q1, q2, q3, q4)

> mymatrix

     q1 q2 q3 q4
[1,]  1  1  5  1
[2,]  2  1  4  1
[3,]  2  2  4  3
[4,]  3  1 NA  3
[5,]  4  5  2  4
[6,]  5  4  5  5
[7,]  5  3  4  4
[8,]  4  5  5  5
```

As you can see, a matrix is a two-dimensional array of values. The numbers to the left side in brackets are the row numbers. The form [1,] means that it is row number one and the *lack of a number* following the comma means that R has displayed all of the columns.

We can get the dimensions of the matrix with the dim function.

```
> dim(mymatrix)

[1] 8 4
```

The first dimension is the number of rows, 8, and the second is the number of columns, 4.

To create a matrix, you do not need to start with separate vectors as we did. You can create one directly with the matrix function. The matrix function call below has four arguments. The first argument is data, which you must enter enclosed in the c function. The next three specify the number of rows, columns, and whether or not you are entering the data by rows. If you leave the byrow=TRUE argument off, you would enter the data turned on its side. We prefer to enter it by rows since it looks more like the format used with Stata data sets.

```
> mymatrix <- matrix(
+    c(1, 1, 5, 1,
+       2, 1, 4, 1,
+       2, 2, 4, 3,
+       3, 1, NA,3,
+       4, 5, 2, 4,
+       5, 4, 5, 5,
+       5, 3, 4, 4,
+       4, 5, 5, 5),
+    nrow=8, ncol=4, byrow=TRUE)

> mymatrix

     [,1] [,2] [,3] [,4]
[1,]    1    1    5    1
[2,]    2    1    4    1
[3,]    2    2    4    3
[4,]    3    1   NA    3
[5,]    4    5    2    4
[6,]    5    4    5    5
[7,]    5    3    4    4
[8,]    4    5    5    5
```

We see that the result is the same as before, except that the columns are no longer named q1, q2, q3, q4. Now let us see what the table, mean and cor functions do with matrices. We will use the earlier version of our matrix, so we will see the variable names.

```
> table(mymatrix)

mymatrix

1 2 3 4 5
6 4 4 8 9

> mean( mymatrix, na.rm=TRUE )

 [1] 3.266667

> cor( mymatrix, use="pairwise" )

            q1          q2          q3          q4
q1   1.0000000   0.7395179  -0.1250000   0.9013878
q2   0.7395179   1.0000000  -0.2700309   0.8090398
q3  -0.1250000  -0.2700309   1.0000000  -0.2182179
q4   0.9013878   0.8090398  -0.2182179   1.0000000
```

The `table` function counts the responses *across all survey questions at once!* That is not something Stata would usually do. It is odd, but not useless. We can see that 9 times people strongly agreed (a value of 5) with any of the questions on our survey.

The `mean` function gets the mean response of them all. Again, it is not of much interest in our situation, but you might find cases where it would be of value.

The `cor` function correlates each item with the others, which is a very common statistical procedure. The fact that the names q1, q1,... appear shows that we are using the version of the matrix we created by combining the vectors with those names.

If you put a matrix into a data frame, its columns will become individual vectors. For example, now that we have mymatrix, we can create our practice data frame in two ways. Both have an identical result:

```
mydata <- data.frame( workshop, gender, q1, q2, q3, q4 )
```

or

```
mydata <- data.frame( workshop, gender, mymatrix )
```

In our case, there is not much difference between the two approaches. However, If you had 100 variables already in a matrix, the latter would be much easier to do.

Selecting Subsets of Matrices

Like data frames, matrices have two dimensions. You can select a subset of a matrix by specifying the two index values in the form

```
mymatrix[rows,columns]
```

For example, we can choose the eighth row and the fourth column using

```
> mymatrix[ 8, 4 ]
```

```
q4
 5
```

We can chose the males, rows five through eight, and variables q3 and q4 using:

```
> mymatrix[ 5:8, 3:4]
```

```
      [,1] [,2]
[1,]    2    4
[2,]    5    5
[3,]    4    4
[4,]    5    5
```

When discussing vectors, we learned that we could select parts of a vector using only one-dimensional indexes. For example, q4[1:4] selects the first four elements of the vector q4. When we leave out one of the two index values for a matrix, we are selecting a vector. Therefore, we can do this very same example by appending [1:4] to mymatrix[,4] as in

```
> mymatrix[ ,4][1:4]
```

```
[1] 1 1 3 3
```

Most of the other methods we have used for selecting elements of vectors or factors work in a similar manner with matrices.

5.3.5 Arrays

An array is a multidimensional extension of the matrix structure. You can think of it as a set of matrices. The use of arrays is beyond our scope.

5.3.6 Lists

A *list* is a very flexible data structure. You can use it to store combinations of any other objects, even other lists. The objects stored in a list are called its *components*. That is a broader term than *variables*, or *elements* of a vector, reflecting the wider range of objects possible.

You can use a list to store related sets of data stored in different formats like vectors and matrices (see the example below). R often uses lists to store different bits of output from the same analysis. For example, results from a linear regression would have equation parameters, residuals and so on. See Chapter 17, "Statistics" for details.

You can also use lists to store sets of arguments to control functions. We will do that later when reading multiple lines of data per case from a text file. Since each record we read will contain a different set of variables—each with a different set of column widths we would need to describe—a list is a perfect way to store them. For an example, see Section 6.5, "Reading Fixed-Width Text Files, Two or More Records per Case."

We will also store arguments when aggregating data by workshop and gender in Section 10.11, "Creating Collapsed or Aggregated Data Sets."

Creating a List

For now, we will focus on storing data in a list. We can combine our variables (vectors) *and our matrix* into a list using the list function.

```
> mylist <- list(workshop, gender, q1, q2, q3, q4, mymatrix)
```

Now let us print it.

```
> mylist

[[1]]
[1] R    Stata R    Stata R    Stata R    Stata
Levels: R Stata SPSS SAS

[[2]]
[1] f    f    f    <NA> m    m    m    m
Levels: f m

[[3]]
[1] 1 2 2 3 4 5 5 4

[[4]]
[1] 1 1 2 1 5 4 3 5

[[5]]
[1]  5  4  4 NA  2  5  4  5

[[6]]
[1] 1 1 3 3 4 5 4 5

[[7]]
     q1 q2 q3 q4
[1,]  1  1  5  1
[2,]  2  1  4  1
[3,]  2  2  4  3
[4,]  3  1 NA  3
[5,]  4  5  2  4
[6,]  5  4  5  5
[7,]  5  3  4  4
[8,]  4  5  5  5
```

Notice how the vector components of the list print sideways now. That allows each variable to have a different length, or even to have a totally different structure, like a matrix. Also notice that it counts the components of the list with an additional index value in double brackets [[1]], [[2]].... Then each component has its usual index values in single brackets.

Recall that when we added our matrix to a data frame, the structure of the matrix vanished and the matrix columns became variables in the data frame. Here though, the matrix is able to maintain its separate identity within the list.

Let us create the list again, this time naming each component.

```
> mylist <- list(
+    workshop=workshop,
+    gender=gender,
+    q1=q1,
+    q2=q2,
+    q3=q3,
+    q4=q4,
+    mymatrix=mymatrix)
```

Now when we print it, the names [[1]], [[2]],... are replaced by the names we supplied.

```
> mylist

$workshop
[1] R       Stata R      Stata R      Stata R      Stata
Levels: R Stata

$gender
[1] f     f     f     <NA> m     m     m     m
Levels: f m

$q1
[1] 1 2 2 3 4 5 5 4

$q2
[1] 1 1 2 1 5 4 3 5

$q3
[1]  5  4  4 NA  2  5  4  5

$q4
[1] 1 1 3 3 4 5 4 5

$mymatrix
     q1 q2 q3 q4
[1,]  1  1  5  1
[2,]  2  1  4  1
[3,]  2  2  4  3
[4,]  3  1 NA  3
[5,]  4  5  2  4
[6,]  5  4  5  5
[7,]  5  3  4  4
[8,]  4  5  5  5
```

Selecting Components of a List

Since a data frame is a specific type of list, any method of selecting components that we discussed for data frames will also apply here. However, since the types of objects a list can store is broader, so too are the techniques for selecting its components.

Selecting Components of a List by Index Numbers

To select the components from a list, we can always use the double-bracketed index values. For example, to select the vector containing gender, we can use

```
> mylist[[2]]
```

```
[1] "f" "f" "f" NA  "m" "m" "m" "m"
```

To select the matrix, we can use

```
> mylist[[7]]
```

```
     [,1] [,2] [,3] [,4]
[1,]   1    1    5    1
[2,]   2    1    4    1
[3,]   2    2    4    3
[4,]   3    1   NA    3
[5,]   4    5    2    4
[6,]   5    4    5    5
[7,]   5    3    4    4
[8,]   4    5    5    5
```

When selecting components from a list, we can continue to add index values to select subsets of that component. Recall that earlier we selected the fifth through eighth rows and third through fourth columns of mymatrix by appending [5:8,3:4] to its name, mymatrix[5:8,3:4]. Now that we can select this matrix by referring to mylist[[7]], we can also append [5:8,3:4] to that:

```
> mylist[[7]][ 5:8, 3:4 ]
```

```
     [,1] [,2]
[1,]   2    4
[2,]   5    5
[3,]   4    4
[4,]   5    5
```

R's indexing approach starts looking pretty confusing at this point, but do not worry. In future chapters we will see that selections usually look far more natural with variable names used to select columns and with logical selections choosing rows.

Selecting Components of a List Using $ Notation

Since we have named our list's components, we can make the same selections by using the form

```
myListName$myComponentName
```

Therefore, to select the component named q1, we can use

```
> mylist$q1

[1] 1 2 2 3 4 5 5 4
```

We can also append index values in square brackets to our selections to choose subsets. Here we select my matrix, then choose the fifth through eighth rows and third and fourth columns:

```
> mylist$mymatrix[ 5:8, 3:4 ]

    q3 q4
[1,]  2  4
[2,]  5  5
[3,]  4  4
[4,]  5  5
```

5.4 Saving Your Work

When learning any new computer program, always do a small amount of work, save it, and get completely out of the software. Then go back in and verify that you really did know how to save your work.

This is a good point at which to stop, clean things up, and save your work. Until you save your work, everything resides in the computer's main random access memory. You never know when a power outage might erase it. R calls this temporary work area its *workspace*. We want to transfer everything we have created from this temporary workspace to a permanent file on our computer's hard drive.

You can use the ls function to see all of the data objects you have created. If you put no arguments between the ls function's parentheses, you will get a list of all your objects. Another more descriptive name for this function is objects. I use ls below instead of objects because it is more popular. That may be due to the fact that Linux and UNIX have an "ls" command that performs a similar function by listing your files.

If you have done the examples from the beginning of this chapter, here are the objects you will see in your workspace.

```
> ls()

[1] "gender"     "mydata"    "mylist"    "mymatrix" "q1"
[6] "q2"         "q3"        "q4"        "workshop" "x"
[11] "y"
```

We want to save some of these objects to our computer's hard drive, but where will they go? The directory or folder that R will store files in is called its *working directory.* Unless you tell it otherwise, R will put any file you save into that directory. On Windows XP or earlier, that is:
C:\Documents and Settings\username\My Documents. On Windows Vista or later, that is: C:\Users\Yourname\My Documents. On Macintosh, the default working directory is /Users/username.

The setwd function *sets* your *w*orking *d*irectory, telling R where you would like your files to go. The getwd function *get*s your *w*orking *d*irectory for you to see.

```
> getwd()

[1] "C:/Documents and Settings/username/My Documents"

> setwd("/myRfolder")

> getwd()

[1] "/myRfolder"
```

Notice that we use a forward slash in "/myRfolder." R can use forward slashes in filenames *even on computers running Windows!* The usual backslashes used in Windows file specifications have a different meaning in R, and in this context will generate an error message:

```
> setwd("\myRfolder") #backslashes are bad in filenames!

Error in setwd("myRfolder") : cannot change working directory

In addition: Warning messages:
1: '\m' is an unrecognized escape in a character string
2: unrecognized escape removed from "\myRfolder"
```

The message warns you that R is trying to figure out what "\m" means. We will discuss why later.

So now we know what is in our workspace and where our working directory resides. We are ready to save our work. However, which objects should we save? Once we have combined our vectors into a data frame, we do not need the individual vectors any more. We will save just our data frame, mydata, and the matrix of survey questions, mymatrix.

The **save** function saves the objects you tell it, to the file you list as its last argument.

```
save(mydata, mymatrix, file="mydata.RData")
```

While Stata users typically only save one data set to a file, R users often save multiple objects to a single file using this approach.

Rather than tell R what you *do* want to save, you could remove the objects that you do *not* want to save and then save everything that remains. We can remove the ones we do not want by listing them as arguments separated by commas on the **remove** function. It also has a more popular shorter name, **rm**.

```
> rm( x,y,workshop,gender,q1,q2,q3,q4,mylist )

> ls()

[1] "mydata" "mymatrix"
```

The **save.image** function will save all objects in your workspace to the file you specify:

```
save.image(file="myWorkspace.RData")
```

When you exit R, it will ask if you want to save your workspace. Since we are saving it to a file we have named, you can tell it no. The next time you start R, you can load your work with the load function.

```
> load("mydata.RData")
```

If you want to see what you have loaded, use the **ls** function:

```
> ls()

[1] "mydata" "mymatrix"
```

For more details, see Chapter 13, *Managing Your Files and Workspace.*

5.5 Comments to Document Your Programs

No matter how simple you may think a program is when you write it, it is good to sprinkle in comments liberally to remind yourself later what you did and why you did it. As we have discussed briefly, R uses the # operator to begin a comment. R comments continue until the end of the line. You can put comments in the middle of statements, but only if they are at the end of the line:

```
# This comment is on its own line, between functions.

workshop <- c(1,2,1,2, #This comment is within the arguments.
              1,2,1,2) #And this is at the end.
```

Unlike Stata /*...*/ style comments, there is no way to comment out a whole block of code that you want to ignore. R users get around that by pretending to define a function whose only goal is to have R ignore the code. For example:

```
BigComment <- function(x)
{
    # Here is code I do not want to run,
    # but I might need to run it later.
mean(x, na.rm=TRUE)
sd(x, na.rm=TRUE)
}
```

While Stata allows errors to exist in the code that has been commented out, R does not. R is actually creating the function, so the code within it must be correct.

A better way to comment out a large block of text is to use a text editor that can easily add (and later remove) the # character to the front of each line in a selected block of code.

5.6 Controlling Functions (Commands)

Stata controls its procedures though commands like `glm` and related options such as # to specify which variables are factors (categorical). Stata commands and functions have options controlling exactly what appears in the output. Modeling statements have a formula syntax. R has analogs to these methods, plus a few unique ones.

5.6.1 Controlling Functions with Arguments

Stata uses options to control what commands calculate and display. R does too, using slightly different terminology. R uses *arguments* to control functions. Let us look at the help file for the `mean` function. The following function call will display its help file:

```
> help(mean)
```

In Fig. 5.1, in the section labeled *Usage*, the help file tells us that the overall form of the function is `mean(x, ...)`. That means you have to provide an R object represented by x, followed by arguments represented by "...." The

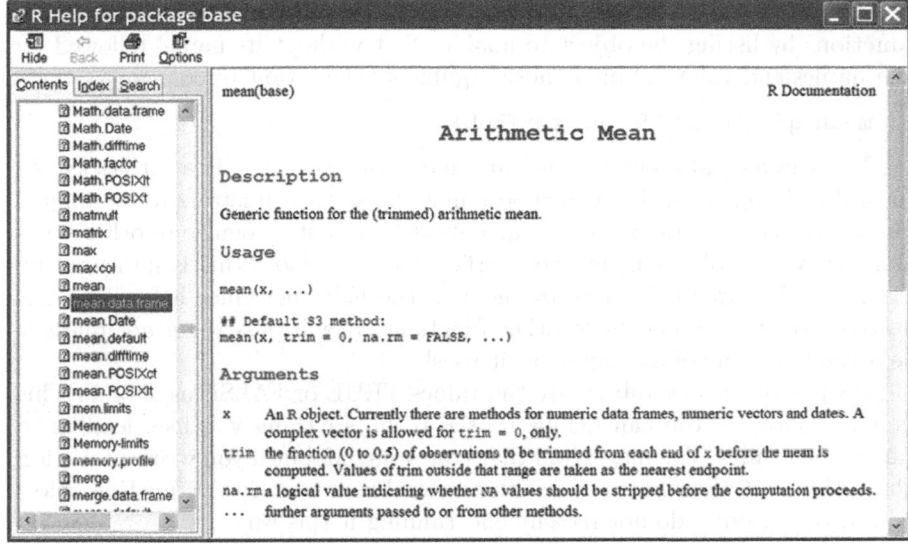

Fig. 5.1. Help file for the mean function.

Default S3 Method section tells us the arguments used by the mean function itself as well as their initial, or default, settings. So if you do not tell it otherwise, it will not trim any data (trim=0) and will not remove missing values (na.rm=FALSE). That means the presence of any missing values will result in the mean being missing or NA too. The "..." means that more arguments are possible, but the mean function will pass those along to other functions that it calls. We will see examples of that later.

The *Arguments* section gets into the details. It tells you that x can be a numeric data frame, numeric vector, or date vector. It also has a comment about *complex* vectors, which are beyond our scope. The trim argument tells R the percent of the extreme values to exclude before calculating the mean. It goes on to define what na.rm and "..." do.

We can run the mean function on our q3 variable by naming each argument. We deleted it previously with the rm function, but imagine that we had not done that. Here we call the function, naming its arguments in the order they appear in the help file and setting their values.

```
mean(x=q3, trim=.25, na.rm=TRUE)
```

If you name all of the arguments, you can use them in any order.

```
mean(na.rm=TRUE, x=q3, trim=.25)
```

We can also run it by listing every argument in their proper positions but without the argument names:

```
mean(q3, .25, TRUE)
```

All of these approaches work equally well. However, people usually run R functions by listing the object to analyze first without its name, followed by the names and values of only those arguments they want to change:

```
mean(q3, trim=.25, na.rm=TRUE)
```

You can also abbreviate some argument names, but it is a bit tricky. As in Stata, the abbreviation you choose must have enough letters to be unique. However, some functions pass arguments they do not recognize to other functions they control. As mentioned earlier in this section, this is indicated by "..." as the function's last argument in the help file. Once a function has started passing arguments to other functions, R will pass them *all* unless it sees the full name of an argument it uses!

People sometimes abbreviate the values TRUE or FALSE as T or F. This is a bad idea, as you can define T or F to be anything you like, leading to undesired results. You may avoid that trap yourself, but if you write a function that others will use, they may use those variable names. So the function below will also run, but I do not recommend running it this way.

```
mean(q3, t=.25 na=T)
```

It is a good idea to avoid abbreviations when naming R arguments.

5.6.2 Controlling Functions with Formulas

An important type of argument is the *formula*. It is the first parameter in functions that do modeling. For example, we can do linear regression, predicting q4 from the others with the following call to the lm function for *l*inear *m*odels.

```
lm( q4 ~ q1+q2+q3, data=mydata )
```

Some modeling functions accept arguments in the form of both formulas and vectors. For example, both of these function calls will compare the genders on the mean of variable q1.

```
t.test( q1 ~ gender, data=mydata )
```

```
t.test( q1[ which(gender=="Female") ],
        q1[ which(gender=="Male")   ],
        data=mydata) #Data ignored!
```

However, there is one very important difference. When using a formula, the data argument can supply the name of a data frame that R will search before looking elsewhere for variables. When not using a formula, as in the second example, the data argument is ignored! We deleted the variables outside the data frame, so R no longer knows where q1 is. The variable q1 still exists in mydata, but even though we use the data argument to point to it, R will find it only for formulas. This approach maintains R's extreme flexibility while helping to keep formulas short. We will clarify this in Section 17.5, "Linear Regression."

The symbols that R uses for formulas are somewhat different from those used by Stata. Table 5.1 shows some common examples using a, b, and c as categorical factors and y, x1, and x2 as continuous numeric variables.

Table 5.1. Example formulas in Stata and R.

Model	Stata	R
Simple regression	MODEL reg y x	y~x
Multiple regression with interaction	MODEL reg y i.x1#i.x2	y~x1+x2+x1:x2
Regression without intercept	MODEL reg y x1, nocons	y~-1+x
One-way analysis of variance	MODEL oneway y a	y~a
Two-way analysis of variance with interaction	MODEL anova y a b a*b	y~a+b+a:b y~a*b
Analysis of covariance	MODEL anova y a, cont(x)	y~a x
Analysis of variance with b nested within a	MODEL anova y b|a	y~b \%in\% a y~a/b

5.6.3 Controlling Functions with an Object's Class

In R, each data structure stores its *class* as an *attribute*, or stored setting, that functions use to determine how to process the object. For objects whose *mode* is numeric, character, or logical, an object's class is its mode. However, for matrices, arrays, factors, lists, or data frames, other values are possible (see Table 5.2).

You can display an object's class with the `class` function:

```
> workshop <- c( 1,2,1,2,1,2,1,2 )

> class(workshop)

[1] "numeric"

> summary(workshop)

   Min. 1st Qu.  Median   Mean 3rd Qu.    Max.
    1.0     1.0     1.5    1.5     2.0     2.0
```

Table 5.2. Modes and classes of various R objects.

Object	Mode	Class
Numeric vector	numeric	numeric
Character vector	character	character
Factor	numeric	factor
Data frame	list	data.frame
List	list	list
Numeric matrix	numeric	matrix
Character matrix	character	matrix
Model	list	lm...
Table	numeric	table

The class *"numeric"* indicates that this version of workshop is a numeric vector, not yet a factor. The summary function provided us with inappropriate information because we failed to tell it that workshop is a factor. Note that when we convert workshop into a factor, we are changing its class to factor and then summary gives us the more appropriate counts instead:

```
> workshop <- factor(workshop,
+     levels=c(1,2,3,4),
+     labels=c("R","Stata","SPSS","SAS") )

> class(workshop)
 [1] "factor"

> summary(workshop)

   R   Stata  SPSS SAS
   4     4     0    0
```

When we first created gender, it was a character vector so its class was character. Later we made its class factor. Numeric vectors like q1 have a class of numeric. The names of some other classes are obvious: factor, data.frame, matrix, list, and array. Objects created by functions have many other classes. For example, the linear model function, lm, stores its output in objects with a class of *lm*.

R has some special functions called *generic functions*. They accept multiple classes of objects and change their processing accordingly. These functions are tiny. Their task is simply to determine the class of the object and then pass it off to another that will do the actual work. The methods function will tell you what other functions a generic function will call. Let us look at the methods that the summary function uses.

```
> methods(summary)

 [1] summary.aov              summary.aovlist
```

```
[3]  summary.connection     summary.data.frame
[5]  summary.Date           summary.default
[7]  summary.ecdf*          summary.factor
[9]  summary.glm            summary.infl
[11] summary.lm             summary.loess*
[13] summary.manova         summary.matrix
[15] summary.mlm            summary.nls*
[17] summary.packageStatus* summary.POSIXct
[19] summary.POSIXlt        summary.ppr*
[21] summary.prcomp*        summary.princomp*
[23] summary.stepfun        summary.stl*
[25] summary.table          summary.tukeysmooth*
   Non-visible functions are asterisked
```

So when we enter summary(mydata), the summary function sees that my-data is a data frame and then passes it to the function summary.data.frame. The functions marked with asterisks above are "non-visible." Visible functions you can be seen by typing their name (without any parentheses). That makes it easy to copy and change them, although only an advanced user would want to do that.

When we discussed the help files, we saw that the **mean** function ended with an argument of "...." That indicates that the function will pass arguments on to other functions. While it is very helpful that generic functions automatically do the "right thing" when you give it various objects to analyze, it complicates the process of using help files.

When written well, the help file for a generic function will refer you to other functions, providing a clear path to all you need to know. However, it does not always go so smoothly. We will see a good example of this in Chapter 15, "Traditional Graphics". The **plot** function is generic. When we call it with our data frame, it will give us a scatter plot matrix. However, to find out all of the arguments we might use to improve the plot, we have to use methods(plot) to find that plot.data.frame exists. We could then use help(plot.data.frame) to find that plot.data.frame calls the **pairs** function, then finally help(pairs) to find the arguments we seek. This is a worst-case scenario, but it is important to realize that this situation does occasionally arise. As you work with R, you may occasionally forget the mode or class of an object you created. This can result in unexpected output. You can always use the **mode** or **class** functions to remind yourself. Table 5.2 shows several R objects and their modes and classes.

5.6.4 Controlling Functions with Extractor Functions

Commands in Stata typically display all their output at once. Ancillary post-estimation commands, however, are commonly used in Stata and add to the scope of statistical output available for a given primary command.

R has simple functions, like the **mean** function, that show all of their results at once. However, R functions that model relationships among variables tend to show you very little output initially. You save the output to a *model object* and then use *extractor functions* to get more information when you need it.

This section is poorly named from an R expert's perspective. Extractor functions do not actually control other functions the way options control Stata output. Instead they show us what the other function has already done. In essence, most modeling in R is done through its equivalent to the Stata postestimation commands.

Let us look at an example of predicting q4 from q1 with linear regression using the **lm** function.

```
> lm( q4~q1+q2+q3, data=mydata)

Call:
lm(formula = q4 ~ q1 + q2 + q3, data = mydata)

Coefficients:
(Intercept)           q1           q2           q3
    -1.3243       0.4297       0.6310       0.3150
```

The output is extremely sparse, lacking the usual tests of significance. Now, instead, we will store the results in a model object called myModel and we will check its class with the **class** function.

```
> myModel <- lm( q4 ~ q1+q2+q3, data=mydata )

> class(myModel)

 [1] "lm"
```

The **class** function tells us that myModel has a class of "*lm*" for *linear model*. We have seen that R functions offer different results (methods) for different types (classes) of objects. So let us see what the **summary** function does with this class of object:

```
> summary(mymodel)

Call:
lm(formula = q4 ~ q1 + q2 + q3, data = mydata)

Residuals:
        1        2        3        5        6        7
-0.31139 -0.42616  0.94283 -0.17975  0.07658  0.02257
        8
-0.12468
```

```
Coefficients:
              Estimate Std. Error t value Pr(>|t|)
(Intercept)   -1.3243     1.2877  -1.028    0.379
q1             0.4297     0.2623   1.638    0.200
q2             0.6310     0.2503   2.521    0.086
q3             0.3150     0.2557   1.232    0.306
---
Signif. codes:  0 *** 0.001 ** 0.01 * 0.05 . 0.1

Residual standard error: 0.6382 on 3 degrees of freedom
  (1 observation deleted due to missingness)

Multiple R-squared: 0.9299,     Adjusted R-squared: 0.8598

F-statistic: 13.27 on 3 and 3 DF,  p-value: 0.03084
```

This is the type of output that Stata shows immediately. There are many other extractor functions that we might use, including **anova** to extract an analysis of variance table, **plot** for diagnostic plots, **predict** to get predicted values, **resid** to get residuals, and so on. We will discuss those in Chapter 17, "Statistics."

What are the advantages of the extractor approach?

- You get only what you need, when you need it.
- The output is in a form that is very easy to use in further analysis.
- You use methods that are consistent across functions in a similar manner to Stata. For example, requests for regression residuals are uniform across R functions and Stata commands.

5.7 How Much Output is There?

In the previous section we discussed saving output and using extractor functions to get more results. However, how do we know what an output object contains? Previously, the **print** function showed us what was in our objects, so let us give that a try. We can do that by simply typing an object's name or by explicitly using the **print** function. To make it perfectly clear that we are using the **print** function, let us actually type out its name.

```
Call:

lm(formula = q4 ~ q1 + q2 + q3, data = mydata)

Coefficients:

(Intercept)          q1          q2          q3
    -1.3243      0.4297      0.6310      0.3150
```

We see that the object contains the original function call complete with its arguments and the linear model coefficients. Now let us check the mode, class, and names of myModel.

```
> mode(myModel)
 [1] "list"

> class(myModel)
 [1] "lm"

> names(myModel)
 [1] "coefficients"  "residuals"     "effects"       "rank"
 [5] "fitted.values" "assign"        "qr"        "df.residual"
 [9] "na.action"     "xlevels"       "call"          "terms"
[13] "model"
```

So we see that myModel is a list, or collection of objects. More specifically, it is a list with a class of "lm." The **names** function shows us the names of all of the objects in it. Why did the **print** function not show them to us? Because the **print** function has a predetermined method for displaying lm class objects. That method says, basically, "If an object's class is lm, then print only the original formula that created the model and its coefficients."

When we put our own variables together into a list, it had a class of simply "list" (its mode was list also). The **print** function's method for that class tells it to print all of the list's components. We can strip away the class attribute of any object with the **unclass** function. In this case, it resets its class to "list." If we do that, then the **print** function will indeed print all of the list's components.

```
> print( unclass(mymodel) )

$coefficients
(Intercept)          q1          q2          q3
 -1.3242616   0.4297468   0.6310127   0.3149789

$residuals
          1            2            3            5            6
-0.31139241 -0.42616034  0.94282700 -0.17974684  0.07658228
          7            8
 0.02257384 -0.12468354

$effects
(Intercept)          q1          q2          q3
 -8.6931829   3.6733345  -1.4475844   0.7861009   0.2801541

   0.7929917  -0.7172223
```

```
$rank
[1] 4

$fitted.values
       1        2        3        5        6        7
1.311392 1.426160 2.057173 4.179747 4.923418 3.977426
       8
5.124684

$assign
[1] 0 1 2 3

$qr
$qr
  (Intercept)         q1         q2          q3
1  -2.6457513 -8.6931829 -7.9372539 -10.9609697
2   0.3779645  3.9279220  3.3096380  -0.3273268
3   0.3779645  0.1677124 -2.6544861   0.7220481
5   0.3779645 -0.3414626  0.4356232   2.4957256
6   0.3779645 -0.5960502 -0.3321400  -0.1051645
7   0.3779645 -0.5960502 -0.7088608   0.4471879
8   0.3779645 -0.3414626  0.4356232  -0.4186885
attr(,"assign")
[1] 0 1 2 3

$qraux
[1] 1.377964 1.167712 1.087546 1.783367

$pivot
[1] 1 2 3 4

$tol
[1] 1e-07

$rank
[1] 4

attr(,"class")
[1] "qr"

$df.residual
[1] 3

$na.action
4
4
```

```
attr(,"class")
[1] "omit"

$xlevels
list()

$call
lm(formula = q4 ~ q1 + q2 + q3, data = mydata)

$terms
q4 ~ q1 + q2 + q3
attr(,"variables")
list(q4, q1, q2, q3)
attr(,"factors")
   q1 q2 q3
q4  0  0  0
q1  1  0  0
q2  0  1  0
q3  0  0  1
attr(,"term.labels")
[1] "q1" "q2" "q3"
attr(,"order")
[1] 1 1 1
attr(,"intercept")
[1] 1
attr(,"response")
[1] 1
attr(,".Environment")
<environment: R_GlobalEnv>
attr(,"predvars")
list(q4, q1, q2, q3)
attr(,"dataClasses")
        q4         q1         q2         q3
 "numeric"  "numeric"  "numeric"  "numeric"

$model
  q4 q1 q2 q3
1  1  1  1  5
2  1  2  1  4
3  3  2  2  4
5  4  4  5  2
6  5  5  4  5
7  4  5  3  4
8  5  4  5  5
```

It looks like the `print` function was doing us a big favor by not printing everything! When you explore the contents of any object, you can take this approach or, just given the names, explore things one at a time. For example, we saw that myModel contained the object named "*$coefficients.*" One way to print one component of a list is to refer to it as mylist$mycomponent. So in this case we can see just the component that contains the model coefficients by entering

```
> myModel$coefficients
```

```
(Intercept)          q1          q2          q3
 -1.3242616   0.4297468   0.6310127   0.3149789
```

That looks like a vector. Let us use the `class` function to check.

```
> class( myModel$coefficients )
```

```
[1] "numeric"
```

Yes, it is a numeric vector. So we can use it with anything that accepts such data. For example, we might get a bar plot of the coefficients with the following (plot not shown). We will discuss bar plots more in Chapter 15, "Traditional Graphics."

```
> barplot( myModel$coefficients )
```

For many modeling functions, it is very informative to perform a similar exploration on the objects created by them.

5.8 Writing Your Own Functions (Macros)

In a similar manner as in Stata, R users may write functions using the same language used for anything else. The resulting function is used in exactly the same way as a function that came with R.

Let us write some variations of a simple function, one that calculates the mean and standard deviation at the same time. For this example, we will apply it to just the numbers 1, 2, 3, 4, and 5.

```
> myvar <- c( 1,2,3,4,5 )
```

We will begin the function called *mystats* and tell it that it is a function of x. What follows in curly brackets is the function itself. We will create this with an error to see what happens.

```
# A bad function.
mystats <- function(x)
{
  mean(x, na.rm=TRUE)
    sd(x, na.rm=TRUE)
}
```

Now let us apply it like any other function.

```
> mystats(myvar)
```

```
[1] 1.5811
```

We got the standard deviation, but what happened to the mean? When we introduced the `print` function, we said that usually you could type an object's name rather than say `print(myobject)`. Well, this is one of the cases where we need to explicitly tell R to print the result. Let us add that to the function.

```
# A good function that just prints.
mystats <- function(x)
{
  print( mean(x, na.rm=TRUE) )
  print(   sd(x, na.rm=TRUE) )
}
```

Now let us run it.

```
> mystats(myvar)
[1] 3
[1] 1.5811
```

That looks better. Let us create our function in a slightly different way, so that it will write our results to a vector for further use. We will use the `c` function to combine the results into a vector.

```
# A function with vector output.
mystats <- function(x)
{
  mymean <- mean(x, na.rm=TRUE)
  mysd   <-   sd(x, na.rm=TRUE)
  c( mean=mymean, sd=mysd )
}
```

Now when we run it, we get the results in vector form.

```
> mystats(myvar)
```

```
  mean     sd
3.0000 1.5811
```

As with any R function that creates a vector, we can assign the result to a variable to use in any way we like.

```
> myVector <- mystats(myvar)

> myVector

   mean      sd
 3.0000  1.5811
```

Many R functions return their results in the form of a list. Recall that each member of a list can be any data structure. Let us use a list to save the original data, as well as the mean and standard deviation. We will use the list function as we did when we combined all our variables into one list.

```
# A function with list output.
mystats <- function(x)
{
  myinput <- x
  mymean  <- mean(x, na.rm=TRUE)
  mysd    <-   sd(x, na.rm=TRUE)
  list(data=myinput, mean=mymean, sd=mysd)
}
```

Now let us run it to see how the results look.

```
mystats(myvar)

$data
 [1] 1 2 3 4 5

$mean
 [1] 3

$sd
 [1] 1.5811
```

We can save the result to mylist and then print just the data.

```
> myStatlist <- mystats(myvar)

> myStatlist$data
 [1] 1 2 3 4 5
```

If you want to see the function itself, simply type the name of the function without any parentheses following.

```
> mystats

function(x)
{
  myinput <- x
  mymean  <- mean(x, na.rm=TRUE)
  mysd    <-   sd(x, na.rm=TRUE)
  list(data=myinput,mean=mymean,sd=mysd)
}
```

You could easily copy this function into a script editor window and change it. You can see and change many R functions this way.

5.9 R Program Demonstrating Programming Basics

Most of the chapters in this book end with equivalent example programs in both Stata and R. This chapter focuses so much on R that we end only with the program for R.

```
# Programming Basics.

# ---Simple Calculations---
2+3

x <- 2
y <- 3
x+y
x*y

# ---Data Structures---

# Vectors
workshop <- c(1,2,1,2,1,2,1,2)
print(workshop)
workshop

gender <- c("f","f","f",NA,"m","m","m","m")
q1 <- c(1,2,2,3,4,5,5,4)
q2 <- c(1,1,2,1,5,4,3,5)
q3 <- c(5,4,4,NA,2,5,4,5)
q4 <- c(1,1,3,3,4,5,4,5)

# Selecting Elements of Vectors
q1[5]
q1[ c(5,6,7,8) ]
```

```
q1[ 5:8 ]
q1[ gender=="m" ]
mean( q1[ gender=="m"], na.rm=TRUE)


# ---Factors---

# Numeric Factors

# First, as a vector
workshop <- c(1,2,1,2,1,2,1,2)
workshop
table(workshop)
mean(workshop)
gender[ workshop==2 ]

# Now as a factor
workshop <- c(1,2,1,2,1,2,1,2)
workshop <- factor( workshop )
workshop
table(workshop)
mean(workshop) #generates error now.
gender[ workshop==2 ]
gender[ workshop=="2" ]

# Recreate workshop, making it a factor
# including levels that don't yet exist.
workshop <- c(1,2,1,2,1,2,1,2)
workshop <- factor(
  workshop,
  levels=c(1,2,3,4),
  labels=c("R","Stata","SPSS","SAS")
)

# Recreate it with just the levels it
# curently has.
workshop <- c(1,2,1,2,1,2,1,2)
workshop <- factor(
  workshop,
  levels=c(1,2),
  labels=c("R","Stata")
)

workshop
table(workshop)
gender[ workshop==2 ]
```

```
gender[ workshop=="2" ]
gender[ workshop=="Stata" ]

# Character factors

gender <- c("f","f","f",NA,"m","m","m","m")
gender <- factor(
  gender,
  levels=c("m","f"),
  labels=c("Male","Female")
)

gender
table(gender)
workshop[ gender=="m" ]
workshop[ gender=="Male" ]

# Recreate gender and make it a factor,
# keeping simpler m and f as labels.
gender <- c("f","f","f",NA,"m","m","m","m")
gender <- factor(gender)
gender

# Data Frames
mydata <- data.frame(workshop,gender,q1,q2,q3,q4)
mydata

# Selecting components by index numbers
mydata[ 8, 6 ] #8th obs, 6th var
mydata[  , 6 ] #All obs, 6th var
mydata[  , 6 ][ 5:8 ] #6th var, obs 5:8

# Selecting components by name
mydata$q1
mydata$q1[ 5:8 ]


# Example renaming gender to sex while
# creating a data frame (left as a comment)
#
# mydata <- data.frame(workshop, sex=gender,
#   q1, q2, q3, q4)

# Matrices
```

```
# Creating from vectors
mymatrix <- cbind(q1, q2, q3, q4)
mymatrix
dim(mymatrix)


# Creating from matrix function
# left as a comment so we keep
# version with names q1, q2...
#
# mymatrix <- matrix(
#   c(1, 1, 5, 1,
#     2, 1, 4, 1,
#     2, 2, 4, 3,
#     3, 1, NA,3,
#     4, 5, 2, 4,
#     5, 4, 5, 5,
#     5, 3, 4, 4,
#     4, 5, 5, 5),
#   nrow=8, ncol=4, byrow=TRUE)
# mymatrix

table(mymatrix)
mean(mymatrix, na.rm=TRUE)
cor(mymatrix, use="pairwise")

# Selecting Subsets of Matrices

mymatrix[ 8, 4]
mymatrix[ 5:8, 3:4]
mymatrix[ ,4][1:4]

# Lists
mylist <- list(workshop, gender,
  q1, q2, q3, q4, mymatrix)
mylist

# List, this time adding names
mylist <- list(
  workshop=workshop,
  gender=gender,
  q1=q1,
  q2=q2,
  q3=q3,
  q4=q4,
```

```
        mymatrix=mymatrix)
mylist

# Selecting components by index numbers.
mylist[[2]]
mylist[[7]]
mylist[[7]][ 5:8, 3:4 ]

# Selecting components by name.
mylist$q1
mylist$mymatrix[ 5:8, 3:4 ]


# ---Saving Your Work---

ls()
objects() #same as ls()

save.image("myall.RData")
save(mydata, file="mydata.RData")


# The 2nd approach is commented to keep
# the q variables for following examples.
# rm(x,y,workshop,gender,q1,q2,q3,q4,
#    mymatrix,mylist)
# ls()
# save.image(file="mydata.RData")

# ---Comments to Document Your Programs---

# This comment is on its own line, between functions.

workshop <- c(1,2,1,2, #This comment is within the arguments.
              1,2,1,2) #And this is at the end.


# ---Controlling Functions---

# Controlling Functions with Arguments

help(mean)

mean(x=q3, trim=.25, na.rm=TRUE)

mean(na.rm=TRUE, x=q3, trim=.25)
```

```
mean(q3, .25, TRUE)

mean(q3, t=.25, na.rm=TRUE)

# Controlling Functions With Formulas

lm( q4 ~ q1+q2+q3, data=mydata )

t.test(q1 ~ gender, data=mydata)

t.test( q1[ which(gender=="Female") ],
        q1[ which(gender=="Male")   ],
        data=mydata) #Data ignored!

# Controlling Functions with Extractor Functions


lm( q4 ~ q1+q2+q3, data=mydata )

myModel <- lm( q4 ~ q1+q2+q3, data=mydata )
class(myModel)
summary(myModel)

# How Much Output Is There?

print(mymodel)

mode(myModel)
class(myModel)
names(myModel)
print( unclass(myModeel) )

myModel$coefficients
class( myModel$coefficients )
barplot( myModel$coefficients )


# ---Writing Your Own Functions (Macros)---

myvar <- c(1,2,3,4,5)

# A bad function.
mystats <- function(x)
{
  mean(x, na.rm=TRUE)
```

```
    sd(x, na.rm=TRUE)
}

mystats(myvar)

# A good function that just prints.
mystats <- function(x)
{
  print( mean(x, na.rm=TRUE) )
  print(   sd(x, na.rm=TRUE) )
}
mystats(myvar)

# A function with vector output.
mystats <- function(x)
{
  mymean <- mean(x, na.rm=TRUE)
  mysd   <-   sd(x, na.rm=TRUE)
  c( mean=mymean, sd=mysd )
}
mystats(myvar)
myVector <- mystats(myvar)
myVector

# A function with list output.
mystats <- function(x)
{
  myinput <- x
  mymean  <- mean(x, na.rm=TRUE)
  mysd    <-   sd(x, na.rm=TRUE)
  list(data=myinput, mean=mymean, sd=mysd)
}
mystats(myvar)
myStatlist <- mystats(myvar)
myStatlist
mystats

save(mydata,mymatrix,mylist,mystats,
  file="myAll.RData")
```

6

Data Acquisition

R can read or import data from a wide range of sources. It includes a data
editor for manual input, and it can access files in text as well as Stata format.
For other topics, such as reading importing data from relational databases,
see the R Data Import/Export manual [39].

6.1 The R Data Editor

R has a simple spreadsheet-style data editor. Unlike Stata, you cannot use it
to create a new data frame. You can only edit an existing one. However, it
is easy to create an empty data frame, which you can then fill in using the
editor:

```
mydata <- edit( data.frame() )
```

The window in Fig. 6.1 will appear. Initially the variables are named *var1*,
var2, and so on. You can easily change these names by clicking on them.
Clicking on the variable name *var1* brought up the *Variable editor* window
shown in the center of Fig. 6.1. We will change it to "id" and leave the
"numeric" button selected so that it will be a numeric variable. We then
close the variable editor window by clicking the usual X in the upper right
corner.

Follow the steps above until you have created the data frame shown in
Fig. 6.2. Make sure to click "character" when defining a character variable.
When you come to the NA values for observation 4, leave them blank. You
could enter the two-character string "NA" for numeric variables, but R will
not recognize that as a missing value for character variables here. Exit the
editor and save changes by choosing *File>Close* or by clicking the Windows
X button. There is no *File>Save* option, which feels quite scary the first time
you use it, but R does indeed save the data.

Notice that the variable in our ID variable matches the row names on
the leftmost edge of Fig. 6.2. R went ahead and created row names of "1,"

R.A. Muenchen, J.M. Hilbe, *R for Stata Users*, Statistics
and Computing, DOI 10.1007/978-1-4419-1318-0_6,
© Springer Science+Business Media, LLC 2010

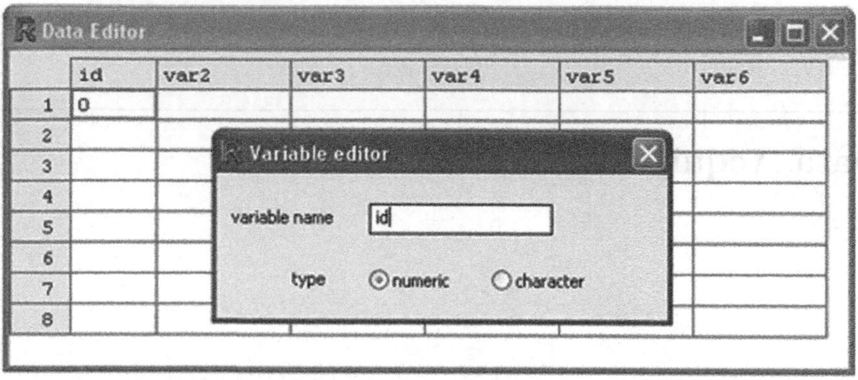

Fig. 6.1. Adding a new variable in the data editor.

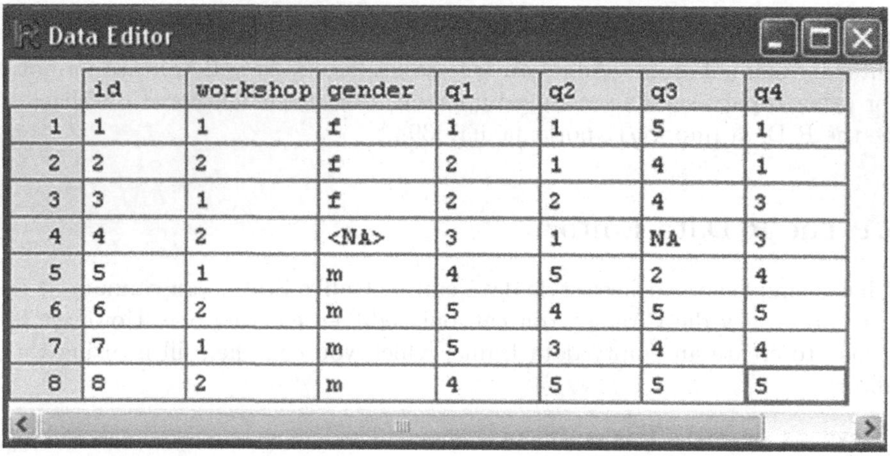

Fig. 6.2. The data editor with our practice data entered.

"2,"... so why did we bother to enter them into the variable id? Because while the data editor allows us to easily change *variable* names, it does not allow us to change *row* names. If you are happy with its default names, you do not need to create your own id variable. However, if you wanted to enter your own row names using the data editor, you can enter them instead into a variable like id and then later set that variable to be row names with the following function call:

```
row.names(mydata) <- mydata$id
```

This function call selects id from mydata using the form,

```
dataframe$variable
```

which we will discuss further in Section 7.7, "Selecting Variables Using $ Notation."

Before using this data, you would also want to use the `factor` function to make workshop and gender into factors.

```
mydata$workshop <- factor(mydata$workshop)
mydata$gender   <- factor(mydata$gender)
```

To see how to do this with fancier value labels, see our discussion in Section 11.1, "Value Labels or Formats (and Measurement Level)."

We now have a data frame that we can analyze, save as a permanent R data file, or export in text format. R does not directly export to Stata.

When we were initially creating the empty data frame, we could have entered the variable names with the following function call

```
mydata <- data.frame(id=0., workshop=0.,
  gender=" ", q1=0., q2=0., q3=0., q4=0.)
```

This is a major time saver when you have to create more than one copy of the data or if you plan to create a similar data set in the future.

R has a `fix` function that actually calls the more aptly named `edit` function and then writes the data back to your original data frame. So

```
fix(mydata)
```

does the same thing as

```
mydata <- edit(mydata)
```

We recommend not using the `edit` function on existing data frames as we find it all too easy to begin editing with just

```
edit(mydata) #Do NOT do this!
```

It will look identical on the screen, but this does not tell `edit` where to save your work. When you exit, your work will appear to be lost. However, R stores the last value you gave it in an object named `.Last.value`. So you can retrieve the data with this function call.

```
mydata <- .Last.value
```

We will use the `edit` function later when renaming variables.

6.2 Reading Delimited Text Files

Delimited text files use special characters, such as spaces, tabs, or commas to separate each data value. We will cover comma- and tab-delimited files in two subsections below, followed by subsections that point out problems you can have reading character (string) values and tabs.

6.2.1 Reading Comma-Delimited Text Files

Let us first read a *comma* *separated* *value* (CSV) file like

```
workshop,gender,q1,q2,q3,q4
1,1,f,1,1,5,1
2,2,f,2,1,4,1
3,1,f,2,2,4,3
4,2, ,3,1, ,3
5,1,m,4,5,2,4
6,2,m,5,4,5,5
7,1,m,5,3,4,4
8,2,m,4,5,5,5
```

There are several important things to notice about this data.

1. The top row contains variable names. This is called the file's *header* line. If you leave the names out, R will name the variables "V1," "V2,"... similar to Stata's "var1," "var2,"... default names.[1]
2. ID numbers are in the leftmost column, but the header line does not contain a name like "ID" for it.
3. Values are separated by commas.
4. Spaces (blanks) represent missing values.
5. There are no blanks before or after the character values of "m" and "f."
6. Each line of data is ended with a single stroke of the *Enter* key, not with a final comma. Your operating system stores either a line feed character, or a carriage return and a line feed. R will treat them the same.

You can read this file using the **read.csv** function call below. If you have already set your working directory in your current R session, you do not need to set it again.

```
> setwd("/myRfolder")

> mydata <- read.csv("mydata.csv")

> mydata
```

```
  workshop gender q1 q2 q3 q4
1        1      f  1  1  5  1
2        2      f  2  1  4  1
3        1      f  2  2  4  3
4        2         3  1 NA  3
5        1      m  4  5  2  4
```

---

[1] Note the inconsistency with R's own data editor, which uses the default names, "var1," "var2,"....

```
6        2       m  5  4  5  5
7        1       m  5  3  4  4
8        2       m  4  5  5  5
```

Notice that it read the id variable and stored it automatically in row names position on the left side of the data frame. It did that because R found eight columns of data but only seven names. Whenever R finds one fewer names than columns, it assumes the first column must be an id variable.

So what does R do when the header line *does* contain a name for the first column, like the following?

```
id,workshop,gender,q1,q2,q3,q4
1,1,f,1,1,5,1
2,2,f,2,1,4,1
. . .
```

If we read the file exactly as before, we would have an additional variable named "id." R would also create row names of "1," "2,"..., but our ID variable may have contained more useful information. Not getting your ID variable into the row names attribute does not cause any major problems, but R will automatically identify observations by their row names, so if you have an ID variable, it makes sense to get it into the row names attribute.

To tell R which variable contains the row names, we add the `row.names` argument.

```
> mydata <- read.csv("mydataID.csv",
+    row.names="id")

> mydata

  workshop gender q1 q2 q3 q4
1        1      f  1  1  5  1
2        2      f  2  1  4  1
. . .
```

When we let R figure out that there was an ID variable, it *had to be* the first column. That is usually where ID variables reside, but if you ever have one in another location, then you will have to use the `row.names` argument to store it in the row names attribute.

6.2.2 Reading Tab-Delimited Text Files

Reading tab-delimited files in R is done very similarly to comma-delimited files, but uses the `read.delim` function.

The following is the tab-delimited text file we will read.

```
workshop    gender    q1    q2    q3    q4
1    1       f         1    1    5    1
2    2       f         2    1    4    1
3    1       f         2    2    4    3
4    2                 3    1         3
5    1       m         4    5    2    4
6    2       m         5    4    5    5
7    1       m         5    3    4    4
8    2       m         4    5    5    5
```

There are several important things to notice about this data.

1. The top row contains variable names, each of which are separated by a *single* tab. *There is no tab before the first variable name, even though adding one would make it line up with the workshop values better!*
2. ID numbers are in the leftmost column, but that column is not named in the header line with the other variable names.
3. The data values are separated by a *single* tab character.
4. Two tab characters in a row represent a missing value. There are no spaces between the tabs. In other words, the space bar was never pressed when this file was created.

As with comma separated values, the fact that R sees eight variables with only seven names tells it that the first column is an ID variable to store in the row names attribute.

```
> setwd("/myRfolder")

> mydata <- read.table("mydata.tab")

> mydata
```

```
  workshop gender q1 q2 q3 q4
1        1      f  1  1  5  1
2        2      f  2  1  4  1
3        1      f  2  2  4  3
4        2   <NA>  3  1 NA  3
5        1      m  4  5  2  4
6        2      m  5  4  5  5
7        1      m  5  3  4  4
8        2      m  4  5  5  5
```

Now let us read a file that includes a name for our ID variable:

```
id    workshop    gender    q1    q2    q3    q4
1     1           f         1    1    5    1
2     2           f         2    1    4    1
...
```

We can read this file format with exactly the same command that we used earlier. However, the ID variable would not end up stored in the row names attribute. So R would not know to use it in functions that identify observations. We can correct that by adding the row.names argument:

```
> mydata <- read.csv("mydataID.csv",
+   row.names="id")

> mydata

  workshop gender q1 q2 q3 q4
1        1      f  1  1  5  1
2        2      f  2  1  4  1
...
```

6.2.3 Missing Values for Character Variables

In the previous two subsections, we ignored a potential problem. The missing value for variable q3 was always displayed as NA, Not Available. However, the missing value for gender was displayed as a blank.

If we had entered R's standard missing value, "NA," where we had missing values, then even the character data would have shown up as missing. However, few other programs write out NA as missing.

Just as in Stata, you can read blanks as character values, and R will not set them to missing unless you specifically tell it to do so. Often, it is not very important to set those values to missing. A person's address is a good example. If we do not know it, there is little need to set it to be missing.

However, when you need to use a character variable in an analysis, setting it to be missing is, of course, very important. Later in the book we *will* use gender in analyses, so we must make sure that blank values are set to missing.

In our comma-delimited file, the missing value for gender was entered as a single space. Therefore, the argument na.char=" " added to any of the comma-delimited examples will set the value to missing. Note there is a single space between the quotes in that argument.

In our tab-delimited file, the missing value for gender was entered as nothing between two tabs (i.e., just two tabs in a row). Therefore, the argument na.char="" added to any of the tab-delimited examples will set the value to missing. Note that there is now *no* space between the quotes in that argument.

However, in both comma- and tab-delimited files, it is very easy to accidentally have blanks where you think there are none or to enter more than you meant. Then your na.char setting will be wrong for some cases.

It is best to use a solution that will get rid of all trailing blanks. That is what the argument strip.white=TRUE does. When you use that, na.char="" will work regardless of how many blanks may have been there before.

Let us try it with our comma-delimited file, since it contains a blank we can get rid of

```
> mydata <- read.csv("mydataID.csv",
+    row.names="id",
+    strip.white=TRUE,
+    na.strings="" )

> mydata

  workshop gender q1 q2 q3 q4
1        1      f  1  1  5  1
2        2      f  2  1  4  1
3        1      f  2  2  4  3
4        2   <NA>  3  1 NA  3
5        1      m  4  5  2  4
6        2      m  5  4  5  5
7        1      m  5  3  4  4
8        2      m  4  5  5  5
```

The only difference between this output and the last one we read for mydataID.csv is that gender is shown as <NA> now instead of blank. R adds angle brackets, "<>'," around the value so you can tell NA stands for Not Available (missing) rather than something meaningful, such as North America.

The strip.white=TRUE argument also provides the benefit of getting rid of trailing blanks that that would set some genders equal to "m" and others to "m " or "m   ". We do not want trailing blanks to accidentally split the males into different groups!

Finally, getting rid of trailing blanks saves space. Since R, like Stata, stores its data in your computer's main memory, saving space is very important.

6.2.4 Trouble with Tabs

In many text editors, including R's, tabs are invisible. That makes it easy to enter an additional tab or two, throwing R off track.

If R complains of too many names in the header line, or not enough values on data lines, or if it creates more variables than you expected, often you have an inconsistent number of tabs somewhere.

Check the header line that contains your variable names and the first few lines of data for extra tabs, especially at the beginning or end of a line. If you have an ID variable in the first column and it is not named in your header line, it is very tempting to put a tab before the first variable name. That will get it to line up over the first column, but it will also tell R that your first variable name is missing!

If you have a data file that has some short values and some very long values in the same column, the person who entered it may have put two tabs after the short values to get the following column to line up again. In that case, you can read it with the `read.table` function. That function has greater flexibility for reading delimited files, and, in fact, the `read.csv` and `read.delim` functions do their work by calling the `read.table` function with several arguments set.

When a file has varying number of tabs between values, `read.table` can read it because its default delimiter is *any number of tabs and/or spaces!* However, this also means that you cannot represent missing values by entering two tabs in a row, or even by putting a space between two tabs. With our practice tabbed data set, it would generate the error message *"line 4 did not have 7 elements."* In that case, you must enter some code to represent missing. The value "NA" is the one that R understands automatically, for both numeric and character values. If you use any other codes, such as "." or "999," see Section 10.5, "Missing Values" to learn how to handle them.

With `read.table`, if you specify the argument, `delim="\t"`, then it uses one single tab as a delimiter.

6.2.5 Skipping Variables in Delimited Files

As with Stata, R must hold all its data in your computer's main memory. This makes skipping columns while reading data particularly important.

The following is the R function call to read the data while skipping the fourth and fifth columns. If you have already set your working directory in your current R session, you do not need to set it again.

```
> setwd("/myRfolder")

> myCols <- read.delim("mydata.tab",
+    strip.white=TRUE,
+    na.strings="",
+    colClasses=c("integer", "integer", "character",
+    "NULL", "NULL", "integer", "integer") )

> myCols
   workshop gender q3 q4
1         1      f  5  1
2         2      f  4  1
3         1      f  4  3
4         2   <NA> NA  3
5         1      m  2  4
6         2      m  5  5
7         1      m  4  4
8         2      m  5  5
>
> # Clean up and save workspace.
> rm(myCols)
```

We used the name myCols to avoid overwriting mydata. You use the colClasses argument to specify the *class* of each column. The classes include logical (TRUE/FALSE), integer (whole numbers), numeric (can include decimals), character (alphanumeric string values), and factor (categorical values like gender). See the help file for other classes like dates. The class we need for this example is NULL. We use it to drop variables.

However, colClasses requires you to specify the classes of all columns, including any initial ID or row names variable. The classes must be included within quotes since they are character strings. The colClasses argument is also helpful for reading other variable types such as dates.

6.2.6 Example Programs for Reading Delimited Text Files

Stata Program for Reading Delimited Text Files

Stata can read comma-delimited files having variable names on the first line, or it can read a file having no imbedded variable names. Use of the "names" option tells Stata that the first line consists of variable names, otherwise it assumes that all observations are to be read as data. For this example, we specify names for the columns of data in a comma-delimited text file called mydataID.txt. The infile command is used for this purpose. Following reading in the data, we use the list command to display the data in the RESULTS window. Note that Stata has a number of alternative data reading capabilities.

In the files we read below, mydataID.csv and mydataID.tab, the id variable is named, along with the other variables, in the first line of the file. That is the style best read by Stata and most other statistics programs.

```
* Filename: ReadDelimited.do

*---comma-delimited File---
clear
insheet using "C:\myRfolder\mydataID.csv", comma names
list

*---tab-delimited File---
clear
insheet using "C:\myRfolder\mydataID.tab", tab names
list
save "C:\myRfolder\mydata.dta", replace
```

R Program for Reading Delimited Text Files

In these examples, the files mydata.csv and mydata.tab both contain an ID variable in column 1. However, the first line of the files, which containing variable names (the header line), does *not* name the ID variable. That is the style that R prefers. The versions named, mydataID.csv and mydataID.tab, include the name of the ID variable.

```
# Filename: ReadDelimited.R

setwd("/myRfolder")

#---comma-delimited File---

# Read comma-delimited file.
# With id variable not named.

mydata <- read.csv("mydata.csv")
mydata

# Read a similar comma-delimited file.
# This time the id variable is named.

mydata <- read.csv("mydataID.csv",
  row.names="id")
mydata

#---tab-delimited File---

# Read a tab-delimited file with un-named ID column.
mydata <- read.delim("mydata.tab")
mydata

# Read a similar tab-delimited file.
# This time the id variable is named.

mydata <- read.delim("mydataID.tab",
  row.names="id")
mydata


#---Stripping Out White Space---

mydata <- read.csv("mydataID.csv",
  row.names="id",
  strip.white=TRUE,
  na.strings="" )
mydata


#---Using colClasses to skip q1 and q2 with NULL---

myCols <- read.delim("mydata.tab",
```

```
      strip.white=TRUE,
      na.strings="",
      colClasses=c("integer", "integer", "character",
      "NULL", "NULL", "integer", "integer") )
myCols

# Clean up and save workspace.
rm(myCols)

save.image(file="mydata.RData")
```

6.3 Reading Text Data Within a Program

It is often useful to have a small data set entered inside a program. This approach is popular when teaching or for an example when you post a question on Internet discussion lists. You only have one file and anyone can copy it and run it without changing it to locate a data file. Stata does this using the **input** command.

Although beginners are often drawn to this approach due to its simplicity, it is not a good idea to use this for more than a few dozen observations. To see the top and bottom of your program requires scrolling past all of the data, which is needlessly time-consuming. As we will soon see, R also displays the data in the console, scrolling potential error messages off the screen if there is more than a screen's worth of data.

We will discuss two ways to read data within an R program: one that is easy and one that is more generally applicable.

6.3.1 The Easy Approach

The easy approach is to nest the **stdin** function within any other R function that reads data. It tells R that the data is coming from the the same place the program is, which is called the *st*andard *in*put.

In our next example, we will use comma separated value (CSV) format, so we will nest a call to the **stdin** function within a call to the **read.csv** function.

```
mydata <- read.csv( stdin() )
workshop,gender,q1,q2,q3,q4
1,1,f,1,1,5,1
2,2,f,2,1,4,1
3,1,f,2,2,4,3
4,2,NA,3,1,NA,3
5,1,m,4,5,2,4
6,2,m,5,4,5,5
```

```
7,1,m,5,3,4,4
8,2,m,4,5,5,5

# Blank line above ends input.
mydata
```

Note that we actually typed "NA" in for missing values, and we were careful to never add any spaces before or after the gender values of "m" or "f." That let us dispense with any additional arguments for the read.csv function. Of course, you could instead enter the data as any example in this chapter, in which case you would need to include the arguments to match the data.

Let us run this example and see what the output looks like.

```
> mydata <- read.csv( stdin() )
0: workshop,gender,q1,q2,q3,q4
1: 1,1,f,1,1,5,1
2: 2,2,f,2,1,4,1
3: 3,1,f,2,2,4,3
4: 4,2,NA,3,1,NA,3
5: 5,1,m,4,5,2,4
6: 6,2,m,5,4,5,5
7: 7,1,m,5,3,4,4
8: 8,2,m,4,5,5,5
9:
> # Blank line above ends input.
> mydata
  workshop gender q1 q2 q3 q4
1        1      f  1  1  5  1
2        2      f  2  1  4  1
3        1      f  2  2  4  3
4        2   <NA>  3  1 NA  3
5        1      m  4  5  2  4
6        2      m  5  4  5  5
7        1      m  5  3  4  4
8        2      m  4  5  5  5
```

We often add blank lines between sections of output to make it easier to read, but given that a blank line is actually used to end the data, we do not do so with this output.

You can see that R displays the data itself, and it prefixes each line with "0:", "1:", "2:".... With all of the data displayed, this is obviously not something you would want to do with hundreds of observations! When we read data from files, we saw that R did not display it in the console.

The ninth line shows that it is blank and the numeric prefixing stops as R returns to its usual ">" prompt. It is the blank line that tells R that there is no more data. If you forget it, R will read your next program lines as data, continuing until it finds a blank line!

Printing the data by entering `mydata` shows us that the row names were correctly assigned and the two missing values are also correct.

6.3.2 The More General Approach

The previous subsection showed how to read data in the middle of an R program, and it required only a minor change. It had one important limitation however: you cannot use `stdin` to read data in programs that are sourced (included) from files.

Since putting data in the middle of a file is often done for interactive demonstrations, that is not often a serious limitation. However, there are times when you want to put the whole program, including data, in a separate file like "myprog.R" and bring it into R with the command

```
source("myprog.R")
```

To do this, we can place the whole data set into a character vector with a *single value* named "mystring":

```
mystring <-
"workshop,gender,q1,q2,q3,q4
1,1,f,1,1,5,1
2,2,f,2,1,4,1
3,1,f,2,2,4,3
4,2,NA,3,1,NA,3
5,1,m,4,5,2,4
6,2,m,5,4,5,5
7,1,m,5,3,4,4
8,2,m,4,5,5,5"
mydata <- read.csv( textConnection(mystring) )
mydata
```

Note that the `c` function is *not* used to combine all of those values into a vector. At the moment, the whole data set is one single character value! The `textConnection` function converts mystring into the equivalent of a file, which R then processes the same way as it would a file.

```
mydata <- read.csv( textConnection(mystring) )
```

6.3.3 Example Programs for Reading Text Data Within a Program

Stata Program for Reading Text Data Within a Program

```
* Filename: ReadWithin.do
```

```
clear all
input id workshop str1 gender q1-q4, automatic
1 1 f 1 1 5 1
2 2 f 2 1 4 1
3 1 f 2 2 4 3
4 2 . 3 1 . 3
5 1 m 4 5 2 4
6 2 m 5 4 5 5
7 1 m 5 3 4 4
8 2 m 4 5 5 5
end
list
```

R Program for Reading Text Data Within a Program

```
# Filename: ReadWithin.R

# The stdin approach.
mydata <- read.csv( stdin() )
workshop,gender,q1,q2,q3,q4
1,1,f,1,1,5,1
2,2,f,2,1,4,1
3,1,f,2,2,4,3
4,2,NA,3,1,NA,3
5,1,m,4,5,2,4
6,2,m,5,4,5,5
7,1,m,5,3,4,4
8,2,m,4,5,5,5

# Blank line above ends input.
mydata

# The textConnection approach
# that works when sourcing files.

mystring <-
"workshop,gender,q1,q2,q3,q4
1,1,f,1,1,5,1
2,2,f,2,1,4,1
3,1,f,2,2,4,3
4,2,NA,3,1,NA,3
5,1,m,4,5,2,4
6,2,m,5,4,5,5
7,1,m,5,3,4,4
8,2,m,4,5,5,5"
```

```
mydata <- read.csv( textConnection(mystring) )
mydata

# Set working directory & save workspace.
setwd("/myRfolder")

save.image(file="mydata.RData")
```

6.4 Reading Fixed-Width Text Files, One Record per Case

Files that separate data values with delimiters such as spaces or commas are convenient for people to work with, but they make a file larger. So many text files dispense with such conveniences and instead keep variable values locked into the exact same column(s) of every record.

If you have a nondelimited text file with one record per case, you can read it using the following approach. R has nowhere near the flexibility in reading fixed-width text files that Stata has. As you will soon see, making an error specifying the width of one variable will result in reading the wrong columns for all those that follow. While Stata offer approaches that would do that too, we do not recommend their use.

Other languages such as Perl or Python are extremely good at reading text files and converting them to a form that R can easily read.

Below is the same data that we used in other examples, but now it is in fixed-width format.

```
011f1151
022f2141
031f2243
042 31 3
051m4524
062m5455
071m5344
082m4555
```

The important things to notice about this file are the following:

1. No names appear on first line.
2. Nothing separates values.
3. The first value of each record is two columns wide; the remainder take only one column each.
4. Blanks represent missing values, but we could use any other character that would fit into the fixed number of columns allocated to each variable.

5. The last line of the file contains data. That is what Stata expects, but R generates a warning that there is an *"incomplete final line found."* It works fine though. If the warning in R bothers you, simply edit the file and press Enter once at the end of the last line.

The R function that reads fixed-width files is `read.fwf`. The following is an example of it reading the above file:

```
> setwd("/myRfolder")

> mydata <- read.fwf(
+     file="mydataFWF.txt",
+     width=c(2,-1,1,1,1,1,1),
+     col.names=c("id", "gender", "q1", "q2", "q3", "q4"),
+     row.names="id",
+     na.strings="",
+     fill=TRUE,
+     strip.white=TRUE)

Warning message:

In readLines(file, n = thisblock) :
  incomplete final line found on 'mydataFWF.txt'

> mydata

  gender q1 q2 q3 q4
1      f  1  1  5  1
2      f  2  1  4  1
3      f  2  2  4  3
4   <NA>  3  1 NA  3
5      m  3  5  2  4
6      m  5  4  5  5
7      m  5  3  4  4
8      m  4  5  5  5
```

The `read.fwf` function call above uses seven arguments:

1. The `file` argument lists the name of the file. It will read it from your current working directory. You can set the working directory with `setwd("path")` or you can specify a path as part of the file specification. We have been using the `file` argument in most of our previous examples, but we never bothered to name it. Since the `file` argument is the first one for this function, people typically just list it first. However, we list it here to remind you that all arguments do have names.

2. The `width` argument provides the width, or number of columns, required by each variable in order. The widths we supplied as a numeric vector are

created using the c function. The first number, 2, tells R to read ID from columns 1 and 2. The next number, −1, tells R to skip one column. In our next example, we will not need to read the workshop variable, so we will put in a −1 to skip it now. The remaining pattern of 1, 1, 1, 1, 1 tells R that each for of the remaining five variables will require one column each. Be very careful at this step! If you made an error and told R that ID was 1 column wide, then `read.fwf` would read all of the other variables from the wrong columns. When you are reading many variables, specifying their length by listing them all like this is tedious. You can make this task much easier by using R's ability to generate vectors of repetitive patterns. For details, see Chapter 12, "Generating Data."

3. The `col.names` argument provides the column or variable names. Those, too, we provide in a character vector. We create it using the c function, `c("id","gender","q1","q2","q3","q4")`. Since the names are character (string) data, we must enclose them in quotes. Names can also be tedious to enter. R's ability to generate vectors of repetitive patterns combined with the `paste` function can generate long sets of variable names. For details, see Chapter 12, "Generating Data."

4. The `row.names` argument tells R that we have a variable that stores a name or identifier for each row. It also tells it which of the variable names from the `col.names` argument that is: "id."

5. The `na.strings=""` argument tells R that an empty field is a missing value. It already is for numeric data, but, as in Stata, a blank is a valid character value. Note that there is no blank between the quotes! That is because we set the `strip.white` option to strip out extra blanks from the end of strings. As you see, R displays missing data for character data within angle brackets as <NA>.

6. The `fill` argument tells R to fill in blank spaces if the file contains lines that are not of the full length (like the Stata `fillin` command). Now is a good time to stop and enter `help(read.fwf)`. Note that there is no `fill` argument offered. It does, however, list its last argument as "...." This means that it will pass any additional arguments on to another function that `read.fwf` might call. In this case, it is the `read.table` function. Clicking the link to that function will reveal the `fill` argument and what it does.

7. The `strip.white` argument tells R to remove any additional blanks it finds in character data values. Therefore, if we were reading a long text string like "Bob   ", it will delete the additional spaces and store just "Bob". That saves space and makes logical comparisons easier. It is all too easy to count the number of blanks incorrectly when making a comparison like `name=="Bob      "`.

The file was read just fine. The warning message about an "incomplete final line" is caused by the lack of a blank line at the end of the file. Stata would not display a warning message about such a condition.

The **read.fwf** function calls the **read.table** function to do its work, so you can use any of those arguments here as well. For example, you could use **stringsAsFactors** to prevent R from converting string variables to factors, as it would do here by default.

6.4.1 Macro Substitution

The above example is a good one to use to begin to learn what Stata would call *macro substitution*. This approach makes your programs much easier to write and maintain. The most interesting aspect to macro substitution in R is that *R has no macro language!* R is powerful enough to do this using its standard features.

Since file paths often get quite long, we will store it in a character vector named *myfile*. This approach also lets you put all of the file references you use at the top of your programs, so you can change them easily. We do this with the assignment

```
myfile <- "mydataFWF.txt"
```

Next, we will store our variable names in another character vector, *myVariableNames*. This makes it much easier to manage when you have a more realistic data set that may contain hundreds of variables:

```
myVariableNames <- c("id", "gender", "q1", "q2", "q3", "q4")
```

Now we will do the same with our variable widths. This makes our next example, which reads multiple records per case, much easier.

```
myVariableWidths <- c(2, -1, 1, 1, 1, 1, 1)
```

Finally we will put it all together in a call to the **read.fwf** function.

```
> mydata <- read.fwf(
+     file=myfile,
+     width=myVariableWidths,
+     col.names=myVariableNames,
+     row.names="id",
+     na.strings="",
+     fill=TRUE,
+     strip.white=TRUE)

Warning message:

In readLines(file, n = thisblock) :
   incomplete final line found on 'mydataFWF.txt'
```

6.4.2 Example Programs for Reading Fixed-Width Text Files, One Record Per Case

These programs do not save the data, since they skip the workshop variable for demonstration purposes.

Stata Program for Fixed-Width Text Files, One Record per Case

```
* Filename: ReadFWF1.do

infix id 1-2 workshop 3 gender 4 q1 5 q2 6 q3 7 q4 8 ///
using c:\myRfolder\mydataFWF.txt, clear
list
```

R Program for Fixed-Width Text Files, One Record per Case

```
# Filename: ReadFWF1.R

setwd("/myRfolder")
mydata <- read.fwf(
   file="mydataFWF.txt",
   width=c(2,-1,1,1,1,1,1),
   col.names=c("id","gender","q1","q2","q3","q4"),
   row.names="id",
   na.strings="",
   fill=TRUE,
   strip.white=TRUE)
mydata

# Now we'll use "macro" substitution to do the same thing.

myfile <- "mydataFWF.txt"
myVariableNames  <- c("id","gender","q1","q2","q3","q4")
myVariableWidths <- c(2,-1,1,1,1,1,1)

mydata <- read.fwf(
   file=myfile,
   width=myVariableWidths,
   col.names=myVariableNames,
   row.names="id",
   na.strings="",
   fill=TRUE,
   strip.white=TRUE)
mydata
```

6.5 Reading Fixed-Width Text Files, Two or More Records per Case

It is common to have to read several records per case. In this section we will read two records per case, but it is easy to generalize from that to any number of records. This section builds on Section 6.4, so if you have not just finished reading it, you will want to do so now. We will only use the macro substitution form in this example.

First, we will store the filename in the character vector named myfile:

```
myfile <- "mydataFWF.txt"
```

Next, we will store the variable names in another character vector. We will pretend that our same file now has two records per case with q1 to q4 on the first record and q5 to q8 in the same columns on the second. Even though id, group, and gender appear on every line, we will not read them again from the second line. Here are our variable names:

```
myVariableNames <- c("id", "group", "gender",
  "q1", "q2", "q3", "q4",
  "q5", "q6", "q7", "q8" )
```

Now we need to specify the columns to read. We must store the column widths for each line of data (per case) in its own vector. Note that on record 2 we begin with −2, −1, −1 to skip the values for id, group, and gender.

```
myRecord1Widths <- c( 2, 1, 1, 1, 1, 1, 1)
myRecord2Widths <- c(-2,-1,-1, 1, 1, 1, 1)
```

Next, we need to store both of the above variables in a list. The following call to the list function combines the two record width vectors into one list named myVariableWidths:

```
myVariableWidths <- list( myRecord1Widths, myRecord2Widths )
```

Let us look at the new list:

```
> myVariableWidths
[[1]]
[1] 2 1 1 1 1 1 1

[[2]]
[1] -2 -1 -1 1 1 1 1
```

You can see that the component labeled [[1]] is the first numeric vector and the one labeled [[2]] is the second. The fact that the list contains two components tells the width argument that we have two records per case. Now we are ready to use the read.fwf function to read the data file:

```
> mydata <- read.fwf(
+    file=myfile,
+    width=myVariableWidths,
+    col.names=myVariableNames,
+    row.names="id",
+    na.strings="",
+    fill=TRUE,
+    strip.white=TRUE)

Warning message:

incomplete final line found by readLines on 'mydataFWF.txt'
in: readLines(file, n = thisblock)

> mydata

  group gender q1 q2 q3 q4 q5 q6 q7 q8
1     1      f  1  1  5  1  2  1  4  1
3     1      f  2  2  4  3  3  1 NA  3
5     1      m  3  5  2  4  5  4  5  5
7     1      m  5  3  4  4  4  5  5  5
```

You can see we now have only four records and eight q variables, so it has
worked well. It is also finally obvious that the row names do not always come
out as simple sequential numbers. It just so happened that is what we have
had until now. Because we are setting our row names from our id variable and
we are reading two records per case, we end up with only the odd-numbered
values. However, if we had let R create its own row names, they would have
ended up, "1," "2," "3," and "4."

As earlier, the warning message is caused by the lack of a blank line at the
end of the file. That does not cause problems.

6.5.1 Example Programs to Read Fixed-Width Text Files with Two Records per Case

Stata Program to Read Two Records per Case

```
* Filename: ReadFWF2.do

clear
#delimit ;
infix 2 lines 1: id 1-2 workshop 3 gender 4 //
q1 5 q2 6 q3 7 q4 8
2: q5 5 q6 6 q7 7 q8 8 using c:\myRfolder\mydataFWF.txt;
#delimit cr
list
```

R Program to Read Two Records per Case

```
# Filename: ReadFWF2.R

setwd("/myRfolder")

# Set all of the values to use.
myfile <- "mydataFWF.txt"
myVariableNames  <- c("id","group", "gender",
   "q1","q2","q3","q4",
   "q5","q6","q7","q8")
myRecord1Widths  <- c( 2, 1, 1, 1, 1, 1, 1)
myRecord2Widths  <- c(-2,-1,-1, 1, 1, 1, 1)
myVariableWidths <- list(myRecord1Widths,myRecord2Widths)

#Now plug them in and read the data:
mydata <- read.fwf(
   file=myfile,
   width=myVariableWidths,
   col.names=myVariableNames,
   row.names="id",
   na.strings="",
   fill=TRUE,
   strip.white=TRUE )
mydata
```

6.6 Importing Data from Stata into R

R can read a Stata data set in a standard "dta" file using R's built-in `foreign` package. That is the most widely-documented approach. However, when we wrote this, that approach read only the older version 8 or 9 format. If the data file is saved as a version 10 file or later, you must save it again using the command `saveold`.

A better way to import data into R from Stata is to use the `stata.get` function from Frank Harrell's `Hmisc` package. It can easily bring in files from any version of Stata, including the latest. It also has the ability to read formatted values, dates, variable labels, and lengths. The `Hmisc` package does not come with R, but it is easy to install. For instructions, see Section 2.1, "Installing Add-on Packages."

Since the `Hmisc` package uses the `foreign` package, we load them both from the library:

```
> library("foreign")

> library("Hmisc")
```

Next, we import the file with a simple call to the `stata.get` function, and print the data:

```
> mydata <- stata.get("c:/myRfolder/mydata.dta")

> mydata
```

	id	workshop	gender	q1	q2	q3	q4
1	1	1	f	1	1	5	1
2	2	2	f	2	1	4	1
3	3	1	f	2	2	4	3
4	4	2		3	1	NA	3
5	5	1	m	4	5	2	4
6	6	2	m	5	4	5	5
7	7	1	m	5	3	4	4
8	8	2	m	4	5	5	5

For more information on using Stata files, see *Data Analysis Using Stata* [25], the *Base Reference Manual* [45], or the *Data-Management Reference Manual* [46]. The latter is a large volume detailing every aspect of managing data in Stata, including the importing and exporting of data.

6.6.1 R Program to Import Data from Stata

```
# Filename: ImportFromStata.R

library("foreign")
library("Hmisc")
mydata <- stata.get("c:/myRfolder/mydata.dta")
mydata
```

6.7 Writing Data to a Comma-Delimited Text File

If you need to export data from R to another package, the comma separated value file is a good way to do it. R can write data to a standard CSV file, and it can write one formatted specifically for Stata, along with a do file to read it.

You can write a comma-delimited CSV file from R using the `write.csv` function. It writes CSV files the same way the `read.csv` function reads them, using many of the same arguments.

```
write.csv(mydata,
  file="mydataExported.csv", na="")
```

The argument, na="" tells R to write out nothing for missing values. If you leave that out, it will write out "NA" instead.

When you are exporting data from R, it is helpful to be able to open the file(s) under program control. That way you can adjust the arguments until you get what you need.

To look at the contents of any text file in R, you can use the file.show function. Let us use it to see the file we just created.

```
> file.show("mydataExported.txt")

"","gender","q1","q2","q3","q4"
"1","f",1,1,5,1
"2","f",2,1,4,1
"3","f",2,2,4,3
"4",NA,3,1,NA,3
"5","m",3,5,2,4
"6","m",5,4,5,5
"7","m",5,3,4,4
"8","m",4,5,5,5
```

The write.csv function actually uses the write.table function with some convenient options set, such as commas as delimiters. If you need to write the file out in a different format, write.table offers a very fine level of control. See help(write.table) for details.

6.7.1 Example Programs for Writing a Comma-Delimited File

Stata Program for Writing a CSV File

```
* Filename: WriteToText.do

use c:\myRfolder\mydata,clear
outfile using c:\myRfolder\mydata.csv, comma
type mydata.csv
```

R Program for Writing a CSV File

```
# Filename: WriteToText.R

write.csv(mydata,
  file="mydataExported.csv", na="")
```

6.8 Exporting Data from R to Stata

The `foreign` package contains a function specifically aimed at exporting data to other packages, including Stata. Its `write.foreign` function writes out a comma-delimited text file along with a matching Stata program file. To complete the importation into Stata, you must edit the program file in Stata, then execute it to read the text file, and, finally, create a data set.

To begin the process, you must load the foreign package.

```
library("foreign")
```

Then you call the `write.foreign` function:

```
write.foreign(mydata,
  datafile="mydataExported.csv",
  codefile="mydataExported.do",
  package="Stata")
```

This function call uses four arguments:

1. The name of the R data frame you wish to export.
2. The `datafile` argument tells R the name of text data file. R will write it to the current working directory unless you specify the full path in the filename.
3. The `codefile` argument tells R the filename of a program that Stata can use to read the text data file. You will have to use this file in Stata to read the data file and create a Stata-formatted file.
4. The `package` argument takes the value `"Stata"` to determine which type of program R writes to the `codefile` location.

We can use the `file.show` function to pop up windows and examine the files.

```
file.show("mydataExported.csv")
file.show("mydataExported.do")
```

The file mydataExported.csv is very similar to the one we wrote out using `write.csv`. Notice that it uses periods as missing values, which Stata will interpret properly.

```
1,1,f,1,1,5,1
2,2,f,2,1,4,1
3,1,f,2,2,4,3
4,2,,3,1,.,3
5,1,m,4,5,2,4
6,2,m,5,4,5,5
7,1,m,5,3,4,4
8,2,m,4,5,5,5
```

The following is the Stata program that R created:

```
infile gender:gender_fmt q1 q2 q3 q4  ///
using  mydataExported.csv , automatic
```

R wrote it as one line; we split it so that it would fit on the page.

Example Program for Exporting Data from R to Stata

This program first writes out a comma-delimited file from R. Then it does it again, along with a matching Stata do file to read it.

```
# Filename: ExportToStata.R

setwd("/myRfolder")

# A standard CSV file.
write.csv(mydata,
  file="mydataExported.csv", na="")
file.show("mydataExported.csv")

# A CSV for Stata with matching do file.

library("foreign")

write.foreign(mydata,
  datafile="mydataExported.csv",
  codefile="mydataExported.do",
  package="Stata")

# Look at the contents of our new files.
file.show("mydataExported.csv")
file.show("mydataExported.do")
```

7

Selecting Variables

In Stata, selecting variables for an analysis is simple, while selecting observations is often a bit more complicated. In R, these two processes can be almost identical. As a result, variable selection in R can at times be somewhat more complex. However, since you need to learn that complexity to select observations, it is not much added effort.

Selecting observations in Stata requires you to use logical conditions with commands like `if` or `in`. You do not usually use that logic to select variables. It is possible to do so, through the use of macros. If you have used Stata for long, you probably know dozens of ways to select observations, but you did not see them all in the first introductory guide you read. With R, it is best to dive in and see all of the methods of selecting variables because understanding them is the key to understanding other documentation, especially the help files and discussions on the R-Help mailing list. Even though you select variables and observations in R using almost identical methods, we will discuss them in two different chapters, with different example programs. This chapter focuses only on selecting variables. The next chapter will use almost identical descriptions with examples for selecting observations. We view that as helpful reinforcement, but no doubt some will view it as rather dull repetition!

7.1 Selecting Variables in Stata

Selecting variables in Stata is rather simple. It is worth reviewing them now before discussing R's approach. Our example data set contains the following variables: workshop, gender, q1, q2, q3, and q4. Stata lets you refer to them by individual names or in contiguous order separated by a dash, "-," as in

    summarize workshop-q4

You can select any variable beginning with the letter "q" using the star operator.

R.A. Muenchen, J.M. Hilbe, *R for Stata Users*, Statistics
and Computing, DOI 10.1007/978-1-4419-1318-0_7,
© Springer Science+Business Media, LLC 2010

```
summarize q*
```

or

```
list q1-q4
```

Finally, if you do not tell it which variable to use, Stata uses them all. For example, if you want Stata to summarize all variables in the data set, type "summarize," or abbreviate it to simply "su."

Now let us turn our attention to how R selects variables.

7.2 Selecting All Variables

In R, if you perform some analyses without selecting any variables, the functions will use all of the variables if they can. For example, to get summary statistics on all variables (and across all observations or rows), use

```
summary(mydata)
```

The variable selection process applies to any R functions that act on variables, not all do. We will use the summary function so you will see it in the context of an analysis.

7.3 Selecting Variables Using Index Numbers

Coming from Stata, you would think a discussion of selecting variables in R would begin with various ways to select variables using their names. R can use variable names, of course, but column *indexes*, also called *subscripts*, are more fundamental to the way R works. That is because objects in R need not name the elements or components they contain, but you can always refer to them by their index numbers.

Our data frame has two dimensions: rows and columns. We reference the rows and columns using square brackets as

```
mydata[rows,columns]
```

If you leave out the row or column indexes, R will process all rows and all columns. Therefore, the following three statements have the same result:

```
summary( mydata )
summary( mydata[ ] )
summary( mydata[ , ] )
```

This chapter focuses on the second parameter, the columns (variables). Our data frame has six variables or columns, which are automatically given index numbers, or indexes of 1, 2, 3, 4, 5, and 6. You can select variables by supplying one index number or a vector of indexes. For example,

```
summary( mydata[ ,3] )
```

selects all rows of the third variable or column, q1. If you leave out an index, it will assume you want them all. If you leave the comma out completely, R assumes you want a column, so

```
summary( mydata[3] )
```

is almost the same as

```
summary( mydata[ ,3] )
```

Both refer to our third variable, q1. While the **summary** function treats the presence or absence of the comma the same, some functions will have problems. That is because with the comma, the variable selection passes a vector and without the comma, it passes a data frame containing only one vector. See Section 10.17, "Converting Data Structures" for details.

To select more than one variable using indexes, you combine the indexes into a vector using the c function. Therefore, this will analyze variables 3 through 6.

```
summary( mydata[ c(3,4,5,6) ] )
```

You will see the c function used in many ways in R. Whenever R requires one object and you need to supply it several, it combines the several into one. In this case, the several index numbers become a single numeric vector.

The colon operator ":" can generate a numeric vector directly, so

```
summary( mydata[3:6] )
```

will use the same variables.

The colon operator is not just shorthand. We saw in an earlier chapter that entering 1:N causes R to generate the sequence, 1, 2, 3,...N. If you use a negative sign on an index, you will exclude those columns. For example:

```
summary( mydata[ -c(3,4,5,6) ] )
```

will analyze all variables except for variables 3, 4, 5, and 6. Your index values must be either all positive or all negative. Otherwise, the result would be illogical. You cannot say, "include only these" and "include all but these" at the same time. Index values of zero are accepted but ignored.

The colon operator can abbreviate sequences of numbers, but you need to be careful with negative numbers. If you want to exclude columns 3:6, the following approach will not work:

```
> -3:6
 [1] -3 -2 -1 0 1 2 3 4 5 6
```

This would, of course, generate an error since you cannot exclude 3 and include 3 at the same time. Adding parentheses will clarify the situation, showing R that you want the minus sign to apply to just the set of numbers from +3 through +6 rather than -3 through +6:

```
> -(3:6)
 [1] -3 -4 -5 -6
```

Therefore, we can exclude variables 3 through 6 with

```
summary( mydata[ -(3:6) ] )
```

If you find yourself working with a set of variables repeatedly, you can easily save a vector of indexes so you will not have to keep looking up index numbers:

```
myQindexes <- c(3,4,5,6)
summary( mydata[myQindexes] )
```

You can list indexes individually or, for contiguous variables, use the colon operator. For a large data set, you could use variables 1, 3, 5 through 20, 25, and 30 through 100 as follows:

```
myindexes <- c(1,3,5:20,25,30:100)
```

This is an important advantage of this method of selecting variables. Most of the other variable selection methods do not easily allow you to select mixed sets of contiguous and noncontiguous variables as you are used to doing in Stata. For another way to do this, see "Selecting Variables Using the Subset Function", Section 7.9.

If your variables follow patterns such as every other variable or every 10th, see Chapter 12, "Generating Data" for ways to generate other sequences of index numbers.

The **names** function will extract a vector of variable names from a data frame. The **data.frame** function, as we have seen, combines one or more vectors into a data frame *and* creates default row names of "1," "2," "3,". . . . Combining these two functions is one way to quickly generate a numbered list of variable names that you can use to look up index values:

```
> data.frame( names(mydata) )

  names.mydata.
1      workshop
2        gender
3            q1
4            q2
5            q3
6            q4
```

It is easy to rearrange the variables to put the four q variables in the beginning of the data frame. In that way, you will easily remember, for example, that q3 has an index value of 3 and so on.

Storing them in a separate data frame is another way to make indexes easy to remember for sequentially numbered variables like these. However, that approach runs into problems if you sort one data frame, as the rows then no longer match up in a sensible way. Correlations between the two sets would be meaningless.

The `ncol` function will tell you the number of columns in a data frame. Therefore, another way to analyze all your variables is

```
summary( mydata[ 1:ncol(mydata)  ]  )
```

If you remember that q1 is the third variable and you want to analyze all of the variables from there to the end, you can use

```
summary( mydata[ 3:ncol(mydata)  ]  )
```

7.4 Selecting Variables Using Column Names

Variables in Stata are required to have names, and those names must be unique. In R, you do not need them since you can refer to variables by index numbers as described in the previous section. Amazingly enough, the names do not have to be unique, although having two variables with the same name would be a terrible idea! R data frames usually include variable names, as does our example data: workshop, gender, q1, q2, q3, q4.

Stata stores its variable names within the respective data sets. However, you do not know exactly where they reside within the data set. Their location is irrelevant. They are in there somewhere, and that is all you need to know. However, in R, they are stored within a data frame in a place called the *names attribute*. The `names` function accesses that attribute, and you can display them by entering

```
> names(mydata)
```

```
[1] "workshop" "gender"   "q1"      "q2"      "q3"      "q4"
```

To select a column by name, you put it in quotes, as in

```
summary( mydata["q1"] )
```

R is still using the form

```
mydata[row,column]
```

However, when you supply only one index value, it assumes it is the column. So

```
summary( mydata[ ,"q1"] )
```

works as well. Note that the addition of the comma before the variable name is the only difference between the two examples above. While the summary function treats the presence or absence of the comma the same, some functions will have problems. That is because with the comma, the selection results in a vector, and without the comma, the selection is a data frame containing only that vector. See Section 10.17 for details.

If you have more than one name, combine them into a single character vector using the c function. For example,

```
summary( mydata[ c("q1","q2","q3","q4") ] )
```

Unfortunately, the colon operator does not work directly with character prefixes as it does with indexes. So the form q1:q4 does not work in this context. However, you can paste the letter "q" onto the numbers you generate using the paste function.

```
myQnames <- paste( "q", 1:4, sep="")
```

```
summary( mydata[myQnames] )
```

The paste function call above has three arguments:

1. The string to paste, which for this example is just the letter "q."
2. The object to paste it to, which is the numeric vector 1, 2, 3, 4 generated by the colon operator 1:4.
3. The *sep*arator character to paste between the two. Since this is set to "", the function will put nothing between "q" and "1," then "q" and "2," and so on. R will store the resulting names "q1," "q2," "q3," "q4" in the character vector myQnames. You can use this approach to generate variable names to use in a variety of circumstances. Note that merely changing the 1:4 above to 1:400 would generate the sequence from q1 to q400. R can easily generate other patterns of repeating values that you can use to create variable names. For details, see Chapter 12, "Generating Data." For another way to select variables by name using the colon operator, see "Selecting Variables Using the Subset Function," Section 7.9.

7.5 Selecting Variables Using Logic

You can select a column by using a logical vector of TRUE/FALSE values. You can enter one manually or create one by specifying a logical condition. Let us begin by entering one manually. For example,

```
summary( mydata[ c(FALSE,FALSE,TRUE,FALSE,FALSE,FALSE) ] )
```

will select the third column, q1, because the third value is TRUE and the third column is q1. In Stata, the digits 1 and 0 can represent TRUE and FALSE, respectively. They can do this in R, but they first require processing by the `as.logical` function. Therefore, we could also select the third variable with

```
summary( mydata[ as.logical( c(0,0,1,0,0,0) ) ] )
```

If we had not converted the 0/1 values to logical FALSE/TRUE, the above function call would have asked for two variables with index values of zero. Zero is a valid value, but it is is ignored. It would have then asked for the variable in column 1, which is workshop. Finally, it would have asked for three more variables in column zero. The result would have been an analysis only for the first variable, workshop. It would have been a perfectly valid, if odd, request!

Luckily, you do not have to actually enter logical vectors like the ones above. Instead, you will generate a vector by entering a logical statement such as

```
names(mydata)=="q1"
```

That logical comparison will generate the following logical vector for you:

```
FALSE, FALSE, TRUE, FALSE, FALSE, FALSE
```

Therefore, another way of analyzing q1 is

```
summary( mydata[ names(mydata)=="q1" ] )
```

While that example is good for educational purposes, in actual use you would prefer one of the shorter approach using variable names:

```
summary( mydata["q1"] )
```

Once you have mastered the various approaches of variable selection, you will find yourself alternating among the methods, as each has its advantages in different circumstances.

The "==" operator compares every element of a vector to a value and returns a logical vector of TRUE/FALSE values. The vector length will match the number of variables, not the number of observations, so we cannot store it in our data frame. So if we have assigned it to an object name, it would just exist as a vector in our R workspace.

As in Stata, the "!" sign represents NOT, so you can also use that vector to get all of the variables except for q1 using the form

```
summary( mydata[ !names(mydata)=="q1" ] )
```

To use logic to select multiple variable names, we can use the OR operator, "—". For example, select q1 through q4 with the following approach. Complex selections like this are much easier when you do it in two steps. First, create the logical vector and store it; then use that vector to do your selection. In the name *myQtf* below, I am using the "tf" part to represent TRUE/FALSE. That will help us remind that this is a logical vector.

```
myQtf <- names(mydata)=="q1" |
         names(mydata)=="q2" |
         names(mydata)=="q3" |
         names(mydata)=="q4"
```

Then we can get summary statistics on those variables using

```
summary( mydata[myQtf] )
```

Whenever you are making comparisons to many values, you can use the %in% operator. This will generate exactly the same logical vector as the OR example above.

```
myQtf <- names(mydata) %in% c("q1","q2","q3","q4")
```

```
summary( mydata[myQtf] )
```

You can easily convert a logical vector into an index vector that will select the same variables. For details, see "Converting Data Structures," Section 10.17.

7.6 Selecting Variables Using String Search

You can select variables by searching all of the variable names for strings of text. This approach uses the methods of selection by index numbers, names, and logic as discussed above, so make sure you have mastered them before trying this.

Stata uses the form

```
keep q*
```

to select all of the variables that begin with the letter q.

R searches variable names for patterns using the grep function. The name grep itself stands for *G*lobal *R*egular *E*xpression *P*rint. It is just a fancy name for a type of search.

The grep function creates a vector containing variable selection criteria we need in the form of indexes, names, or TRUE/FALSE logical values. The grep function and the rules that it follows, called *regular expressions*, appear in many different software packages and operating systems.

Below we will use the grep function to find the index numbers for names for those that begin with the letter q:

```
myQindexes <- grep("^q", names(mydata), value=FALSE)
```

The grep function call above uses three arguments:

1. The first is the command string, or regular expression, "^p", which means, "find strings that begin with lowercase p." The symbol "^" represents "begins with." You can use any regular expression here, allowing you to search for a wide range of patterns in variable names. We will discuss using wildcard patterns later.
2. The second argument is the character vector that you wish to search, which, in our case, is our variable names. Substituting names(mydata) here will extract those names.
3. The value argument tells it what to return when it finds a match. The goal of grep in any computer language or operating system is to find patterns. A value of TRUE here will tell it to return the variable names that match the pattern we seek. However, in R, indexes are more important than names, so the default setting is FALSE to return indexes instead. We could leave it off in this particular case, but we will use it the other way in the next example so we will list it here for educational purposes.

The contents of myQindexes will be 3, 4, 5, 6. In all our examples that use that name, it will have those same values.

To analyze those variables, we can then use

```
summary( mydata[myQindexes] )
```

Now let us do the same thing but have the grep function save the actual variable names. All we have to do is set value=TRUE.

```
myQnames <- grep("^q", names(mydata), value=TRUE)
```

The character vector myQnames now contains the variable names "q1," "q2," "q3," and "q4" and we can analyze those variables with

```
summary( mydata[myQnames] )
```

This approach gets what we expected: variable names. Since it uses names, it makes much more sense to a Stata user. So, why we did not do this first? Because in R, indexes are more flexible than variable names.

Finally, let us see how we would use this search method to select variables using logic. The %in% function works just like the in operator in Stata.

It finds things that occur in a list. We will use it to find when a member of all our variable names appears in the list of names beginning with "q" (stored in myQnames). The result will be a logical set of TRUE/FALSE values that indicate that the q variables are the last four:

```
FALSE, FALSE, TRUE, TRUE, TRUE, TRUE
```

We will store those values in the logical vector myQtf:

```
myQtf <- names(mydata) %in% myQnames
```

Now we can use the myQtf vector in any analysis we like:

```
summary( mydata[myQtf] )
```

It is important to note that since we were searching for variables that begin with the letter "q," our program would have also found variables qA and qB if they had existed. We can narrow our search with a more complex search expression that says the letter "q" precedes at least one digit. This would give us the ability to simulate Stata's ability to refer to variables that have a numeric suffix, such as "var1-var100."

This is actually quite easy, although the regular expression is a bit cryptic. It requires changing the myQnames line in the example above to the following:

```
myQnames <- grep("^q[1-9]", names(mydata), value=TRUE)
```

This regular expression means "any string that begins with "q," and is followed by one or more numerical digits." Therefore, if they existed, this would select q1, q27, q1old but not qA or qB. You can use it in your programs by simply changing the letter "q" to the root of the variable name you are using.

You may be more familiar with the search patterns using wildcards in Microsoft Windows. That system uses "*" to represent any number of characters and "?" to represent any single character. So the wildcard version of any variable name beginning with the letter q is "q*." Computer programmers call this type of symbol a "glob," short for global. R lets you convert globs to regular expressions with the glob2rx function. Therefore, we could do our first grep again in the form

```
myQindexes <- grep(glob2rx("q*"), names(mydata), value=FALSE)
```

Unfortunately, wildcards or globs are limited to simple searches and cannot do our example of q ending with any number of digits.

7.7 Selecting Variables Using $ Notation

You can select a column using $ notation, which combines the name of the data frame and the name of the variable within it, as in

```
summary( mydata$q1 )
```

This is referred to several ways in R, including "$ prefixing," "prefixing by dataframe$," or "$ notation." When you use this method to select multiple variables, you need to combine them into a single object like a data frame, as in

```
summary( data.frame( mydata$q1, mydata$q2 ) )
```

Having seen the c function, your natural inclination might be to use it for multiple variables as in

```
summary( c( mydata$q1, mydata$q2 ) ) #Not good!
```

This would indeed make a single object, but certainly not the one a Stata user expects. The c function would combine them both into a single variable with twice as many observations! The **summary** function would then happily analyze the new variable. When the **data.frame** function combines vectors into a single data frame, they remain separate vectors within that data frame. That is what we want here.

7.8 Selecting Variables Using Component Names

This section introduces using simple component names for variables stored in a data frame, like gender instead of mydata$gender. The technical details we will cover in Chapter 13, "Managing Your Files and Workspace."

In Stata, you refer to variables by simple names like gender or q1. You might have many data sets that contain a variable named gender, but there is no confusion since you have to specify the data set in advance.

In Stata you clarify which data set you want to use by opening it with
use mydata.dta

In R, the potential for confusing variable names is greater because it is much more flexible. For example, you can actually correlate a variable stored in one data frame with a variable stored in a *different data frame*! all of the variable selection methods discussed above made it perfectly clear which data frame to use, but they required extra typing. You can avoid this extra typing in several ways.

7.8.1 The attach Function

One approach R offers to simplify the selection of variables is the **attach** function. You attach a data frame using the following function call:

```
attach(mydata)
```

Once you have done that, you can refer to just q1, and R will know which one you mean. With this approach, getting summary statistics might look like

```
summary(q1)
```

or

```
summary( data.frame(q1, q2, q3, q4) )
```

If you finish with that data set and wish to use another, you can detach it with

```
detach( mydata )
```

Objects will detach automatically when you quit R, so using `detach` is not that important unless you need to use those variable names stored in a different data frame. In that case, detach one file before attaching the next.

The `attach` function works well when selecting existing variables, but it is best avoided when creating them. An attached data frame can be thought of as a temporary copy, so changes to existing variables will be lost. Therefore, when adding new variables to a data frame, you need to use any of the other above methods that make it absolutely clear where to store the variable. Afterward, you can detach the data and attach it again to gain access to the modified or new variables. We will look at the `attach` function more thoroughly in Chapter 13, "Managing Your Files and Workspace."

7.8.2 The `with` Function

The `with` function is another way to use short variable names. It is similar to using the `attach` function, followed by any other *single* function, and then followed by a `detach` function. The following is an example:

```
with( mydata, summary( data.frame(q1, q2, q3, q4) ) )
```

It lets you use simple component names and even lets you create variables safely. The downside is that you must repeat it with every function, whereas you might need the `attach` function only once at the beginning of your program. The added set of parentheses also increases your odds of making a mistake. To help avoid errors, you can type this as

```
with( mydata,
   summary( data.frame(q1, q2, q3, q4) )
)
```

7.8.3 Using Component Names in Formulas

A third way to use short variable (component) names works only with *modeling functions*. Modeling functions use formulas to perform analyses like linear regression or analysis of variance. They also have a `data` argument that specifies which data frame to use. This keeps formulas much shorter.

Here are two ways to perform a linear regression. First, using dollar notation,

```
lm( mydata$q4 ~ mydata$q1 + mydata$q2 + mydata$q3 )
```

The following is the same regression, using the `data` argument to tell the function which data frame to use:

```
lm( q4 ~ q1+q2+q3, data=mydata)
```

As formulas get longer, this second approach becomes much easier. For functions that accept formulas, this is the approach we recommend. It is easier to use than either the **attach** or **with** functions. It also offers other benefits when making predictions from the model. We will defer that discussion to Chapter 17, "Statistics."

To use this approach, all of the data must reside in the same data frame, making it less flexible. However, it is usually a good idea to have all of the variables in the same data frame anyway.

It is important to know that the **data=mydata** applies *only* to the variables specified in the **formula** argument. Some modeling functions can specify which variables to use *without* specifying a formula. In that case, you must use an alternate approach (**attach** or **with**) if you wish to use shorter variable names. We will see an example of this when doing t-tests in Chapter 17.

7.9 Selecting Variables with the **subset** Function

R has a **subset** function that you can use to select variables (and observations). It is the easiest way to select contiguous sets of variables by name, such as in this Stata example:

```
sum q1-q4
```

It follows the form

```
subset(mydata, select=q1:q4)
```

For example, when used with the **summary** function, it would appear as

```
summary( subset(mydata, select=q1:q4 ) )
```

or

```
summary( subset(mydata, select=c(workshop, q1:q4) ) )
```

The second example above contains three sets of parentheses. It is very easy to make mistakes with so many nested functions. A syntax-checking editor like JGR's or Emacs will help. Another thing that helps is to split them across multiple lines:

```
summary(
  subset(mydata, select=c(workshop, q1:q4) )
)
```

It is interesting to note that when using the c function within the **subset** function's **select** argument, it is combining the variable names, not the vectors themselves. So the following example will analyze the two variables separately:

```
summary(
    subset(mydata, select=c(q1,q2) ) # Good.
)
```

That is very different from

```
summary( c(mydata$q1,mydata$q2) ) # Not good.
```

which combines the two vectors into one long one before analysis. The `subset` function's unique syntax irritates some R users. We find that its usefulness outweighs its quirks.

7.10 Selecting Variables Using List Index

Our data frame is also a list. The components of the list are vectors that form the columns of the data frame. You can address these components of the list using an index value enclosed in two square brackets. For example, to select our third variable, we can use

```
summary( mydata[[3]] )
```

With this approach, the colon operator will not extract variables 3 through 6:

```
mydata[[3:6]]   # Will NOT get variables 3 through 6.
```

7.11 Generating Indexes A to Z from Two Variable Names

We have seen how the colon operator can help us analyze variables 3 through 6 using the form

```
summary( mydata[3:6] )
```

With that method, you have to know the index numbers, and digging through lists of variables can be tedious work. However, we can have R do that work for us, finding the index value for any variable name we like. This call to the `names` function

```
names(mydata)== "q1"
```

will generate the logical vector

```
FALSE, FALSE, TRUE, FALSE, FALSE, FALSE, FALSE
```

because q1 is the third variable. The `which` function will tell us the index values of any TRUE values in a logical vector, so

```
which( names(mydata)== "q1" )
```

will yield a value of 3. Putting these ideas together, we can find the index number of the first variable we want, store it in myqA, then find the last variable, store it in myqZ and then use them with the colon operator to analyze our data from A to Z:

```
myqA <- which( names(mydata)=="q1" )
myqZ <- which( names(mydata)=="q4" )

summary( mydata[ ,myqA:myqZ ] )
```

7.12 Saving Selected Variables to a New Dataset

You can use any variable selection method to create a new data frame that contains only those variables. If we wanted to create a new data frame that contained only the q variables, we could do so using any method described ealier. Here are a few variations:

```
myqs <- mydata[3:6]

myqs <- mydata[ c("q1","q2","q3","q4") ]
```

This next example will work, but R will name the variables "mydata.q1," "mydata.q2"...showing the data frame from which they came.

```
myqs <- data.frame(mydata$q1, mydata$q2,
                   mydata$q3, mydata$q4)
```

You can add variable name indicators to give them any name you like. With this next one, we are manually specifying original names.

```
myqs <- data.frame(q1=mydata$q1, q2=mydata$q2,
                   q3=mydata$q3, q4=mydata$q4)
```

Using the attach function, the data.frame function leaves the variable names in their original form.

```
attach(mydata)
myqs <- data.frame(q1, q2, q3, q4)
detach(mydata)
```

Finally, we have the subset function with its unique and convenient use of the colon operator directly on variable names.

```
myqs <- subset(mydata, select=q1:q4)
```

7.13 Example Programs for Variable Selection

In the examples throughout this chapter, we used the `summary` function to demonstrate how a complete analysis request would look. However, here we will use the `print` function to make it easier to see the result of each selection when you run these programs. Even though

```
mydata["q1"]
```

is equivalent to

```
print( mydata["q1"] )
```

because `print` is the default function, we will use the longer form because it is more representative of its look with most functions. As you learn R, you will quickly opt for the shorter approach when printing.

For most of the programming examples in this book, the Stata programs are shorter because the R programs demonstrate R's somewhat greater flexibility, at least in some instances. However, in the case of variable selection, Stata has a significant advantage in ease of use. These programs demonstrate roughly equivalent features.

7.13.1 Stata Program to Select Variables

```
* Filename: SelectingVars.do

use c:\myRfolder\mydata, clear
list workshop gender q1 q2 q3 q4
list workshop-q4
list workshop gender q*

* Creating a data set from selected variables;
keep q*
save c:\myRfolder\myqs
```

7.13.2 R Program to Select Variables

```
# Filename: SelectingVars.R

# Uses many of the same methods as selecting observations.

setwd("/myRfolder")
load(file="mydata.RData")

# This refers to no particular variables,
```

```
# so all are printed.
print(mydata)

#---Selecting Variables by Index Numbers---

# These also select all variables by default.
print( mydata[ ] )
print( mydata[ , ] )

# Select just the 3rd variable, q1.
print( mydata[ ,3] ) #Passes q3 as a vector.
print( mydata[3] )    #Passes q3 as a data frame.

# These all select the variables q1,q2,q3 and q4 by indexes.
print( mydata[ c(3, 4, 5, 6) ] )
print( mydata[ 3:6 ] )

# These exclude variables q1,q2,q3,q4 by indexes.
print( mydata[ -c(3, 4, 5, 6) ] )
print( mydata[ -(3:6) ] )

# Using indexes in a numeric vector.
myQindexes <- c(3, 4, 5, 6)
myQindexes
print( mydata[myQindexes] )
print( mydata[-myQindexes] )

# This displays the indexes for all variables.
print( data.frame( names(mydata) ) )

# Using ncol to find the last index.
print( mydata[ 1:ncol(mydata) ] )
print( mydata[ 3:ncol(mydata) ] )

#---Selecting Variables by Column Names---

# Display all variable names.
names(mydata)

# Select one variable.
print( mydata["q1"] ) #Passes q1 as a data frame.
print( mydata[ ,"q1"] ) #Passes q1 as a vector.

# Selecting several.
print( mydata[ c("q1","q2","q3","q4") ] )
```

```
# Save a list of variable names to use.
myQnames <- c("q1","q2","q3","q4")
print(myQnames)
print( mydata[myQnames] )

# Generate a list of variable names.
myQnames <- paste( "q", 1:4, sep="")
print(myQnames)
print( mydata[myQnames] )

#---Selecting Variables Using Logic---

# Select q1 by entering TRUE/FALSE values.
print( mydata[ c(FALSE,FALSE,TRUE,FALSE,FALSE,FALSE) ] )

# Manually create a vector to get just q1.
print( mydata[ as.logical( c(0,0,1,0,0,0) ) ] )

# Automatically create a logical vector to get just q1.
print( mydata[ names(mydata)=="q1" ] )

# Exclude q1 using NOT operator "!".
print( mydata[ !names(mydata)=="q1" ] )

# Use the OR operator, "|" to select q1 through q4,
# and store the resulting logical vector in myqs.
myQtf <- names(mydata)=="q1" |
         names(mydata)=="q2" |
         names(mydata)=="q3" |
         names(mydata)=="q4"
print(myQtf)
print( mydata[myQtf] )

# Use the %in% operator to select q1 through q4.
myQtf <- names(mydata) %in% c("q1","q2","q3","q4")
print(myQtf)
print( mydata[myQtf] )

#---Selecting Variables by String Search---

# Use grep to save the q variable indexes.
myQindexes <- grep("^q", names(mydata), value=FALSE)
print(myQindexes)
print( mydata[myQindexes] )
```

```r
# Use grep to save the q variable names (value=TRUE now).
myQnames <- grep("^q", names(mydata), value=TRUE)
print(myQnames)
print( mydata[myQnames] )

# Use %in% to create a logical vector
# to select q variables.
myQtf <- names(mydata) %in% myQnames
print(myQtf)
print( mydata[myQtf] )

# Repeat example above but searching for any
# variable name that begins with q, followed
# by one digit, followed by anything.
myQnames <- grep("^q[[:digit:]]\{1\}",
   names(mydata), value=TRUE)
print(myQnames)
myQtf <- names(mydata) %in% myQnames
print(myQtf)
print( mydata[myQtf] )

# Example of how glob2rx converts q* to ^q.
glob2rx("q*")

#---Selecting Variables Using $ Notation---

print( mydata$q1 )
print( data.frame(mydata$q1, mydata$q2) )

#---Selecting Variables by Component Names---

# Using the "attach" function.
attach(mydata)
print(q1)
print( data.frame(q1, q2, q3, q4) )
detach(mydata)

# Using the "with" function.
with( mydata,
  summary( data.frame(q1, q2, q3, q4) )
)

#---Selecting Variables Using subset Function---
```

```
print( subset(mydata, select=q1:q4) )
print( subset(mydata,
  select=c(workshop, q1:q4)
) )

#---Selecting Variables by List Index---

print( mydata[[3]] )

#---Generating Indexes A to Z from Two Variables---

myqA <- which( names(mydata)=="q1" )
print(myqA)
myqZ <- which( names(mydata)=="q4" )
print(myqZ)
print( mydata[myqA:myqZ] )

#---Creating a New Data Frame---

# Equivalent ways to create a data frame
# of just the q vars.

myqs <- mydata[3:6]
print(myqs)
myqs <- mydata[ c("q1","q2","q3","q4") ]
print(myqs)
myqs <- data.frame(mydata$q1, mydata$q2,
                   mydata$q3, mydata$q4)
print(myqs)
myqs <- data.frame(q1=mydata$q1, q2=mydata$q2,
                   q3=mydata$q3, q4=mydata$q4)
print(myqs)

attach(mydata)
myqs <- data.frame(q1,q2,q3,q4)
print(myqs)
detach(mydata)

myqs <- subset(mydata, select=q1:q4)
print(myqs)
```

8

Selecting Observations

It bears repeating that the approaches that R uses to select observations are, for the most part, the same as those discussed in the previous chapter for selecting variables. This chapter focuses only on selecting observations, and it does so in the same order as the chapter on selecting variables. The next chapter will cover the selection of variables and observations at the same time but will do so in much less detail.

8.1 Selecting Observations in Stata

There are many ways to select observations in Stata, and it is outside our scope to discuss them all here. However, we will look at some approaches for comparison purposes. For Stata, if you do not select observations, it assumes you want to analyze all of the data. So in Stata

```
describe workshop-q4;
```

will analyze all of the observations.

To select a subset of observations (e.g., the males), Stata uses the "if" option.

```
describe workshop-q4 if gender=="m"
```

It is also common to create a logical 0/1 value in the form

```
gen female=gender=="f"
```

which you could then apply with,

```
describe workshop=q4 if female
```

R.A. Muenchen, J.M. Hilbe, *R for Stata Users*, Statistics and Computing, DOI 10.1007/978-1-4419-1318-0_8, © Springer Science+Business Media, LLC 2010

8.2 Selecting All Observations

In R, if you perform an analysis without selecting any observations, the function will use all of the observations it can. For all descriptive analyses, Stata works in the same manner.

For example, to get summary statistics on all observations (and all variables), we could use

```
summary(mydata)
```

which is similar to Stata's version:

```
summary mydata
```

The methods to select observations apply to all R functions that accept variables (vectors and so forth) as input. We will use the summary function so you will see the selection in the context of an analysis.

8.3 Selecting Observations Using Index Numbers

Although it is as easy to select observations by index numbers, you need to be careful doing it. This is because sorting a data frame is something you do often, and sorting changes the index number of each row (if you save the sorted version of course). Variables rarely change order, so this approach is much more widely used to select them. That said, let us dive in and see how R does it.

Our data frame has two dimensions: rows and columns. R refers to these in the form

```
mydata[rows,columns]
```

If you leave out the row or column indexes, R will process all rows and all columns. Therefore, the following three statements have the same result:

```
summary( mydata )
summary( mydata[ ] )
summary( mydata[ , ] )
```

Since this section focuses on selecting observations, we will now discuss just the first index, the rows. Our data frame has eight observations or rows, which are automatically given index numbers, or indexes of 1, 2, 3, 4, 5, 6, 7, and 8. You can select observations by supplying one index number or a vector of indexes. For example,

```
summary( mydata[5 , ] )
```

selects all of the variables for only row 5. There is not much worth analyzing with that selection! Note that the comma is *very* important, even though we request no columns in the example above. If you leave the comma out, R will assume that any index values it sees are column indexes, and you will end up selecting *variables* instead of observations!

As long as you include the comma, this selection goes across columns of a data frame, so it must return a one-row data frame. A data frame can contain variables that are numeric, character, or factor. Only a data frame could store such a mixture. That is the opposite of selecting the fifth variable with `mydata[ ,5]` because that would select a vector. In many cases, this distinction would not matter, but it might.

To select more than one observation using indexes, you must combine them into a numeric vector using the c function. Therefore, this will select rows 5 through 8, which happen to be the males:

```
summary( mydata[ c(5,6,7,8) , ] )
```

You will see the c function used in many ways in R. Whenever R requires one object and you need to supply it several, it combines the several into one. In this case, the several index numbers become a single numeric vector. Again, take note of the comma that precedes the right square bracket. If we left that comma out, R would try to analyze variables 5 through 8 instead of observations 5 through 8! Since we have only six variables, that would generate an error message. However, if we had more variables, the analysis would run, giving us the wrong result with no error message. We added extra spaces in this example to help you notice the comma. You do not need additional spaces in R, but you can have as many as you like to enhance readability.

The colon operator ":" can generate a numeric vector directly, so

```
summary( mydata[5:8, ] )
```

selects the same observations.

The colon operator is not just shorthand. Entering 1:N at the R console will cause it to generate the sequence, 1,2,3,...,N.

If you use a negative sign on an index, you will exclude those observations. For example

```
summary( mydata[ -c(1,2,3,4) , ] )
```

will exclude the first four records, three females and one with a gender of NA. R will then analyze the males.

Your index values must be either all positive or all negative. Otherwise, the result would be illogical. You cannot say "include only these observations" and "include all but these observations" at the same time.

The colon operator can abbreviate sequences of numbers, but you need to be careful with negative numbers. If you want to exclude rows 1 through 4, the following sequence will not work:

```
> -1:4
```

```
[1] -1  0  1  2  3  4
```

This would, of course, generate an error because they must all have the same sign. Adding parentheses will clarify the situation, showing R that you want the minus sign to apply to just the set of numbers from +1 through +4 rather than –1 through +4:

```
> -(1:4)
```

```
[1] -1 -2 -3 -4
```

```
> summary( mydata[ -(1:4) , ] )
```

If you find yourself working with a set of observations repeatedly, you can easily save a vector of indexes so you will not have to keep looking up index numbers. In this example, we are storing the indexes for the males in myMindexes (M for male). If we were not trying to make a point about indexes, we would choose a simpler name like just "males."

```
myMindexes <- c(5,6,7,8)
```

From now on, we can use that variable to analyze the males:

```
summary( mydata[myMindexes, ] )
```

For a more realistic data set, typing all of the observation index numbers you need would be absurdly tedious and error prone. We will use logic to create that vector in "Observation Selection, Advanced Topics," Section 8.8. You can list indexes individually or, for contiguous observations, use the colon operator. For a larger data set, you could use observations 1, 3, 5 through 20, 25, and 30 through 100 as follows

```
mySubset <- c(1,3,5:20,25,30:100)
```

See the Chapter 12, "Generating Data" for ways to generate other sequences of index numbers.

It is easy to have R list the index for each observation in a data frame. Simply create an index using the colon operator and append it to the front of the data frame.

```
> data.frame(myindex=1:8, mydata)
```

```
  myindex workshop gender q1 q2 q3 q4
1       1        R      f  1  1  5  1
2       2    Stata      f  2  1  4  1
3       3        R      f  2  2  4  3
```

```
4       4       Stata  <NA> 3  1 NA  3
5       5           R     m  4  5  2  4
6       6       Stata     m  5  4  5  5
7       7           R     m  5  3  4  4
8       8       Stata     m  4  5  5  5
```

Note that the unlabeled column on the left contains the row names. In our case, the row names look like indexes. However, the row names could have been descriptive strings like "Bob," so there is no guarantee of a relationship between row names and indexes. Index values are dynamic, like the case numbers displayed in the Stata data editor. When you sort or rearrange the data, they change. Row names, on the other hand, are fixed when you create the data frame. Sorting or rearranging the rows will not change row names.

You can use the **nrow** function to find the number of rows in a data frame. Therefore, another way to analyze all your observations is

```
summary( mydata[ 1:nrow(mydata) , ]  )
```

If you remember that the first male is the fifth record and you want to analyze all of the observations from there to the end, you can use

```
summary( mydata[ 5:nrow(mydata) , ]  )
```

8.4 Selecting Observations Using Row Names

Stata data sets have variable names but not observation or case names. In R, data frames always name the observations and store those names in the row names attribute. When we read our data set from a text file, we told it that the first column would be our row names. The row.names function will display them:

```
row.names(mydata)
```

R will respond with

```
"1", "2", "3", "4", "5", "6", "7", "8"
```

The quotes around them show that R treats them as characters, not as numbers. If you do not provide an ID or name variable for R to use as row names, it will always create them in this form. Therefore, if we had not had an ID variable, we would have ended up in exactly the same state. I included an ID variable because it emphasizes the need to be able to track your data back to its most original source when checking for data entry errors. With such boring row names, there is little need to use them. Indexes are numerically more useful. So let us change the names so we will have an example that makes sense. We will create a new character vector of names:

```
> mynames <- c("Ann","Cary","Sue","Carla",
               "Bob","Scott","Mike","Rich")
```

Now we will write those names into the row names attribute of our data frame:

```
row.names(mydata) <- mynames
```

This is a very interesting assignment! It shows that the `row.names` function does not just show you the names, it provides access to the names attribute itself. Assigning mynames to that vector renames all of the rows! In Section 10.6, "Renaming Variables (and Observations)," we will see this again with several variations.

Let us see how this has changed our data frame.

```
> mydata
```

```
      workshop gender q1 q2 q3 q4
Ann          R      f  1  1  5  1
Cary     Stata      f  2  1  4  1
Sue          R      f  2  2  4  3
Carla    Stata   <NA>  3  1 NA  3
Bob          R      m  4  5  2  4
Scott    Stata      m  5  4  5  5
Mike         R      m  5  3  4  4
Rich     Stata      m  4  5  5  5
```

Now that we have some interesting names to work with, let us see what we can do with them. If we wanted to look at the data for "Ann," we could use

```
mydata["Ann", ]
```

You might think that if we had several records per person, we could use row names to select all of the rows for any person. R, however, requires that row names be unique, which is a good idea. You could always use an id number that is unique for row names, then have the subjects' names on each record in their set and a counter like time 1, 2, 3, 4. We will look at just that structure in Section 10.15, "Reshaping Variables to Observations and Back."

To select more than one row name, you must combine them into a single character vector using the `c` function. For example, we could analyze the females using

```
summary( mydata[ c("Ann","Cary","Sue","Carla"), ] )
```

With a more realistically sized data frame, we would probably want to save the list of names to a character vector that we could use repeatedly. Here we use *F* to represent females and *names* to remind us of what is in the vector:

```
myFnames <- c("Ann","Cary","Sue","Carla")
```

Now we will analyze the females again using this vector:

```
summary( mydata[ myFnames, ] )
```

Note that, in Stata, observations are selected using the in operator such as:

```
summ age in 1/4
```

or

```
summ age if q1==1
```

8.5 Selecting Observations Using Logic

You can select observations by using a logical vector of TRUE/FALSE values. You can enter one manually or create by specifying a logical condition. Let us begin by entering one manually. For example, the following will print the first four rows of our data set:

```
> myRows <- c(TRUE, TRUE, TRUE, TRUE,
+    FALSE, FALSE, FALSE, FALSE)

> print( mydata[myRows, ]  )

  workshop gender q1 q2 q3 q4
1        R      f  1  1  5  1
2    Stata      f  2  1  4  1
3        R      f  2  2  4  3
4    Stata   <NA>  3  1 NA  3
```

In Stata, the digits 1 and 0 can represent TRUE and FALSE. Let us see what happens when we try this in R.

```
> myBinary <- c(1, 1, 1, 1, 0, 0, 0, 0)

> print( mydata[myBinary, ] )

    workshop gender q1 q2 q3 q4
1          R      f  1  1  5  1
1.1        R      f  1  1  5  1
1.2        R      f  1  1  5  1
1.3        R      f  1  1  5  1
```

What happened? Remember that putting a 1 in for the row index asks for row 1. So our request asked for row 1 four times in a row and then asked for row 0 four times. Index values of zero are ignored. We can get around this problem by using the as.logical function.

```
> myRows <- as.logical(myBinary)
```

Now, myRows contains the same TRUE/FALSE values it had in the previous example and would work fine. While the above examples make it clear how R selects observations using logic, they are not very realistic. Hundreds of records would require an absurd amount of typing. Rather than typing such logical vectors, you can generate them with logical statement such as

```
> mydata$gender=="f"
```

```
[1]  TRUE  TRUE  TRUE    NA FALSE FALSE FALSE FALSE
```

The "==" operator compares every value of a vector, like gender, to a value, like "f", and returns a logical vector of TRUE/FALSE values. These logical conditions can be as complex as you like, including all of the usual logical conditions. See Table 10.2, "Logical operators," for details.

The length of the resulting logical vector will match the number of observations in our data frame. Therefore, we could store it our data frame as a new variable.

Unfortunately, we see that the fourth logical value is NA. That is because the fourth observation has a missing value for gender. Up until this point, we have been mirroring Chapter 7, "Selecting Variables." Logical comparisons of variable names did not have a problem with missing values. Now, however, we must take a different approach. First, let us look at what would happen if we continued down this track.

```
> print( mydata[ mydata$gender=="f", ] )
```

```
   workshop gender  q1 q2 q3 q4
1         R      f   1  1  5  1
2     Stata      f   2  1  4  1
3         R      f   2  2  4  3
NA     <NA>   <NA>  NA NA NA NA
```

What happened to the fourth observation? It had missing values only for gender and q3. Now *all* of the values for that observation are missing. R has noticed that we were selecting rows based on only gender. Not knowing what we would do with the selection, it had to make all of the other values missing too. Why? Because we might have been wanting to correlate q1 and q4. Those two had no missing values in the original data frame. If we want to correlate them only for the females, even their values must be set to missing.

We could select observations using this logic and then count on R's other functions to remove the bad observations as they would any others with missing values. However, there is little point in storing them. Their presence could also affect future counts of missing values for other analyses, perhaps when females are recombined with males.

Luckily, there is an easy way around this problem. The `which` function gets the index values for the TRUE values of a logical vector. Let us see what it does.

```
> which( mydata$gender=="f" )

[1] 1 2 3
```

It has ignored both the NA value and the FALSE values to show us that only the first three values of our logical statement were TRUE. We can save these index values in myFemales.

```
> myFemales <- which( mydata$gender=="f" )

> myFemales
  [1] 1 2 3
```

We can then analyze just the females with the following:

```
summary( mydata[ myFemales , ] )
```

Negative index values exclude those rows, so we could analyze the non-females (males and missing) with the following:

```
summary( mydata[-myFemales , ] )
```

We could, of course, get males and exclude missing the same way we got the females.

We can select observations using logic that is more complicated. For example, we can use the AND operator "&" to analyze subjects who are both male and who "strongly agree" that the workshop they took was useful. Compound selections like this are much easier when you do it in two steps. First, create the logical vector and store it; then use that vector to do your selection.

```
> HappyMales <- which(mydata$gender=="m"
+    & mydata$q4==5)

> HappyMales
  [1] 6 8
```

So we could analyze these observations with

```
summary( mydata[HappyMales , ] )
```

Whenever you are making comparisons to many values, you can use the `%in%` operator. Let us select observations who have taken the R or Stata workshop. With just two target workshops, you could use a simple `workshop="R" | workshop="Stata"`, but the longer the target list, the happier you will be to save all of the repetitive typing.

```
> myRstata <-
+   which( mydata$workshop %in% c("R","Stata") )

> myRstata
 [1] 1 3 5 7
```

Then we can get summary statistics on those observations using

```
summary( mydata[myRstata, ] )
```

The various methods we described in Chapter 7, "Selecting Variables" make a big difference in how complicated the logical commands to select observations appear. Here are several different ways to analyze just the females:

```
myFemales <- which( mydata$gender=="f")

myFemales <- which( mydata[2] == "f")

myFemales <- which( mydata["gender"] == "f")

with(mydata,
  myFemales <- which(gender=="f")
)

attach(mydata)
  myFemales <- which(gender=="f")
detach(mydata)
```

You could then use any of these to analyze the data using

```
summary( mydata[ myFemales, ] )
```

You can easily convert a logical vector into index vector that will select the same observations. For details, see "Converting Data Structures," Section 10.17.

8.6 Selecting Observations Using String Search

If you have character variables, or useful row names, you can select observations by searching their values for strings of text. This approach uses the methods of selection by indexes, row names, and logic discussed ealier, so make sure you have mastered them before trying these.

R searches variable names for patterns using the **grep** function. The name **grep** itself stands for *G*lobal *R*egular *E*xpression *P*rint. It is just an acronym for a type of search.

The **grep** function creates a vector containing variable selection criteria that we need in the form of indexes, names, or TRUE/FALSE logical values.

The `grep` function and the rules that it follows, called *regular expressions*, appear in many different software packages and operating systems.

We previously replaced our original row names, "1," "2,"..., with more interesting ones, "Ann", "Cary,".... Now we will use the `grep` function to search for row names that begin with the letter "C":

```
myCindexes <- grep("^C", row.names(mydata), value=FALSE)
```

This `grep` function call uses three arguments:

1. The first is the command string, or regular expression, "^C," which means "find strings that begin with a capital letter C." The symbol "^" represents "begins with." You can use any regular expression here, allowing you to search for a wide range of patterns in variable names. We will discuss using wildcard patterns later.
2. The second argument is the character vector that you wish to search. In our case, we want to search the row names of mydata, so we use the `row.names` function here.
3. The `value` argument tells it what to store when if finds a match. The goal of grep in any computer language or operating system is to find patterns. A value of TRUE here will tell it to save the row names that match the pattern we seek. However, in R, indexes are more fundamental than names, which are optional, so the default setting is FALSE to save indexes instead. We could leave it off in this particular case, but we will use it the other way in the next example, so we will list it here for educational purposes. The contents of myCindexes will be 2 and 4 because Cary and Carla are the second and fourth observations. If we wanted to save this variable, it does not match the eight values of our other variables, so we cannot store it in our data frame. We would instead just store it in the workspace as a vector outside our data frame.

To analyze those observations, we can then use

```
summary( mydata[myCindexes , ] )
```

Now let us do the same thing but have **grep** save the actual variable names. All we have to do is change to **value=TRUE**:

```
myCnames <- grep("^C", row.names(mydata), value=TRUE)
```

The character vector myCnames now contains the row names "Cary" and "Carla" and we can analyze those observations with

```
summary( mydata[myCnames , ] )
```

Finally, let us do a similar search using the **%in%** function. In R, it works just like the **in** option in Stata. It finds matches between two sets of values. We will use it to find which of our row names appears in this set of target names:

```
myTargetNames <- ("Carla","Caroline",
  "Cary","Cathy","Cynthia")
```

```
myMatches <- row.names(mydata) %in% myTargetNames
```

The result will be a logical set of TRUE/FALSE values that indicate that the names that match are in the second and fourth positions:

```
FALSE, TRUE, FALSE, TRUE, FALSE, FALSE, FALSE, FALSE
```

Now we can use the myMatches vector in any analysis like summary:

```
summary( mydata[myMatches, ] )
```

You may be more familiar with the search patterns using wildcards in Microsoft Windows. They use "*" to represent any number of characters and "?" to represent any single character. So the wildcard version of any variable name beginning with the letter "C" is "C*." Computer programmers call this type of symbol a "glob," short for *glob*al. R lets you convert globs to *regular expressions* with the glob2rx function. Therefore, we could do our first grep again in the form

```
myCindexes <- grep( glob2rx("C*"),
  row.names(mydata), value=FALSE )
```

8.7 Selecting Observations Using the subset Function

You can select observations using the subset function. You simply list your logical condition under the subset argument, as in

```
subset(mydata, subset=gender=="f")
```

Note that an equal sign follows the subset argument because that is what R uses to set argument values. The gender=="f" comparison is still done using "==" because that is the symbol R uses for logical comparisons. You can use subset to analyze your selection using the form

```
summary(
  subset(mydata, subset=gender=="f")
)
```

The following is a slightly more complicated selection, in which we select the males who were happy with their workshop. In R, the logic is a single object, a logical vector, regardless of its complexity.

```
summary(
  subset( mydata, subset=gender=="m" & q4==5 )
)
```

Since the first argument to the subset function is the data frame to use, you do not have to write out the longer forms of names like mydata$q1 or mydata$gender. Also, its logical selections automatically exclude cases for which the logic would be missing. So it acts like the which function that is built into every selection. That is a very helpful function!

8.8 Generating Indexes A to Z from Two Row Names

We have discussed various observation selection techniques. Now we are ready to examine combination methods that use a blend of row names, logic, and index numbers. If you have not mastered the previous examples, now would be a good time to review them!

We have seen how the colon operator can help us analyze the males, who are observations 5 through 8, using the form

```
summary( mydata[5:8, ] )
```

However, you had to know the index numbers, and digging through lists of observation numbers can be tedious work. However, we can use the row.names function and the which function to get R to find the index values we need. The function call

```
row.names(mydata)=="Bob"
```

will generate the logical vector

```
FALSE, FALSE, FALSE, FALSE, TRUE, FALSE, FALSE, FALSE
```

because Bob is the fifth observation. The which function will tell us the index values of any TRUE values in a logical vector, so

```
which(FALSE, FALSE, FALSE, FALSE,
   TRUE, FALSE, FALSE, FALSE)
```

will yield a value of 5. Putting these ideas together, we can find the index number of the first observation we want, store it in myMaleA, then find the last observation, store it in myMaleZ, and then use them with the colon operator to analyze our data from A to Z:

```
myMaleA <- which( names(mydata)=="Bob" )
myMaleZ <- which( names(mydata)=="Rich" )
summary( mydata[ myMaleA:myMaleZ, ] )
```

8.9 Variable Selection Methods with No Counterpart for Selecting Observations

As we have seen, the methods that R uses to select variables and observations are almost identical. However, there are several techniques for selecting variables that have no equivalent in selecting observations:

* The $ prefix form (e.g., mydata$gender).
* The **attach** function's approach to short variable names.
* The **with** function's approach to short variable names.
* The use of formulas.
* The list form (e.g., mydata[[2]]).

8.10 Saving Selected Observations to a New Data Frame

You can create a new data frame that is a subset of your original one by using any of the methods for selecting observations. You simply assign the data to a new data frame. The examples below all select the males and assign them to the myMales data frame:

```
myMales <- mydata[5:8, ]

myMales <- mydata[ which(mydata$gender=="m") , ]

myMales <- subset( mydata, subset=gender=="m" )
```

8.11 Example Programs for Selecting Observations

The examples below demonstrate the many ways to select observations. Throughout this chapter we used the **summary** function to demonstrate how a complete analysis request would look. Here we will instead use the **print** function to make it easier to see the result of each selection when you run the programs. Even though

```
mydata[5:8, ]
```

is equivalent to

```
print( mydata[5:8, ] )
```

because **print** is the default function, we will use the longer form because it is more representative of its look with most functions. As you learn R, you will quickly opt for the shorter approach when you only want to print data.

8.11.1 Stata Program to Select Observations

```
* Filename: SelectingObs.do

use c:\myRfolder\mydata, clear
describe workshop-q4;
describe workshop-q4 if gender=="m"
gen female=gender=="f"
describe workshop=q4 if female
summ
```

8.11.2 R Program to Select Observations

```
# Filename: SelectingObs.R .

setwd("/myRfolder")
load(file="mydata.RData")
print(mydata)

#---Selecting Observations by Index---

# Print all rows.
print( mydata[ ] )
print( mydata[ , ] )
print( mydata[1:8, ] )

# Just observation 5.
print( mydata[5 , ] )

# Just the males:
print( mydata[ c(5,6,7,8) , ] )
print( mydata[ 5:8        , ] )

# Excluding the females with minus sign.
print( mydata[ -c(1,2,3,4), ] )
print( mydata[ -(1:4)    , ] )

# Saving the Male (M) indexes for reuse.
myMindexes <- c(5,6,7,8)
summary( mydata[myMindexes, ] )

# Print a list of index numbers for each observation.
data.frame(myindex=1:8,mydata)

# Select data using length as the end.
```

```
print( mydata[ 1:nrow(mydata),  ]  )
print( mydata[ 5:nrow(mydata),  ]  )

#---Selecting Observations by Row Name---

# Display row names.
row.names(mydata)

# Select rows by their row name.
print( mydata[ c("1","2","3","4"), ] )

# Assign more interesting names.
mynames <- c("Ann","Cary","Sue","Carla",
             "Bob","Scott","Mike","Rich")
print(mynames)

# Store the new names in mydata.
row.names(mydata) <- mynames
print(mydata)

# Print Ann's data.
print( mydata["Ann" , ] )
mydata["Ann" , ]

# Select the females by row name.
print( mydata[ c("Ann","Cary","Sue","Carla"), ] )

# Save names of females to a character vector.
myFnames <- c("Ann","Cary","Sue","Carla")
print(myFnames)

# Use character vector to select females.
print( mydata[ myFnames, ] )

#---Selecting Observations Using Logic---

#Selecting first four rows using TRUE/FALSE.
myRows <- c(TRUE, TRUE, TRUE, TRUE,
  FALSE, FALSE, FALSE, FALSE)
print( mydata[myRows, ]  )

# Selecting first four rows using 1s and 0s.
myBinary <- c(1, 1, 1, 1, 0, 0, 0, 0)
print( mydata[myBinary, ] )
myRows <- as.logical(myBinary)
```

```
print( mydata[ myRows, ] )

# Use a logical comparison to select the females.
mydata$gender=="f"
print( mydata[ mydata$gender=="f", ] )
which( mydata$gender=="f" )
print( mydata[ which(mydata$gender=="f") , ] )

# Select females again, this time using a saved vector.
myFemales <- which( mydata$gender=="f" )
print(myFemales)
print( mydata[ myFemales , ] )

# Excluding the females using the "!" NOT symbol.
print( mydata[-myFemales , ] )

# Select the happy males.
HappyMales <- which(mydata$gender=="m"
  & mydata$q4==5)
print(HappyMales)
print( mydata[HappyMales , ] )

# Selecting observations using %in%.
myRstata <-
  which( mydata$workshop %in% c("R","Stata") )
print(myRstata)
print( mydata[myRstata , ] )

# Equivalent selections using different
# ways to refer to the variables.

print( subset(mydata, gender=='f') )

attach(mydata)
  print( mydata[ gender=="f" , ] )
detach(mydata)

with(mydata,
  print ( mydata[ gender=="f" , ] )
)

print( mydata[ mydata["gender"]=="f" , ] )

print( mydata[ mydata$gender=="f" , ] )
```

```
#---Selecting Observations by String Search---

# Search for row names that begin with "C".
myCindexes <- grep("^C", row.names(mydata), value=FALSE)
print( mydata[myCindexes , ] )

# Again, using wildcards.
myCindexes <- grep( glob2rx("C*") ,
  row.names(mydata), value=FALSE)
print( mydata[myCindexes , ] )


#---Selecting Observations Using subset Function---

subset(mydata,subset=gender=="f")

summary(
  subset( mydata, subset=gender=="m" & q4==5 )
)


#---Generating Indexes A to Z From Two Row Names---

myMaleA <- which( row.names(mydata)=="Bob" )
print(myMaleA)
myMaleZ <- which( row.names(mydata)=="Rich" )
print(myMaleZ)
print( mydata[myMaleA:myMaleZ , ] )


#---Creating A New Data Frame---

# Creating a new data frame of only males (all equivalent).
myMales <- mydata[5:8, ]
print(myMales)
myMales <- mydata[ which( mydata$gender=="m" ) , ]
print(myMales)
myMales <- subset( mydata, subset=gender=="m" )
print(myMales)

# Creating a new data frame of only females (all equivalent).
myFemales <- mydata[1:3, ]
print(myFemales)
myFemales <- mydata[ which( mydata$gender=="f" ) , ]
print(myFemales)
myFemales <- subset( mydata, subset=gender=="f" )
print(myFemales)
```

9

Selecting Variables and Observations

In the previous two chapters, we focused on selecting variables and observations separately. You can combine those approaches to select both variables and observations at the same time. As an example, we will use the various methods to select the variables workshop and q1 to q4 for only the males.

Previously we began with index numbers because they are so fundamental to understanding how R works. This time we will discuss the more practical approaches first.

The explanations in this chapter are much sparser. If you need clarification, see the detailed discussions of each approach in the previous two chapters.

9.1 The subset Function

Although you can use any of the methods introduced in the previous two chapters to select both variables and observations, you would usually choose variables by name and choose observations by logic. The subset function lets us use that combination easily.

When selecting variables, subset allows you to use the colon operator on lists of contiguous variables, like gender:q4. Variable selections that are more complex than a single variable or two contiguous variables separated by a colon must be combined with the c function, as usual.

When selecting observations, you perform logic like gender=="m" without having to use which(gender=="m") to get rid of the observations that have missing values for gender. The logic can be as complex as you like, so we can select the males who are happy with their workshop using gender=="m" & q4==5. Note that the result of a logical condition is always a single logical vector, so you never need the c function for logic. See Table 10.2, "Logical operators," for details.

We can perform our selection by nesting the subset function directly within other functions:

R.A. Muenchen, J.M. Hilbe, *R for Stata Users*, Statistics
and Computing, DOI 10.1007/978-1-4419-1318-0_9,
© Springer Science+Business Media, LLC 2010

```
summary(
  subset(mydata,
    subset=gender=="m",
    select=c(workshop, q1:q4) )
)
```

Since R allows you to skip the names of arguments as long as you have them in proper order, you often see subset used in the form

```
summary(
  subset(mydata, gender=="m",
    c(workshop, q1:q4) )
)
```

If you plan to use a subset like this repeatedly, it would make more sense to save the subset in a data frame. Here we will add the print function just to make the point that selection is done once and then used repeatedly with different functions. Here we are using the name myMalesWQ to represent the males with workshop and the q variables.

```
myMalesWQ <- subset(mydata,
    subset=gender=="m",
    select=c(workshop, q1:q4)
)

print(myMalesWQ)
summary(myMalesWQ)
```

Performing the task in two steps like that often makes the code easier to read and less error-prone.

9.2 Selecting Observations by Logic and Variables by Name

Another very useful approach is to use logic to select observations and to use names to select variables.

```
summary(
  mydata[ which(gender=="m") ,
        c("workshop","q1","q2","q3","q4") ]
)
```

This is very similar to what we did with the subset function, but with character index values, we cannot use the form q1:q4 to choose contiguous variables. So if you had many variables, you would want to use the shortcut described in Section 7.11, "Generating Indexes A to Z from Two Variable Names."

We could make our example more legible by defining the row and column indexes in a separate step:

```
myMales <- which(gender=="m")
myVars  <- c("workshop","q1","q2","q3","q4")

summary( mydata[ myMales, myVars] )
```

This has the added benefit of allowing us to analyze just the males, for all variables (we are not selecting any specifically) with

```
summary( mydata[ myMales, ] )
```

We can also analyze males and females (by *not* choosing only males) for just my Vars:

```
summary( mydata[ , myVars] )
```

If we did not need that kind of flexibility and we planned to use this subset repeatedly, we would save it to a data frame.

```
myMalesWQ <- mydata[ myMales, myVars]

summary(myMalesWQ)
```

9.3 Using Names to Select Both Observations and Variables

The above two approaches usually make the most sense. You usually know variable names and subset values to select. For completeness sake, we will continue on with additional combinations, but if you feel you understood the previous two chapters and the examples above, feel free to skip these examples and go to Section 9.6, "Saving and Loading Subsets."

Since the males have character row names of "5" through "8," we could use both row names and column with

```
summary( mydata[
  c("5","6","7","8"),
  c("workshop","q1","q2","q3","q4")
] )
```

This is an odd approach for selecting rows. We do not often bother to learn such meaningless row names. If we had row names that made more sense, like "Ann," "Bob," "Carla,"..., this approach would make more sense. However, we can at least be assured that the row names will not be affected by the addition of new observations or by sorting. Such manipulations do not change row names as they do numeric index values.

If you plan on using these character index vectors often or if you have many values to specify, it is helpful to store them separately. This also helps document your program, since a name like myMales will remind you, or your colleagues, what you were selecting.

```
myMales <- c("5","6","7","8")

myVars  <- c("workshop","q1","q2","q3","q4")
```

Now we can repeat the same examples that we used in the section immediately above. Once you have a vector of index values, it does not matter if they are character names, logical values, or numeric values.

Here we analyze our chosen observations and variables:

```
summary( mydata[ myMales, myVars] )
```

Here we analyze only the males, but include all variables:

```
summary( mydata[ myMales, ] )
```

Here we select all of the observations but analyze only our chosen variables:

```
summary( mydata[ , myVars] )
```

9.4 Using Numeric Index Values to Select Both Observations and Variables

The males have numeric index values of 5 through 8, and we want the first variable and the last four, so we can use numeric index vectors to choose them as in either of these two equivalent approaches:

```
summary( mydata[ c(5,6,7,8), c(1,3,4,5,6) ] )

summary( mydata[ 5:8, c(1,3:6) ] )
```

This selection is impossible to interpret without a thorough knowledge of the data frame. When you are hard at work on an analysis, you may well recall these values. However, such knowledge fades fast, so you would do well to add comments to your programs reminding yourself what these values select.

Adding new variables or observations to the beginning of the data frame, or sorting it, would change these index values. This is a risky approach!

As we discussed in the last section, we can save the numeric index vectors for repeated use.

```
myMales <- c(5,6,7,8)

myVars  <- c(1,3:6)
```

Again, we can repeat the same examples that we used in the sections above. Once you have a vector of index values, it does not matter if they are character names or numeric indexes.

Here we analyze our chosen observations and variables:

```
summary( mydata[ myMales, myVars] )
```

Here we analyze only the males, but include all variables:

```
summary( mydata[ myMales, ] )
```

Here we select all of the observations but analyze only our chosen variables:

```
summary( mydata[ , myVars] )
```

9.5 Using Logic to Select Both Observations and Variables

Selecting observations with logic makes perfect sense, but selecting variables using logic is rarely worth the effort. The following is how we would use this combination for our example:

```
summary(
  mydata[which(gender=="m"),
    names(mydata) %in% c("workshop","q1","q2","q3","q4") ]
)
```

Let us reconsider using variable names directly. For this example, it is clearly simpler:

```
summary(
  mydata[ which(gender=="m") ,
    c("workshop","q1","q2","q3","q4") ]
)
```

However, once we save these values, you use them with no more work than earlier.

```
myMales <- which(gender=="m")
```

```
myVars  <- names(mydata) %in%
  c("workshop","q1","q2","q3","q4")
```

Here we analyze our chosen observations and variables:

```
summary( mydata[ myMales, myVars] )
```

Here we analyze only the males but include all variables:

```
summary( mydata[ myMales, ] )
```

Here we select all of the observations but analyze only our chosen variables:

```
summary( mydata[ , myVars] )
```

9.6 Saving and Loading Subsets

All of the methods we used to create subsets result in a temporary copy that exists only in our workspace. To use it in future R sessions, we will need to write it out to our computer's hard drive using the `save` or `save.image` functions. The more descriptive a name you give it, the better.

```
myMalesWQ <- subset(mydata,
    subset=gender=="m",
    select=c(workshop,q1:q4)
)
```

If your files are not too large, you can save your original data and your subset with

```
save(mydata, myMalesWQ, file="mydata.RData")
```

The next time you start R, you can load both data frames with

```
load("mydata.RData")
```

If you are working with large files, you can save only the subset.

```
save(myMalesWQ, file="myMalesWQ.RData")
```

Now when you start R, you can load and work with just the subset to save space.

```
load("myMalesWQ.RData")

summary(myMalesWQ)
```

9.7 Example Programs for Selecting Variables and Observations

9.7.1 Stata Program for Selecting Variables and Observations

```
* Filename: SelectingVarsAndObs.do

use c:\myRfolder\mydata, clear
display
```

```
* ---Equivalent to the Subset Function---
list workshop q* if gender=="m"
preserve
keep if gender=="m"
keep workshop q*
save c:\myRfolder\mymalesWQ
list
summ

* ---Logic for Obs, Names for Vars---
list
gen id = 0
replace id=_n+4
order id workshop q*
save c:\myRfolder\mymaleWQ, replace
list
restore
list
use c:\myRfolder\mymalesWQ, clear
list

* ---Names for Both---
list
gen id = 0
replace id=_n+4
order id workshop q*
list
restore
list workshop q*

* ---Numeric Indexes for Both---
di gender[1] // display value first observation of gender
di q1[1] + q1[4] // sum of 1st and 4th observations of q1
di q1[2] * q2[2] // product of 2nd obs of q1 and q2

* ---Saving and Loading Subsets---
use c:\myRfolder\mymalesWQ, clear
keep workshop q*
save, replace
list
```

9.7.2 R Program for Selecting Variables and Observations

```
# Filename: SelectingVarsAndObs.R
```

```
setwd("/myRfolder")
load(file="mydata.RData")
attach(mydata)
print(mydata)

#---The subset Function---

print(
  subset(mydata,
    subset=gender=="m",
    select=c(workshop, q1:q4) )
)

myMalesWQ <- subset(mydata,
    subset=gender=="m",
    select=c(workshop, q1:q4)
)

print(myMalesWQ)
summary(myMalesWQ)

#---Logic for Obs, Names for Vars---

print(
  mydata[ which(gender=="m") ,
          c("workshop","q1","q2","q3","q4") ]
)

myMales <- which(gender=="m")
myVars  <- c("workshop","q1","q2","q3","q4")

print( mydata[ myMales, myVars] )
print( mydata[ myMales, ] )
print( mydata[ , myVars] )


#---Names for Both---

print( mydata[
  c("5","6","7","8"),
  c("workshop","q1","q2","q3","q4")
] )

myMales <- c("5","6","7","8")
myVars  <- c("workshop","q1","q2","q3","q4")
```

```
print( mydata[ myMales, myVars] )
print( mydata[ myMales, ] )
print( mydata[ , myVars] )


#---Numeric Indexes for Both---

print( mydata[ c(5,6,7,8), c(1,3,4,5,6) ] )
print( mydata[ 5:8, c(1,3:6) ] )

myMales <- c(5,6,7,8)
myVars  <- c(1,3:6)

print( mydata[ myMales, myVars] )
print( mydata[ myMales, ] )
print( mydata[ , myVars] )


#---Logic for Both---

summary(
  mydata[ which(gender=="m"),
          names(mydata) %in%
            c("workshop","q1","q2","q3","q4") ]
)


# Switching to names for vars for comparison
summary(
  mydata[ which(gender=="m") ,
          c("workshop","q1","q2","q3","q4") ]
)


myMales <- which(gender=="m")

myVars  <- names(mydata) %in%
  c("workshop","q1","q2","q3","q4")

print( mydata[ myMales, myVars] )

print( mydata[ myMales, ] )

print( mydata[ , myVars] )
```

```
#---Saving and Loading Subsets---

myMalesWQ <- subset(mydata,
    subset=gender=="m",
    select=c(workshop,q1:q4)
)

save(mydata, myMalesWQ, file="myBoth.RData")
load("myBoth.RData")

save(myMalesWQ, file="myMalesWQ.RData")
load("myMalesWQ.RData")

print(myMalesWQ)
```

10

Data Management

There is an old rule of thumb that says 80% of your data analysis time is spent transforming, reshaping, merging, and otherwise managing your data. Stata has a reputation of being more flexible than R for data management. However, as you will see in this chapter, R can do everything that Stata can do on these important tasks.

10.1 Transforming Variables

Unlike Stata, R has no separation of phases for data modification and analysis. Like Stata, anything that you have read into or created in your R workspace you can modify at any time.

R performs transformations such as adding or subtracting variables on the whole variable at once, as does Stata. It calls that vector arithmetic. R has loops, but you do not need them for this type of manipulation. R can nest one function call within another within any other. This applies to transformations as well. For example, taking the logarithm of our q4 variable and then getting summary statistics on it, you have a choice of a two-step process like

```
mydata$q4Log <- log(mydata$q4)
summary( mydata$q4Log )
```

or you could simply nest the log function within the summary function:

```
summary( log(mydata$q4) )
```

If you planned to do several things with the transformed variable, saving it under a new name would lead to less typing and quicker execution. Table 10.1 shows basic transformations in both packages. In Chapter 7, "Selecting Variables," we chose variables using various methods: by index, by column name, by logical vector, using the style mydata$myvar, by using simply the variable

R.A. Muenchen, J.M. Hilbe, *R for Stata Users*, Statistics and Computing, DOI 10.1007/978-1-4419-1318-0_10, © Springer Science+Business Media, LLC 2010

Table 10.1. Mathematical operators in Stata and R.

	R	Stata
Addition	x+y	x+y
Antilog, base 10	10^x	10^x
Antilog, natural	exp(x)	exp(x)
Division	x/y	x/y
Exponentiation	x^2	x^2
Logarithm, base 10	log10(x)	log10(x)
Logarithm, natural	log(x)	log(x)
		or ln(x)
Multiplication	x*y	x*y
Round off	round(x)	round(x)
Square root	sqrt(x)	sqrt(x)
Subtraction	x-y	x-y

name after you have attached a data frame, and using the subset or with functions.

Here are several examples that perform the same transformation using different variable selection approaches. The within function is a variation of the with function that has some advantages for variable creation that are beyond our scope. We have seen that R has a mean function, but we will calculate the mean the long way just for demonstration purposes.

```
mydata$meanQ <- (mydata$q1 + mydata$q2
          + mydata$q3 + mydata$q4)/4

mydata[,"meanQ"] <- (mydata[ ,"q1"] + mydata[ ,"q2"]
              + mydata[ ,"q3"] + mydata[ ,"q4"] )/4

within( mydata,
  meanQ <- (q1 + q2 + q3 + q4)/4
)
```

Another way to use the shorter names is with the transform function. It is similar to attaching a data frame, performing as many transformations as you like using short variable names, and then detaching the data (we do that example next). It looks like

```
mydata <- transform(mydata, meanQ=(q1+q2+q3+q4)/4 )
```

It may seem strange to use the "=" now in an equation instead of "<-," but in this form, meanQ is a named argument, and those are always specified using "=." If you have many transformations, it is easier to read them on separate lines:

```
mydata <- transform( mydata,
  score1=(q1+q2)/2,
```

```
score2=(q3+q4)/2
)
```

The `transform` function reads the data before it begins, so if you want to continue to transform variables you just created, you must do it in a second call to that function. For example, to get the means of score1 and score2, you cannot do the following:

```
mydata <- transform( mydata,
  score1=(q1+q2)/2,
  score2=(q3+q4)/2,
  meanscore=score1+score2/2  #does not work!
)
```

It will not know what score1 and score2 are for the creation of meanscore. You can could do that in two steps:

```
mydata <- transform( mydata,
  score1=(q1+q2)/2,
  score2=(q3+q4)/2
)
mydata <- transform( mydata,
  meanscore=score1+score2/2  #this works.
)
```

You can create a new variable using the index method too, but it requires a bit of extra work. Let us load the data set again since we already have a variable named meanQ in the current one.

```
load(file="mydata.RData")
```

Now we will add a variable at index position 7 (we currently have six variables). Using the index approach, it is easier to initialize a new variable by binding a new variable to mydata. Otherwise, R will automatically give it a column name of V7 that we would want to rename later. We used the column bind function, `cbind`, to create mymatrix earlier. Here we will use it to name the new variable, meanQ, initialize it to zero, and then bind it to mydata.

```
mydata <- data.frame( cbind( mydata, meanQ=0.) )
```

Now we can add the values to column 7.

```
mydata[7] <- (mydata$q1 + mydata$q2 +
              mydata$q3 + mydata$q4)/4
```

Let us examine what happens when you create variables using the `attach` function. **WARNING!** *The attach function is hazardous for variable creation!* You can think of the `attach` function as creating a temporary copy of the data frame, so changing that is worthless. You can use the attach method to simplify naming variables only on the right side of the equation. This is a safe example, because the variable being created uses the long dataframe$varname style:

```
attach(mydata)

mydata$meanQ <- (q1+q2+q3+q4)/4

detach(mydata)
```

If you were to modify a variable in your data frame, you would have to re-attach it before you would see it. In the following example, we attach mydata and look at q1:

```
> attach(mydata)

> q1

[1] 1 2 2 3 4 5 5 4
```

So we see what q1 looks like. Next, we will see what it looks like squared and then write it to mydata$q1 (choosing a new name would be wiser but would not make this point clear). By specifying the full name mydata$q1, we know R will write it to the original data frame, not the temporary working copy:

```
> mydata$q1^2

[1]   1   4   4   9 16 25 25 16

> mydata$q1 <- q1^2
```

However, what does the simple name of q1 show us? The unmodified temporary version!

```
> q1
[1] 1 2 2 3 4 5 5 4
```

If we **attach** the file again, it will essentially make a new temporary copy and q1 finally shows that we did indeed square it:

```
> attach(mydata)

The following object(s) are masked from mydata (position 3):
  gender q1 q2 q3 q4 workshop

> q1

[1]   1   4   4   9 16 25 25 16
```

The message warning about masked objects is telling you that there were other objects with those names that are now not accessible. Those are just the ones we attached earlier, so that is fine. We could have avoided this message by detaching mydata before attaching it a second time. The only problem that presents us now is a bit of wasted workspace.

Just like Stata, R does *all* its of calculations in the computer's main memory. You can use them immediately, but they will exist only in your current session unless you save your workspace. We recommend using either the **save** or the **save.image** function to write your work to a file:

```
setwd("/myRfolder")
save.image("myWorkspace.RData")
```

See Chapter 13, "Managing Your Files and Workspace" for more ways to save new variables.

10.1.1 Example Programs for Transforming Variables

Stata Program for Transforming Variables

```
* Filename: Transform.do

use c:\myRfolder\mydata, clear
gen totalq = q1+q2+q3+q4
gen logtotalq = log10(totalq)
gen mean1 = totalq/4
egen mean2 = mean(q1-q4)
save c:\myRfolder\mydataT
```

R Program for Transforming Variables

```
# Filename: Transform.R

setwd("/myRfolder")
load(file="mydata.RData")
mydata

#Transformation in the middle of another function.
summary( log(mydata$q4) )

#Creating meanQ with dollar notation.
mydata$meanQ <- (mydata$q1 + mydata$q2
                + mydata$q3 + mydata$q4)/4
mydata
```

```
# Creating meanQ using attach.
attach(mydata)
mydata$meanQ <- (q1+q2+q3+q4)/4
detach(mydata)
mydata

# Creating meanQ using transform.
mydata <- transform(mydata,
  meanQ=(q1+q2+q3+q4)/4 )
mydata

# Creating two variables using transform.
mydata <- transform( mydata,
  score1=(q1+q2)/2,
  score2=(q3+q4)/2 )
mydata

# Creating meanQ using index notation on the left.
load(file="mydata.RData")
mydata <- data.frame( cbind( mydata, meanQ=0.) )
mydata[7] <- (mydata$q1 + mydata$q2 +
              mydata$q3 + mydata$q4)/4
mydata

save.image(file="mydataT.RData")
```

10.2 Functions or Commands? The `apply` Function Decides

The last section described data transformations but said little about statistical functions. Stata has two independent ways to calculate statistics: functions and commands. Statistics may also be calculated using Mata, Stata's matrix language facility. In general, Stata functions and commands work as follows: Statistical *functions* work within each observation to calculate a statistic like the mean of our q variables for each observation. Statistical *commands* work within a variable to calculate statistics like the mean of our q4 variable across all observations.

R, on the other hand, has only one way to calculate: *functions*. What determines if the function is working on variables or observations is how you *apply* it!

In the previous subsection, we created a mean variable using

```
mydata$meanQ <- (mydata$q1 + mydata$q2
                 mydata$q3 + mydata$q4) / 4
```

This approach gets tedious with long lists of variables. It also has a problem with missing values. The meanQ variable will be missing if any of the variables has a missing value. The **mean** function solves that problem.

10.2.1 Applying the mean Function

We have previously seen that R has both a **mean** function and a **summary** function. For numeric objects, the **mean** function returns a single value, wherease the **summary** function returns the minimum, first quartile, median, mean, third quartile, and maximum. We could use either of these functions to create a meanQ variable. However, the **mean** function returns only the value we need, so it is better for this purpose.

Let us start examining our options by first putting our q variables into a matrix. Simply selecting the variables with the command below will not work, because even though variables 3 through 6 are all numeric, it will maintain its form as a data frame.

```
myQmatrix <- mydata[ ,3:6]  #Not a matrix!
```

The proper way to convert the data is with the **as.matrix** function:

```
> myQmatrix <- as.matrix( mydata[ ,3:6] )

> myQmatrix

  q1 q2 q3 q4
1  1  1  5  1
2  2  1  4  1
3  2  2  4  3
4  3  1 NA  3
5  4  5  2  4
6  5  4  5  5
7  5  3  4  4
8  4  5  5  5
```

Let us review what happens if we use the **mean** function on myQmatrix:

```
> mean( myQmatrix )
[1] NA
```

The result is NA, or missing, because the matrix contains an NA value. The default method of dealing with missing values in R is to set the resulting value to missing. To remove missing values, most basic statistical functions have the **na.rm** argument. The value is FALSE by default, so we will set it to TRUE to get our grand mean:

```
> mean( myQmatrix, na.rm=TRUE )
[1] 3.322581
```

This is an interesting ability, but it is not that useful in our case. What is of much more interest is the mean of each variable, as a Stata command would do, or the mean of each observation, as a Stata function would do. We can do either by using the `apply` function. Let us start by getting the means of the variables:

```
> apply(myQmatrix, 2, mean, na.rm=TRUE)

      q1       q2       q3       q4
3.250000 2.750000 4.142857 3.250000
```

The `apply` function call above has three arguments and passes a fourth to the `mean` function.

1. The name of the matrix (or array) you wish to analyze.
2. The *margin* you want to apply the function over, with 1 representing rows and 2 representing columns. This is easy to remember since R uses the index order of [rows,columns], so the margins values are [1,2] respectively.
3. The function you want to apply to each row or column. In our case, this is the `mean` function.
4. The `apply` function passes any other arguments on to the function you are applying. In our case, `na.rm=TRUE` is an argument for the `mean` function, not the `apply` function. If you look at the help file for the `apply` function, you will see its form is `apply(X, MARGIN, FUN, ...)`. That means it only has three arguments but will pass other arguments, indicated by the ellipses "...," to the function "FUN" (`mean` in our case). So `na.rm=TRUE` means nothing to the `apply` function other than something to pass to the function it is applying.

Applying the `mean` function to *rows* is as easy as changing the value 2, representing columns, to 1, representing rows:

```
> apply(myQmatrix, 1, mean, na.rm=TRUE)

       1        2        3        4        5
2.000000 2.000000 2.750000 2.333333 3.750000
       6        7        8
4.750000 4.000000 4.750000
```

Since means and sums are such popular calculations, there are specialized functions to get them: `rowMeans`, `colMeans`, `rowSums`, and `colSums`. For example, to get the row means of myQmatrix, we can do

```
> rowMeans(myQmatrix, na.rm=TRUE)

       1        2        3        4        5
2.000000 2.000000 2.750000 2.333333 3.750000
```

```
      6        7        8
4.750000 4.000000 4.750000
```

To add a new variable to our data frame that is the mean of the q variables, we could any *one* of the following forms:

```
> mydata$meanQ <- apply(myQmatrix, 1, mean, na.rm=TRUE)

> mydata$meanQ <- rowMeans(myQmatrix, na.rm=TRUE)

> mydata <- transform(mydata,
+   meanQ=rowMeans(myQmatrix, na.rm=TRUE)
+ )

> mydata
```

```
  workshop gender q1 q2 q3 q4     meanQ
1        R      f  1  1  5  1 2.000000
2    Stata      f  2  1  4  1 2.000000
3        R      f  2  2  4  3 2.750000
4    Stata   <NA>  3  1 NA  3 2.333333
5        R      m  4  5  2  4 3.750000
6    Stata      m  5  4  5  5 4.750000
7        R      m  5  3  4  4 4.000000
8    Stata      m  4  5  5  5 5.750000
```

Finally, we can apply a function to each vector in a data frame by using the `lapply` function. A data frame is a type of list, and the letter "l" in `lapply` stands for *list*. The function applies other functions to lists, and it returns its results in a list. Since it is clear we want to apply the function to each component in the list, there is no need for a row/column margin argument.

```
> lapply(mydata[ ,3:6], mean, na.rm=TRUE)

$q1
[1] 3.25

$q2
[1] 2.75

$q3
[1] 4.1429

$q4
[1] 3.25
```

Since the output is in the form of a list, it takes up more space when printed than the vector output from the `apply` function. You can also use the `sapply` function on a data frame. Its simplified vector output would be much more compact. The "s" in `sapply` means it simplifies its output whenever possible to vector, matrix, or array form. Both the `lapply` and `sapply` functions can apply functions that return more than one value, because lists and matrices or arrays can store much more information than the vectors to which the `apply` function is restricted.

```
> sapply(mydata[ ,3:6], mean, na.rm=TRUE)

       q1       q2       q3       q4
3.250000 2.750000 4.142857 3.250000
```

Since the result is a vector, it is very easy to get the mean of the means:

```
> mean(
+    sapply(mydata[ ,3:6], mean, na.rm=TRUE)
+ )

[1] 3.3482
```

Other statistical functions that work very similarly are `sd` for standard deviation, `var` for variance, and `median`. The `length` function is similar to the Stata `length` function but different enough to deserve its own section (below).

10.2.2 Finding N or NVALID

In Stata saying, `egen varok = rownonmiss(q1 q2 q3 q4)`, would count the valid values of those variables for each observation. Running descriptive statistical procedures would give you the number of valid observations for each variable. R has several variations on this theme. First, let us look at the `length` function.

```
> length(mydata[ ,"q3"] )

[1] 8
```

The variable q3 has seven valid values and one missing value. The `length` function is telling us the number of total responses. Another approach is to ask for values that are not missing. The "!" sign means "not," so let us try the following:

```
> !is.na( mydata[ ,"q3"] )

[1]  TRUE  TRUE  TRUE FALSE  TRUE  TRUE  TRUE  TRUE
```

That identified them logically. Since statistical functions will interpret TRUE as 1 and FALSE as 0, summing them will give us the number of valid values.

```
> sum( !is.na( mydata[ ,"q3"] ) )
```

```
[1] 7
```

Jim Lemon and Philippe Grosjean's `prettyR` package has a function that does that very calculation. Let us load that package from our library and apply the function to our data frame using `sapply`.

```
> library("prettyR")
```

```
> sapply(mydata, valid.n)
```

```
workshop   gender      q1       q2       q3       q4
       8        7       8        8        7        8
```

That is the kind of output we would get from descriptive statistics procedures in Stata. In Chapter17, "Statistics" we will see functions that provide that information and much more, like means and standard deviations.

What about applying it across rows, like the Stata `rownonmiss` function? Let us create a myQn variable that contains the number of valid responses in q1 through q4. First, we will pull those variables out into a matrix. That will let us use the `apply` function to the rows.

```
> myMatrix <- as.matrix( mydata[ ,3:6] )
```

```
> myMatrix
```

```
  q1 q2 q3 q4
1  1  1  5  1
2  2  1  4  1
3  2  2  4  3
4  3  1 NA  3
5  4  5  2  4
6  5  4  5  5
7  5  3  4  4
8  4  5  5  5
```

Now we use the `apply` function with the `margin` argument set to 1, which asks it to go across rows.

```
> apply(myMatrix, 1, valid.n)
```

```
1 2 3 4 5 6 7 8
4 4 4 3 4 4 4 4
```

So we see that all of the observations have four valid values except for the fourth. Now let us do that again, but this time save it in our data frame as variable myQn.

```
> mydata$myQn <- apply(myMatrix, 1, valid.n)

> mydata
```

```
  workshop gender q1 q2 q3 q4 myQn
1        1      f  1  1  5  1    4
2        2      f  2  1  4  1    4
3        1      f  2  2  4  3    4
4        2   <NA>  3  1 NA  3    3
5        1      m  4  5  2  4    4
6        2      m  5  4  5  5    4
7        1      m  5  3  4  4    4
8        2      m  4  5  5  5    4
```

Another form of the apply function is tapply. It exists to create *tables*, by applying a function repeatedly to groups in the data. For details, see the Section 10.11, "Creating Collapsed or Aggregated Data Sets."

Finally, there is the mapply function, which is a multivariate version of sapply. See help(mapply) for details.

The functions we have examined in this section are very basic. Their sparse output is similar to Stata functions. For R functions that act more like Stata commands, see Chapter 17, *Statistics*. Still, R does not differentiate one type of function from another as Stata does for its functions and commands.

10.2.3 Example Programs for Applying Statistical Functions

Stata Program for Applying Statistical Functions

```
* Filename: FunctionsCommands.do

use c:\myRfolder\mydata, clear
preserve

* Some statistical functions
egen mymean = rowmean(q1-q4)
egen mysum = rowtotal(q1-q4)
gen myn = mysum/mymean
restore

* A statistical command
summ
```

R Program for Applying Statistical Functions

```
# Filename: FunctionsCommands.R

setwd("/myRfolder")
load(file="mydata.RData")
mydata
attach(mydata)

# Create myQmatrix.
myQmatrix <- as.matrix( mydata[ ,3:6] )
myQmatrix
# Get mean of whole matrix.
mean( myQmatrix )
mean( myQmatrix,na.rm=TRUE )

# Get mean of matrix columns
apply(myQmatrix,2,mean,na.rm=TRUE)

# Get mean of matrix rows.
apply(myQmatrix,1,mean,na.rm=TRUE)
rowMeans(myQmatrix,na.rm=TRUE)

# Add row means to mydata.
mydata$meanQ <- apply(myQmatrix, 1, mean, na.rm=TRUE)
mydata$meanQ <- rowMeans(myQmatrix,na.rm=TRUE)
mydata <- transform(mydata,
  meanQ=rowMeans(myQmatrix, na.rm=TRUE)
mydata

# Means of data frames & their vectors.
mean(mydata, na.rm=TRUE)
lapply(mydata[ ,3:6], mean, na.rm=TRUE)
sapply(mydata[ ,3:6], mean, na.rm=TRUE)
mean(
  sapply(mydata[ ,3:6], mean, na.rm=TRUE)
)

# Length of data frames & their vectors.
length(mydata[ ,"q3"] )
is.na( mydata[ ,"q3"] )
!is.na( mydata[ ,"q3"] )
sum( !is.na( mydata[ ,"q3"] ) )
```

```
# Like the Stata count from stat procedures.
library("prettyR")
sapply(mydata, valid.n)

# Like the Stata count function.
apply(myMatrix, 1, valid.n)
mydata$myQn <- apply(myMatrix, 1, valid.n)
mydata
```

10.3 Conditional Transformations

Conditional transformations apply different formulas to various groups in your data. For example, the formulas for recommended daily allowances of vitamins differ for males and females. The `ifelse` function does conditional transformations in a way that is similar to the Stata approach. The general form of the function is

```
ifelse(logic, true, false)
```

where "logic" is a logical condition to test, "true" is the value to return when the logic is true, and "false" is the value to return when the logic is false. For example, to create a variable that has a value of 1 for people who strongly agree with question 4 on our survey, we could use

```
> mydata$q4Sagree <- ifelse( q4 == 5, 1, 0 )

> mydata$q4Sagree

[1] 0 0 0 0 0 1 0 1
```

This is such a simple outcome that we can also do this using

```
mydata$q4Sagree <- as.numeric( q4 == 5 )
```

However, the latter approach only allows the outcomes of 1 and 0, whereas the former version allows for any value. The statement `q4==5` will result in a vector of logical TRUE/FALSE values. The `as.numeric` function converts it into zeros and ones.

R has some slightly different symbols and rules for logical comparisons. The table of logical operators, Table 10.2, shows the symbols and some of the rules used by each package.

If we want a variable to indicate when people agree with question 4, (i.e., they responded with agree or strongly agree), we can use

```
> mydata$q4agree <- ifelse( q4 >= 4, 1,0)

> mydata$q4agree

[1] 0 0 0 0 1 1 1 1
```

Table 10.2. Logical operators in Stata and R.

	R	Stata
Equals	==	==
Less than	<	<
Greater than	>	>
Less than or equal	<=	<=
Greater than or equal	>=	>=
Not equal	!=	~= or !=
And	&	&
Or	|	|
0<=x<=1	(x >= 0) & (x<=1)	0<=x<=1
Missing value size	Missing values have no size	Missing values are greater than all numbers in logical comparisons
Logic for missing values	x=NA can never be true. Use is.na(x) instead.	x=. can be true

The logical condition can be as complicated as you like. The following is one that creates a score of 1 when people took workshop 1 (abbreviated ws1) and agreed that it was good:

```
> mydata$ws1agree <- ifelse( workshop == 1 & q4 >=4 , 1,0)

> mydata$ws1agree

[1] 0 0 0 0 1 0 1 0
```

We can fill in equations that will supply values under the two conditions. The following equations for males and females are a bit silly, but they make the point obvious. You might think that if gender were missing, the gender=="f" condition would be false and the second equation would apply. However, in this circumstance, R, like Stata, sets the result to missing.

```
> mydata$score <- ifelse( gender=="f",(2*q1)+q2,(3*q1)+q2 )
```

The following is our resulting data frame:

```
> mydata
```

	workshop	gender	q1	q2	q3	q4	q4Sagree	q4agree	ws1agree	score
1	1	f	1	1	5	1	0	0	0	3
2	2	f	2	1	4	1	0	0	0	5
3	1	f	2	2	4	3	0	0	0	6
4	2	<NA>	3	1	NA	3	0	0	0	NA
5	1	m	4	5	2	4	0	1	1	17
6	2	m	5	4	5	5	1	1	0	19
7	1	m	5	3	4	4	0	1	1	18
8	2	m	4	5	5	5	1	1	0	17

10.3.1 Example Programs for Conditional Transformations

Stata Program for Conditional Transformations

```
* Filename: TransformIF.do

use c:\myRfolder\mydata, clear
preserve
if q4 == 5 {
gen x1=1
}
else {
gen x1=0
}
if q4>=4 {
gen x2=1
}
else {
gen x2=0
}
if workshop == 1 & q4>=5 {
gen x3=1
}
else {
gen x3=0
}
if gender=="f" {
gen scoreA = 2*q1+q2
}
else {
gen scoreA = 3*q1+q2
}
if workshop==1 & q4>5 {
gen scoreB = 2*q1+q2
}
else {
gen scoreB = 3*q1+q2
}
restore
```

R Program for Conditional Transformations

```
# Filename: TransformIF.R

setwd("/myRfolder")
```

```
load(file="mydata.RData")
mydata
attach(mydata)

#Create a series of dichotomous 0/1 variables
# The new variable q4SAgree will be 1 if q4 equals 5,
# (Strongly agree) otherwise zero.
mydata$q4Sagree <- ifelse( q4 == 5, 1,0)
mydata$q4Sagree

# This does the same as above.
mydata$q4Sagree <- as.numeric( q4 == 5 )
mydata$q4Sagree

# Create a score for people who agree with q4.
mydata$q4agree <- ifelse( q4 >= 4, 1,0)
mydata$q4agree

# Find the people only in workshop1 agree to item 5.
mydata$ws1agree <- ifelse( workshop == 1 & q4 >=4 , 1,0)
mydata$ws1agree

# Use equations to calculate values.
mydata$score <- ifelse( gender=="f",(2*q1)+q2,(3*q1)+q2 )
mydata
```

10.4 Multiple Conditional Transformations

Conditional transformations apply different formulas to different subsets of your data. If you have only a single formula to apply to each group, read Section 10.3, "Conditional Transformations." Like Stata, R uses the same approach for *single* conditional transformations as it does for *multiple* conditional transformations. It does, however, let us look at some interesting variations in R.

The simplest approach is to use the `ifelse` function a few times. Here we create two scores, cleverly named score1 and score2, which are calculated differently for the males and the females:

```
mydata$score1 <- ifelse( gender=="f",(2*q1)+q2,(20*q1)+q2 )
mydata$score2 <- ifelse( gender=="f",(3*q1)+q2,(30*q1)+q2 )
```

As earlier, the calls to the `ifelse` functions have three arguments:

1. The `gender=="f"` argument provides the logical condition to test.
2. The first formula applies to the TRUE condition, for the females.
3. The second formula applies to the FALSE condition, for the males.

We can do the same thing using the index approach, but it is a bit trickier. First, let us add the new score names to our data frame so that we can refer to the columns by name:

```
> mydata <- data.frame( mydata, score1=NA, score2=NA )

> mydata

  workshop gender q1 q2 q3 q4 score1 score2
1        R      f  1  1  5  1     NA     NA
2    Stata      f  2  1  4  1     NA     NA
3        R      f  2  2  4  3     NA     NA
4    Stata   <NA>  3  1 NA  3     NA     NA
5        R      m  4  5  2  4     NA     NA
6    Stata      m  5  4  5  5     NA     NA
7        R      m  5  3  4  4     NA     NA
8    Stata      m  4  5  5  5     NA     NA
```

This initializes the scores to zero. We could also have initialized them to missing by changing "score1=0, score2=0", to "score1=NA, score2=NA".

Next, we want to differentiate between the genders. We can use the form gender=="f", but we do not want to use it directly as indexes to our data frame because gender has a missing value. What would R do with mydata[NA,]? Luckily, the which function only cares about TRUE values, so we will use that to locate the observations we want:

```
> gals <- which( gender=="f" )

> gals

[1] 1 2 3

> guys <- which( gender=="m" )

> guys

[1] 5 6 7 8
```

We can now use the gals and guys variables (American slang for women and men) to make the actual formula with the needed indexes much shorter:

```
> mydata[gals,"score1"] <-  2*q1[gals] + q2[gals]
> mydata[gals,"score2"] <-  3*q1[gals] + q2[gals]
> mydata[guys,"score1"] <- 20*q1[guys] + q2[guys]
```

```
> mydata[guys,"score2"] <- 30*q1[guys] + q2[guys]

> mydata
  workshop gender q1 q2 q3 q4 score1 score2
1        1      f  1  1  5  1      3      4
2        2      f  2  1  4  1      5      7
3        1      f  2  2  4  3      6      8
4        2   <NA>  3  1 NA  3      0      0
5        1      m  4  5  2  4     85    125
6        2      m  5  4  5  5    104    154
7        1      m  5  3  4  4    103    153
8        2      m  4  5  5  5     85    125
```

We can see that this approach worked, but look closely at the index values. We are selecting observations based on the rows. So where is the required comma? When we attached the data frame, the variables q1 and q2 became accessible by their simple component names. In essence, they are vectors now, albeit temporary ones. Vectors can use index values too, but since they only have one dimension, they only use one index. If we had not attached the file, we would have had to write the formulas as

```
2* mydata[gals, "q1"] + mydata[gals, "q2"]
```

We no longer need the guys and gals variables, so we can remove them from our workspace.

```
rm(guys,gals)
```

10.4.1 Example Programs for Multiple Conditional Transformations

Stata Program for Multiple Conditional Transformations

```
* Filename: TransformIF2.do

use c:\myRfolder\mydata, clear
preserve
if gender=="m" {
gen score1 = (1.1*q1)+q2
gen score2 = (1.2*q1)+q2
}
else if gender=="f" {
gen score1 = (2.1*q1) + q2
gen score2 = (2.2*q1) + q2
}
restore
```

R Program for Multiple Conditional Transformations

```
# Filename: TransformIF2.R

# Read the file into a data frame and print it.
setwd("/myRfolder")
load(file="mydata.RData")
attach(mydata)
mydata

# Using the ifelse approach.
mydata$score1 <-
  ifelse( gender=="f",(2*q1)+q2,(20*q1)+q2 )
mydata$score2 <-
  ifelse( gender=="f",(3*q1)+q2,(30*q1)+q2 )
mydata

# Using the index approach.
load(file="mydata.RData")

# Create names in data frame.
mydata <- data.frame( mydata, score1=0, score2=0 )
attach(mydata)
mydata

# Find which are males and females.
gals <- which( gender=="f" )
gals
guys <- which( gender=="m" )
guys
mydata[gals,"score1"] <-  2*q1[gals] + q2[gals]
mydata[gals,"score2"] <-  3*q1[gals] + q2[gals]
mydata[guys,"score1"] <- 20*q1[guys] + q2[guys]
mydata[guys,"score2"] <- 30*q1[guys] + q2[guys]
mydata

# Clean up.
rm(guys, gals)
```

10.5 Missing Values

We have discussed missing values briefly in several previous chapters. Let us bring those various topics together to review and expand on. R represents missing values with NA, for Not Available. The letters NA are also an object in R that you can use to assign missing values. In Stata, numeric missing values are indicated with a period, while a string missing value is simply displayed in double quotes, " ". Stata also has extended missing numeric values ranging from .a, .b, through .z in ascending order. Relational operators such as these missing value indicators are stored as very high numeric values, (i.e., higher than the range of real numbers).

When importing numeric data, R reads blanks as missing (except when blanks are delimiters). R reads the string NA as missing for both numeric and character variables. When importing a text file, Stata recognizes a period as a missing value for numeric variables. R will, instead, read the whole variable as a character vector! If you have control of the source of the data, it is best not to write them out that way. If not, you can use a text editor to replace the periods with NA, but you have to be careful to do so in a way that does not also replace valid decimal places. Some editors make that easier than others. A safer method would be to fix it in R, which we do below.

When other values represent missing, you will, of course, have to tell R about them. The `read.table` function provides an argument, `na.strings`, which allows you to provide a set of missing values. However, it applies that value to every variable, so its usefulness is limited. The following is a data set that we will use to demonstrate the various ways to set missing values. The data frame we use, mydataNA, is the same as mydata in our other examples, except that it uses several missing value codes:

```
> mydataNA <- read.table("mydataNA.txt")

> mydataNA
```

	workshop	gender	q1	q2	q3	q4
1	1	f	1	1	5	1
2	2	f	2	1	4	99
3	.	f	9	2	4	3
4	2	.	3	9	99	3
5	1	m	4	5	2	4
6	.	m	9	9	5	5
7	1	.	5	3	99	4
8	2	m	4	5	5	99

In the data we see that workshop and gender have periods as missing values, q1 and q2 have 9's, and q3 and q4 have 99's. Do not be fooled by the periods in workshop and gender; they are not already set to missing! If so, they would have appeared as NA instead. R has seen the periods and has converted both variables to character (string) variables. Since `read.table` converts string variables to factors unless the `as.is=TRUE` argument is added, both workshop and gender are now factors. We can set all three codes to missing by simply adding the `na.strings` argument to the `read.table` function:

```
> mydataNA <- read.table("mydataNA.txt",
+   na.strings=c(".", "9", "99") )

> mydataNA

  workshop gender q1 q2 q3 q4
1        1      f  1  1  5  1
2        2      f  2  1  4 NA
3       NA      f NA  2  4  3
4        2    <NA>  3 NA NA  3
5        1      m  4  5  2  4
6       NA      m NA NA  5  5
7        1    <NA>  5  3 NA  4
8        2      m  4  5  5 NA
```

If the data did not come from a text file, we could still easily scan every variable for 9 and 99 to replace with missing values using

```
mydataNA[mydataNA==9 | mydataNA==99] <- NA
```

Both of the above approaches treat all variables alike. If any variables, like age, had valid values of 99, it would set them to missing too! For how to handle that situation, see Section 10.5.3, "When "99" Has Meaning." Of course "." never has meaning by itself, so getting rid of them all with `na.strings="."` is usually fine.

10.5.1 Substituting Means for Missing Values

There are several methods for replacing missing values with estimates of what they would have been. These methods include simple mean substitution, regression, and,—the gold standard—multiple imputation. We will just do mean substitution.

Any logical comparison on NAs results in an NA outcome, so `q1==NA` will never be TRUE, even when q1 is indeed NA. Therefore, if you wanted to substitute another value such as the mean, you would need to use the `is.na` function. Its output is TRUE when a value is NA. The following shows how you can use it to substitute missing values.

```
attach(mydataNA)
```

```
mydataNA$q1[ is.na(q1) ] <- mean( q1, na.rm=TRUE )
```

On the left-hand side, the statement above selects mydataNA$q1 as a vector and then finds its missing elements with `is.na(mydata$q1)`. On the right, it calculates the mean of q1 across all observations to assign to those NA values on the left. We are attaching mydata so we can use short variables names to simplify the code, but we are careful to use the long form, mydataNA$q1, where we write the result. This ensures that the result will be stored within the data frame, mydata, rather than in the attached copy. See Section 13.3, "Attaching Data Frames" for details.

10.5.2 Finding Complete Observations

You can omit all observations that contain any missing values with the na.omit function. The new data frame, myNoMissing, contains no missing values for any variables.

```
> myNoMissing <- na.omit(mydataNA)

> myNoMissing

  workshop gender q1 q2 q3 q4
1        1      f  1  1  5  1
5        1      m  4  5  2  4
```

Yikes! We do not have much data left. Thank goodness this is not our dissertation data. The complete.cases function returns a value of TRUE when a case is complete —that is, when an observation has no missing values:

```
> complete.cases(mydataNA)

[1]  TRUE FALSE FALSE FALSE  TRUE FALSE FALSE FALSE
```

Therefore, we can use this to get the cases that have no missing values (the same result as the na.omit function) by doing

```
> myNoMissing <- mydataNA[ complete.cases(mydataNA), ]

> myNoMissing

  workshop gender q1 q2 q3 q4
1        1      f  1  1  5  1
5        1      m  4  5  2  4
```

Since we already saw na.omit do that, it is of more interest to do the reverse. If we want to see which observations contain any missing values, we can use "!" for NOT:

```
> myIncomplete <- mydataNA[ !complete.cases(mydataNA), ]

> myIncomplete
```

```
  workshop gender q1 q2 q3 q4
2        2      f  2  1  4 NA
3       NA      f NA  2  4  3
4        2   <NA>  3 NA NA  3
6       NA      m NA NA  5  5
7        1   <NA>  5  3 NA  4
8        2      m  4  5  5 NA
```

10.5.3 When "99" Has Meaning

Occasionally, data sets use different missing values for different sets of variables. In that case, the methods described earlier would not work because they assume every missing value code applies to all variables.

Variables often have several missing value codes to represent things like, "not applicable," "do not know," and "refused to answer." Early statistics programs used to read blanks as zeros, so researchers got used to filling their fields with as many 9's as would fit. For example, a two-column variable such as years of education would use 99, to represent missing. The data set might also have a variable like age, for which 99 is a valid value. Age, requiring three columns, would have a missing value of 999. Data archives like the Interuniversity Consortium of Political and Social Research (ICPSR) have many data sets coded with multiple values for missing.

We will use conditional transformations, covered earlier in this chapter, to address this problem. Let us read the file again and put NAs in for the values 9 and 99 independently:

```
> mydataNA <- read.table("mydataNA.txt", na.strings=".")

> attach(mydataNA)

> mydataNA$q1[q1==9 ] <- NA
> mydataNA$q2[q2==9 ] <- NA
> mydataNA$q3[q3==99] <- NA
> mydataNA$q4[q4==99] <- NA

> mydataNA

  workshop gender q1 q2 q3 q4
1        1      f  1  1  5  1
2        2      f  2  1  4 NA
3       NA      f NA  2  4  3
4        2   <NA>  3 NA NA  3
5        1      m  4  5  2  4
```

```
6        NA      m NA NA  5  5
7         1   <NA>  5  3 NA  4
8         2      m  4  5  5 NA
```

That approach can handle any values we might have and assign NAs only where appropriate, but it would be quite tedious with hundreds of variables. We have used the `apply` family of functions to execute the same function across sets of variables. We can use that method here. First, we need to create some functions, letting x represent each variable. We can do this using the index method:

```
my9isNA    <- function(x) { x[x==9  ] <- NA; x}
my99isNA   <- function(x) { x[x==99 ] <- NA; x}
```

or we could use the `ifelse` function:

```
my9isNA   <- function(x) { ifelse( x==9,  NA, x) }
my99isNA  <- function(x) { ifelse( x==99, NA, x) }
```

Either of these approaches create functions that will return a value of NA when x==9 or x==99 and will return a value of just x if they are false. If you leave off that last "...x}" above, what will the functions return when the conditions are false? That would be undefined, so every value would become NA!

Now we need to apply each function where it is appropriate, using the `lapply` function.

```
> mydataNA <- read.table("mydataNA.txt", na.strings=".")

> attach(mydataNA)

> mydataNA[3:4] <- lapply( mydataNA[3:4], my9isNA  )
> mydataNA[5:6] <- lapply( mydataNA[5:6], my99isNA )

> mydataNA
```

```
  workshop gender q1 q2 q3 q4
1        1      f  1  1  5  1
2        2      f  2  1  4 NA
3       NA      f NA  2  4  3
4        2   <NA>  3 NA NA  3
5        1      m  4  5  2  4
6       NA      m NA NA  5  5
7        1   <NA>  5  3 NA  4
8        2      m  4  5  5 NA
```

The `sapply` function could have done this too. With our small data frame, this has not saved us much effort. However, to handle thousands of variables, all we would need to change are the above indices from 3:4 and 5:6 to perhaps 3:4000 and 4001:6000.

10.5.4 Example Programs to Assign Missing Values

Stata Program to Assign Missing Values

```
* Filename: MissingValues.do

use c:\myRfolder\mydata, clear
preserve
replace q1=. if q1==9
replace q2=. if q2==9
replace q3=. if q3==99
replace q4=. if q4==99

* Same thing but is quicker for lots of vars
restore
forvalues i = 1/2 {
replace q'i'=. if q'i'==9
}
forvalues i = 3/4 {
replace q'i'=. if q'i'==90
}
restore
```

R Program to Assign Missing Values

```
# Filename: MissingValues.R

setwd("/myRfolder")
# Read the data to see what it looks like.

mydataNA <- read.table("mydataNA.txt")
mydataNA

# Now read it so that ".", 9, 99 are
# converted to missing.
mydataNA <- read.table("mydataNA.txt",
  na.strings=c(".", "9", "99") )
mydataNA

# Convert 9 and 99 manually
```

```
mydataNA <- read.table("mydataNA.txt",
  na.strings=".")
mydataNA[mydataNA==9 | mydataNA==99] <- NA
mydataNA
# Substitute the mean for missing values.
mydataNA$q1[is.na(mydataNA$q1)] <-
  mean(mydataNA$q1, na.rm=TRUE)
mydataNA

# Eliminate observations with any NAs.
myNoMissing <- na.omit(mydataNA)
myNoMissing

# Test to see if each case is complete.
complete.cases(mydataNA)

# Use that result to select compete cases.
myNoMissing <- mydataNA[ complete.cases(mydataNA), ]
myNoMissing

# Use that result to select incomplete cases.
myIncomplete <- mydataNA[ !complete.cases(mydataNA), ]
myIncomplete

# When "99" Has Meaning...
# Now read it and set missing values
# one variable at a time.
mydataNA <- read.table("mydataNA.txt", na.strings=".")
mydataNA
attach(mydataNA)

# Assign missing values for q variables.
mydataNA$q1[q1==9]  <- NA
mydataNA$q2[q2==9]  <- NA
mydataNA$q3[q3==99] <- NA
mydataNA$q4[q4==99] <- NA
mydataNA
detach(mydataNA)

# Read file again, this time use functions.
mydataNA <- read.table("mydataNA.txt",na.strings=".")
mydataNA
attach(mydataNA)

#Create a functions that replaces 9, 99 with NAs.
```

```
my9isNA   <- function(x) { x[x==9  ] <- NA; x}
my99isNA  <- function(x) { x[x==99 ] <- NA; x}

# Now apply our functions to the data frame using lapply.
mydataNA[3:4] <- lapply( mydataNA[3:4], my9isNA )
mydataNA[5:6] <- lapply( mydataNA[5:6], my99isNA )
mydataNA
```

10.6 Renaming Variables (and Observations)

In Stata, you do not know where variable names are stored or how. You just
know they are in the data set somewhere. Renaming is simply a matter of
matching the new name to the old name with a `rename` command. In R,
however, both row and column names are stored in attributes—essentially
character vectors—within the data frame. In essence, they are just another
form of variable that you can manipulate.

If you use Microsoft Windows, you can see the names in the data editor,
and changing them there by hand is a very easy way to rename them. The
function call `fix(mydata)` brings up the data editor. Clicking on the name of
a variable opens a box that enables you to change its name. In Fig. 10.1, we
are in the midst of changing the name of the variable q1 (see the name in the
spreadsheet) to x1.

Closing the Variable Name box, the Data Editor completes your changes.
If you use Macintosh or Linux, the `fix` function does not work this way.
However, on any operating system, you can use functions to change variable
names. The programming approach to changing names that feels the closest
to Stata is the `rename` function in Hadley Wickham's `reshape` package [53].
To use it, install the package and then load it with the `library` function.
Then create a character vector whose *values* are the new names. The *names*
of the vector elements are the old variable names. This approach makes it
particularly easy to to rename only a subset of your variables. It also feels
very familiar to Stata users since it follows the **old-name=new-name** style of
their `rename` command.

```
> library("reshape")

> myChanges <- c(q1="x1", q2="x2", q3="x3", q4="x4")

> myChanges

   q1    q2    q3    q4
 "x1"  "x2"  "x3"  "x4"
```

Now it is very easy to change names with

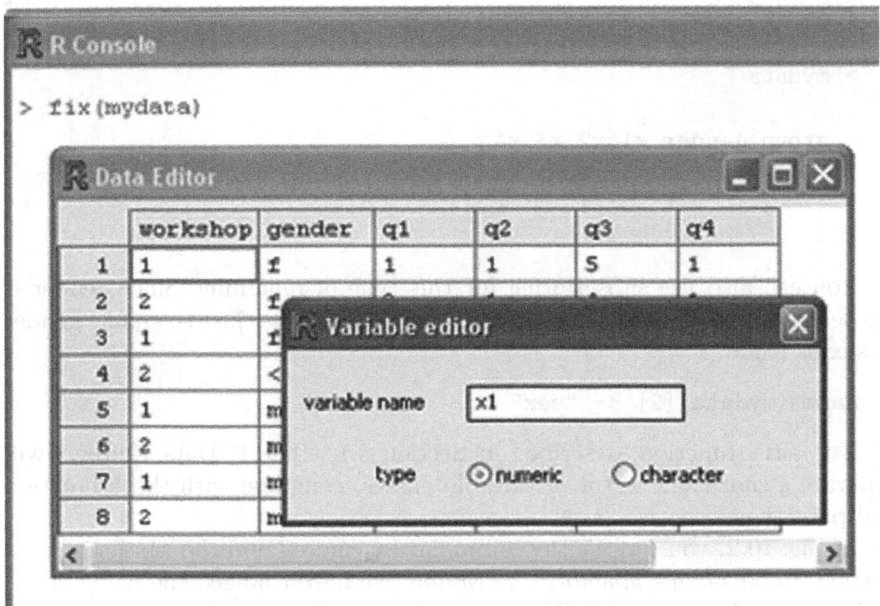

Fig. 10.1. Renaming a variable using R's data editor.

```
> mydata <- rename(mydata, myChanges)

> mydata

  workshop gender x1 x2 x3 x4
1        1      f  1  1  5  1
2        2      f  2  1  4  1
3        1      f  2  2  4  3
4        2   <NA>  3  1 NA  3
5        1      m  4  5  2  4
6        2      m  5  4  5  5
7        1      m  5  3  4  4
8        2      m  4  5  5  5
```

R's built-in approach to renaming variables is to use the **names** function. Simply entering **names(mydata)** causes R to print out the names vector.

```
> names(mydata)
```

```
[1] "group"   "gender"  "q1"      "q2"      "q3"      "q4"
```

You can also assign a character vector of equal length to that function, which renames the variables. With this approach, you can supply a name for every variable.

```
> names(mydata) <- c("group","gender","x1","x2","x3","x4")

> mydata

  group gender x1 x2 x3 x4
1     1      f  1  1  5  1
2     2      f  2  1  4  1
...
```

You can also use subscripting for this type of renaming. Since gender is the second variable in our data frame, you could change just the name gender to sex as follows:

```
names(mydata)[2] <- "sex"
```

The `edit` function, described in Section 6.1, "The R Data Editor," will generate a character vector of variable names, complete with the c function and parentheses.

In Fig. 10.2, you can see the command we entered and the window that it opened, titled *names(mydata) – R Editor*. We have changed the name of the variable "gender" to "sex." When we finish our changes, closing the box will execute the command.

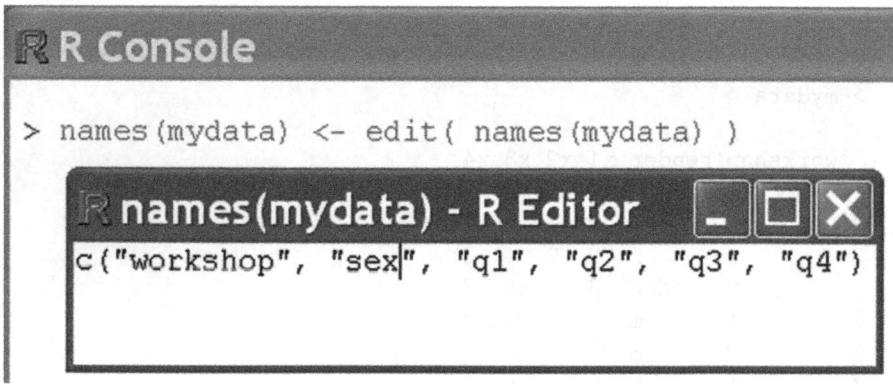

Fig. 10.2. Renaming variables using the `edit` function.

10.6.1 Renaming Variables—Advanced Examples

The methods shown above are often sufficient to rename your variables. You can view the next few sections as either beating the topic to death or as a wonderful opportunity to extend what you have learned about R into further examples. I think it is worthwhile because if you read the R-help e-mail support list, you will see these methods used to rename variables. The approach used in Section 10.6.4, "Renaming Many Sequentially Numbered Variable Names," can be a real time saver.

10.6.2 Renaming by Index

Let us extract the names of our variables using the names function.

```
> mynames <- names(mydata)

> mynames

[1] "group"  "gender" "q1"     "q2"     "q3"     "q4"
```

Now we have a character vector whose values we can change using the R techniques we have covered elsewhere. We would like to get the index value of each variable name. Recall that whenever a data frame is created, row names are added that are sequential numbers by default. So we can use the data.frame function to number our variable names:

```
> data.frame(mynames)

  mynames
1   group
2  gender
3      q1
4      q2
5      q3
6      q4
```

We see from the above list that q1 is the third name and q4 is the sixth. We can now use that information to enter new names directly into this vector and print the result so that we can see if we had made errors:

```
> mynames[3] <- "x1"
> mynames[4] <- "x2"
> mynames[5] <- "x3"
> mynames[6] <- "x4"

> mynames

[1] "group"  "gender" "x1"     "x2"     "x3"     "x4"
```

That looks good, so let us place those new names into the names attribute of our data frame and look at the results:

```
> names(mydata) <- mynames
> mydata
```

```
  group gender x1 x2 x3 x4
1     1        f  1  1  5  1
2     2        f  2  1  4  1
...
```

As you will see in the program below, each time we do another method of name changes, we need to restore the old names to demonstrate the new techniques. We can accomplish that by either reloading our original data frame or by using

```
names(mydata) <- c("group","gender","q1","q2","q3","q4")
```

10.6.3 Renaming by Column Name

If you prefer to use variable names instead of index numbers, that is easy to do. We will make another copy of mynames:

```
> mynames <- names(mydata)

> mynames
```

```
[1] "group"  "gender" "q1"     "q2"     "q3"     "q4"
```

Now we will make the same changes but using a logical match to find where mynames=="q1" and so on and assigning the new names to those locations.

```
> mynames[ mynames=="q1" ] <- "x1"
> mynames[ mynames=="q2" ] <- "x2"
> mynames[ mynames=="q3" ] <- "x3"
> mynames[ mynames=="q4" ] <- "x4"

> mynames
```

```
[1] "group"  "gender" "x1"     "x2"     "x3"     "x4"
```

Finally, we put the new set mynames into the names attribute of our data frame, mydata.

```
> names(mydata) <- mynames

> mydata
```

```
  group gender x1 x2 x3 x4
1     1        f  1  1  5  1
2     2        f  2  1  4  1
...
```

You can combine all these steps into one, but we find it very confusing to read.

```
names(mydata)[names(mydata)=="q1"] <- "x1"
names(mydata)[names(mydata)=="q2"] <- "x2"
names(mydata)[names(mydata)=="q3"] <- "x3"
names(mydata)[names(mydata)=="q4"] <- "x4"
```

10.6.4 Renaming Many Sequentially Numbered Variable Names

Our next example works well if you are changing many variable names, like 100 variables named x1, x2,... over to similar names like y1, y2,.... You occasionally have to make changes like this when you measure many variables at different times and you need to rename the variables in each data set before joining them all.

We learned how the **paste** function can append sequential numbers onto any string in Section 7.4, "Selecting Variables by Column Name." We will use it here to create the new variable names:

```
> myXs <- paste( "x", 1:4, sep="")

> myXs

[1] "x1" "x2" "x3" "x4"
```

Now we need to find out where to put the new names. We already know this of course, but we found that out in the previous example by listing all of the variables. If we had thousands of variables, that would not be a very good method. We will use the method we covered previously (and in more detail) in Section 7.11, "Generating Indexes A to Z from Two Variable Names":

```
> myA <- which( names(mydata)=="q1" )

> myA

[1] 3

> myZ <- which( names(mydata)=="q4" )

> myZ

[1] 6
```

Now we know the indexes of the variable names to replace; we can replace them with the following:

```
> names(mydata)[myA:myZ] <- myXs

> mydata

   group gender x1 x2 x3 x4
1      1      f  1  1  5  1
2      2      f  2  1  4  1
...
```

10.6.5 Renaming Observations

R has row names that work much the same as variable names, but they apply to observations. These names must be unique and often come from an ID variable. When reading a text file using `read.table`, the `row.names` argument allows you to specify an ID variable. See Section 6.2, "Reading Delimited Text Files" for details.

Row names are stored in a vector called the *row names attribute*. Therefore, when renaming rows using a variable, you must select it so that it will pass as a vector. In the examples below, the first three select a variable named "id" as a vector, so they work. The last approach looks almost like the first, but it selects id as a data frame, which will not fit in the row names attribute. Recall that leaving out the comma in `mydata["id"]` makes R select a variable as a data frame. The moral of the story is that when renaming observations using index values, *keep the comma*!

```
> row.names(mydata) <- mydata[ ,"id"] #This works.

> row.names(mydata) <- mydata$id        #This works too.

> row.names(mydata) <- mydata[["id"]] #This does too.

> row.names(mydata) <- mydata["id"]   #This does not.

Error in 'row.names<-.data.frame'('*tmp*',
   value = list(id = c(1, 2, 3,   :
   invalid 'rowrow.names' names length
```

10.6.6 Example Programs for Renaming Variables

For many of our programming examples, the R programs are longer because they demonstrate a wider range of functionality. In this case, renaming variables is definitely easier in Stata. R does have a greater flexibility in this area, but it is an ability that only a fanatical programmer could love!

Stata Program for Renaming Variables

```
* Filename: Rename.do

use c:\myRfolder\mydata, clear
preserve
rename q1 x1
rename q2 x2
rename q3 x3
rename q4 x4

* or
restore
forvalues i = 1/4 {
rename q'i' x'i'
}
```

R Program for Renaming Variables

```
# Filename: Rename.R
setwd("/myRfolder")
load(file="mydata.RData")
mydata

# Using the data editor.

fix(mydata)
mydata

# Restore original names for next example.
names(mydata) <- c("group", "gender",
  "q1", "q2", "q3", "q4")

# Using the reshape package.

library("reshape")
myChanges <- c(q1="x1",q2="x2",q3="x3",q4="x4")
myChanges

mydata <- rename(mydata, myChanges)
mydata
```

```
# Restore original names for next example.
names(mydata) <- c("group", "gender",
  "q1", "q2", "q3", "q4")


# The standard R approach.
names(mydata) <- c("group", "gender",
  "x1", "x2", "x3", "x4")
mydata


# Restore original names for next example.
names(mydata) <- c("group", "gender",
  "q1", "q2", "q3", "q4")


# Using the edit function.
names(mydata) <- edit( names(mydata) )
mydata


# Restore original names for next example.
names(mydata) <- c ("workshop", "gender",
  "q1", "q2", "q3", "q4")

#---Selecting Vaiables by Index Numbers---

mynames <- names(mydata)

# Data.frame adds index numbers to names.
data.frame(mynames)

# Then fill in index numbers in brackets.
mynames[3] <- "q1"
mynames[4] <- "q2"
mynames[5] <- "q3"
mynames[6] <- "q4"

# Finally, replace old names with new.
names(mydata) <- mynames
mydata

# Restore original names for next example.
names(mydata) <- c("group", "gender",
  "q1", "q2", "q3", "q4")
```

```
#---Selecting Variables by Name---
# Make a copy to work on.
mynames <- names(mydata)
mynames

# Replace names in copy.
mynames[ mynames=="q1" ] <- "x1"
mynames[ mynames=="q2" ] <- "x2"
mynames[ mynames=="q3" ] <- "x3"
mynames[ mynames=="q4" ] <- "x4"
mynames

# Then replace the old names.
names(mydata) <- mynames
mydata

# Restore original names for next example.
names(mydata) <- c ("group", "gender",
  "q1", "q2", "q3", "q4")

#---Same as Above, but Confusing!---

names(mydata)[names(mydata)=="q1"] <- "x1"
names(mydata)[names(mydata)=="q2"] <- "x2"
names(mydata)[names(mydata)=="q3"] <- "x3"
names(mydata)[names(mydata)=="q4"] <- "x4"
print(mydata)

# Restore original names for next example.
names(mydata) <- c("group", "gender",
  "q1", "q2", "q3", "q4")

#---Replacing Many Numbered Names---

# Examine names
names(mydata)

# Generate new numbered names.
myXs <- paste( "x", 1:4, sep="")
myXs

# Find out where to put the new names.
myA <- which( names(mydata)=="q1" )
myA
myZ <- which( names(mydata)=="q4" )
```

```
myZ
# Replace names at index locations.
names(mydata)[myA:myZ] <- myXs(mydata)

#remove the unneeded objects.
rm(myXs, myA, myZ)
```

10.7 Recoding Variables

Recoding is just a simpler way of doing a set of related IF/THEN conditional transformations. Survey researchers often collapse five-point Likert-scale items to simpler three-point Disagree/Neutral/Agree scales to summarize results. This can also help when a cross-tabulation (or similar analysis) with other variables creates tables that are too sparse to analyze.

Recoding can also reverse the scale of negatively worded items so that a large numeric value has the same meaning across all items. It is easier to reverse scales by subtracting each score from 6 as in

```
mydata$qr1 <- 6-mydata$q1
```

That results in 6-5=1, 6-4=2, and so on.

There are two important issues to consider when recoding data. First, collapsing a scale loses information and power. You will lessen your ability to find significant, and hopefully useful, relationships. Second, recoding nominal categorical variables like race can be disastrous. For example, inexperienced researchers often recode race into Caucasian and Other without checking to see how reasonable that is beforehand. You should do an analysis to see if the groups you are combining show similar patterns with regard to your dependent variable of interest. Given how much time that can add to the overall analysis, it is often far easier to set values to missing. Simply focus your analysis on the groups for which you have sufficient data rather than combine groups without justification.

Stata has a specific recode command by that name and offers a "label" option that allows value labels to follow the recoding.

You can also recode the data with a series of IF/THEN statements. We show both methods below. For simplicity, we leave the value labels out of the Stata and R programs. We cover those in Section 11.1, "Value Labels or Formats (and Measurement Level)."

For recoding continuous variables into categorical, see the cut function in base R and the cut2 function in Frank Harrell's Hmisc package. For choosing optimal cut points with regard to a target variable, see the rpart function in the rpart package or the tree function in the Hmisc package.

It is wise to avoid modifying your original data, so recoded variables are typically stored under new names. If you named your original variables q1, q2,... then you might name the recoded ones qr1, qr2,..., with "r" representing *recoded*.

10.7.1 Recoding a Few Variables

We will work with the `recode` function from John Fox's `car` package, which you will have to install before running this. See Chapter 2, "Installing and Updating R," for details. We will apply it below to collapse our five-point scale down to a three-point one representing just disagree, neutral, and agree.

```
> library("car")

> mydata$qr1 <- recode(q1, "1=2; 5=4")
> mydata$qr2 <- recode(q2, "1=2; 5=4")
> mydata$qr3 <- recode(q3, "1=2; 5=4")
> mydata$qr4 <- recode(q4, "1=2; 5=4")

> mydata
```

	workshop	gender	q1	q2	q3	q4	qr1	qr2	qr3	qr4
1	1	f	1	1	5	1	2	2	4	2
2	2	f	2	1	4	1	2	2	4	2
3	1	f	2	2	4	3	2	2	4	3
4	2	<NA>	3	1	NA	3	3	2	NA	3
5	1	m	4	5	2	4	4	4	2	4
6	2	m	5	4	5	5	4	4	4	4
7	1	m	5	3	4	4	4	3	4	4
8	2	m	4	5	5	5	4	4	4	4

The `recode` function needs only two arguments: the variable you wish to recode and a string of values in the form "old1=new1; old2=new2;...."

10.7.2 Recoding Many Variables

The above approach worked fine with our tiny data set, but in a more realistic situation, we would have many variables to recode. So let us scale this example up. We learned how to rename many variables in Section 10.6.4, so we will use that knowledge here.

```
> myQnames <- paste( "q", 1:4, sep="")

> myQnames

[1] "q1" "q2" "q3" "q4"

> myQRnames <- paste( "qr", 1:4, sep="")

> myQRnames

[1] "qr1" "qr2" "qr3" "qr4"
```

Now we will use the original names to extract the variables we want to recode to a separate data frame.

```
> myQRvars <- mydata[ ,myQnames]
> myQRvars

  q1 q2 q3 q4
1  1  1  5  1
2  2  1  4  1
3  2  2  4  3
4  3  1 NA  3
5  4  5  2  4
6  5  4  5  5
7  5  3  4  4
8  4  5  5  5
```

We will use our other set of variable names to rename the variables we just selected.

```
> names(myQRvars) <- myQRnames

> myQRvars

  qr1 qr2 qr3 qr4
1   1   1   5   1
2   2   1   4   1
3   2   2   4   3
4   3   1  NA   3
5   4   5   2   4
6   5   4   5   5
7   5   3   4   4
8   4   5   5   5
```

Now we need to create a function that will allow us to apply the recode function to each of the selected variables. Our function only has one argument, x, which will represent each of our variables.

```
myRecoder <- function(x) { recode(x,"1=2;5=4") }
```

Here is how we can use myRecoder on a single variable. Notice that the qr1 variable had a 1 for the first observation, which myRecoder made a 2. It also had values of 5 for the sixth and seventh observations, which became 4s.

```
> myQRvars$qr1

[1] 1 2 2 3 4 5 5 4
```

```
> myRecoder(myQRvars$qr1)
```

```
[1] 2 2 2 3 4 4 4 4
```

To apply this function to our whole data frame, myQRvars, we can use the sapply function.

```
> myQRvars <- sapply( myQRvars, myRecoder)
```

```
> myQRvars
```

```
      qr1 qr2 qr3 qr4
[1,]    2   2   4   2
[2,]    2   2   4   2
[3,]    2   2   4   3
[4,]    3   2  NA   3
[5,]    4   4   2   4
[6,]    4   4   4   4
[7,]    4   3   4   4
[8,]    4   4   4   4
```

The sapply function has converted our data frame to a matrix, but that is fine. We will use the cbind function to bind these columns to our original data frame.

```
> mydata <- cbind(mydata,myQRvars)
```

```
> mydata
```

```
  workshop gender q1 q2 q3 q4 qr1 qr2 qr3 qr4
1        1      f  1  1  5  1   2   2   4   2
2        2      f  2  1  4  1   2   2   4   2
3        1      f  2  2  4  3   2   2   4   3
4        2   <NA>  3  1 NA  3   3   2  NA   3
5        1      m  4  5  2  4   4   4   2   4
6        2      m  5  4  5  5   4   4   4   4
7        1      m  5  3  4  4   4   3   4   4
8        2      m  4  5  5  5   4   4   4   4
```

Now we can use either the original variables or their recoded counterparts in any analysis we choose. In this simple case, it was not necessary to create the myRecorder function. We could have used the form,

```
sapply(myQRvars, recode, "1=2;5=4")
```

However, you can generalize the approach we took to far more situations.

10.7.3 Example Programs for Recoding Variables

Stata Program for Recoding Variables

```
* Filename: Recode.do

use c:\myRfolder\mydata, clear
recode q1-q4 (1=2) (5=4)
```

R Program for Recoding Variables

```
# Filename: Recode.R

setwd("/myRfolder")
load(file="mydata.RData")
mydata
attach(mydata)

library("car")
mydata$qr1 <- recode(q1, "1=2; 5=4")
mydata$qr2 <- recode(q2, "1=2; 5=4")
mydata$qr3 <- recode(q3, "1=2; 5=4")
mydata$qr4 <- recode(q4, "1=2; 5=4")
mydata

# Do it again, stored in new variable names.
load(file="mydata.RData")
attach(mydata)

# Generate two sets of var names to use.
myQnames <-  paste( "q",  1:4, sep="")
myQnames
myQRnames <- paste( "qr", 1:4, sep="")
myQRnames

# Extract the q variables to a separate data frame.
myQRvars <- mydata[ ,myQnames]
myQRvars

# Rename all of the variables with R for Recoded.
names(myQRvars) <- myQRnames
myQRvars

# Create a function to apply the labels to lots of variables.
myRecoder <- function(x) { recode(x,"1=2;5=4") }
```

```
# Here's how to use the function on one variable.
myQRvars$qr1
myRecoder(myQRvars$qr1)

#Apply it to all of the variables.
myQRvars <- sapply( myQRvars, myRecoder)
myQRvars

# Save it back to mydata if you want.
mydata <- cbind(mydata,myQRvars)
mydata
summary(mydata)
```

10.8 Keeping and Dropping Variables

In Stata, you use the **keep** and **drop** commands to determine which variables to save in your data set. In R, the main methods to do this within a data frame are in Chapter 7, "Selecting Variables." For example, if we want to keep variables on the left side of our data frame, workshop through q2 (variables 1 through 4), an easy way to do this is with

```
myleft <- mydata[ ,1:4]
```

We will strip off the ones on the right side in a future example on merging data frames.

Another way to drop variables is to assign the NULL object to the variable:

```
mydata$varname <- NULL
```

This has the advantage of removing a variable without having to make a copy of the data frame. That may come in handy with data frames so large that your workspace will not hold a copy, but it is usually much safer to work on copies when you can. Mistakes happen! You can apply NULL repeatedly with the form

```
myleft <- mydata
```

```
myleft$q3 <- myleft$q4 <- NULL
```

NULL is only used to remove components from data frames and lists. You cannot use it to drop elements of a vector nor can you use it to remove a vector by itself from your workspace.

In Section 13.5, "Removing Objects from Your Workspace," we will discuss removing objects using the **rm** function. That function removes only whole objects; it cannot remove variables from within a data frame:

```
rm( mydata$q4 )  #This does NOT work.
```

10.8.1 Example Programs for Keeping and Dropping Variables

Stata Program for Keeping and Dropping Variables

```
* Filename: KeepDrop.do

use c:\myRfolder\mydata, clear
keep id workshop gender q1 q2

* Or equivalently;
* drop q3 q4

save c:\myRfolder\myleft, replace
```

R Program for Keeping and Dropping Variables

```
# Filename: KeepDrop.R

setwd("/myRfolder")
load(file="mydatda.RData")

# Using variable selection.
myleft <- mydata[ ,1:4]
myleft

# Using NULL.
myleft <- mydata
myleft$q3 <- myleft$q4 <- NULL
myleft
```

10.9 Stacking/Appending Data Sets

Often we find data with observations divided into two or more sets due to collection at different times or places. Combining them is an important step prior to analysis. Stata calls this *appending* data sets and accomplishes this with the append command. R, with its row/column orientation calls it *binding rows*.

To demonstrate this, let us take our practice data set and split it into separate ones for females and males. Then we will bind the rows back together. A split function exists to do this type of task, but it puts the resulting data frames into a list, so we will use an alternate approach.

First, let us get the females:

```
> females <- mydata[ which(gender=="f"), ]
> females
```

```
  workshop gender q1 q2 q3 q4
1        1      f  1  1  5  1
2        2      f  2  1  4  1
3        1      f  2  2  4  3
```

Now we get the males:

```
> males <- mydata[ which(gender=="m"), ]
> males

  workshop gender q1 q2 q3 q4
5        1      m  4  5  2  4
6        2      m  5  4  5  5
7        1      m  5  3  4  4
8        2      m  4  5  5  5
```

We can put them right back together by binding their rows with the `rbind` function. The "r" in `rbind` stands for *row*.

```
> both <- rbind(females, males)

> both

  workshop gender q1 q2 q3 q4
1        1      f  1  1  5  1
2        2      f  2  1  4  1
3        1      f  2  2  4  3
5        1      m  4  5  2  4
6        2      m  5  4  5  5
7        1      m  5  3  4  4
8        2      m  4  5  5  5
```

This works fine when the two data frames share the exact same variables. Often the data frames you will need to bind have a few variables missing. We will drop variable q2 in the males data frame to create such a mismatch.

```
> males$q2 <- NULL
> males

  workshop gender q1 q3 q4
5        1      m  4  2  4
6        2      m  5  5  5
7        1      m  5  4  4
8        2      m  4  5  5
```

Note that variable q2 is indeed gone. Now let us try to put the two data frames together again.

```
> both <- rbind(females, males)

Error in match.names(clabs, names(xi)) :
    names do not match previous names
```

It fails because the `rbind` function needs both data frames to have the exact same variable names. Luckily, Hadley Wickham's `reshape` package has a function, `rbind.fill`, that binds whichever variables it finds that match and then fills in missing values for those that do not. This next example assumes that you have installed the `reshape` package. See Chapter 2, "Installing and Updating R," for details.

```
> library("reshape")

> both <- rbind.fill(females, males)

> both

  workshop gender q1 q2 q3 q4
1        1      f  1  1  5  1
2        2      f  2  1  4  1
3        1      f  2  2  4  3
5        1      m  4 NA  2  4
6        2      m  5 NA  5  5
7        1      m  5 NA  4  4
8        2      m  4 NA  5  5
```

We can do the same thing with the built-in `rbind` function, but we have to first determine which variables we need to add and then add them manually with the `data.frame` function and set them to NA.

```
> males <- data.frame( males, q2=NA )

> males

  workshop gender q1 q3 q4 q2
5        1      m  4  2  4 NA
6        2      m  5  5  5 NA
7        1      m  5  4  4 NA
8        2      m  4  5  5 NA
```

The males data frame now has a variable q2 again and so we can bind the two data frames using `rbind`. The fact that q2 is now on at the end will not matter. The data frame you list first on the `rbind` function call will determine the order of the final data frame. However, if you use index values to refer to your variables, you need to be aware of the difference!

```
> both <- rbind(females, males)

> both

  workshop gender q1 q2 q3 q4
1        1      f  1  1  5  1
2        2      f  2  1  4  1
3        1      f  2  2  4  3
5        1      m  4 NA  2  4
6        2      m  5 NA  5  5
7        1      m  5 NA  4  4
8        2      m  4 NA  5  5
```

This was an easy way to do it with such a tiny data frame. In situations that are more realistic, rbind.fill is usually a great time saver.

10.9.1 Example Programs for Stacking/Appending Data Sets

Stata Program for Stacking/Appending Data Sets

```
* Filename: Append.do

use c:\myRfolder\mydata, clear
preserve

keep if gender=="m"
save c:\myRfolder\mymale
restore

keep if gender=="f"
save c:\myRfolder\myfemale
use c:\myRfolder\mymale, clear

append using c:\myRfolder\myfemale
save c:\myRfolder\both
```

R Program for Stacking/Appending Data Sets

```
# Filename: Append.R

setwd("/myRfolder")
load(file="mydata.RData")
mydata
attach(mydata)
# Create female data frame.
```

```
females <- mydata[ which(gender=="f"), ]
females

# Create male data frame.
males <- mydata[ which(gender=="m"), ]
males

#Bind their rows together with the rbind function.
both <- rbind(females, males)
both

# Drop q2 to see what happens.
males$q2 <- NULL
males

# See that row bind will not work.
both <- rbind(females, males)

# Use reshape's rbind.fill.
library("reshape")
both <- rbind.fill(females, males)
both

# Add a q2 variable to males.
males <- data.frame( males, q2=NA )
males

# Now rbind can handle it.
both <- rbind(females,males)
both
```

10.10 Joining/Merging Data Sets

One of the most frequently used data manipulation methods is joining or merging two data sets, each of which contains variables that the other lacks. Stata does this with its merge command.

If you have a one-to-many join, it will create a row for every possible match. A common example is a short data frame containing household-level information such as family income joined to a longer data set of individual family member variables. A complete record of each family member along with his or her household income will result. Duplicates in more than one data frame are possible, but you should study them carefully for errors.

So that we will have an ID variable to work with, let us read our practice data without the `row.names` argument. That will keep our ID variable as is and fill in row names with 1, 2, 3, ...

```
> mydata <- read.table("mydata.csv",
+   header=TRUE,sep=",",na.strings=" ")

> mydata

  id workshop gender q1 q2 q3 q4
1  1        1      f  1  1  5  1
2  2        2      f  2  1  4  1
3  3        1      f  2  2  4  3
4  4        2   <NA>  3  1 NA  3
5  5        1      m  4  5  2  4
6  6        2      m  5  4  5  5
7  7        1      m  5  3  4  4
8  8        2      m  4  5  5  5
```

Now we will split the left half of the data frame into one called myleft:

```
> myleft <- mydata[ c("id","workshop","gender","q1","q2") ]

> myleft

  id workshop gender q1 q2
1  1        1      f  1  1
2  2        2      f  2  1
3  3        1      f  2  2
4  4        2   <NA>  3  1
5  5        1      m  4  5
6  6        2      m  5  4
7  7        1      m  5  3
8  8        2      m  4  5
```

We then do the same for the variables on the right, but we will keep id and workshop to match on later.

```
> myright <- mydata[ c("id","workshop","q3","q4") ]

> myright

  id workshop q3 q4
1  1        1  5  1
2  2        2  4  1
3  3        1  4  3
4  4        2 NA  3
```

```
5  5        1  4   4
6  6        2  5   5
7  7        1  4   4
8  8        2  5   5
```

Now we can use the `merge` function to put the two data frames back together.

```
> both <- merge(myleft, myright, by="id")

> both
```

```
  id workshop.x gender q1 q2 workshop.y q3 q4
1  1          1      f  1  1          1  5  1
2  2          2      f  2  1          2  4  1
3  3          1      f  2  2          1  4  3
4  4          2   <NA>  3  1          2 NA  3
5  5          1      m  4  5          1  2  4
6  6          2      m  5  4          2  5  5
7  7          1      m  5  3          1  4  4
8  8          2      m  4  5          2  5  5
```

This call to the `merge` function has three arguments.

1. The first data frame to merge.
2. The second data frame to merge.
3. The `by` argument that has either a single variable name in quotes or a character vector of names.

If you leave out the `by` argument, it will match by all variables with common names! That is quite unlike Stata, which would simply match the two row-by-row. That is what the R `cbind` function will do. It is much safer to match on some sort of ID variable(s) though. Very often, rows do not match up as well as you think.

Sometimes the same variable has two different names in the data frames you need to merge. For example, one may have "id" and another "subject." If you have such a situation, you can use the `by.x` argument to identify the first variable or set of variables and the `by.y` argument to identify the second. The `merge` function will match them up in order and do the proper merge. In this next example, we do just that. In our case variables have the same name, but now they would not have to.

```
> both <- merge(myleft,    myright,
+                  by.x="id", by.y="id")

> both
```

	id	workshop	gender	q1	q2	q3	q4
1	1	1	f	1	1	5	1
2	2	2	f	2	1	4	1
3	3	1	f	2	2	4	3
4	4	2	<NA>	3	1	NA	3
5	5	1	m	4	5	2	4
6	6	2	m	5	4	5	5
7	7	1	m	5	3	4	4
8	8	2	m	4	5	5	5

If you have multiple variables in common, but you only want to match on a subset of them, you can use the form

```
both <- merge( myleft,myright,
               by=c("id","workshop") )
```

If each file had variables with slightly different names, you could use the form

```
both <- merge( myleft,myright,
  by.x=c("id",      "workshop"),
  by.y=c("subject","shortCourse")
)
```

By default, Stata keeps all records regardless of whether or not they match (a full outer join). For observations that do not have matches in the other file, the merge function will fill in with missing values. R takes the opposite approach, keeping only those that have a record in both (an inner join). To get merge to keep all records, use the argument all=TRUE. You can also use all.x=TRUE to keep all of the records in the first file regardless of whether or not they have matches in the second. The all.y=TRUE argument does the reverse.

While Stata can merge any number of files at once, base R can only do two at a time. To do more, you can use the merge_all function in the reshape package.

10.10.1 Example Programs for Joining/Merging Data Sets

Stata Program for Joining/Merging Data Sets

```
* Filename: Merge.do

use c:\myRfolder\mydata, clear
drop q3 q4
save c:\myRfolder\myleft

use c:\myRfolder\mydata, clear
drop workshop-q2
```

```
save c:\myRfolder\myright

use c:\myRfolder\myleft, clear
sort id

merge id using c:\myRfolder\myright
save c:\myRfolder\both, replace
```

R Program for Joining/Merging Data Sets

```
# Filename: Merge.R

setwd("/myRfolder")

# Read data keeping ID as a variable.
mydata <- read.table("mydata.csv",
  header=TRUE,sep=",",na.strings=" ")
mydata

#Create a data frame keeping the left two q variables.
myleft <- mydata[ c("id","workshop","gender","q1","q2") ]
myleft

#Create a data frame keeping the right two q variables.
myright <- mydata[ c("id","workshop","q3","q4") ]
myright

#Merge the two dataframes by ID.
both <- merge(myleft,myright,by="id")
both

#Merge the two dataframes by ID.
both <- merge(myleft,    myright,
            by.x="id", by.y="id" )

#Merge dataframes by both ID and workshop.
both <- merge(myleft,myright,by=c("id","workshop"))
both

#Merge dataframes by both ID and workshop,
#while allowing them to have different names.
both <- merge(myleft,
            myright,
            by.x=c("id","workshop"),
            by.y=c("id","workshop") )
both
```

10.11 Creating Collapsed or Aggregated Data Sets

We often have to work on data that is a summarization of other data. For example, you might work on household-level data that you aggregated from a data set that had each family member as its own observation. Stata calls this *collapsing* data and performs it with the `collapse` command. Database programmers call this *rolling up* data.

R has three distinct advantages over Stata aggregation.

1. It is possible to perform multilevel calculations and selections in a single step. We will perform some of each below.
2. R can aggregate *with every function it has and any function you write!* It is not limited to the few that Stata has in its `collapse` command.
3. R has data structures optimized to hold aggregate results. Other functions offer methods to take advantage of those structures.

10.11.1 The `aggregate` Function

We will use the `aggregate` function to calculate the mean of the q1 variable by gender and save it to a new (very small!) data frame.

```
> attach(mydata)

> myAgg1 <- aggregate(q1,
+    by=data.frame(gender),
+    mean, na.rm=TRUE)

> myAgg1

  gender        x
1      f 1.666667
2      m 4.500000
```

The `aggregate` function call above has four arguments.

1. The variable you wish to aggregate.
2. One or more grouping factors. Unlike Stata, the data does not have to be sorted by these factors. This must be in the form of a list (or data frame, which is a type of list). Recall that single subscripting of a data frame creates a list. So `mydata["gender"]` and `mydata[2]` work. Adding the comma to either one will prevent them from working. Therefore, `mydata[ ,"gender"]` or `mydata[ ,2]` will not work. If you have attached the data frame, `data.frame(gender)` will work. The function call `list(gender)` will also work, but it loses track of the grouping variable names.

3. The function that you wish to apply—in this case, the **mean** function. An important limitation of the **aggregate** function is that it can apply only functions that return a *single* value. If you need to apply a function that returns multiple values, you can use the **tapply** function.
4. Arguments to pass to the function applied. Here **na.rm=TRUE** is passed to the **mean** function to remove missing, or NA, values.

Next we will aggregate by two variables: workshop and gender. To keep our by-factors in the form of a list (or data frame), we can use any one of the following forms:

```
mydata[ c("workshop","gender")]
```

or

```
mydata[ c(2,3) ]
```

or if you have attached the data frame,

```
data.frame( workshop, gender)
```

In this example, we will use the latter form.

```
> myAgg2 <- aggregate(q1,
+    by=data.frame(workshop, gender),
+    mean, na.rm=TRUE)

> myAgg2

  workshop gender   x
1        R      f 1.5
2    Stata      f 2.0
3        R      m 4.5
4    Stata      m 4.5
```

Now let us use the **mode** and **class** functions to see the type of object the **aggregate** function creates is a data frame.

```
> mode(myAgg2)

[1] "list"

> class(myAgg2)

[1] "data.frame"
```

It is small, but ready for further analysis.

10.11.2 The `tapply` Function

In the last subsection we discussed the **aggregate** function. That function has an important limitation: You can only use it with functions that return single values. The **tapply** function works very similarly to the **aggregate** function but can perform aggregation using any R function. To gain this ability, it has to abandon the convenience of creating a data frame. Instead, its output is in the form of a matrix or an array.

Let us first duplicate the last example from the above subsection using tapply.

```
> myAgg2 <- tapply(q1,
+    data.frame(workshop,gender),
+    mean, na.rm=TRUE)

> myAgg2
```

```
          gender
workshop    f     m
    R      1.5   4.5
    Stata  2.0   4.5
```

The **tapply** function call above uses four arguments.

1. The variable to aggregate.
2. One or more grouping factors. Unlike Stata, the data does not have to be sorted by these factors. This must be in the form of a list (or data frame, which is a list). Recall that single subscripting of a data frame creates a list. So `mydata["gender"]` and `mydata[2]` work. Adding the comma to either one will prevent them from working. Therefore, `mydata[ ,"gender"]` or `mydata[ ,2]` will not work. If you have attached the data frame, `data.frame(gender)` will work. The function call `list(gender)` will also work, but it loses track of the grouping variable names.
3. The function to apply—in this case, the **mean** function. This function can return any result, not just single values.
4. Any additional parameters to pass to the applied function. In this case, `na.rm=TRUE` is used by the **mean** function to remove NA or missing values.

The actual means are, of course, the same as we obtained earlier using the **aggregate** function. However, the result is now a numeric matrix rather than a data frame.

```
> class(myAgg2)
[1] "matrix"

> mode(myAgg2)
[1] "numeric"
```

Now let us do an example that the **aggregate** function could not perform. The **range** function returns two values: the minimum and maximum for each variable.

```
> myAgg2 <- tapply(q1,
+    data.frame(workshop,gender),
+    range, na.rm=TRUE)

> myAgg2
         gender
workshop f          m
    R      Numeric,2 Numeric,2
    Stata Numeric,2 Numeric,2
```

This output looks quite odd! It is certainly not formatted for communicating results to others. Let us see how it is stored.

```
> mode(myAgg2)

[1] "list"

> class(myAgg2)

[1] "matrix"
```

It is a matrix, whose elements are lists. Let us look at the entry for the females who took the R workshop. That result is stored in the first row and first column.

```
> class( myAgg2[1,1] )

[1] "list"

> myAgg2[1,1]

[[1]]
[1] 1 2
```

So we see that each component in this matrix is a list that contains a single vector of minimum and maximum values. The opinions of the females who took the R workshop range from 1 to 2.

While this output is not very useful for communicating results, it is very useful as input for further programming.

10.11.3 Merging Aggregates with Original Data

It is often useful to add aggregate values back to the original data frame. This allows you to perform multilevel transformations that involve both individual-level and aggregate-level values. A common example of such a calculation is a Z score, which subtracts a variable's mean and then divides by its standard deviation (the scale function performs this particular calculation more easily).

Another important use for merging aggregates with original data is to perform multilevel selections of observations. To select individual-level observations based on aggregate-level values requires access to both at once. For example, we could create a subset of subjects who fall below their group's mean value.

This is an area in which R has a distinct advantage over Stata. R's greater flexibility allows it to do both multi-level transformations and selections in a single step.

Now let us calculate a Z-score for variable q1 with the single following statement. Note that we are specifying the long form of the name for our new variable, mydata$Zq1, so that it will go into our data frame.

```
> mydata$Zq1 <- (q1 - mean(q1) ) / sd(q1)

> mydata

  workshop gender q1 q2 q3 q4        Zq1
1        R      f  1  1  5  1 -1.5120484
2    Stata      f  2  1  4  1 -0.8400269
3        R      f  2  2  4  3 -0.8400269
4    Stata   <NA>  3  1 NA  3 -0.1680054
5        R      m  4  5  2  4  0.5040161
6    Stata      m  5  4  5  5  1.1760376
7        R      m  5  3  4  4  1.1760376
8    Stata      m  4  5  5  5  0.5040161
```

You can also select the observations that were below average with this single statement.

```
> mySubset <- mydata[ q1 < mean(q1), ]

> mySubset
  workshop gender q1 q2 q3 q4        Zq1
1        R      f  1  1  5  1 -1.5120484
2    Stata      f  2  1  4  1 -0.8400269
3        R      f  2  2  4  3 -0.8400269
4    Stata   <NA>  3  1 NA  3 -0.1680054
```

Stata cannot perform such calculations and selections in one step. You would have to create the aggregate-level data and then merge it back into the individual-level data set. R can use that approach too, and as the number of levels you consider increases, it becomes more reasonable to do so.

So let us now merge myAgg2, created in Section 10.11.1, "The `aggregate` Function." to mydata. To do that, we will rename the mean of q1 from x to mean.q1. We will use the `rename` function from the `reshape` package. If you do not have that installed, see Chapter 2, "Installing and Maintaining R."

```
> library("reshape")

> myAgg3 <- rename(myAgg2, c(x="mean.q1"))

> myAgg3

  workshop gender mean.q1
1        R      f     1.5
2    Stata      f     2.0
3        R      m     4.5
4    Stata      m     4.5
```

Now we merge the mean onto each of the original observations.

```
> mydata2 <- merge(mydata, myAgg3,
+   by=c("workshop","gender") )

> mydata2

  workshop gender q1 q2 q3 q4        Zq1 mean.q1
1        R      f  1  1  5  1 -1.5120484     1.5
2        R      f  2  2  4  3 -0.8400269     1.5
3        R      m  4  5  2  4  0.5040161     4.5
4        R      m  5  3  4  4  1.1760376     4.5
5    Stata      f  2  1  4  1 -0.8400269     2.0
6    Stata      m  5  4  5  5  1.1760376     4.5
7    Stata      m  4  5  5  5  0.5040161     4.5
```

The `merge` function call above has only two arguments.

1. The two data frames to merge. Unlike Stata, which can merge many data sets at once, R can only do two at a time.
2. The `by` argument specifies the variables to match on. In this case, they have the same name in both data frames. They can, however, have different names. See the `merge` help files for details. While some other functions require `by` variables in list form, here you provide more than one variable in the form of a character vector.

We could now perform multilevel transformations or selections on mydata2.

10.11.4 Tabular Aggregation

The aim of table creation in Stata is to communicate the results to people. You can create simple tables of frequencies and percents using the Stata `tabulate` command. However, no other procedures are programmed to process these tables further automatically.

While R can create tables that are nicely formatted for presentation, its output is usually sparse and optimized for further use by other functions. They are a different form of aggregated data set. See Chapter 17, "Statistics," for other uses of tables.

Let us revisit simple frequencies using the `table` function. First, let us look at just workshop attendance (the data frame is attached, so we are using short variable names).

```
> table(workshop)

workshop
  R Stata
  4    4
```

And now gender and workshop.

```
> table(gender,workshop)
        workshop

gender R Stata
    f 2    1
    m 2    2
```

Let us save this table to an object myCounts and check its mode and class.

```
> myCounts <- table(gender, workshop)

> mode(myCounts)

[1] "numeric"

> class(myCounts)

[1] "table"
```

We see that the mode of myCounts is numeric and its class is *table*. Other functions that exist to work with presummarized data know what to do with table objects. In Chapter 15, "Traditional Graphics," we will see the kinds of plots we can make from tables. In Chapter 17, "Statistics," we will also work with table objects to calculate related values like row and column percents.

Other functions prefer count data in the form of a data frame. This is the type of output created by the Stata `collapse` command. The `as.data.frame` function makes quick work of it.

```
> myCountsDF <- as.data.frame(myCounts)

> myCountsDF
```

```
      gender workshop Freq
1        f        R    2
2        m        R    2
3        f     Stata    1
4        m     Stata    2

> class(myCountsDF)
[1] "data.frame"
```

This approach is particularly useful for people who use analysis of variance. You can get cell counts for very complex models in a form that is very easy to read and use in further analyses.

10.11.5 The reshape Package

If you perform a lot of aggregation, you will want to learn how to use Hadley Wickham's powerful **reshape** package [53].

10.11.6 Example Programs for Collapsing/Aggregating Data

Stata Program for Collapsing/Aggregating Data

```
* Filename: Collapse.do

use c:\myRfolder\mydata
* Get means of q1 for each gender
tabstat q1, by(gender)

* Get means of q1 by workshop and gender;
tabulate outwork gender, summarize(q1) means

* Strip out just the mean and matching variables;
collapse (mean) workshop gender, by(q1)

* Merge aggregated data back into mydata.
* mydata assumed to be sorted by q1
sort q1
merge q1 using mydata
```

R Program for Collapsing/Aggregating Data

```
# Filename: Collapse.R

setwd("/myRfolder")
```

```
load(file="mydata.RData")
attach(mydata)
mydata

# The aggregate Function.
# Means by gender.
myAgg1 <- aggregate(q1,
  by=data.frame(gender),
  mean, na.rm=TRUE)
myAgg1

# Now by workshop and gender.
myAgg2 <- aggregate(q1,
  by=data.frame(workshop, gender),
  mean, na.rm=TRUE)

myAgg2
mode(myAgg2)
class(myAgg2)

# Aggregation with tapply.
myAgg2 <- tapply(q1,
  data.frame(workshop,gender),
  mean, na.rm=TRUE)

myAgg2
class(myAgg2)
mode(myAgg2)

myAgg2 <- tapply(q1,
  data.frame(workshop,gender),
  range, na.rm=TRUE)
myAgg2

mode(myAgg2)
class(myAgg2)
class( myAgg2[1,1] )
myAgg2[1,1]

# Example multi-level transformation.
mydata$Zq1 <- (q1 - mean(q1) ) / sd(q1)
mydata
mySubset <- mydata[ q1 < mean(q1), ]
mySubset
```

```
# Rename x to be mean.q1.
library("reshape")
myAgg3 <- rename(myAgg2, c(x="mean.q1"))
myAgg3

# Now merge means back with mydata.
mydata2 <- merge(mydata,myAgg3,
  by=c("workshop","gender") )
mydata2

# Tables of Counts
table(workshop)
table(gender,workshop)
myCounts <- table(gender, workshop)

mode(myCounts)
class(myCounts)

# Counts in Summary/Aggregate style.
myCountsDF <- as.data.frame(myCounts)
myCountsDF
class(myCountsDF)

# Clean up
mydata["Zq1"] <- NULL
rm(myAgg1, myAgg2, myAgg3,
  myComplete, myMeans, myCounts, myCountsDF)
```

10.12 By or Split-File Processing

When you want to repeat an analysis for every level of a categorical variable, you can use the by command in Stata. Stata requires you to sort the data by the factor variable(s) first, but R does not.

R has a by function, which repeats analysis for levels of factors. In Section 10.11, "Creating Collapsed or Aggregated Data Sets," we did similar things while creating summary data sets. When we finish with this topic, we will compare the two approaches.

Let us look at the by function first and then discuss how it compares to similar functions. We will use the by function to apply the mean function. First, let us use the mean function by itself just for review. To get the means of our q variables, we can use

```
> mean( mydata[ c("q1","q2","q3","q4") ] ,
+         na.rm=TRUE)
```

```
    q1      q2      q3      q4
3.25003.2500 2.7500 4.1429 3.7500
```

Now let us get means for the males and females using the by function:

```
> myBYout <- by( mydata[ c("q1","q2","q3","q4") ] ,
+       mydata["gender"],
+       mean,na.rm=TRUE)

> myBYout

gender: f
      q1       q2       q3       q4
1.666667 1.333333 4.333333 1.666667
----------------------------------------------------
gender: m
  q1   q2   q3   q4
4.50 4.25 4.00 4.50
```

The by function call above has four arguments.

1. The data frame name and/or variables to analyze,
   mydata[c("q1","q2","q3","q4")].
2. One or more grouping factors. Unlike Stata, the data does not have
   to be sorted by these factors. This must be in the form of a list (or
   data frame, which is a type of list). Recall that single subscripting of
   a data frame creates a list. So mydata["gender"] and mydata[2] work.
   Adding the comma to either one will prevent them from working. Therefore, mydata[,"gender"] or mydata[,2] will not work. If you have attached the data frame, data.frame(gender) will work. The function call
   list(gender) will also work, but it loses track of the grouping variable
   names.
3. The function to apply—in this case, the mean function. The by function can apply functions that calculate more than one value (unlike the
   aggregate function).
4. Any additional arguments are ignored by the by function and simply
   passed to the applied function. In this case, na.rm=TRUE is simply passed
   to the mean function.

Let us check to see what the mode and class are of the output
object.

```
> mode(myBYout)

[1] "list"
```

```
> class(myBYout)
```

```
[1] "by"
```

It is a list, with a class of "by." If we would like to convert that to a data frame, we can do so with the following. The **as.table** function gets the data into a form that the **as.data.frame** function can then turn into a data frame.

```
> myBYdata <- as.data.frame( (as.table(myBYout) ) )
```

```
> myBYdata
```

```
    gender   Freq.f Freq.m
q1       f 1.666667   4.50
q2       m 1.333333   4.25
q3       f 4.333333   4.00
q4       m 1.666667   4.50
```

Now let us break the mean down by both workshop and gender. To keep our by factors in the form of a list (or data frame), we can use any one of these forms:

```
mydata[ c("workshop","gender")]
```

or

```
mydata[ c(2,3) ]
```

or, if you have attached the data frame,

```
data.frame( workshop, gender)
```

This starts to look messy, so let us put both our variable list and our factor list into character vectors:

```
myVars <- c("q1","q2","q3","q4")
```

```
myBys  <- mydata[ c("workshop","gender") ]
```

By using our character vectors as arguments for the by function, it is much easier to read. This time, let us use the **range** function to show that the by function can apply functions that return more than one value.

```
> myBYout <- by( mydata[myVars],
+   myBys, range, na.rm=TRUE )
```

```
> myBYout
```

```
workshop: R
gender: f
[1] 1 5
--------------------------------------------------------
workshop: Stata
gender: f
[1] 1 4
--------------------------------------------------------
workshop: R
gender: m
[1] 2 5
--------------------------------------------------------
workshop: Stata
gender: m
[1] 4 5
```

That output is quite readable. Recall that when we did this same analysis using the tapply function, the results were in a form that were optimized for further analysis rather than communication. However, we can save the data to a data frame if we like. The approach it takes is most interesting. Let us see what type of object we have.

```
> mode(myBYout)
[1] "list"

> class(myBYout)
[1] "by"

> names(myBYout)
NULL
```

It is a list with a class of "by" and no names. Let us look at one of its components.

```
> myBYout[[1]]
[1] 1 5
```

This is the first set of ranges from the printout above. If we wanted to create a data frame from these, we could bind them into the rows of a matrix and then convert that to a data frame with

```
> myBYdata <- data.frame(
+    rbind( myBYout[[1]], myBYout[[2]],
+           myBYout[[3]], myBYout[[4]] )
+ )

> myBYdata
```

```
  X1 X2
1  1  5
2  1  4
3  2  5
4  4  5
```

That approach is easy to understand but not much fun to use if we had many more factor levels! Luckily the do.call function can call a function you choose once, on all of the components of a list, just as if you had entered them individually. That is quite different from the lapply function, which applies the function you choose repeatedly on each separate component. All we have to do is give it the function to feed the components into, rbind in this case, and the list name, byBYout.

```
> myBYdata <- data.frame( do.call(rbind, myBYout) )

> myBYdata

  X1 X2
1  1  5
2  1  4
3  2  5
4  4  5
```

10.12.1 Comparing Summarization Methods

So we have seen that the capability of the by function closely mirrors that of the aggregate and tapply functions. Table 10.3, can help you choose which to use.

Table 10.3. Comparison of summarization functions.

	Input	Functions it can apply	Output
by	Data frame	Any function	List with class of "by." Easier to read but not as easy to program
aggregate	Data frame	Only functions that return single values	Data frame. Easy to read and program
tapply	List or data frame	Any function	List. Easy to access components for programming. Not as nicely formatted for reading.
table	Factors	Does counting only	Table object. Easy to read and easy to analyze further.

10.12.2 Example Programs for By or Split-file Processing

Stata Program for By or Split-File Processing

```
* Filename: By.do

use c:\myRfolder\mydata, clear
sort gender
by gender: sum gender
tabstat q1 q2 q3 q4, stat(mean sd min max)
tabstat q1 q2 q3 q4, stat(mean sd min max) by(gender)
```

R Program for By or Split-File Processing

```
# Filename: By.R

setwd("/myRfolder")
load(file="mydata.RData")
attach(mydata)
options(width=64)
mydata

# Get means of q variables for all observations.
mean( mydata[ c("q1","q2","q3","q4") ] ,
      na.rm=TRUE)

# Now get means by gender.
myBYout <- by( mydata[ c("q1","q2","q3","q4") ] ,
    mydata["gender"],
    mean,na.rm=TRUE)
myBYout
mode(myBYout)
class(myBYout)
myBYdata <- as.data.frame( (as.table(myBYout) ) )
myBYdata

# Get range by workshop and gender
myVars <- c("q1","q2","q3","q4")
myBys  <- mydata[ c("workshop","gender") ]
myBYout <- by( mydata[myVars],
  myBys, range, na.rm=TRUE )
myBYout

# Converting output to data frame.
mode(myBYout)
```

```
class(myBYout)
names(myBYout)
myBYout[[1]]

# A data frame the long way.
myBYdata <- data.frame(
  rbind(myBYout[[1]], myBYout[[2]],
        myBYout[[3]], myBYout[[4]])
)
myBYdata

# A data frame using do.call.
myBYdata <- data.frame( do.call( rbind, myBYout) )
myBYdata
mode(myBYdata)
class(myBYdata)
```

10.13 Removing Duplicate Observations

Duplicate observations frequently creep into data sets, especially those that are merged from various other data sets. The Stata approach is to use the **duplicates** command, but there are several other ways duplicate can be dropped. For example, the **collapse** command may be used with **sort** and **keep** to get rid of duplicates without examining them.

First, we will create a data frame that takes the top two observations from mydata and appends them to the bottom with the **rbind** function:

```
> myDuplicates <- rbind( mydata, mydata[1:2,] )

> myDuplicates

   workshop gender q1 q2 q3 q4
1         R      f  1  1  5  1   <- We are copying
2     Stata      f  2  1  4  1   <- these two...
3         R      f  2  2  4  3
4     Stata   <NA>  3  1 NA  3
5         R      m  4  5  2  4
6     Stata      m  5  4  5  5
7         R      m  5  3  4  4
8     Stata      m  4  5  5  5
9         R      f  1  1  5  1   <- ...down here
10    Stata      f  2  1  4  1   <- as duplicates.
```

Next we will use the **unique** function to find and delete them.

```
> myNoDuplicates <- unique(myDuplicates)

> myNoDuplicates
  workshop gender q1 q2 q3 q4
1        R      f  1  1  5  1
2    Stata      f  2  1  4  1
3        R      f  2  2  4  3
4    Stata  <NA>  3  1 NA  3
5        R      m  4  5  2  4
6    Stata      m  5  4  5  5
7        R      m  5  3  4  4
8    Stata      m  4  5  5  5
```

So the unique function removed them but did not show them to us. In
a more realistic data set, we would certainly not want to print the whole
thing and examine the duplicates visually as we did above. However, knowing
more about the duplicates might help us prevent them from creeping into our
future analyses. Let us put the duplicates back and see what the duplicated
function can do.

```
> myDuplicates <- rbind( mydata, mydata[1:2,] )

> myDuplicates$Duplicated <- duplicated(myDuplicates)

> myDuplicates

   workshop gender q1 q2 q3 q4 Duplicated
1         R      f  1  1  5  1      FALSE
2     Stata      f  2  1  4  1      FALSE
3         R      f  2  2  4  3      FALSE
4     Stata  <NA>  3  1 NA  3      FALSE
5         R      m  4  5  2  4      FALSE
6     Stata      m  5  4  5  5      FALSE
7         R      m  5  3  4  4      FALSE
8     Stata      m  4  5  5  5      FALSE
9         R      f  1  1  5  1       TRUE
10    Stata      f  2  1  4  1       TRUE
```

The duplicated function added the variable aptly named *Duplicated* to our
data frame. Its TRUE values show us that R has indeed located the duplicate
records. It is interesting to note that now we technically no longer have complete duplicates! The original first two records now have values of FALSE,
whereas the last two, which up until now had been exact duplicates, have
values of TRUE. So they have ceased to be exact duplicates! Therefore, the
unique function would no longer get rid of the last two records. That is OK

because now we will just get rid of those marked TRUE after we print a report of duplicate records.

```
> attach(myDuplicates)

> myDuplicates[ Duplicated, ]

   workshop gender q1 q2 q3 q4 Duplicated
9         R      f  1  1  5  1       TRUE
10     Stata     f  2  1  4  1       TRUE
```

Finally, we will choose those not duplicated (i.e., !Duplicated) and drop the seventh variable, which is the TRUE/FALSE variable itself.

```
> myNoDuplicates <- myDuplicates[ !Duplicated, -7]

> myNoDuplicates

   workshop gender  q1 q2 q3 q4
1         R      f   1  1  5  1
2      Stata     f   2  1  4  1
3         R      f   2  2  4  3
4      Stata   <NA>  3  1 NA  3
5         R      m   4  5  2  4
6      Stata     m   5  4  5  5
7         R      m   5  3  4  4
8      Stata     m   4  5  5  5
```

Now our data is back to its original, duplicate-free state.

10.13.1 Example Programs for Removing Duplicate Observations

Stata Program for Removing Duplicate Observations

```
* Filename: Duplicates.do

use c:\myRfolder\mydata, clear
duplicates drop id workshop gender q1-q4, force
list
```

R Program for Removing Duplicate Observations

```
# Filename: Duplicates.R

setwd("/myRfolder")
load("mydata.RData")
mydata
```

```
# Create some duplicates.
myDuplicates <- rbind( mydata, mydata[1:2,] )
myDuplicates

# Get rid of duplicates without seeing them.
myNoDuplicates <- unique(myDuplicates)
myNoDuplicates

# This checks for location of duplicates
# before getting rid of them.
myDuplicates <- rbind( mydata, mydata[1:2,] )
myDuplicates
myDuplicates$Duplicated <- duplicated(myDuplicates)
myDuplicates

# Print a report of just the duplicates.
myDuplicates[ Duplicated, ]

# Remove duplicates and Duplicated variable.
attach(myDuplicates)
myNoDuplicates <- myDuplicates[ !Duplicated, -7]
myNoDuplicates
```

10.14 Selecting First or Last Observations per Group

When a data set contains groups, members within each group are often sorted in a useful order. For example, a company may have divisions divided into departments. Each department might have salary information for each person and a running total. So the last person's running total value would be the total for each department.

The Stata approach on this problem is quite flexible. Simply saying,

```
use mydata
sort workshop gender
```

which sorts the data by workshop and within workshop, by gender. A Stata user may then keep the first, last, or any specified observation within the grouping, dropping the others.

The R approach to this problem demonstrates R's extreme flexibility. It does not have a function aimed directly at this problem. However, it is easy to create one using several other functions. We have seen the head function print the top few observations of a data frame. The tail function does the same for the last few. We have also used the by function to apply a function to groups within a data frame. We can use the by function to apply the head function to get the first observation in each group or use the tail function to get the last. Since the **head** and **tail** functions both have an "**n=**" argument, we can not only use **n=1** to get the single first or last, but also we could use **n=2** to get the first two or last two observations per group, and so on.

The last record per group is often of greatest interest since it contains the value of interest when you have a sum, like salaries, that is added cumulatively for each observation. So we will look at how to select the last observation per group. The idea readily extends to the first record(s) per group.

First, we will put our by variables into a data frame. By using workshop and then gender, we will soon be selecting the last male in each workshop.

```
myBys <- data.frame(mydata$workshop, mydata$gender)
```

Next, we use the **by** function to apply the **tail** function to mydata by workshop and gender. We are saving the result to mylast, which is in the form of a list.

```
mylastList <- by( mydata, myBys, tail, n=1 )

mylastList
```

The following is the resulting list:

```
mydata.workshop: 1
mydata.gender: f
  workshop gender q1 q2 q3 q4
3        1      f  2  2  4  3
----------------------------------------------------------------
mydata.workshop: 2
mydata.gender: f
  workshop gender q1 q2 q3 q4
4        2      f  3  1 NA  3
----------------------------------------------------------------
mydata.workshop: 1
mydata.gender: m
  workshop gender q1 q2 q3 q4
7        1      m  5  3  4  4
----------------------------------------------------------------
mydata.workshop: 2
mydata.gender: m
  workshop gender q1 q2 q3 q4
8        2      m  4  5  5  9
```

We would like to put this into a data frame by combining all of the vectors from that list in the form of rows. The **do.call** function does this. It essentially takes all of the elements of a list and feeds them into a single call to the function you choose. In this case, that is the **rbind** function.

```
mylastDF <- do.call( rbind, as.list(mylast) )
```

The following are the records we desired.

```
mylastDF
  workshop gender q1 q2 q3 q4
3        1      f  2  2  4  3
4        2      f  3  1 NA  3
7        1      m  5  3  4  4
8        2      m  4  5  5  9
```

That single call to the do.call function does this for you:

```
mylastDF <- rbind( (mylastList)[[1]],
                   (mylastList)[[2]],
                   (mylastList)[[3]],
                   (mylastList)[[4]]  )
```

If we had hundreds of groups, the do.call function would be a big time saver!

10.14.1 Example Programs for Selecting Last Observation per Group

Stata Program for Selecting Last Observation per Group

```
* Filename: FirstLastObs.do

use c:\myRfolder\mydata, clear
sort workshop gender
by workshop gender: keep if _n==_N
list
```

R Program for Selecting Last Observation per Group

```
# Filename: FirstLastObs.R

setwd("/myRfolder")
load(file="mydata.RData")
mydata
myBys <- data.frame(mydata$workshop,mydata$gender)
mylastList <- by( mydata,myBys,tail,n=1 )
mylastList

#Back into a data frame:
mylastDF <- do.call(rbind, mylastList)
mylastDF
```

```
# Another way to create the dataframe:
mylastDF <- rbind(mylastList[[1]],
                  mylastList[[2]],
                  mylastList[[3]],
                  mylastList[[4]])
mylastDF
```

10.15 Reshaping Variables to Observations and Back

A common data management problem is reshaping data from "wide" format to "long" and back. If we assume our variables q1, q2, q3, and q4 are the same item measured at four times, we will have the standard wide format for repeated measures data.

Converting this to the long format consists of writing out four records, each of which has just one measure—we will call it Y—and a counter variable, often called time, that goes 1, 2, 3, and 4. So in the simplest case, just two variables, Y and time could replace dozens of variables. Going from wide to long is just the reverse.

Stata can do this using the **reshape** command.

In R, Hadley Wickham's **reshape** package is quite powerful and easy to use. It uses the analogy of *melting* your data so that you can *cast* it into a different mold. In addition to reshaping, the package makes quick work of a wide range of aggregation problems.

We will need an ID variable. For this example, we will create one named subject using the colon operator:

```
> mydata$subject <- 1:8

> print(mydata)
```

```
  workshop gender q1 q2 q3 q4 subject
1        1      f  1  1  5  1       1
2        2      f  2  1  4  1       2
3        1      f  2  2  4  3       3
4        2   <NA>  3  1 NA  3       4
5        1      m  4  5  2  4       5
6        2      m  5  4  5  5       6
7        1      m  5  3  4  4       7
8        2      m  4  5  5  5       8
```

Now we will load the **reshape** package, attach the data so that we can use short variable names, and "melt" it into the long form. The **melt** function needs only two arguments: the name of the data frame to reshape and the variables that identify each unique value.

```
> library("reshape")

> attach(mydata)

> mylong <- melt(mydata,
    id=c("subject","workshop","gender") )

> mylong
```

```
   subject workshop gender variable value
1        1        1      f       q1     1
2        2        2      f       q1     2
3        3        1      f       q1     2
4        4        2   <NA>       q1     3
5        5        1      m       q1     4
6        6        2      m       q1     5
7        7        1      m       q1     5
8        8        2      m       q1     4
9        1        1      f       q2     1
10       2        2      f       q2     1
11       3        1      f       q2     2
12       4        2   <NA>       q2     1
13       5        1      m       q2     5
14       6        2      m       q2     4
15       7        1      m       q2     3
16       8        2      m       q2     5
17       1        1      f       q3     5
18       2        2      f       q3     4
19       3        1      f       q3     4
20       4        2   <NA>       q3    NA
21       5        1      m       q3     2
22       6        2      m       q3     5
23       7        1      m       q3     4
24       8        2      m       q3     5
25       1        1      f       q4     1
26       2        2      f       q4     1
27       3        1      f       q4     3
28       4        2   <NA>       q4     3
29       5        1      m       q4     4
30       6        2      m       q4     5
31       7        1      m       q4     4
32       8        2      m       q4     5
```

Now let us cast it back into the wide format.

```
> mywide <- cast(mylong, subject+workshop+gender ~ variable)
```

```
> mywide

  subject workshop gender q1 q2 q3 q4
1       1        1      f  1  1  5  1
2       2        2      f  2  1  4  1
3       3        1      f  2  2  4  3
4       4        2   <NA>  3  1 NA  3
5       5        1      m  4  5  2  4
6       6        2      m  5  4  5  5
7       7        1      m  5  3  4  4
8       8        2      m  4  5  5  5
```

The **cast** function needs only two arguments: the data to reshape and a formula. The formula has the identifying variables on the left side separated by plus signs, then a tilde, "~", and the variable that will contain the new variables' values.

As we have seen with the **reshape** package and others, R's ability to extend its power with packages can be very useful. However, it also occasionally leads to confusion among names. R comes with a *function* named **reshape**, and the **Hmisc** package has one named **reShape**. They are totally different due to the capital "S"! They can both do the task at hand, but the **reshape** *package* is the one we are using. While the package is named **reshape**, the functions to do the reshaping are named **melt** and **cast**.

10.15.1 Example Programs for Reshaping Variables to Observations and Back

Stata Program for Reshaping Data

```
* Filename: Reshape.do

use c:\myRfolder\mydata, clear

reshape long q, i(subject) j(item)
list

reshape wide q, i(subject) j(item)
list
```

R Program for Reshaping Data

```
# Filename: Reshape.R

setwd("/myRfolder")
load(file="mydata.RData")
```

```
# Create an id variable.
mydata$subject <- 1:8
mydata
library("reshape")
attach(mydata)

# Melt data into "long" format.
mylong <- melt(mydata,
   id=c("subject","workshop","gender") )
mylong

# Cast data back into "wide" format.
mywide <- cast(mylong,
   subject+workshop+gender ~ variable)
mywide
```

10.16 Sorting Data Frames

Sorting is one of the areas that R differs most from Stata. In Stata, sorting is critical prerequisite for two frequent tasks:

1. In Stata, using the by operator to perform separate analyses on a variable or set of variables requires that the data be sorted on the variable to which the by operator refers. Stata's sort command is used for this purpose. The gsort command allows sorting in either ascending or descending order. The bysort command allows the user to use the by operator immediately without having to previously sort the data.
2. Stata also requires that both files be sorted on a matched variable before merging files is allowed. Usually, that matching variable is a subject or id.

As we have seen, R does not need the data sorted for either of these tasks. Still, sorting is useful in a variety of contexts.

R sorts in a very different way. It does not directly sort a data frame. Instead, it determines the order that the rows would be in if sorted and then applies them to do the sort.

Consider the names Ann, Eve, Carla, Dave, and Bob. They are almost sorted in ascending order. Since the number of names is small, it is easy to determine the order that the names would require to sort them. We need the first name, Ann, followed by the fifth name, Bob, followed by the third name, Carla, the fourth name, Dave, and, finally, the second name, Eve. The order function would get those index values for us: 1, 5, 3, 4, 2.

To understand how these index values will help us sort, let us review briefly how data frame indexes work. One way to select rows from a data frame is to use the form `mydata[rows,columns]`. If you leave them all out, as in `mydata[ , ]`, then you will get all rows and all columns. You can select the first four records with

```
> mydata[ c(1,2,3,4), ]

  id workshop gender q1 q2 q3 q4
1 1         1      f  1  1  5  1
2 2         2      f  2  1  4  1
3 3         1      f  2  2  4  3
4 4         2   <NA>  3  1 NA  3
```

We can select them in reverse order with

```
> mydata[ c(4,3,2,1), ]

  id workshop gender q1 q2 q3 q4
4 4         2   <NA>  3  1 NA  3
3 3         1      f  2  2  4  3
2 2         2      f  2  1  4  1
1 1         1      f  1  1  5  1
```

Now let us create a variable to store the order of the observations if sorted by workshop:

```
> myW <- order( mydata$workshop )

> myW
[1] 1 3 5 7 2 4 6 8
```

We can use this variable as the row index to mydata to see it sorted by workshop:

```
> mydata[ myW, ]

  id workshop gender q1 q2 q3 q4
1 1         1      f  1  1  5  1
3 3         1      f  2  2  4  3
5 5         1      m  4  5  2  4
7 7         1      m  5  3  4  4
2 2         2      f  2  1  4  1
4 4         2   <NA>  3  1 NA  3
6 6         2      m  5  4  5  5
8 8         2      m  4  5  5  5
```

The `order` function is one of the few R functions that allow you to specify multiple variables without combining them in some way, like into a vector with the c function. So we can create an order variable to sort the data by

gender and then workshop within gender with the following. GW stands for
Gender then Workshop.

```
> myGW <- order( mydata$gender, mydata$workshop )

> mydata[ myGW, ]
```

	id	workshop	gender	q1	q2	q3	q4
1	1	1	f	1	1	5	1
3	3	1	f	2	2	4	3
2	2	2	f	2	1	4	1
5	5	1	m	4	5	2	4
7	7	1	m	5	3	4	4
6	6	2	m	5	4	5	5
8	8	2	m	4	5	5	5
4	4	2	<NA>	3	1	NA	3

The default order is ascending (small to large). To reverse this, place the minus
sign before any variable. Therefore, this will sort by workshop in descending
order and then, within that, gender in ascending order:

```
> mydata$myWG <- order( -mydata$workshop, mydata$gender )

> mydata$myWG
```

```
[1] 2 6 8 4 1 3 5 7
```

The WG part of myWG is an acronym for Workgroup, Gender. Stata and
R both view missing values as the highest, or last, values to sort. You can
use the argument na.last=FALSE to cause R to place NAs first. You can also
remove records with missing values by setting na.last=NA.

To see mydata in sorted order, we then use myWG in the row index
position:

```
> myWdG <- order( -mydata$workshop, mydata$gender )

> mydata[ myWdG, ]
```

	id	workshop	gender	q1	q2	q3	q4
2	2	2	f	2	1	4	1
6	6	2	m	5	4	5	5
8	8	2	m	4	5	5	5
4	4	2	<NA>	3	1	NA	3
1	1	1	f	1	1	5	1
3	3	1	f	2	2	4	3
5	5	1	m	4	5	2	4
7	7	1	m	5	3	4	4

Since it is so easy to create a variable to store your various order indexes in, you do not need to store the whole data frame in sorted form to have easy access to it. However, if you want to, you can save the data frame in sorted form by using

```
> mydataSorted <- mydata[ myWdG,  ]

> mydataSorted
```

	id	workshop	gender	q1	q2	q3	q4
2	2	2	f	2	1	4	1
6	6	2	m	5	4	5	5
8	8	2	m	4	5	5	5
4	4	2	<NA>	3	1	NA	3
1	1	1	f	1	1	5	1
3	3	1	f	2	2	4	3
5	5	1	m	4	5	2	4
7	7	1	m	5	3	4	4

10.16.1 Example Programs for Sorting Data Sets

Stata Program for Sorting Data

```
* Filename: Sort.do

use c:\myRfolder\mydata, clear

* sort workshop ascending order
sort workshop
list

* sort gender and workshop, both ascending order
sort gender workshop
list

* sort workshop descending and gender in ascending order.
gsort - workshop + gender
list
```

R Program for Sorting Data

```
# Filename: Sort.R

setwd("/myRfolder")
load(file="mydata.RData")
mydata
```

```
# Show first four observations in order.
mydata[ c(1,2,3,4), ]

# Show them in reverse order.
mydata[ c(4,3,2,1), ]

# Create order variable for workshop.
myW <- order( mydata$workshop )
myW
mydata[ myW, ]

# Create order variable for gender then workshop.
myGW <- order( mydata$gender, mydata$workshop )
myGW
mydata[ myGW, ]

# Create order variable for
# descending (-) workshop then gender
myWdG <- order( -mydata$workshop, mydata$gender )
myWdG

# Print data in WG order.
mydata[ myWdG, ]

# Save data in WdG order.
mydataSorted <- mydata[ myWdG,  ]
mydataSorted
```

10.17 Converting Data Structures

In Stata, there is only one main data structure—the data set—although it may be established as a time series panel data set using the **tsset** command. Within the data set, there are variables. It seems absurdly obvious, but we need to say it: All Stata commands accept variables as input. Of course, you have to learn that putting a character variable in where a numeric one is expected causes an error. Occasionally, a character variable contains numbers and we must convert them. Putting a categorical variable in where a continuous variable belongs may not yield an error message, but perhaps it should.

As we have seen, R has several data structures, including vectors, factors, data frames, matrices, and lists. For many functions (what Stata calls commands), R can automatically provide output optimized for the data structure you give it. Said more formally, *generic functions apply different methods to*

different classes of objects. So to control a function, you have to know several
things:

1. The classes of objects the function is able to accept.
2. What the function will do with each class; that is, what its method is
   for each. Although many important functions in R offer multiple methods
   (they are generic), not all are.
3. The data structure you are supplying to the function—that is, what the
   class of your object is. As we have seen, the way you select data determines
   its data structure or class.
4. If necessary, how to convert from the data structure you have to one you
   need.

In Chapter 7, "Selecting Variables," we learned that both of these commands select our variable q1 and pass the data in the form of a data frame:

```
mydata[3]
mydata["q1"]
```

while these, with their additional comma, also select variable q1 but instead
pass the data in the form of a vector:

```
mydata[ ,3]
mydata[ ,"q1"]
```

Many functions would work just fine on either result. However, some procedures are fussier than others and require very specific data structures. If
you are having a problem figuring out which form of data you have, there are
functions that will tell you. For example

```
class(mydata)
```

will tell you its class is "data frame." Knowing a data frame is a type of list,
you will know that functions that require either of those structures will accept
it. As with the **print** function, it may produce different output, but it will
accept it. There are also functions that test the status of an object, and they
all begin with "**is.**" For example

```
is.data.frame( mydata[3] )
```

will display TRUE, but

```
is.vector( mydata[3] )
```

will display FALSE.

Some of the functions you can use to convert from one structure to another are listed in Table 10.4. Let us apply one to our data. First, we will
remind ourselves how the **print** function prints our data frame in a vertical
format.

Table 10.4. Data conversion functions.

Conversion to Perform	Example
Index vector to logical vector	`myQindexes <- c(3, 4, 5, 6)`
	`myQtf <- 1:6 %in% myQindexes`
Vectors to columns of a data frame	`data.frame(x,y,z)`
Vectors to rows of a data frame	`data.frame( rbind(x,y,z) )`
Vectors to columns of a matrix	`cbind(x,y,z)`
Vectors to rows of a matrix	`rbind(x,y,z)`
Vectors combined into one long one	`c(x,y,z)`
Data frame to matrix (must be same type)	`as.matrix(mydataframe)`
Matrix to data frame	`as.data.frame(mymatrix)`
A vector to an r by c matrix	`matrix(myvector,nrow=r,ncol=c)`
	(note this is not as.matrix!)
Matrix to one very long vector	`as.vector(mymatrix)`
List to one long vector	`unlist(mylist)`
Lists or data frames into lists	`c(list1,list2)`
List of vectors, matrices to rows of matrix	`myMatrix <- ( do.call(rbind, myList) )`
List of vectors, matrices to cols of matrix	`myMatrix <- ( do.call(cbind, myList) )`
Logical vector to index vector	`myQtf <- c(FALSE, FALSE,`
	`      TRUE, TRUE, TRUE, TRUE)`
	`myQindexes <- which(myQtf)`
Table to data frame	`as.data.frame(mytable)`
Remove the class completely	`unclass(myobject)`

```
> print(mydata)

  workshop gender q1 q2 q3 q4
1        R      f  1  1  5  1
2    Stata      f  2  1  4  1
3        R      f  2  2  4  3
4    Stata   <NA>  3  1 NA  3
5        R      m  4  5  2  4
6    Stata      m  5  4  5  5
7        R      m  5  3  4  4
8    Stata      m  4  5  5  9
```

Now let us print it in list form by adding the `as.list` function. Essentially, the data frame becomes a list at the moment of printing, giving us the horizontal orientation that we saw earlier when printing a true list.

```
> print( as.list(mydata) )
```

```
$workshop
[1] R     Stata R    Stata R    Stata R    Stata
Levels: R SAS SPSS STATA

$gender
[1] f     f     f     <NA> m     m     m     m
Levels: f m

$q1
[1] 1 2 2 3 4 5 5 4

$q2
[1] 1 1 2 1 5 4 3 5

$q3
[1]  5  4  4 NA  2  5  4  5

$q4
[1] 1 1 3 3 4 5 4 9
```

10.17.1 Converting from Logical to Numeric Index and Back

We have looked at various ways to select variables and observations using both logical and numerical indexes. Now let us look at how to convert from one to the other.

The which function will examine a logical vector and tell you which of them are true; that is, it will tell you the index values of those that are true. We can create a logical vector that chooses our q variables many ways. Let us use the vector that selects the last four variables in our practice data frame. For various ways to create a vector like this, See Chapter 7, "Selecting Variables" or Chapter 8, "Selecting Observations." We will just enter it manually.

```
myQtf <- c(FALSE, FALSE, TRUE, TRUE, TRUE, TRUE)
```

We can convert that to a numeric index vector that gives us the index numbers for each occurrence of the value TRUE using the which function.

```
myQindexes <- which(myQtf)
```

Now myQindexes contains 3, 4, 5, 6 and we can analyze just the q variables using

```
summary( mydata[myQindexes] )
```

To go in the reverse direction, we would want to know of all of the variable indexes—1, 2, 3, 4, 5, 6—which of them were, in a logical sense, in our list of 3, 4, 5, 6.

```
myQindexes <- c(3, 4, 5, 6)
```

Now we will use the %in% function to create it using logical comparisons:

```
myQtf <- 1:6 %in% myQindexes
```

Now myQtf has the values FALSE, FALSE, TRUE, TRUE, TRUE, TRUE and we can analyze just the Q variables with

```
summary( mydata[myQtf] )
```

Why are there two methods? The logical method is the most direct, since calling the which function is often an additional step. However, if you have 20,000 variables, as researchers in genetics often have, the logical vector will contain 20,000 values. The numeric index vector will have only as many values as there are variables in your subset. The which function also has a critical advantage. Since it looks only to see which values are TRUE, the NA missing values do not affect it. Using a logical vector, R will look at all values, TRUE, FALSE, even the missing values of NA. However, the selection mydata[NA ,] is undefined, causing problems. See Chapter 8, "Selecting Observations" for details.

11

Enhancing Your Output

As we have seen, R output is quite sparse and not nicely formatted for word processing. As in Stata, you can improve R's output by adding value and variable labels. You can also format the output to make beautiful tables to use with word processors, web pages, and document preparation systems.

11.1 Value Labels or Formats (and Measurement Level)

This section blends two topics because in R they are inseparable. In Stata, assigning labels to values is independent of the variable's measurement level. In R, you can assign value labels only to variables whose measurement level is *factor*. To be more precise, only objects whose class is factor can have label attributes.

In Stata, a variable's measurement level of nominal, ordinal, or interval is not stored. Instead, how you use the variable dictates whether a variable is viewed as continuous, categorical, or even binary. You can model a binary predictor as if it were continuous, although this would not be wise.

Stata uses value labels in a two-step process. For a categorical variable, you first define the various levels of the variable using the "label define" command, and then you specify that the defined levels correspond to values provided to the levels. We will show an example below.

R has the measurement level of factor for nominal data, ordered factor for ordinal data, and numeric for interval or scale data. You set these in advance and then the statistical and graphical procedures use them in an appropriate way automatically. When creating a factor, assigning labels is optional. If you do not use labels, the variable's original values are stored as character labels. R stores value labels in the factor itself.

R.A. Muenchen, J.M. Hilbe, *R for Stata Users*, Statistics
and Computing, DOI 10.1007/978-1-4419-1318-0_11,
© Springer Science+Business Media, LLC 2010

11.1.1 Character Factors

Let us review how the `read.table` function deals with character variables. If we do not tell it what to do, it will convert all character data to factors.

```
> mydata <- read.table("mydata.tab")

> mydata

    workshop gender q1 q2 q3 q4
1          1      f  1  1  5  1
2          2      f  2  1  4  1
3          1      f  2  2  4  3
4          2   <NA>  3  1 NA  3
5          1      m  4  5  2  4
6          2      m  5  4  5  5
7          1      m  5  3  4  4
8          2      m  4  5  5  5
```

You cannot tell what gender is by looking at it, but the `class` function can tell us that gender is a factor.

```
> class( mydata[ ,"gender"] )

[1] "factor"
```

In our case, this is helpful. However, there are times when you want to leave character data as simply characters. When reading people's names or addresses from a database, for example, you do not want to store them as factors. The argument `stringsAsFactors=FALSE` will tell the `read.table` function to leave such variables as character.

```
> mydata2 <- read.table("mydata.tab",
+    stringsAsFactors=FALSE)

> mydata2

    workshop gender q1 q2 q3 q4
1          1      f  1  1  5  1
2          2      f  2  1  4  1
3          1      f  2  2  4  3
4          2   <NA>  3  1 NA  3
5          1      m  4  5  2  4
6          2      m  5  4  5  5
7          1      m  5  3  4  4
8          2      m  4  5  5  5
```

This sets how all of the character variables are read, so if some of them do need to be factors, you can convert those afterward. The data looks just the same, but the `class` function can verify that gender is indeed now a character variable.

```
> class( mydata2[ ,"gender"] )
```

```
[1] "character"
```

Many functions will not do what you expect with character data. For example, we have seen the `summary` function count factor levels. However, it will not count them in character form. If these were names or addresses, there would be little use in counting them to see that they were virtually all unique. Instead, `summary` simply gives you the grand total (length) and the variable's class and mode:

```
> summary( mydata2$gender )
```

```
  Length      Class       Mode
       8  character  character
```

We will focus on the first data frame that has gender as a factor. As `read.table` scans the data, it assigns the numeric values to the character values in alphabetical order. Therefore, gender gets 1 for "f" and 2 for "m" since "f" precedes "m" in the alphabet. R always uses the numbers 1, 2, ... However, if you use the factor in an analysis, say as a regression predictor, it will do the proper coding for you automatically. For character data, these defaults are often sufficient. If you supply the `levels` argument in the `factor` function, you can use it to specify the order of label assignment:

```
mydata$genderF <- factor(
   mydata$gender,
   levels=c("m","f"),
   labels=c("Male","Female") )
```

The `factor` function call above has three arguments.

1. The name of the factor.
2. The `levels` argument with the levels *in order*. Since "m" appears first, it will be associated with 1 and "f" with 2.
3. The `labels` argument provides labels in the same order as the `levels` argument. This example sets "m" as 1 and "f" as 2 and uses the fully written out labels. If you leave the labels out, R will use the levels themselves as labels. In this case, the labels would be simply "m" and "f." That is how we will leave our practice data set, as it keeps the examples shorter.

There is a danger in setting value labels with character data that does not appear at all in Stata. In the function call above, if we instead set

```
levels=c("m","F")
```

R would set the values for all females to missing (NA), because the actual values are lowercase. There are no capital F's in the data! This danger applies, of course, to other more obvious misspellings.

11.1.2 Numeric Factors

Workshop is a categorical measure, but initially R assumes it is numeric because it is entered as 1 and 2. If we do any analysis on workshop, it will be as an integer variable.

```
> class( mydata$workshop )

[1] "integer"

> summary( mydata$workshop )

  Min. 1st Qu.  Median    Mean 3rd Qu.    Max.
   1.0     1.0     1.5     1.5     2.0     2.0
```

We can nest a call to the **as.factor** function into any analysis to overcome this problem.

```
> summary( as.factor(mydata$workshop) )

1 2
4 4
```

So we see four people took workshops 1 and 2. The values 1 and 2 are merely labels at this point.

We can use the **factor** function to convert it to a factor and optionally assign labels. Factor labels in R are stored in the factor itself.

```
mydata$workshop <- factor(
  mydata$workshop,
  levels=c(1,2,3,4),
  labels=c("R","Stata","SPSS","SAS")
)
```

Notice that we have assigned four labels to four values even though our data only contain the values 1 and 2. This can ensure consistent value label assignments regardless of the data we currently have on hand. If we collected another data set in which people only took SPSS and Stata workshops, we do not want 1=R in one data set and 1=SPSS in another!

To simplify our other examples, we will use only the labels that appear in this small data set.

```
mydata$workshop <- factor(
  mydata$workshop,
  levels=c(1,2,3,4),
  labels=c("R","Stata")
)
```

Now let us convert our q variables to factors. Since we will need to specify the same levels repeatedly, let us put them in a variable.

```
> myQlevels <- c(1,2,3,4,5)

> myQlevels

[1] 1 2 3 4 5
```

Now we will do the same for the labels.

```
> myQlabels <- c("Strongly Disagree",
+                "Disagree",
+                "Neutral",
+                "Agree",
+                "Strongly Agree")

> myQlabels

[1] "Strongly Disagree" "Disagree"          "Neutral"
[4] "Agree"             "Strongly Agree"
```

Finally, we will use the `ordered` function to complete the process. It works just like the `factor` function but tells R that the data values have order. In statistical terms, it sets the variable's measurement level to ordinal. Ordered factors allow you to perform logical comparisons of greater than or less than. R's statistical modeling functions also try to treat ordinal data appropriately. However, some methods are influenced by the assumption that the ordered values are equally spaced, which may not be the case in your data.

We will put the factors into new variables with an "f" for *f*actor in their names, like qf1 for q1. The f is just there to help us remember; it has no meaning to R. We will keep both sets of variables because people who do survey research often want to view this type of variable as numeric for some analyses and as categorical for others. It is not necessary to do this if you prefer converting back and forth on the fly.

```
> mydata$qf1 <- ordered( mydata$q1, myQlevels, myQlabels)
> mydata$qf2 <- ordered( mydata$q2, myQlevels, myQlabels)
> mydata$qf3 <- ordered( mydata$q3, myQlevels, myQlabels)
> mydata$qf4 <- ordered( mydata$q4, myQlevels, myQlabels)
```

Now we can use the **summary** function to get frequency tables on them, complete with value labels.

```
> summary( mydata[ c("qf1","qf2","qf3","qf4") ] )
```

```
                    qf1                      qf2                      qf3
Strongly Disagree:1  Strongly Disagree:3  Strongly Disagree:0
Disagree         :2  Disagree         :1  Disagree         :1
Neutral          :1  Neutral          :1  Neutral          :0
Agree            :2  Agree            :1  Agree            :3
Strongly Agree   :2  Strongly Agree   :2  Strongly Agree   :3
                                          NA's             :1
                    qf4
Strongly Disagree:3
Disagree         :0
Neutral          :2
Agree            :2
Strongly Agree   :1
```

11.1.3 Making Factors of Many Variables

The approach used above works fine for small numbers of variables. However, if you have hundreds, it is needlessly tedious. We do the same thing again, this time in a form that would handle any number of variables whose names follow the format string1 to stringN. Our practice data only has q1 to q4, but the same number of commands would handle q1 to q4000.

First, we will generate variable names to use. We will use qf to represent the q variables in factor form. This is an optional step, needed only if you want to keep the variables in both forms.

```
> myQnames <- paste( "q",  1:4, sep="")

> myQnames

[1] "q1" "q2" "q3" "q4"

> myQFnames <- paste( "qf", 1:4, sep="")

> myQFnames

[1] "qf1" "qf2" "qf3" "qf4"
```

Now we will use the myQnames character vector as column names to select from our data frame. We will store those in a separate data frame.

```
> myQFvars <- mydata[ ,myQnames]
```

```
> myQFvars
```

```
  q1 q2 q3 q4
1  1  1  5  1
2  2  1  4  1
3  2  2  4  3
4  3  1 NA  3
5  4  5  2  4
6  5  4  5  5
7  5  3  4  4
8  4  5  5  5
```

Next, we will use the myQFnames character vector to rename these variables.

```
> names(myQFvars) <- myQFnames
```

```
> myQFvars
```

```
  qf1 qf2 qf3 qf4
1   1   1   5   1
2   2   1   4   1
3   2   2   4   3
4   3   1  NA   3
5   4   5   2   4
6   5   4   5   5
7   5   3   4   4
8   4   5   5   5
```

Now we need to make up a function to apply to the variables.

```
myLabeler <- function(x) {
  ordered(x, myQlevels, myQlabels)
}
```

The mylabeler function will apply myQlevels and myQlabels (defined in Subsection 11.1.2) to any variable, x, that we supply to it. Let us try it on a single variable.

```
> summary( myLabeler( myQFvars[ ,"qf1"] ) )
```

```
Strongly Disagree      Disagree      Neutral        Agree
                1             2            1            2
   Strongly Agree
                2
```

It is important to understand that the mylabeler function will work only on vectors, since the ordered function requires them. Removing the comma in the above command would select a data frame containing only q1f, instead of a vector, and this would not work.

```
> summary( myLabeler(myQFvars["qf1"]) ) # Doesn't work!
```

```
Strongly Disagree        Disagree      Neutral          Agree
                0               0            0              0
    Strongly Agree           NA's
                0               1
```

Now we will use the **sapply** function to apply **myLabeler** to myQFvars.

```
myQFvars <- data.frame( sapply( myQFvars, myLabeler ) )
```

The **sapply** function simplified the result to a matrix and the **data.frame** function converted that to a data frame. Now the **summary** function will count the values and display their labels.

```
> summary(myQFvars)
```

```
                     qf1                    qf2                   qf3
 Agree             :2  Agree             :1  Agree             :3
 Disagree          :2  Disagree          :1  Disagree          :1
 Neutral           :1  Neutral           :1  Strongly Agree    :3
 Strongly Agree    :2  Strongly Agree    :2  NA's              :1
 Strongly Disagree :1  Strongly Disagree :3
                     qf4
 Agree             :2
 Neutral           :2
 Strongly Agree    :2
 Strongly Disagree :2
```

If you care to, you can bind myQFvars to our original data frame.

```
mydata <- cbind(mydata, myQFvars)
```

11.1.4 Converting Factors into Numeric or Character Variables

R has functions for converting factors into numeric or character vectors (variables). To extract the numeric values from a factor like gender, we can use the **as.numeric** function.

```
> mydata$genderNums <- as.numeric( mydata$gender )
```

```
> mydata$genderNums
```

```
[1]  1  1  1 NA  2  2  2  2
```

If we want to extract the labels themselves to use in a character vector, we can do so with the as.character function.

```
> mydata$genderChars <- as.character( mydata$gender)

> mydata$genderChars

[1] "f" "f" "f" NA  "m" "m" "m" "m"
```

We can apply the same two functions to variable qf1. Since we were careful to set all of the levels, even for those that did not appear in the data, this works fine. First, we will do it using as.numeric.

```
> mydata$qf1Nums <- as.numeric(mydata$qf1)

> mydata$qf1Nums

[1] 1 2 2 3 4 5 5 4
```

Now let us do it again using the as.character function.

```
> mydata$qf1Chars <- as.character(mydata$qf1)

> mydata$qf1Chars

[1] "Strongly Disagree" "Disagree"  "Disagree"
[4] "Neutral"           "Agree"     "Strongly Agree"
[7] "Strongly Agree"    "Agree"
```

Where you can run into trouble is when you do not specify the original numeric values, and they are not simply 1, 2, 3,.... For example, let us create a variable whose original values are 10, 20, 30:

```
> x <- c(10,20,30)

> x

[1] 10 20 30

> xf <- as.factor(x)

> xf

[1] 10 20 30
Levels: 10 20 30
```

So far, the factor xf looks fine. However, when we try to extract the original values with the as.numeric function, we get, instead, the levels 1, 2, 3!

```
> as.numeric(xf)
[1] 1 2 3
```

If we use **as.character** to get the values, there are no nice value labels, so we get character versions of the original values.

```
> as.character(xf)
```

```
[1] "10" "20" "30"
```

If we want those original values in a numeric vector like the one we began with, we can use **as.numeric** to convert them. To extract the original values and store them in a variable x10, we can use the following:

```
> x10 <- as.numeric( as.character(xf) )
```

```
> x10
```

```
[1] 10 20 30
```

The original values were automatically stored as value labels. If you had specified value labels of your own, like low, medium, and high, the original values would have been lost. You would then have to recode the values to get them back. For details, see Section 10.7, "Recoding Variables."

11.1.5 Dropping Factor Levels

Earlier in this chapter, we created labels for factor levels that did not exist in our data. While it is not at all necessary, it is helpful if you were to enter more data or merge your data frame with others that have a full set of values. However, when using such variables in analysis, it is often helpful to get rid of such empty levels.

To get rid of the unused levels, append [,drop=TRUE] to the variable reference. For example, if you want to include the empty levels, skip the **drop** argument.

```
> summary( workshop )

   R   Stata  SPSS SAS
   4     4     0    0
```

However, when you need to get rid of empty levels, add the **drop** argument.

```
> summary( workshop[ ,drop=TRUE])

   R Stata
   4    4
```

11.1.6 Example Programs for Value Labels or Formats

Stata Program to Assign Value Labels

Note: In Stata, one may not label strings. Therefore, given that gender is coded as a string with values of "f" and "m," it cannot be further labeled. It is, though, common in Stata to have a labeled categorical numeric variable. The labels are displayed on the screen unless one uses the NOLABEL option.

```
* Filename: ValueLabels.do

use c:\myRfolder\mydata, clear
label define workshop 1 "R" 2 "Stata"
label values workshop workshop
label define agreement 1 "Strongly Disagree" 2 "Disagree" //
3 "Neutral" 4 "Agree" 5 "Strongly Agree"
label values q1-q4 agreement
```

R Program to Assign Value Labels and Factor Status

```
# Filename: ValueLabels.R

setwd("f:/myRfolder")

#---Character Factors---

# Read gender as factor.
mydata <- read.table("mydata.tab")
mydata
class( mydata[ ,"gender"] )

# Read gender as character.
mydata2 <- read.table("mydata.tab", as.is=TRUE)
mydata2
class( mydata2[ ,"gender"] )
summary( mydata2$gender )
rm(mydata2)

#---Numeric Factors---

class( mydata$workshop )
summary( mydata$workshop )

summary( as.factor(mydata$workshop) )
```

```
# Now change workshop into a factor:
mydata$workshop <- factor( mydata$workshop,
  levels=c(1,2,3,4),
  labels=c("R","SAS","SPSS","Stata") )
mydata

# Now summary only counts workshop attendance.
summary(mydata$workshop)

#---Making the Q Variables Factors---

# Store levels to use repeatedly.
myQlevels <- c(1,2,3,4,5)
myQlevels

# Store labels to use repeatedly.
myQlabels <- c("Strongly Disagree",
               "Disagree",
               "Neutral",
               "Agree",
               "Strongly Agree")
myQlabels

mydata$qf1 <- ordered( mydata$q1, myQlevels, myQlabels)
mydata$qf2 <- ordered( mydata$q2, myQlevels, myQlabels)
mydata$qf3 <- ordered( mydata$q3, myQlevels, myQlabels)
mydata$qf4 <- ordered( mydata$q4, myQlevels, myQlabels)

# Get summary and see that workshops are now counted.
summary( mydata[ c("qf1","qf2","qf3","qf4") ] )

#---An Approach for Many Numbered Variables---

# Generate two sets of var names to use.
myQnames  <- paste( "q",  1:4, sep="")
myQnames
myQFnames <- paste( "qf", 1:4, sep="")
myQFnames

# Extract the q variables to a separate data frame.
myQFvars <- mydata[ ,myQnames]
myQFvars

# Rename all of the variables with F for Factor.
names(myQFvars) <- myQFnames
```

```
myQFvars

# Create a function to apply the labels to lots of variables.
myLabeler <- function(x) {
  ordered(x, myQlevels, myQlabels)
}

# Using the function on one variable.
summary( myLabeler(myQFvars[,"qf1"]) )
summary( myLabeler(myQFvars["qf1"]) ) # Doesn't work!

# Appling it to all of the variables.
myQFvars <- data.frame( sapply( myQFvars, myLabeler ) )

# Get summary again, this time with labels.
summary(myQFvars)

# Joining the new factors to mydata.
mydata <- cbind(mydata,myQFvars)
mydata

#---Converting Factors to Character/Numeric---

# Converting the gender factor, first with as.numeric.
mydata$genderNums <- as.numeric( mydata$gender )
mydata$genderNums

# Again with as.character.
mydata$genderChars <- as.character( mydata$gender)
mydata$genderChars

# Converting the qf1 factor.
mydata$qf1Nums <- as.numeric(mydata$qf1)
mydata$qf1Nums

mydata$qf1Chars <- as.character(mydata$qf1)
mydata$qf1Chars

# Example with bigger values.
x <- c(10,20,30)
x
xf <- factor(x)
xf
as.numeric(xf)
as.character(xf)
```

```
x10 <- as.numeric( as.character(xf) )
x10
```

11.2 Variable Labels

Perhaps the most fundamental feature missing from the main R distribution is support for variable labels. It does have a *comment attribute* that you can apply to each variable, but only the `comment` function itself will display it.

In Stata, you might name a variable BP and want your publication-ready output to display "Systolic Blood Pressure" instead. Stata does this using the `label define` command. We discussed this in part in the previous chapter.

Survey researchers in particular rely on variable labels. They often name their variables Q1, Q2, and so on and assign labels as the full text of the survey items. R is the only statistics package that we are aware of that lacks this feature.

11.2.1 Variable Labels in The Hmisc Package

It is a testament to R's openness and flexibility that a user can add such a fundamental feature. Frank Harrell did just that in his `Hmisc` package [14]. It adds a *label attribute* to the data frame and stores the labels there. The fact that variable labels were not included in the main distribution means that most procedures do not take advantage of what `Hmisc` adds. The many wonderful functions in the `Hmisc` package do, of course.

Unfortunately, some functions, like `barplot`, no longer work with the variables once you have labeled them. So it is best to make a copy of your data frame, apply the labels to it, and only use that version of your data set when using functions from the `Hmisc` package. Use your original copy for your other analyses.

The `Hmisc` package creates variable labels using its `label` function.

```
library("Hmisc")

label(mydata$q1) <- "The instructor was well prepared."
label(mydata$q2) <- "The instructor communicated well."
label(mydata$q3) <- "The course materials were helpful."
label(mydata$q4) <- "Overall, I found this workshop useful."
```

Now the `Hmisc` `describe` function will take advantage of the labels.

```
> describe( mydata[ ,3:6] )

mydata[, 3:6]

  4  Variables      8  Observations
```

```
----------------------------------------------------------
q1 : The instructor was well prepared.
       n missing  unique     Mean
       8       0       5     3.25
              1  2  3  4  5
Frequency  1  2  1  2  2
%            12 25 12 25 25
----------------------------------------------------------
q2 : The instructor communicated well.
       n missing  unique     Mean
       8       0       5     2.75
              1  2  3  4  5
Frequency  3  1  1  1  2
%            38 12 12 12 25
----------------------------------------------------------
q3 : The course materials were helpful.
       n missing  unique     Mean
       7       1       3    4.143
2 (1, 14%), 4 (3, 43%), 5 (3, 43%)
----------------------------------------------------------
q4 : Overall, I found this workshop useful.
       n missing  unique     Mean
       8       0       4     3.25
1 (2, 25%), 3 (2, 25%), 4 (2, 25%), 5 (2, 25%)
----------------------------------------------------------
```

As we see below, built-in functions such as **summary** ignore the labels.

```
> summary( mydata[ ,3:6] )
```

```
      q1              q2              q3              q4
 Min.   :1.00   Min.   :1.00   Min.   :2.00   Min.   :1.00
 1st Qu.:2.00   1st Qu.:1.00   1st Qu.:4.00   1st Qu.:2.50
 Median :3.50   Median :2.50   Median :4.00   Median :3.50
 Mean   :3.25   Mean   :2.75   Mean   :4.14   Mean   :3.25
 3rd Qu.:4.25   3rd Qu.:4.25   3rd Qu.:5.00   3rd Qu.:4.25
 Max.   :5.00   Max.   :5.00   Max.   :5.00   Max.   :5.00
                               NA's   :1.00
```

11.2.2 Long Variable Names as Labels

You can use illegal variable names of any length by enclosing them in quotes.
This has the advantage of working with most R functions.

```
> names(mydata) <- c("Workshop","Gender",
+    "The instructor was well prepared.",
```

```
+    "The instructor communicated well.",
+    "The course materials were helpful.",
+    "Overall, I found this workshop useful.")
```

Notice here that names like q1, q2,... do not exist now. The labels *are* the variable names.

```
> names(mydata)
```

```
[1] "Workshop"
[2] "Gender"
[3] "The instructor was well prepared."
[4] "The instructor communicated well."
[5] "The course materials were helpful."
[6] "Overall, I found this workshop useful."
```

Now many R functions, even those built-in, will use the labels. Here we select the variables by their numeric index values rather than their names:

```
> summary( mydata[ ,3:6] )
 The instructor was well prepared.
 Min.    :1.00
 1st Qu.:2.00
 Median :3.50
 Mean    :3.25
 3rd Qu.:4.25
 Max.    :5.00

 The instructor communicated well.
 Min.    :1.00
 1st Qu.:1.00
 Median :2.50
 Mean    :2.75
 3rd Qu.:4.25
 Max.    :5.00
 ...
```

You can still select variables by their names, but now typing the whole name out is an absurd amount of work!

```
> summary( mydata["Overall, I found this workshop useful."] )

 Overall, I found this workshop useful.
 Min.    :1.00
 1st Qu.:2.50
 Median :3.50
 Mean    :3.25
```

```
3rd Qu.:4.25
Max.    :5.00
```

In addition to selecting variables by their index number, it is also easy to search for keywords in long variable names using the **grep** function. For details, see Section 7.6, "Selecting Variables by String Search." The **grep** function call below finds the two variable names containing the string "instructor" in variables 3 and 4 and then stores their locations in a numeric index vector:

```
> myvars <- grep( 'instructor', names(mydata) )

> myvars

[1] 3 4
```

Now we can use those indexes to analyze the selected variables:

```
> summary ( mydata[myvars] )

The instructor was well prepared.
Min.    :1.00
1st Qu.:2.00
Median :3.50
Mean    :3.25
3rd Qu.:4.25
Max.    :5.00

The instructor communicated well.
Min.    :1.00
1st Qu.:1.00
Median :2.50
Mean    :2.75
3rd Qu.:4.25
Max.    :5.00
```

Some important R functions, such as **data.frame**, convert the spaces in the labels to periods.

```
> newdata <- data.frame( mydata )

> names( newdata[ ,3:6] )
[1] "The.instructor.was.well.prepared."
[2] "The.instructor.communicated.well."
[3] "The.course.materials.were.helpful."
[4] "Overall..I.found.this.workshop.useful."
```

To avoid this change, add the **check.names=FALSE** argument to the **data.frame** function call.

```
> newdata <- data.frame(mydata, check.names=FALSE)

> names( newdata[ ,3:6] )

[1] "The instructor was well prepared."
[2] "The instructor communicated well."
[3] "The course materials were helpful."
[4] "Overall, I found this workshop useful."
```

11.2.3 Other Packages That Support Variable Labels

There are at least two other packages that support variable labels. Unfortunately, we have not had a chance to use them. Martin Elff's memisc package [10] offers a wide range of tools for survey research. Jim Lemon and Philippe Grosjean's prettyR package [30] stores variable labels as character variables.

11.2.4 Example Programs for Variable Labels

Stata Program for Variable Labels

```
* Filename: VarLabels.do

use c:\myRfolder\mydata, clear
label var q1 "The instructor was well prepared"
label var q2 "The instructor communicated well"
label var q3 "The course materials were helpful"
label var q4 "Overall, I found this workshop useful"

* summarize the q variables
sum q*
```

R Program for Variable Labels

```
# Filename: VarLabels.R

setwd("/myRfolder")
load(file="mydata.RData")
options(width=64)
mydata

# Using the Hmisc label attribute.
library("Hmisc")
label(mydata$q1) <- "The instructor was well prepared."
label(mydata$q2) <- "The instructor communicated well."
label(mydata$q3) <- "The course materials were helpful."
```

```
label(mydata$q4) <-
  "Overall, I found this workshop useful."

# Hmisc describe function uses the labels.
describe( mydata[ ,3:6] )

# Buit-in summary function ignores the labels.
summary( mydata[ ,3:6] )

#Assign long variable names to act as variable labels.
names(mydata) <- c("Workshop","Gender",
  "The instructor was well prepared.",
  "The instructor communicated well.",
  "The course materials were helpful.",
  "Overall, I found this workshop useful.")

names(mydata)

# Now summary uses the long names.
summary( mydata[ ,3:6] )

# You can still select variables by name.
summary( mydata["Overall, I found this workshop useful."] )

# Searching for strings in long variable names.
myvars <- grep('instructor',names(mydata))
myvars
summary ( mydata[myvars] )

# Data.frame replaces spaces with periods.
newdata <- data.frame( mydata )
names( newdata[ ,3:6] )

# Data.frame now keeps the spaces.
newdata <- data.frame( mydata, check.names=FALSE )
names( newdata[ ,3:6] )
```

11.3 Output for Word Processing and Web Pages

Hypertext Markup Language, or *HTML*, is the format used for displaying results on web pages. Most word processors can also easily incorporate HTML files. For technical writing, the popular LATEX document preparation system and the LyX document processor share a common format for displaying tables of results.

In Stata, getting tabular results into your word processor or web page is as easy as selecting it and choosing, *Edit>Copy, Copy Table* or *Copy Table as HTML*. Then you just paste it where you need it. It also has specialized, user-written commands like `outreg2` and `outtex`.

In R, the output in the console is just text. It does not even have tabs between columns. You can cut and paste it into a word processor, but it would only appear in neat columns when displayed with a mono-spaced font like Courier.

However, there are a number of packages and functions that enable you to create nicely formatted results.

Table 11.1. Our practice data set printed in LATEX.

	workshop	gender	q1	q2	q3	q4
1	R	f	1.00	1.00	5.00	1.00
2	SAS	f	2.00	1.00	4.00	1.00
3	R	f	2.00	2.00	4.00	3.00
4	SAS		3.00	1.00		3.00
5	R	m	4.00	5.00	2.00	4.00
6	SAS	m	5.00	4.00	5.00	5.00
7	R	m	5.00	3.00	4.00	4.00
8	SAS	m	4.00	5.00	5.00	5.00

11.3.1 The `xtable` Package

David Dahl's `xtable` package [8] can convert your R results into both HTML and LATEX. The following is our practice data frame as it appears from the `print` function.

```
> print(mydata)

  workshop gender q1 q2 q3 q4
1        R      f  1  1  5  1
2      SAS      f  2  1  4  1
3        R      f  2  2  4  3
4      SAS   <NA>  3  1 NA  3
5        R      m  4  5  2  4
6      SAS      m  5  4  5  5
7        R      m  5  3  4  4
8      SAS      m  4  5  5  5
```

In Table 11.1, you can see mydata printed again after loading the `xtable` package. How did we get such nice output? The following are the function calls and output:

```
> library("xtable")

> myXtable <- xtable(mydata)

> print(myXtable, type="latex")

% latex table generated in R 2.9.2 by xtable 1.5-5 package
% Sat Oct 17 11:55:58 2009
\begin{table}[ht]
\begin{center}
\begin{tabular}{rllrrrr}
  \hline
 & workshop & gender & q1 & q2 & q3 & q4 \\
  \hline
1 & R & f & 1.00 & 1.00 & 5.00 & 1.00 \\
  2 & SAS & f & 2.00 & 1.00 & 4.00 & 1.00 \\
  3 & R & f & 2.00 & 2.00 & 4.00 & 3.00 \\
  4 & SAS &  & 3.00 & 1.00 &  & 3.00 \\
  5 & R & m & 4.00 & 5.00 & 2.00 & 4.00 \\
  6 & SAS & m & 5.00 & 4.00 & 5.00 & 5.00 \\
  7 & R & m & 5.00 & 3.00 & 4.00 & 4.00 \\
  8 & SAS & m & 4.00 & 5.00 & 5.00 & 5.00 \\
   \hline
\end{tabular}
\end{center}
\end{table}
```

Notice that the **print** command has a new method for handling objects with a class of *xtable*, and a new **type** argument. The value, **type="latex"** is the default, so we did not need to list it here. However, it makes it easy to guess that **type="html"** is the way to get HTML output.

The LATEX output begins with the line "% latex table generated in R...." If you are not accustomed to the LATEX language, it may see quite odd, but when we pasted it into this chapter, it came out looking nice.

If we had instead used **type="html"**, we could have used the output on web pages or in most any word processor.

The following is another example, this time using the output from a linear model that we will examine later in Section 17.5, "Linear Regression."

```
> mymodel <- lm( q4~q1+q2+q3, data=mydata)

> myXtable <- xtable(mymodel)
```

Before printing the result, let us add a label and caption to the result. If this were an HTML file, these commands would add an anchor and a title, respectively.

```
> label(myXtable) <- c("xtableOutput")

> caption(myXtable) <-
+   c("Linear model results formatted by xtable.")

> print(myXtable,type="latex")

% latex table generated in R 2.9.2 by xtable 1.5-5 package
% Sat Oct 17 12:49:59 2009
\begin{table}[ht]
\begin{center}
\begin{tabular}{rrrrr}
  \hline
 & Estimate & Std. Error & t value & Pr($>$$|$$t$|$) \\
  \hline
(Intercept) & -1.3243 & 1.2877 & -1.03 & 0.3794 \\
  q1 & 0.4297 & 0.2623 & 1.64 & 0.1999 \\
  q2 & 0.6310 & 0.2503 & 2.52 & 0.0861 \\
  q3 & 0.3150 & 0.2557 & 1.23 & 0.3058 \\
   \hline
\end{tabular}
\caption{Linear model results formatted by xtable.}
\label{xtableOutput}
\end{center}
\end{table}
```

The caption and label appear near the bottom of the output. You can see the nicely formatted table in Table 11.2. We cheated a bit on the previous table by adding the caption manually.

Table 11.2. Linear model results formatted by xtable

	Estimate	Std. Error	t value	Pr($>|t|$)
(Intercept)	-1.3243	1.2877	-1.03	0.3794
q1	0.4297	0.2623	1.64	0.1999
q2	0.6310	0.2503	2.52	0.0861
q3	0.3150	0.2557	1.23	0.3058

11.3.2 Other Options for Formatting Output

There several other packages that can provide nicely formatted output. Roger Koenker's quantreg package [24] includes the latex.table function, which creates LaTeX output. Eric Lecoutre'S R2HTML package [28] includes over a dozen functions for writing output in HTML format.

Perhaps the most interesting options to get nice output are the Sweave function and ODFweave package. Friedrich Leisch's Sweave function [29] comes with the main R installation. It allows you to "weave" your R program into your LaTeX or LyX file. When you compile your document, the R programming code is replaced with R output! This means that you have a single document that contains both your analysis and the resulting report.

The odfWeave package [26] by Max Kuhn and Steve Weaston works similarly to Sweave but using the *Open Document Format*, or *ODF*. Many word processors, including Microsoft Word and OpenOffice, can work with ODF files.

11.3.3 Example Programs for Formatting Output

Stata Program for Creating Nice Output

```
* Filename: NiceOutput.do

use c:\myRfolder\mydata, list
regress q4  q1 q2 q3
outtex
```

R Program for Creating Nice Output

```
# Filename: NiceOutput.R

options(width=60)
setwd("/myRfolder")
load("mydata.RData")
attach(mydata)

library("xtable")

# Formatting a Data Frame

print(mydata)
myXtable <- xtable(mydata)
class(myXtable)

print(myXtable, type="html")
print(myXtable, type="latex")

# Formatting a Linear Model
```

```
mymodel <- lm( q4~q1+q2+q3, data=mydata)
myXtable <- xtable(mymodel)

label(myXtable) <- c("xtableOutput")
caption(myXtable) <-
  c("Linear model results formatted by xtable")

print(myXtable,type="html")
print(myXtable,type="latex")
```

12

Generating Data

Stata can generate data in a number of ways. The simplest is by use of the **generate** command. It can generate data in loops and through the use of matrix operations as well.

Generating data is important to both R and Stata users. As we have seen, many R functions are controlled by numeric, character, or logical vectors. You can generate those vectors using the methods in this chapter, making quick work of otherwise tedious tasks.

The following are some of the ways we have used vectors as arguments to R functions.

- To create variable names that follow a pattern like q1, q2,... using the **paste** function For an example, see Chap 7.
- To create a set of index values to select variables, as with **mydata[,3:6]**. Here the colon operator generates the simple values 3, 4, 5, 6. The methods below can generate a much wider range of patterns.
- To generate sets of column widths when reading data from fixed-width text files. Our example used a very small vector of value widths, but the methods in this chapter could generate long sets of patterns to read hundreds of variables with a single command.

Generating data is also helpful in more general ways for situations similar to those in other statistics packages.

- Generating data allows you to demonstrate various analytic methods, as we are doing in this book. It is not easy to find one data set to use for all of the methods you might like to use.
- Generating data lets you create very small examples that can help you debug an otherwise complex problem. Debugging a problem on a large data set often introduces added complexities and slows down each new attempted execution. When you can demonstrate a problem with the smallest possible set of data, it helps you focus on the exact nature of the

R.A. Muenchen, J.M. Hilbe, *R for Stata Users*, Statistics and Computing, DOI 10.1007/978-1-4419-1318-0_12, © Springer Science+Business Media, LLC 2010

problem. This is usually the best way to report a problem when requesting technical assistance. If possible, provide a small generated example
when you ask questions to the R-help e-mail support list.

• When you are designing an experiment, the levels of the experimental
variables usually follow simple repetitive patterns. You can generate those
and then add the measured outcome values to it manually. With such a
nice neat data set to start with, it is tempting to collect data in that order.
However, it is important to collect it in random order whenever possible
so that factors such as human fatigue or machine wear do not bias the
results of your study.

Some of our data generation examples use R's random number generator.
It will give a different result each time you use it unless you use the `set.seed`
function before each function that generates random numbers.

12.1 Generating Numeric Sequences

R generates data using specialized functions. We have used the simplest one:
the colon operator. We can generate a simple sequence with

```
> 1:10
```

```
[1]   1   2   3   4   5   6   7   8   9  10
```

You can store the results of any of our data generation example in a vector
using the assignment operator. So we can create the id variable we used with

```
> id <- 1:8
```

```
> id
```

```
[1] 1 2 3 4 5 6 7 8
```

The `seq` function generates sequences like this too, and it offers more
flexibility. The following is an example:

```
> seq(from=1, to=10, by=1)
```

```
[1]   1   2   3   4   5   6   7   8   9  10
```

The `seq` function call above has three arguments.

1. The `from` argument tells it where to begin the sequence.
2. The `to` argument tells it where to stop.
3. The `by` argument tells it the increments to use between each number.

The following is an example that goes from 5 to 50 in increments of 5.

```
> seq(from=5, to=50, by=5)
```

```
[1]   5 10 15 20 25 30 35 40 45 50
```

Of course, you do not need to name the arguments if you use them in order. So you can do the above example using this form too.

```
> seq(5, 50, 5)
```

```
[1]   5 10 15 20 25 30 35 40 45 50
```

12.2 Generating Factors

The **gl** function *generates* *levels* of factors. The following is an example that generates the series 1,2,1,2...:

```
> gl(n=2, k=1, length=8)
```

```
[1] 1 2 1 2 1 2 1 2
```

```
Levels: 1 2
```

The **gl** function call above has three arguments.

1. The **n** argument tells it how many levels your factor will have.
2. The **k** argument tells it how many of each level to repeat before incrementing to the next value.
3. The **length** argument is the total number of values generated. Although this would usually be divisible by n*k, it does not have to be.

To generate our gender variable, we just need to change k to be 4.

```
> gl(n=2, k=4, length=8)
```

```
[1] 1 1 1 1 2 2 2 2
```

```
Levels: 1 2
```

There is also an optional **label** argument. Here we use it to generate workshop and gender, complete with value labels.

```
> workshop <- gl(n=2, k=1, length=8, label=c("R","Stata") )
```

```
> workshop
```

```
[1] R    Stata R    Stata R    Stata R    Stata
Levels: R Stata
```

```
> gender <- gl( n=2, k=4, length=8, label=c("f","m") )

> gender

[1] f f f f m m m m
Levels: f m
```

12.3 Generating Repetitious Patterns (Not Factors)

When you need to generate repetitious sequences of values, you are often creating levels of factors, which is covered in the previous section. However, sometimes you need similar patterns that are numeric, not factors. The `rep` function generates these.

```
> gender <- rep(1:2, each=4, times=1)

> gender

[1] 1 1 1 1 2 2 2 2
```

The call to the `rep` function above has three simple arguments.

1. The set of numbers to repeat. We have used the colon operator to generate the values 1 and 2. You could use the `c` function here to list any set of numbers you need.
2. The `each` argument tells it often to repeat each number in the set. Here we need four of each number.
3. The `times` argument tells it the number of times to repeat the (set by `each`) combination. For this example, we only needed one.

Note that while we are generating the gender variable as an easy example, `rep` did not create gender as a factor. To make it one, you would have to use the `factor` function. You could instead generate it directly as a factor using the more appropriate `gl` function.

Next, we generate the workshop variable by repeating each number in the 1:2 sequence only one time each but repeat that set four times.

```
> workshop <- rep(1:2, each=1, times=4)

> workshop

[1] 1 2 1 2 1 2 1 2
```

By comparing the way we generated gender and workshop, the meaning of the `rep` function's arguments should become clear.

Now we come to the only example that we actually needed for the `rep` function in this book. To generate a constant! We use a variation of this in Chapter 15, *Traditional Graphics*, to generate a set of zeros to use on a histogram.

```
> myZeros <- rep(0, each=8)

> myZeros

[1] 0 0 0 0 0 0 0 0
```

12.4 Generating Integer Measures

R's ability to generate samples of integers is easy to use and is in some respects similar to that of Stata. In other respects, as we will discover, they are quite dissimilar. You provide a list of possible values and then use the `sample` function to generate your data. First, we put the Likert scale values 1, 2, 3, 4, and 5 into myValues.

```
> myValues <- c(1, 2, 3, 4, 5)
```

Next, we set the random number seed using the `set.seed` function, so you can see the same result when you run it.

```
> set.seed(1234) #Set random number seed.
```

Finally, we generate a random sample size of 1,000 from myValues using the `sample` function. We are sampling with replacement so we can use the five values repeatedly.

```
> q1 <- sample(myValues, size=1000, replace=TRUE)
```

Now we can check its mean and standard deviation.

```
> mean(q1)

[1] 3.029

> sd(q1)

[1] 1.412854
```

To generate a sample using the same numbers but with a roughly normal distribution, we can change the values to have more as you reach the center.

```
> myValues <- c(1, 2, 2, 3, 3, 3, 4, 4, 5)
> set.seed(1234)
> q2 <- sample( myValues, 1000, replace = TRUE)

> mean(q2)
[1] 3.012

> sd(q2)
[1] 1.169283
```

You can see from the bar plots in Fig. 12.1 that our first variable follows a uniform distribution (left) and our second one follows a normal distribution (right). Do not worry about how we created the plot; we will cover than that in Chapter 15, "Traditional Graphics."

We could have done the latter example more precisely by generating 1,000 samples from a normal distribution and then chopping it into 5 equally spaced groups. We will cover generating samples from continuous samples in the next section.

```
> barplot( table(q1) )
> barplot( table(q2) )
```

If you would like to generate two Likert-scale variables that have a mean difference, you can do so by providing them with different sets of values from which to sample. In the example below, we nest the call to the c function, to generate a vector of values, within the call to the **sample** function. Notice that the vector for q1 has no values greater than 3 and q2 has none less than 3. This difference will create the mean difference. Here we are only asking for a sample size of 8.

```
> set.seed(1234)
```

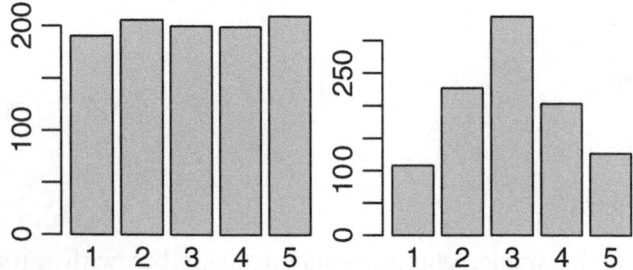

Fig. 12.1. Barplots showing the distributions of our generated integer variables.

```
> q1 <- sample( c(1, 2, 2, 3), size=8, replace = TRUE)

> mean(q1)
[1] 1.75

> set.seed(1234)

> q2 <- sample( c(3, 4, 4, 5), size=8, replace = TRUE)

> mean(q2)
[1] 3.75
```

12.5 Generating Continuous Measures

You can generate continuous random values from a uniform distribution using the runif function.

```
> set.seed(1234)

> x1 <- runif(n=1000)

> mean(x1)
[1] 0.5072735

> sd(x1)
[1] 0.2912082
```

where the n argument is the number of values to generate. You can also provide min and max arguments to set the lowest and highest possible values, respectively. So you might generate 1,000 pseudo-test-scores that range from 60 to 100 with

```
> set.seed(1234)

> x2 <- runif(n=1000, min=60, max=100)

> mean(x2)
[1] 80.29094

> sd(x2)
[1] 11.64833
```

Normal distributions with a mean of 0 and standard deviation of 1 have many uses. You can use the rnorm function to generate 1,000 values from such a distribution with

```
> set.seed(1234)

> x3 <- rnorm(n=1000)

> mean(x3)
[1] -0.0265972

> sd(x3)
[1] 0.9973377
```

You can specify other means and standard deviations as in the following example:

```
> set.seed(1234)

> x4 <- rnorm(n=1000, mean=70, sd=5)

> mean(x4)
[1] 69.86701

> sd(x4)
[1] 4.986689
```

We can use the hist function to see what two of these distributions look like, see Fig. 12.2.

```
> hist(x2)
> hist(x4)
```

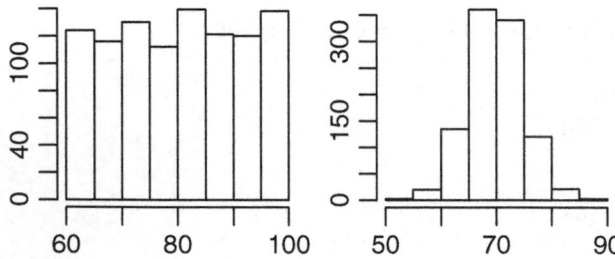

Fig. 12.2. Histograms showing the distributions of our continuous generated data.

12.6 Generating a Data Frame

Putting all of the above ideas together, we can use the following function calls to create a data frame similar to our practice data set, with a couple of test scores added. We are not bothering to set the random number generator seed, so each time you run this, you will get different results.

```
> id <- 1:8

> workshop <- gl( n=2, k=1,
+   length=8, label=c("R","Stata") )

> gender <-    gl( n=2, k=4,
+   length=8, label=c("f","m")    )

> q1 <- sample( c(1, 2, 2, 3), 8, replace = TRUE)
> q2 <- sample( c(3, 4, 4, 5), 8, replace = TRUE)
> q3 <- sample( c(1, 2, 2, 3), 8, replace = TRUE)
> q4 <- sample( c(3, 4, 4, 5), 8, replace = TRUE)

> pretest    <- rnorm( n=8, mean=70, sd=5)
> posttest   <- rnorm( n=8, mean=80, sd=5)

> myGenerated <- data.frame(id, gender, workshop,
+   q1, q2, q3, q4, pretest, posttest)

> myGenerated
  id gender workshop   q1 q2 q3 q4  pretest posttest
1  1      f        R    1  5  2  3 67.77482 77.95827
2  2      f    Stata    1  4  2  5 58.28944 78.11115
3  3      f        R    2  3  2  4 68.60809 86.64183
4  4      f    Stata    2  5  2  4 64.09098 83.58218
5  5      m        R    1  5  3  4 70.16563 78.83855
6  6      m    Stata    2  3  3  3 65.81141 73.86887
7  7      m        R    2  4  3  4 69.41194 85.23769
8  8      m    Stata    1  4  1  4 66.29239 72.81796
```

A more complex example is presented in Appendix D.

12.7 Example Programs for Generating Data

12.7.1 Stata Program for Generating Data

```
* Filename: GenerateData.do
```

```
clear
set obs 8

* ID
gen byte id = _n

* workshop
gen byte workshop = mod(_n, 2)
replace workshop = 2 if workshop==0

* gender
gen gender = int(runiform()+.5)
label define gender 0 "f" 1 "m"
label values gender gender


* Q variables
forvalues i = 1/8 {
forvalues j = 1/4 {
 cap gen q'j' = round(runiform() * 'i' *'j')+1
   }
}

* Pretest and Posttest
gen pretest  = int(normal(runiform())*100)
gen posttest = int(normal(runiform())*100)

list
```

12.7.2 R Program for Generating Data

```
# Filename: GenerateData.R

# Simple sequences.

1:10
seq(from=1,to=10,by=1)
seq(from=5,to=50,by=5)
seq(5,50,5)

# Generating our ID variable
id <- 1:8
id
```

```
# gl function Generates Levels.

gl(n=2,k=1,length=8)
gl(n=2,k=5,length=8)

#Adding labels.

workshop <- gl(n=2,k=1,length=8,label=c("R","Stata"))
workshop

gender <- gl( n=2,k=4,length=8, label=c("f","m") )
gender

# The rep function.

# Simple sequences.

1:10
seq(from=1,to=10,by=1)
seq(from=5,to=50,by=5)
seq(5,50,5)

# Generating our ID variable
id <- 1:8
id

# gl function Generates Levels.

gl(n=2,k=1,length=8)
gl(n=2,k=5,length=8)

#Adding labels.

workshop <- gl(n=2,k=1,length=8,label=c("R","Stata"))
workshop

gender <- gl( n=2,k=4,length=8, label=c("f","m") )
gender

# Generating uniformly distributed Likert data

myValues <- c(1, 2, 3, 4, 5)
set.seed(1234)


# Simple sequences.
```

```
1:10
seq(from=1, to=10, by=1)
seq(from=5, to=50, by=5)
seq(5, 50, 5)

# Generating our ID variable
id <- 1:8
id

# gl function Generates Levels.

gl(n=2,k=1,length=8)
gl(n=2,k=5,length=8)

#Adding labels.

workshop <- gl(n=2,k=1,length=8,label=c("R","Stata"))
workshop

gender <- gl( n=2,k=4,length=8, label=c("f","m") )
gender

# Generating repetitious Patterns (Not Factors).

gender <- rep(1:2, each=4, times=1)
gender

workshop <- rep(1:2, each=1, times=4)
workshop

myZeros <- rep(0, each=8)
myZeros

# Generating uniformly distributed Likert data

myValues <- c(1, 2, 3, 4, 5)
set.seed(1234)
q1 <- sample( myValues, size=1000, replace = TRUE)
mean(q1)
sd(q1)

# Generating normally distributed Likert data

myValues <- c(1, 2, 2, 3, 3, 3, 4, 4, 5)
```

```
set.seed(1234)
q2 <- sample( myValues , size=1000, replace = TRUE)
mean(q2)
sd(q2)


# Plot details in Traditional Graphics chapter.
par( mar=c(2, 2, 2, 1)+0.1 )
par( mfrow=c(1, 2) )
barplot( table(q1) )
barplot( table(q2) )
# par( mfrow=c(1, 1) ) #Sets back to 1 plot per page.
# par( mar=c(5, 4, 4, 2)+0.1 )


# Two Likert scales with mean difference
set.seed(1234)
q1 <- sample( c(1, 2, 2, 3), size=8, replace = TRUE)
mean(q1)

set.seed(1234)
q2 <- sample( c(3, 4, 4, 5), size=8, replace = TRUE)
mean(q2)


# Generating continuous data

# From uniform distribution.
# mean=0.5
set.seed(1234)
x1 <- runif(n=1000)
mean(x1)
sd(x1)


# From a uniform distribution
# between 60 and 100
set.seed(1234)
x2 <- runif(n=1000, min=60, max=100)
mean(x2)
sd(x2)


# From a normal distribution.

set.seed(1234)
x3 <- rnorm(n=1000)
mean(x3)
sd(x3)
```

```
set.seed(1234)
x4 <- rnorm(n=1000, mean=70, sd=5)
mean(x4)
sd(x4)

# Plot details are in Traditional Graphics chapter.
par( mar=c(2,2,2,1)+0.1 )
par( mfrow=c(1,2) )
hist(x2)
hist(x4)
# par( mfrow=c(1,1) ) #Sets back to 1 plot per page.
# par( mar=c(5,4,4,2)+0.1 )

# Generating a Data Frame.

id <- 1:8
workshop <- gl( n=2, k=1,
  length=8, label=c("R","Stata") )
gender <-    gl( n=2, k=4,
  length=8, label=c("f","m")   )
q1 <- sample( c(1, 2, 2, 3), 8, replace = TRUE)
q2 <- sample( c(3, 4, 4, 5), 8, replace = TRUE)
q3 <- sample( c(1, 2, 2, 3), 8, replace = TRUE)
q4 <- sample( c(3, 4, 4, 5), 8, replace = TRUE)
pretest    <- rnorm( n=8, mean=70, sd=5)
posttest   <- rnorm( n=8, mean=80, sd=5)

myGenerated <- data.frame(id, gender, workshop,
  q1, q2, q3, q4, pretest, posttest)
myGenerated
```

13

Managing Your Files and Workspace

Stata and R both have commands that replicate many of your computer's operating system functions such as listing names of objects, deleting them, setting search paths, and so on. Learning how to use these commands is especially important because, like Stata, R stores its data in your computer's limited random access memory. You need to make the most of your computer's memory when handling large data sets or when a command is highly iterative.

13.1 Loading and Listing Objects

You can see what objects are in your workspace with the ls function. To list all objects such as data frames, vectors, and functions, use

```
ls()
```

The objects function does the same thing and its name is more descriptive, but ls is more widely used since it is the same command that UNIX, Linux, and MacOS X users can use to list the files in a particular directory or folder (without the parentheses).

When you first start R, using the ls function will tell you there is nothing in your workspace. How it does this is quite odd by Stata's standards. It tells you that the list of objects in memory is a character vector with zero values.

```
> ls()
```

```
character(0)
```

The file *myall.RData* contains all of the objects we created in Chapter 5, "Programming Language Basics." After loading that into our workspace using the load function, ls will show us the objects that are available.

```
> load("myall.RData")
```

R.A. Muenchen, J.M. Hilbe, *R for Stata Users*, Statistics and Computing, DOI 10.1007/978-1-4419-1318-0_13,

```
> ls()

[1] "gender"    "mydata"    "mylist"    "mymatrix" "q1"
[6] "q2"        "q3"        "q4"        "workshop"
```

You can use the **pattern** argument to search for any regular expression. Therefore, to get a list of all objects that begin with the string *"my,"* you can use the following:

```
> ls(pattern="my")

[1] "mydata"    "mylist"    "mymatrix"
```

The **ls** function does not look inside data frames to see what they contain, and it does not even tell you when an object is a data frame. You can use many of the functions we have already covered to determine what an object is and what it contains.

To review, typing its name or using the **print** function will show you the whole object or at least something about it. What **print** shows you depends on the class of the object. The **head** and **tail** functions will show you the top or bottom few lines of vectors, matrices, tables, data frames, or functions.

The **class** function will tell you if an object is a data frame, list, or some other object. The **names** function will show you object names within objects such as data frames, lists, vectors, and matrices. The **attributes** function will display all of the attributes that are stored in an object such as variable names, the object's class, and any labels that it may contain.

```
> attributes(mydata)

$names

[1] "id"    "workshop" "gender"    "q1"    "q2"    "q3"    "q4"

$class

[1] "data.frame"

$row.names

[1] 1 2 3 4 5 6 7 8
```

The **str** function displays the *str*ucture of any R object in a compact form.

```
> str(mydata)

'data.frame':    8 obs. of  6 variables:
```

```
$ workshop: Factor w/ 4 levels "R","Stata","SPSS",..:
           1 2 1 2 1 2 1 2

$ gender  : Factor w/ 2 levels "f","m": 1 1 1 NA 2 2 2 2

$ q1       : num  1 2 2 3 4 5 5 4

$ q2       : num  1 1 2 1 5 4 3 5

$ q3       : num  5 4 4 NA 2 5 4 5

$ q4       : num  1 1 3 3 4 5 4 5
```

The `str` function works on functions too. The following is the structure it shows for the `lm` function.

```
> str( lm )

function (formula, data, subset, weights, na.action,

method = "qr", model = TRUE, x = FALSE, y = FALSE,

qr = TRUE, singular.ok = TRUE, contrasts = NULL, offset, ...)
```

The `ls.str` function applies the `str` function to every object in your workspace. It is essentially a combination of the `ls` function and the `str` function. The following is the structure of all of the objects we had in our workspace as we wrote this paragraph.

```
> ls.str()

myCounts :   'table' int [1:2, 1:2] 2 2 1 2

myCountsDF : 'data.frame':     4 obs. of  3 variables:

 $ gender  : Factor w/ 2 levels "f","m": 1 2 1 2

 $ workshop: Factor w/ 2 levels "R","Stata": 1 1 2 2

 $ Freq    : int  2 2 1 2

mydata : 'data.frame':  8 obs. of  6 variables:

 $ workshop: int  1 2 1 2 1 2 1 2
```

```
$ gender   : Factor w/ 2 levels "f","m": 1 1 1 NA 2 2 2 2

$ q1        : int  1 2 2 3 4 5 5 4

$ q2        : int  1 1 2 1 5 4 3 5

$ q3        : int  5 4 4 NA 2 5 4 5

$ q4        : int  1 1 3 3 4 5 4 5
```

Frank Harrell's `Hmisc` package has a `contents` function that is modeled after the SAS Contents procedure. It also lists names and other attributes as shown below. However, it works only with data frames.

```
> library("Hmisc")

Attaching package: 'Hmisc'
...

> contents(mydata)

Data frame:mydata    8 observations and 7 variables
Maximum # NAs:1

          Levels Storage NAs
id                integer  0
workshop          integer  0
gender          2 integer  1
q1                integer  0
q2                integer  0
q3                integer  1
q4                integer  0


+--------+------+
|Variable|Levels|
+--------+------+
| gender |  f,m |
+--------+------+
```

13.2 Understanding Your Search Path

Once you have data in your workspace, where exactly is it? It is in an *environment* called *.GlobalEnv*. The `search` function will show us where that resides in R's search path. Since the search path is affected by any packages

or data files you load, we will start R with a clean workspace and load our
practice data frame, mydata.

```
> setwd("/myRfolder")

> load("mydata.RData")

> ls()
```

[1] "mydata"

Now let us examine R's search path.

```
> search()
```

[1] ".GlobalEnv"   "package:stats" "package:graphics"

[4] "package:grDevices" "package:utils" "package:datasets"

[7] "package:methods"   "Autoloads"   "package:base"

Since our workspace, .GlobalEnv, is in position 1, R will search it first.
By supplying no arguments to the ls function, we were asking for a listing of
objects in the first position of the search path. Let us see what happens if we
apply ls to different levels. We can either use the path position value, 1, 2,
3,... or their names.

```
> ls(1) #This uses position number.
```

[1] "mydata"

```
> ls(".GlobalEnv") #This uses name.
```

[1] "mydata"

The *package:stats* at level 2 contains some of R's built-in statistical functions. There are a lot of them, so let us use the **head** function to show us just
the top few results.

```
> head( ls(2) )
```

[1] "acf"   "acf2AR"   "add.scope" "add1"
[5] "addmargins" "aggregate"

```
> head( ls("package:stats") ) #Same result.
```

[1] "acf"   "acf2AR"   "add.scope" "add1"
[5] "addmargins" "aggregate"

13.3 Attaching Data Frames

Understanding the search path is essential to understanding what the `attach` function really does. We will attach mydata and see what happens.

```
> attach(mydata)

> search()

 [1] ".GlobalEnv"        "mydata"
 [3] "package:stats"     "package:graphics"
 [5] "package:grDevices" "package:utils"
 [7] "package:datasets"  "package:methods"
 [9] "Autoloads"         "package:base"

> ls(2)

[1] "gender"    "id"        "q1"       "q2"       "q3"
[6] "q4"        "workshop"
```

You can see that `attach` has made virtual copies of the variables stored in mydata and placed them in search position 2. When we refer to just "gender" rather than "mydata$gender," R looks for it in position 1 first. It does find anything with just that simple name even though mydata$gender is in that position. R then goes on to position 2 and finds it. This is the process that makes it so easy to refer to variables by their simple component names. It also makes them very confusing to work with if you create new variables! Let us say we want to take the square root of q4:

```
> q4 <- sqrt(q4)

> q4

[1] 1.000000 1.000000 1.732051 1.732051 2.000000 2.236068
[7] 2.000000 2.236068
```

This looks like it worked fine. However, let us list the contents of search positions 1 and 2 to see what really happened:

```
> ls(1)

[1] "mydata" "q4"

> ls(2)

[1] "gender"    "id"        "q1"       "q2"       "q3"
[6] "q4"        "workshop"
```

R created the new version of q4 as a separate vector in our main workspace. The copy of q4 that the `attach` function put in position 2 was never changed! Since search position 1 dominates, asking for q4 will cause R to show us the one in our workspace. Asking for mydata$q4 will cause R to go inside the data frame and show us the original, untransformed values.

There are two important lessons to learn from this:

1. If you want to create a new variable inside a data frame, either fully specify the name using `mydata$varname` or `mydata[ ,"varname"]`, or use the `tranform` function described in Section 10.1, *Transforming Variables*.
2. When two objects have the same name, R will always choose the object higher in the search path.

When the `attach` function places objects in position 2 of the search path (a position you can change but rarely need to), those objects will block, or *mask*, any others of the same name in lower positions (i.e., further toward the end of the search list). In the following example, I started with a fresh launch of R, loaded mydata, and attached it twice to see what happens.

```
> attach(mydata)
> attach(mydata)

The following object(s) are masked from mydata (position 3):
        gender id q1 q2 q3 q4 workshop

> search()

 [1] ".GlobalEnv"      "mydata"           "mydata"
 [4] "package:stats"   "package:graphics" "package:grDevices"
 [7] "package:utils"   "package:datasets" "package:methods"
[10] "Autoloads"       "package:base"
```

Note that above mydata is now in search positions 2 and 3. If you refer to any variable or any object, R has to settle which one you mean (they do not need to be identical, as in this example.) The message about masked objects in position 3 tells us that the second attach brought in variables with those names into position 2. The variables from the first attach were then moved to position 3, and those with common names were masked (all of them in this example). Therefore, we can no longer refer to them by their simple names; those names are already in use somewhere higher in the search path. In this case, the variables from the second attach went to position 2 and they will be used. However, if objects with any of those names were in our main workspace (not in a data frame), they would be used instead.

When we first learned about vectors, we created q1, q2, q3, and q4 as vectors and then formed them into a data frame. If we had left them as separate vectors in our main workspace, even the first attach would have given us a similar message. The vectors in position 1 would have blocked those with the same names in positions 2 and 3.

This masking effect can block access to any object. In Section 2.2, "Loading an Add-on Package," we saw that when two packages share a function name, the most recent one loaded from the library is the one R will use. You can avoid getting the warning about masked objects by first detaching packages or data frames you previously attached, before attaching the second.

13.4 Attaching Files

So far, we have only used the **attach** function with data frames. It can also be very useful with R data files. If you load a file, it brings all objects into your workspace. However, if you attach the file, you can bring in only what you need and then detach it.

For example, let us create a variable x and then add only the vector q4 from the file myall.RData, a file that contains the objects we created in Chapter 5, "Programming Language Basics." Recall that in that chapter, we created each of our practice variables first as vectors and then converted them to factors, a matrix, a data frame, and a list.

```
> x <- c(1,2,3,4,5,6,7,8)

> attach("myall.RData")

> search()

 [1] ".GlobalEnv"        "file:myall.RData"  "package:stats"
 [4] "package:graphics"  "package:grDevices" "package:utils"
 [7] "package:datasets"  "package:methods"   "Autoloads"
[10] "package:base"

> q4 <- q4
```

The last statement looks quite odd! What is going on? The **attach** function loaded myall.RData, but put it at position 2 in the search path. R will place any variables you create in your workspace (position 1) and the attached copy allows R to find q4 in position 2. So it copies it from there to your workspace. Let us look at what we now have in both places.

```
> ls(1) # Your workspace.

[1] "q4" "x"

> ls(2) # The attached file.
```

```
[1] "gender"    "mydata"    "mylist"    "mymatrix" "q1"
[6] "q2"        "q3"        "q4"        "workshop"
```

```
> detach(2)
```

So we have succeeded in copying a single vector, q4, from a data frame into our workspace. The final `detach` removes `"file:myall.RData"` from the search path.

13.5 Removing Objects from Your Workspace

To delete an object from your workspace, use the `remove` function or the equivalent `rm` function as in

```
rm(mydata)
```

The `rm` function is one of the few functions that will accept multiple objects separated by commas; that is, the names do not have to be in a single character vector. In fact, the names *cannot* simply be placed into a single vector. We will soon see why.

Let us load myall.RData, so we will have lots of objects to remove.

```
> load(file="myall.RData")
```

```
> ls()
```

```
[1] "mystats" "gender"    "mydata"    "mylist"    "mymatrix"
[6] "q1"        "q2"        "q3"        "q4"        "workshop"
```

We do not need our vectors, workshop, gender, and the q variable since they are in our dataframe, mydata. To remove these extraneous variables, we can use

```
rm(workshop,gender,q1,q2,q3,q4)
```

If we had lots of variables, manually entering each name would get quite tedious. We can instead use any of the shortcuts for creating sets of variable names described in Chapter 7, "Selecting Variables." Let us use the `ls` function with its `pattern` argument to find all of the objects that begin with the letter "q."

```
> myQvars <- ls(pattern="q")
```

```
> myQvars
```

```
[1] "q1" "q2" "q3" "q4"
```

Now let us use the c function to combine workshop and gender with myQ-vars:

```
> myDeleteItems <- c("workshop","gender",myQvars)

> myDeleteItems

[1] "workshop" "gender"    "q1"        "q2"        "q3"
[6] "q4"
```

Note that myQvars is *not* enclosed in quotes in the first line. It is already a character vector that we are adding to the character values of "workshop" and "gender."

Finally, we can delete them all at once by adding the list argument to the rm function:

```
> rm(list=myDeleteItems)
>
> ls()
[1] "mydata"     "myDeleteItems" "mylist"     "mymatrix"
[5] "myQvars"    "mystats"
```

Finally, we can remove myQvars and myDeleteItems.

```
> rm(myQvars,myDeleteItems)

> ls()

[1] "mydata"     "mylist"     "mymatrix" "mystats"
```

It may appear that a good way to delete the list of objects in myDeleteItems would be to use

```
rm(myDeleteItems)
```

or, equivalently,

```
rm( c("workshop","gender","q1","q2","q3","q4") )
```

However, that would delete only the *list of item names*, not the items themselves! That is why the rm function needs a list argument when dealing with character vectors.

Once you are happy with the objects remaining in your workspace, you can save them all with

```
save.image("myFavorites.RData")
```

If you want to delete all of the visible objects in your workspace, you can do the following. Be careful, there is no "undo" function for this radical step!

```
myDeleteItems <- ls()
```

```
rm( list=myDeleteItems )
```

Doing this in two steps makes it clear what is happening, but, of course, you can nest these two functions. This approach looks quite cryptic at first, but I hope the above steps make it much more obvious what is occurring.

```
rm( list=ls() )
```

To conserve workspace by saving only the variables you need within a data frame, see Section 10.8, "Keeping and Dropping Variables." The rm function cannot drop variables stored within a data frame.

13.6 Minimizing Your Workspace

Removing unneeded objects from your workspace is one important way to save space. You can also use the cleanup.import function from Frank Harrell's Hmisc package. It automatically stores the variables in a data frame in their most compact form. You use it as

```
library("Hmisc")
```

```
mydata <- cleanup.import(mydata)
```

If you have not installed Hmisc, see Chapter 2, "Installing R and Add-on Packages," for details.

13.7 Setting Your Working Directory

Your working directory is the location R uses to retrieve or store files, if you do not otherwise specify the full path for filenames. On Windows, the default working directory is *My Documents*. On Windows XP or earlier, that is C:\Documents and Settings\username\My Documents. On Windows Vista or later, that is C:\Users\Yourname\My Documents. On Macintosh, the default working directory is /Users/username.

The getwd function will tell you the current location of your working directory:

```
> getwd()
```

```
[1] "C:/Users/Muenchen/My Documents"
```

Windows users can see and/or change their working directory by choosing *File>Change dir....* R will then display a window that you use to browse to any folder you like.

On any operating system, you can change the working directory with the setwd function. This is the equivalent to the Stata cd command. Simply provide the full path between the quotes:

```
setwd("/myRfolder")
```

We discussed earlier that R uses the forward slash "/" even on computers running Windows. That is because within strings, R uses "\t," "\n" and "\\" to represent the single characters tab, newline, and backslash, respectively. In general, a backslash followed by another character may have a special meaning. So when using R on Windows, always specify the paths with either a single forward slash or two backslashes in a row. This book uses the single forward slash because that works with R on all operating systems.

You can set your working directory automatically by putting it in your .Rprofile. For details, see Appendix C, "Automating Your R Setup."

13.8 Saving Your Workspace

Throughout this book we manually save the objects we create, naming them as we do so. That is the way almost all other computer programs work. R also has options for saving your workspace automatically when you exit.

13.8.1 Saving Your Workspace Manually

To save the entire contents of your workspace, you can use the save.image function:

```
save.image(file="myWorkspace.RData")
```

This will save all your objects, data, functions, everything. Therefore, it is usually good to remove unwanted objects first, using the rm function. See Section 13.5, "Removing Objects from Your Workspace," for details.

If you are a Windows user, R does not automatically append the .RData extension, as do most Windows programs, so make sure you enter it yourself.

Later, when you start R, you can use *File>Load Workspace* to load it from the hard drive back into the computer's memory. You can also restore them using the load function.

```
load(file="myWorkspace.RData")
```

If you want to save only a subset of your workspace, the save function allows you to list the objects to save, separated by commas, before the file argument:

```
save(mydata, file="mydata.RData")
```

This is one of the few functions that can accept many objects separated by commas, so might save three as in the example below.

```
save(mydata, mylist, mymatrix, file="myExamples.RData")
```

It also has a `list` argument that lets you specify a character vector of objects to save.

You exit R by choosing *File>Exit* or by entering the function call `quit()` or just `q()`. R will then offer to save your workspace. If you have used either the `save` or the `save.image` functions recommended above, you should say "No."

13.8.2 Saving Your Workspace Automatically

Every time you exit R, it offers to save your workspace for you automatically. If you click "Yes," it stores it in a file named ".RData" in your working directory (see how to set that in the Section 13.7. The next time you start R from the same working directory, it automatically loads that file back into memory, and you can continue working.

While this method saves a little time, it also has problems. The name .RData is an odd choice, because most operating systems hide files that begin with a period. So, initially, you cannot copy or rename your project files! That is true on Windows, Macintosh, and Linux/UNIX systems. Of course, you can tell your operating system to show you such files (shown below).

Since all your projects end up in a file with the same name, it is harder to find the one you need via search engines or backup systems. If you accidentally moved an .RData file to another folder, you would not know which project it contained without first loading it into R.

13.9 Getting Operating Systems to Show You ".*RData*" Files

While the default workspace file, ".*RData*," is hidden on most operating system, you can tell them to show you those files.

To get Windows XP to show you .RData, in Windows Explorer uncheck the option below and *uncheck* the option *Tools> Folder Options> View> Hide extensions to known file types*. Then click *Apply to all folders*. Then click *OK*.

In Windows Vista, use the following selection: *Start>Control Panel> Appearance and Personalization> Folder Options> View> Show hidden files and folders*. Then click *OK*.

In Windows 7 or later, start File Explorer, then follow this menu path, and *uncheck* the option *Organize> Folder and search options> View> Hide extensions for known file types*. Then click *OK*.

Note that this will still not allow you to click on a filename like myProject.RData and rename it to just .RData. The Windows Rename message box will tell you "You must type a filename."

Linux/UNIX users can see files named .RData with the command "ls -a."

Macintosh users can see files named .RData by starting a terminal window with *Applications> Utilities> Terminal.* In the terminal window, enter

```
defaults write com.apple.finder AppleShowAllFiles TRUE
killall Finder
```

To revert back to normal file view, simply type the same thing, but with "FALSE" instead of "TRUE."

13.10 Organizing Projects with Windows Shortcuts

If you are a Windows user and like using shortcuts, there is another way to keep your various projects organized. You can create an R shortcut for each of your analysis projects. Then you right-click the shortcut, choose *Properties*, and set the *Start in folder* to a unique folder. When you use that shortcut to start R, on exit it will store the .RData file for that project. Although neatly organized into separate folders, each project workspace will still be in a file named .RData.

13.11 Saving Your Programs and Output

R users who prefer the graphical user interface can easily save programs, called scripts, and output to files in the usual way. Just click anywhere on the window you wish to save, choose *File>Save as*, and supply a name. The standard extension for R programs is ".R" and for output is simply ".txt". You can also save bits of output to your word processor using the typical cut/paste steps.

On Windows, R will not automatically append ".R" to each filename. You must specify that yourself. When you forget this, and you will, later choosing *File>Open script* will not let you see the file! You will have to specify "*.*" as the filename to get the file to appear.

R users who prefer to use the command-line interface often use text editors such as Emacs, or the one in JGR, that will check their R syntax for errors. Those files are no different from any other file created in a given editor.

Windows and Macintosh users can cut and paste graphics output into their word processors or other applications. Users of any operating system can rerun graphs, directing their output to a file. See Chapter 14, "Graphics Overview" for details.

13.12 Saving Your History

The R console displays function calls you enter (or that menus enter for you) and their output. It is a good idea to submit function calls from a script window (program editor), but sometimes you enter them directly into the console and then later realize that you need to save the program. You could save the input and output in the console window, but you would need to edit out the output to create a usable program.

R has a *history* file that saves all of the function calls in a given session. This is similar to the Stata LOG file. However, unlike Stata, the history file is not cumulative on Windows computers. It is cumulative on Linux and Macintosh, however.

You can save the current session's history to a file in your working directory with the `savehistory` function. To route the history to a different folder, use the `setwd` function to change it before using `savehistory`, or simply specify the file's full path in the `file=` argument.

```
savehistory(file="myHistory.Rhistory")
```

You can later recall it using the `loadhistory` function.

```
loadhistory(file="myHistory.Rhistory")
```

Note that the filename can be anything you like, but the extension should be ".Rhistory." In fact the entire filename will be simply ".Rhistory" if you do not provide one. We prefer to save a cumulative history file automatically. It takes little disk space and you never know when it will help you recover work that you thought you would never need. For details, see Appendix C, "Automating Your R Setup."

All of the file and workspace functions we have discussed are summarized in Table 13.1.

13.13 Large Data Set Considerations

All of the topics we have covered in this chapter are helpful for managing the amount of free space you have available in your workspace. Since R, like Stata, stores its data in your computer's random access memory, R cannot analyze huge data sets.

An exception to this is Thomas Lumley's `biglm` package [31], which processes data in "chunks" for some linear and generalized linear models.

When the physical memory in your computer fills up, it is possible to use use your computer's hard drive to simulate more memory (known as virtual memory), but it is extremely inefficient and time-consuming. Given the low cost of memory today this is much less of a problem than you might think. R can handle hundreds of thousands of records on a computer with 2 gigabytes of

Table 13.1. Workspace management functions

Function to perform	Example
List object names, including .First, .Last	`objects(all.names=TRUE)`
List object names, of most objects	`ls()` or `objects()`
List object attributes	`attributes(mydata)`
Load workspace	`load(file="myWorkspace.RData")`
Remove a variable from a data frame	`mydata$myvar <- NULL`
Remove all objects (non hidden ones)	`rm( list=ls() )`
Remove an object	`rm(mydata)`
Remove several objects	`rm(mydata, mymatrix, mylist)`
Save all objects	`save.image(file="myWorkspace.RData")`
Save some objects	`save(x,y,z,file="myObjects.RData")`
Show structure of all objects	`ls.str( all.names=TRUE )`
Show structure of most objects	`ls.str()`
Show structure of data frame only (requires Hmisc)	`contents(mydata)`
Show structure of objects by name	`str(mydata), str(lm)`
Store data efficiently (requires Hmisc)	`mydata <- cleanup.import(mydata)`
Working directory, getting	`getwd ()`
Working directory, setting	`setwd("/mypath/myfolder")`
	Even Windows uses forward slashes,

memory available to R. That is the current memory limit for a single process or program in 32-bit operating systems. To have 2 gigabytes free just for R, you would you would want to have perhaps 3 gigabytes of total memory so that your operating system would have the room it needs.

Operating systems capable of 64-bit memory spaces are the norm on newer systems. The huge amounts of memory they can handle mitigate this problem.

Another way around the limitation is to store your data in a relational database and use its facilities to generate a sample to analyze. A sample size of a few thousand is sufficient for many analyses.

However, if you need to ensure that certain small groups (e.g., those who have a rare disease, the small proportion that defaulted on a loan) then you may end up taking a complex sample, which complicates your analysis considerably. R has specialized packages to help analyze such samples, including `pps`, `sampfling`, `sampling`, `spsurvey`, and `survey`. See CRAN at http://cran.r-project.org/ for details.

An alternative for R users is to purchase S-PLUS, a commercial package that has an almost identical language to R. S-PLUS has functions to handle what it calls "big data." It solves the problem in a way similar to that used in packages such as SAS and SPSS. However, while S-PLUS can run many R programs written using R's core functions, it cannot run R's add-on packages.

13.14 Example R Program for Managing Files and Workspace

Most chapters in this book end with the Stata and R programs that summarize the topics in the chapter. However this chapter has been very specific to R. Therefore, we present only the R program below.

```
# Filename: ManagingFilesWorkspace.R

ls()

setwd("/myRfolder")
load("myall.RData")
ls()

# List objects that begin with "my".
ls(pattern="my")

# Get attributes and structure of mydata.
attributes(mydata)
str(mydata)

# Get structure of the lm function.
str( lm )

# List all objects' structure.
ls.str()

# Use the Hmisc contents function.
install.packages("Hmisc")
library("Hmisc")
contents(mydata)

# ---Understanding Search Paths---
# After restarting R to purge it of
# packages added by loading Hmisc...

setwd("/myRfolder")
load("mydata.RData")
ls()
search()
```

```
ls(1) #This uses position number.
ls(".GlobalEnv") # This does the same using name.

head( ls(2) )
head( ls("package:stats") ) #Same result.

# See how attaching mydata change the path.
attach(mydata)
search()
ls(2)

# Create a new variable.
q4 <- sqrt(q4)
q4
ls(1)
ls(2)

# Attaching data frames.
detach(mydata)
attach(mydata)
attach(mydata)
search()

# Clean up for next example,
# or restart R with an empty workspace.
detach(mydata)
detach(mydata)
rm( list=ls() )

# Attaching files.
x <- c(1,2,3,4,5,6,7,8)
attach("myall.RData")
search()
q4 <- q4

ls(1) # Your workspace.
ls(2) # The attached file.
detach(2)

# Removing objects.
rm(mydata)
load(file="myall.RData")
ls()
# Example not run:
# rm(workshop,gender,q1,q2,q3,q4)
```

```
myQvars <- ls(pattern="q")
myQvars

myDeleteItems <- c("workshop","gender",myQvars)
myDeleteItems

myDeleteItems
rm( list=myDeleteItems )

ls()
rm( myQvars, myDeleteItems )
ls()

# Wrong!
rm(myDeleteItems)
rm( c("workshop","gender","q1","q2","q3","q4") )

save.image("myFavorites.RData")

# Removing all workspace items.
# The clear approach:

myDeleteItems <- ls()
myDeleteItems
rm( list=myDeleteItems )

# The usual approach:
rm( list=ls() )

# Setting your working directory.

getwd()
setwd("/myRfolder")

# Saving your workspace.

load(file="myall.RData")

# Save everything.
save.image(file="myPractice1.RData")

# Save some objects.
save(mydata,file="myPractice2.RData")
save(mydata,mylist,mymatrix,file="myPractice3.RData")
```

```
# Remove all objects and reload myPractice3.
rm( list=ls() )
load("myPractice3.RData")
ls()

# Save and load history.
savehistory(file="myHistory.Rhistory")
loadhistory(file="myHistory.Rhistory")
```

14

Graphics Overview

Graphics is perhaps the most difficult topic to compare between Stata and R. Both packages contains at least two graphical approaches, each with dozens of options and each with entire books devoted to them. Therefore, we will focus on only two main approaches in R, and we will discuss many more examples in R than in Stata. This chapter focuses on a broad, high-level comparison. The next chapter focuses on R's traditional graphics. The one after that focuses just on the grammar of graphics approaches used in both R and Stata.

Dynamic visualization allows you explore your data by interacting with plots. Selections you make in one graph, such as the females in a bar chart, are reflected in all graphs. Although dynamic visualization is outside our scope, R has this capability through two excellent packages that we will review briefly.

The `iplots` package [49] offers a wide array of interactive plots. These include histograms, bar charts, scatter plots, box plots, fluctuation diagrams, parallel coordinates plots, and spine plots. They all include interactive abilities such as linked highlighting and color brushing. The package was developed by Simon Urbanek, Tobias Wichtrey, Alex Gouberman, and Martin Theus.

R can also link to a separate interactive graphics package, GGobi [47], available for free at http://www.ggobi.org/. GGobi's plots include scatter plots, bar charts, and parallel coordinates plots. One of its most interesting features is called *projection pursuit*. This approach displays a 3-dimensional scatter plot, which it rotates as it searches for your goal in the data. For example, searching for "holes" might help you find clusters of observations in your data. This helpful software was written by Deborah F. Swayne, Duncan Temple Lang, Andreas Buja, and Dianne Cook.

You can link to GGobi very easily from Graham Williams' `rattle` graphical user interface for data mining, discussed in Section 3.6.2.

You can also link to GGobi from within R using function calls provided by the `rggobi` package [27]. The `rggobi` package was developed by Duncan Temple Lang, Debby Swayne, Hadley Wickham, and Michael Lawrence. It is available with all other R packages on the Comprensive R Archive Network, but you also need to install GGobi itself separately.

R.A. Muenchen, J.M. Hilbe, *R for Stata Users*, Statistics and Computing, DOI 10.1007/978-1-4419-1318-0_14,

14.1 Stata Graphics

Stata's graphics come as part of the package. It is not an add-on and it is not written as open source code. Nearly all of Stata's graphic commands and functions are hard-coded in C into the Stata executable. However, beginning with Stata version 10, Stata provides users with a host of graphic primitives that they can use to construct and develop new types of graphics. Version 10 also comes with a graphics editor, which can be used to annotate a produced graph in a number of ways. Stata comes with built-in capabilities to construct most every variety of two-dimensional graph. Its built-in three-dimensional graphic capabilities are limited, although it is possible for a knowledgeable user to create these types of graphs.

Stata comes with a 618-page reference manual completely devoted to graphics. Stata's publishing company, called Stata Press, has a volume specifically aimed at helping Stata users to better understand and create graphs. Authored by Michael N. Mitchell, *A Visual Guide to Stata Graphics* [33], is a 471-page text covering most every aspect of Stata graphics, including the handling of various primitives.

14.2 R Graphics

R offers three main types of graphics: traditional, lattice [41], and ggplot2 [54].

R's traditional graphics functions (also called base graphics) come with the main R installation. Traditional graphics include high-level functions such as bar plots, histograms, and scatter plots. These functions are brief and the default settings are good.

While Stata requires you specify your complete plot in advance, R's traditional graphics allow you to plot repeatedly on the same graph. For example, you might start with a scatter plot and then add a regression line. As you add new features, each writes on top of the previous ones, so the order of function calls is important. Once written, a particular feature cannot be changed without starting the plot over from the beginning.

R's traditional graphics also includes low-level functions for drawing things like points, lines, and axes. These provide flexibility and control that people can use to invent new types of graphs. Their use has resulted in many add-on graphics packages for R. The level of control is so fine that you can even use it for artistic graphics that have nothing to do with data. See Paul Murrell's book *R Graphics* [35] for examples.

The second major graphics package added to R was lattice, written by Deepayan Sarkar [41]. It implements W. S. Cleveland's Trellis graphics system [6]. Now as part of the base R distribution, it does an excellent job of creating multiframe plots. A good book on that package is Deepayan Sarkar's *Lattice: Multivariate Data Visualization with R* [40]. We will not examine lattice

Table 14.1. A comparison of R's three main graphics packages

	Traditional (or base)	lattice	ggplot2
Automatic output for different objects	Yes	No	No
Automatic legends	No	Sometimes	Yes
Easily repeats plots for different groups	No	Yes	Yes
Easy to use with multiple data sources	Yes	No	Yes
Allows you to build plots piece-by-piece	Yes	No	Yes
Allows you to replace pieces after creation	No	No	Yes
Consistent functions	No	No	Yes
Attractiveness of default settings	Good	Good	Excellent
Can do mosaic plots	Yes	Yes	No
Control extends beyond data graphics	Yes	No	No
Underlying graphics system	Traditional	Grid	Grid

graphics, as the next system covers most of its abilities and offers additional advantages.

The third major package, ggplot2 [54], written by Hadley Wickham, is based on the grammar of graphics described in the next section. It offers an excellent balance between power and ease of use.

We will cover ggplot2 in Chapter 16 Although ggplot2 has advantages over lattice, most of our ggplot2 examples can be created as well in the lattice package. A comparison of these three main packages is given in Table 14.1.

14.3 The Grammar of Graphics

Leland Wilkinson's watershed work, *The Grammar of Graphics* [56], forms the foundation of Hadley Wickham's ggplot2 package, as well as the graphics in the SPSS Statistics package. Wilkinson's key insight was the realization that general principals form the foundation of all data graphics. Once you design a graphics language to follow those principals, the language should then be able to do any existing data graphics as well as variations that people had not previously considered.

An example is a stacked bar chart that shows how many students took each workshop (i.e., one divided bar). This not a popular graph, but if you change its coordinate system from rectangular to circular (Cartesian to polar), it becomes a pie chart. So rather than requiring separate procedures, you can have one that includes changing coordinates. That type of generalization applies to various other graphical elements as well.

A much more interesting example is Charles Joseph Minard's famous plot of Napoleon's march to Moscow and back in 1812 (Fig. 14.1). The light gray line shows the army's advance toward Moscow, and the dark grey line shows its retreat. The thickness of the line reflects the size of the army. Through

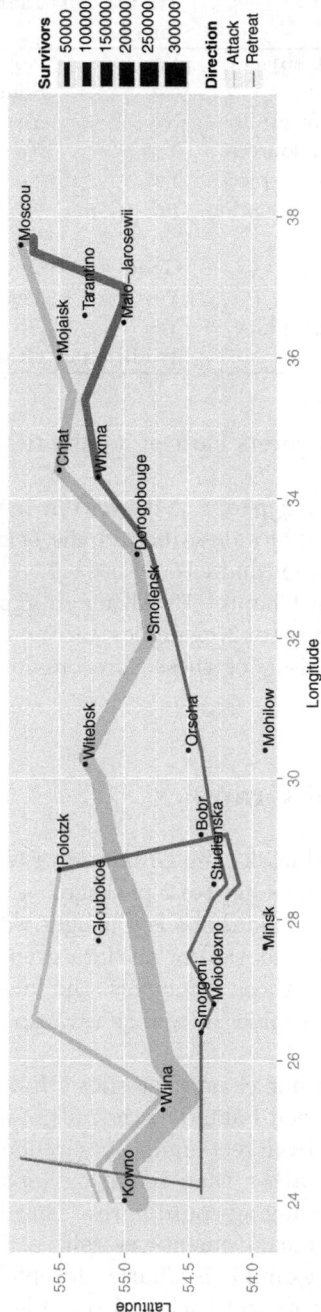

Fig. 14.1. Minard's plot of Napoleon's march created with the `ggplot2` package.

a very substantial effort, you can get many graphics packages to create this graph, including R's traditional graphics. However, R's `ggplot2` package can do it easily using the same general concepts that it uses for any other plots.

It may seem that people are unlikely to use this type of plot again, but minor variations of it are used to diagram computer network throughput, the transmission of disease, and the communication of product awareness in marketing.

The point is that `ggplot2` gives you the broadest range of graphical options that R offers. The `ggplot2` web site has many interesting examples of the range of plots that this package can create.

14.4 Other Graphics Packages

There are many other graphics packages that we will not have space to examine. Two notable ones are the **maps** package [2] for creating geographic maps and the vcd package [32] for visualizing categorical data. The latter was written by David Meyer, Achim Zeileis, and Kurt Hornik   and was inspired by Michael Friendly's book *Visualizing Categorical Data* [15]. That book describes how to do its plots using SAS macros. The fact that plots initially implemented in SAS were also possible to add to R is testament to R's graphical flexibility.

There are comprehensive collections of graphs and the R programs to make them at the R Graph Gallery at `http://addictedtor.free.fr/graphiques/` and the Image Browser at `http://bg9.imslab.co.jp/Rhelp/`. You can also use the **demo** function in R to have it show you a sample of what it can do. Enter the demo function calls below in the R console, and each will generate several example plots.

```
demo(graphics)
demo(persp)
library("lattice")
demo(lattice)
```

14.5 Graphics Procedures and Graphics Systems

R has many add-on packages that contain similar high-level graphics functions.

At a lower level are graphics systems. This is where a function call to do something like a scatter plot is turned into the precise combinations of lines and points needed. Controlling the graphics system allows you to change settings that affect all graphs, like text fonts, fill patterns, and line or point types. In Stata, you can find out how to control these settings using the symbolstyle and linestyle options. A Stata user may also access information using the menu system–for example *Graphics> Manage Graphs> Query styles and schemes* or *Graphics> Change scheme/size*. Stata also allows you to control these settings when you create a template to apply to future graphs.

Graphics systems are more visible in R because there are two of them. The traditional graphics system controls the high-level traditional graphics functions such as `plot`, `barplot`, and `pie` as well as some add-on packages such as `maps`. It also controls low-level traditional graphics functions that do things like draw lines or rectangles.

The packages `lattice` and `ggplot2` instead use the `grid` graphics system. The implications of this will become much more obvious as we look at examples. The grid graphics system was written by Paul Murrell and is documented in his book *R Graphics* [35]. That book is a good reference for both graphics systems as well as high-level traditional graphics procedures. It also gives an introduction to lattice graphics.

14.6 Graphics Devices

At the lowest level of graphics control is the graphics device itself. Regardless of the graphics package or system in R you use, the way you see or save the result is the same: the graphics device.

By default, R writes to your screen, each plot taking the place of the previous one. Windows users can buffer the plots for viewing with the Page Up/Page Down keys, by choosing *History> Recording* in your plot window.

R has functions named for the various graphics devices. So to write a plot to an encapsulated postscript file, you could use

```
postscript( file="myPlot.eps",
  paper="special",
  width=4,
  height=3.5)                    #Opens the device.

plot(pretest,posttest)           #Does the plot.

dev.off()                        #Closes the device.
```

The `paper="special"` argument lets you set the size of the plot using the `width` and `height` arguments. Measurements are in inches.

The last command, `dev.off()`, is optional, since R will close the device when you exit R. However, any additional plots you create will go to that file until you either call the `dev.off()` function or explicitly choose to use the screen device again.

Although bitmap file formats are generally lower-resolution than postscript or PDF, in some cases you may need one. For example, this book was written in a version of the LATEXdocument preparation system that prefers encapsulated postscript files. Although that is a high-resolution format, it does not support transparency used by some plots. So we switched to a high-resolution Portable Network Graphics (PNG) file for the plots that used transparency. The following is the format we used:

```
png(file="transparencyDemo.png",
  res=600,
  width=2400,
  height=2100)


plot(pretest, posttest)


dev.off()
```

The png function measures width and height in dots per inch (dpi) of resolution. So at 600 dpi, 2400 by 2100 yields a 4 by 3.5 inch plot.

Screen device functions are windows(), quartz(), and x11() for Microsoft Windows, Macintosh OS X, and UNIX or Linux, respectively. Other popular device functions include jpeg, pdf, pictex (for LaTeX), png, and win.metafile for Microsoft Windows. The JPG file format is popular for photographs but is best avoided for most data graphics as its compression blurs the sharp boundaries that make up lines, points, and numbers.

Multiple plots can go to the file in the above example because Postscript (and PDF) support multiple pages. Other formats like Microsoft Windows Metafile do not. For that type of format you can send multiple plots to separate files, using the following form. The part of the filename "%03d" tells R to append 1, 2,... to the end of each filename. The numbers are padded by blanks or zeros depending on the operating system.

```
win.metafile( file="myPlot%03d.wmf" )

barplot( table(workshop) ) #1st plot goes to myPlot  1.wmf

hist(posttest)             #2nd plot goes to myPlot  2.wmf

plot(pretest,posttest)     #2rd plot goes to myPlot  3.wmf

dev.off()
```

The ggplot2 package has its own ggsave function to save its plots to files. For details, see Chapter 16, "Graphics with ggplot2."

```
ggsave(file = "march.jpeg", width=16, height=4)
```

For much greater depth on these and many other graphics subjects, see *R Graphics* [35].

14.7 Practice Data: mydata100

The following examples use a longer version of our practice data set called mydata100. It has 100 observations, includes people who have taken all 4 workshops, and adds test scores taken before and after the workshops (pretest and posttest). The file also contains full variable and value labels. It is also attached, so all of the examples use short variable names. The following is the top part of the data.

```
> head(mydata100)

  gender workshop q1 q2 q3 q4 pretest posttest
1 Female        R  4  3  4  5      77       76
2   Male     SPSS  3  4  3  4      75       78
3 Female     SPSS  3  2  3  3      79       81
4 Female     SPSS  5  4  5  3      85       85
5 Female    Stata  4  4  3  4      80       84
6 Female     SPSS  5  4  3  5      77       80
```

15

Traditional Graphics

In the previous chapter, we discussed the various graphics packages in R and Stata. Now we will delve into R's traditional, or base, graphics.

15.1 Bar Plots

Bar plots using R's traditional graphics are easy to do, but they use a method quite different from Stata. While Stata assumes that your data need summarizing and requires options to tell it when they are presummarized, many of R's base graphics functions assume just the opposite. We will first look at bar plots of counts, then grouped counts, and, finally, various types of bar plots for means.

15.1.1 Bar Plots of Counts

The `barplot` function call below makes a plot with just two bars: one for each value (Fig. 15.1). They could be counts, means, or any other measure. The main point is that we get a bar for *every observation*. We are ignoring options for the moment, so the plot lacks labels and its axis values are tiny.

```
barplot( c(40,60) )
```

If we apply the same function to variable q4, we get a bar representing each observation in the data frame (Fig. 15.2).

```
barplot( q4 ) # Not good.
```

Notice that the *y*-axis is labeled 1 through 5. It is displaying the raw values for every observation rather than summarizing them. That is not a very helpful plot!

Recall that the `table` function gets frequency counts.

R.A. Muenchen, J.M. Hilbe, *R for Stata Users*, Statistics and Computing, DOI 10.1007/978-1-4419-1318-0_15,
© Springer Science+Business Media, LLC 2010

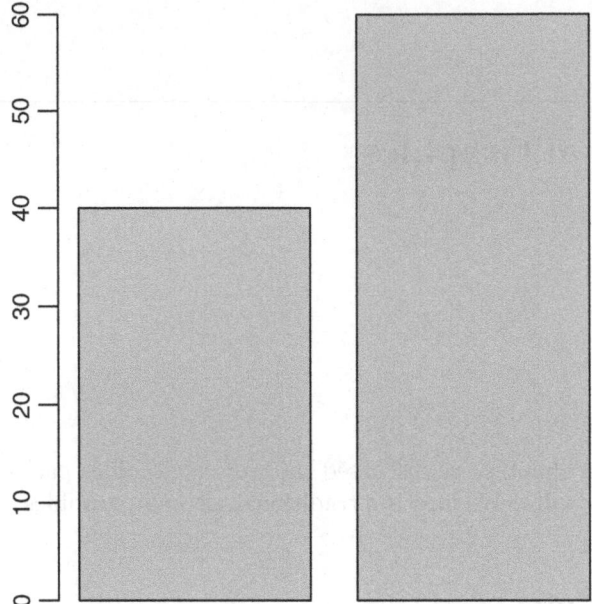

Fig. 15.1. Unlabeled bar plot using traditional graphics.

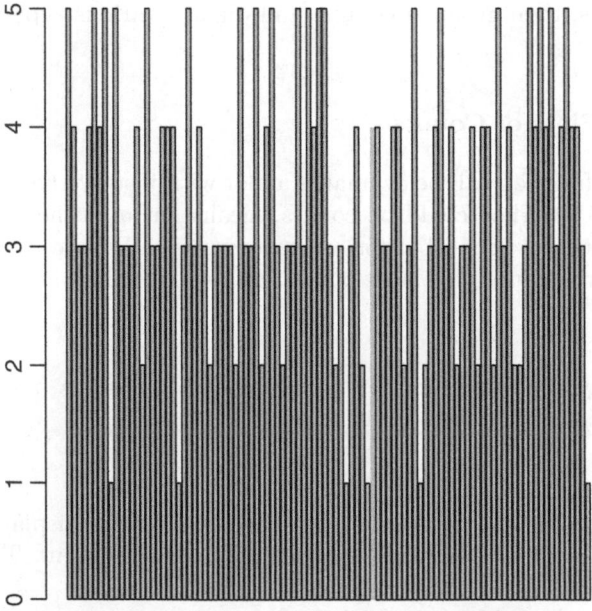

Fig. 15.2. Bad bar plot of unsummarized variable q4.

```
> table(q4)

q4

 1  2  3  4  5
 6 14 34 26 20
```

Since the `table` function gets the data in the form we need for a bar plot, we can simply nest one function within the other to finally get a reasonable plot (Fig. 15.3).

```
> barplot( table(q4) )
```

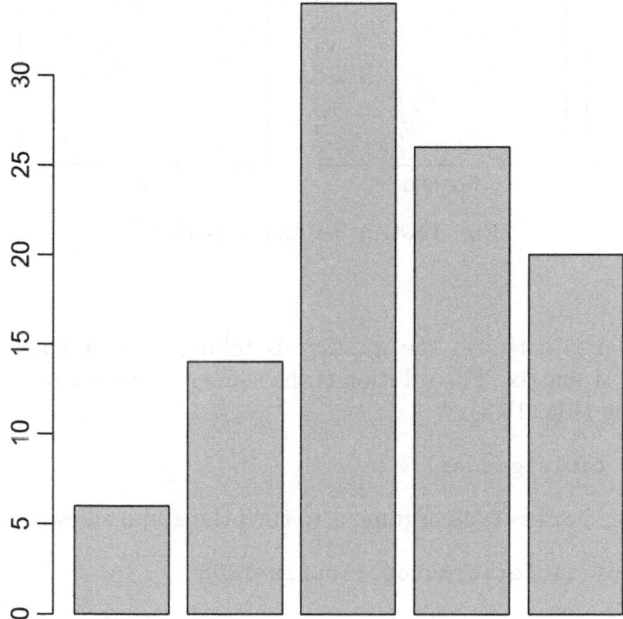

Fig. 15.3. A more reasonable bar plot for variable q4, this time summarized first.

When we make that same mistake with a bar plot on gender, we see a different message.

```
> barplot(gender)
```

```
Error in bar plot.default(gender) :
  'height' must be a vector or a matrix
```

If gender was coded 1 or 2 and was not stored as a factor, it would have created one bar for every subject, each with a height of 1 or 2. However,

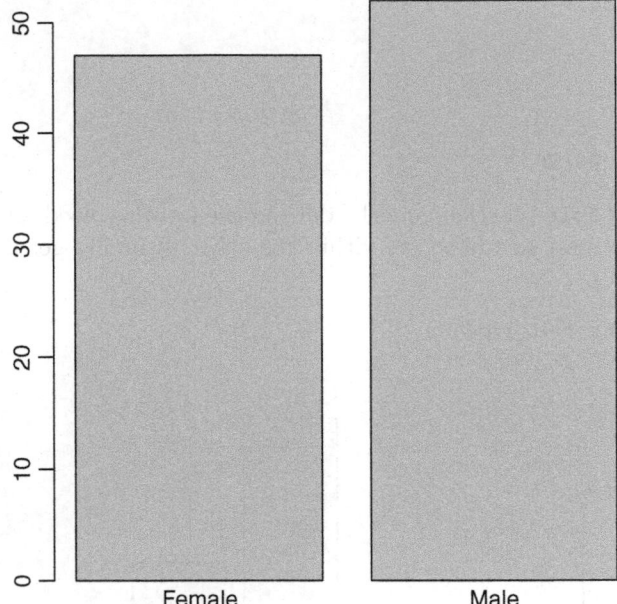

Fig. 15.4. A bar plot of gender.

because gender is a factor, the message is telling us that `barplot` accepts only a vector or matrix. The solution is the same as before: count the genders before plotting (Fig. 15.4).

```
barplot( table(gender) )
```

We can use the `horiz=TRUE` argument to turn the graph sideways (Fig. 15.5).

```
> barplot( table(workshop), horiz=TRUE )
```

If we are interested in viewing groups as a proportion of the total, we can stack the bars into a single one (Fig. 15.6). As we will see in the next chapter, this is essentially a pie chart in rectangular Cartesian co-ordinates, rather than circular polar coordinates. To do this, we use the `as.matrix` function to convert the table into the form we need and use the `beside=FALSE` argument to prevent the bars from appearing beside each other.

```
barplot( as.matrix( table(workshop) ),
  beside = FALSE)
```

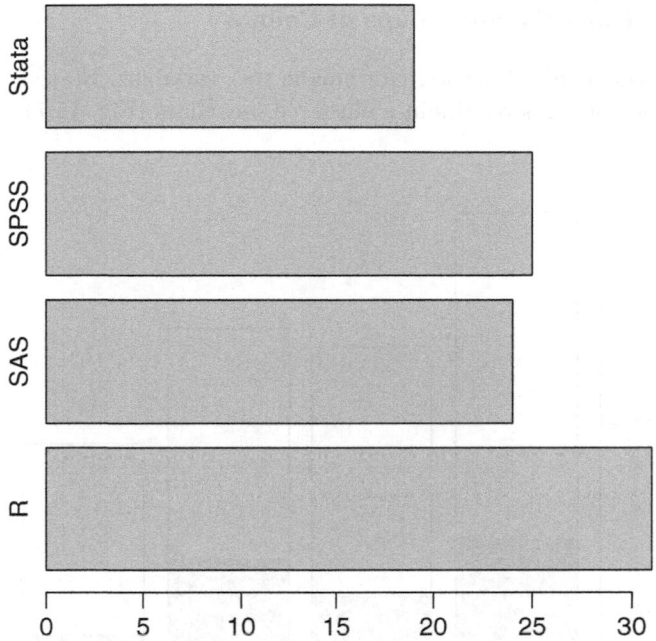

Fig. 15.5. A horizontal bar plot of workshop flipped using `horiz=TRUE`.

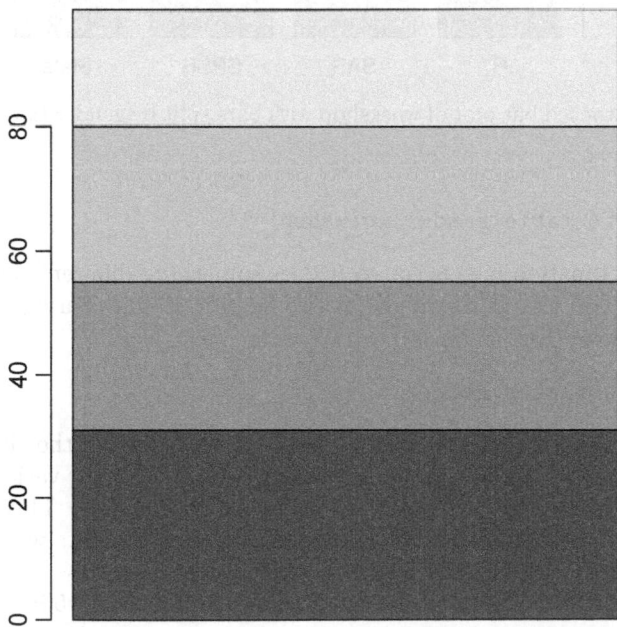

Fig. 15.6. An unlabeled stacked bar plot of workshop.

15.1.2 Bar Plots for Subgroups of Counts

Recall that the `table` function can handle two variables. Nested within the `barplot` function, this results in a clustered bar chart (Fig. 15.7).

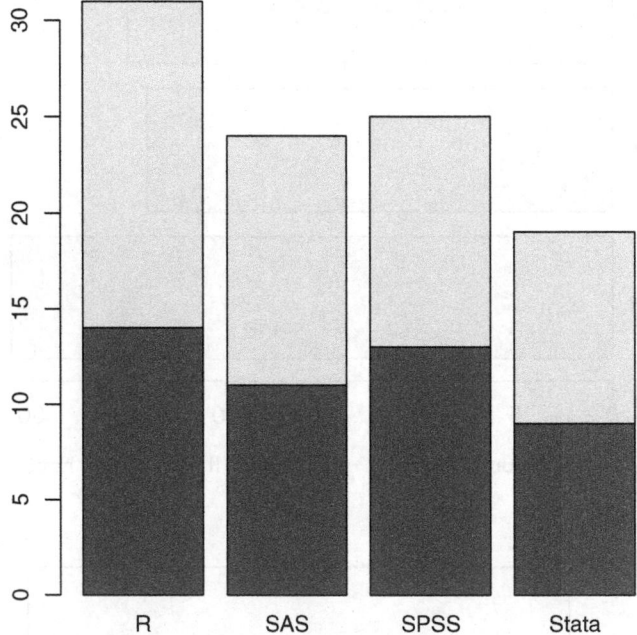

Fig. 15.7. A stacked bar plot of workshop with bars split by gender (lacking legend).

```
> barplot( table(gender,workshop) )
```

The `plot` function is generic, so it does something different depending on the variables you give it. If we give it two factors, it will create a plot similar to the one above (Fig. 15.8).

```
> plot( workshop,gender )
```

The difference is that the bars fill the plot vertically so the shading gives us proportions instead of counts. Also, the width of each bar varies, reflecting the marginal proportion of observations in each workshop. This is called a *spine plot*. Notice that we did not need to summarize the data with the `table` function. The `plot` function takes care of that for us.

The `mosaicplot` function does something similar (Fig. 15.9).

```
> mosaicplot( table(workshop,gender) )
```

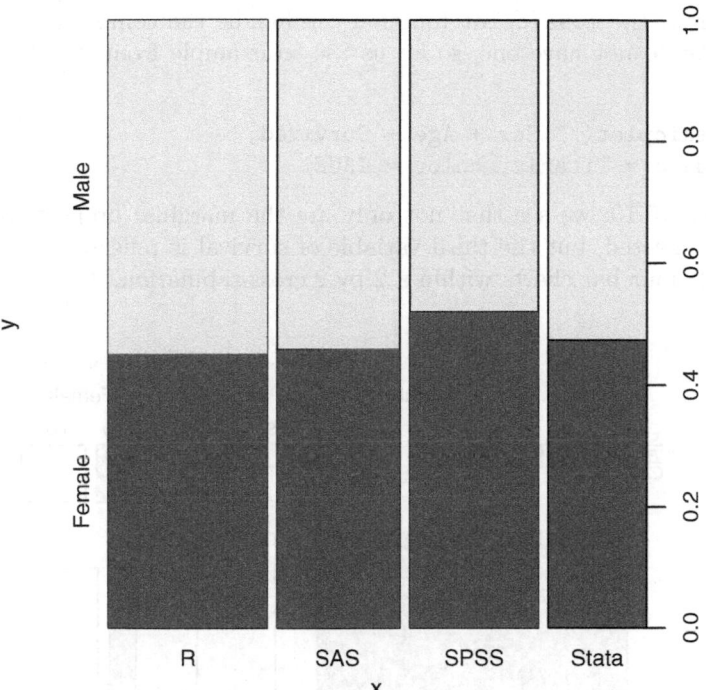

Fig. 15.8. A mosaic plot of workshop by gender, done using the `plot` function. Gender is labeled automatically.

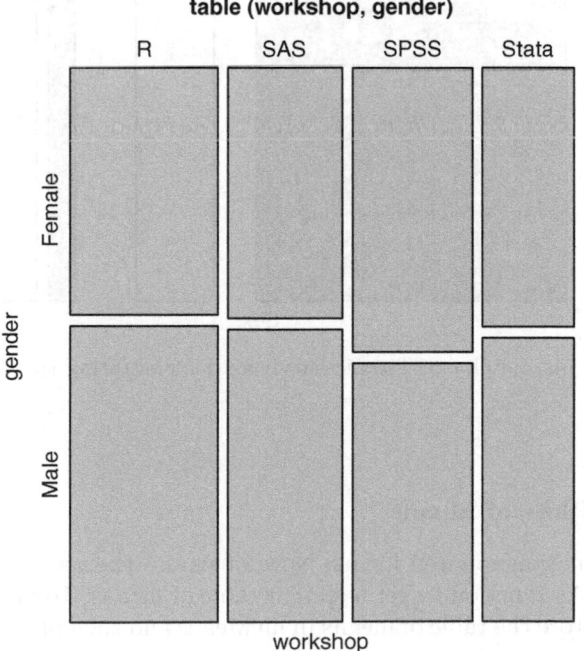

Fig. 15.9. A mosaic plot of workshop by gender, done using the `mosaicplot` function.

However, the `mosaicplot` function can handle the complexity of a third factor. We do not have one, so let us use an example from the `mosaicplot` help file.

```
> mosaicplot( ~ Sex + Age + Survived,
+    data = Titanic, color = TRUE)
```

In Fig. 15.10, we see that not only are the marginal proportions of sex and age reflected, but the third variable of survival is reflected as well. It is essentially four bar charts within a 2 by 2 cross-tabulation.

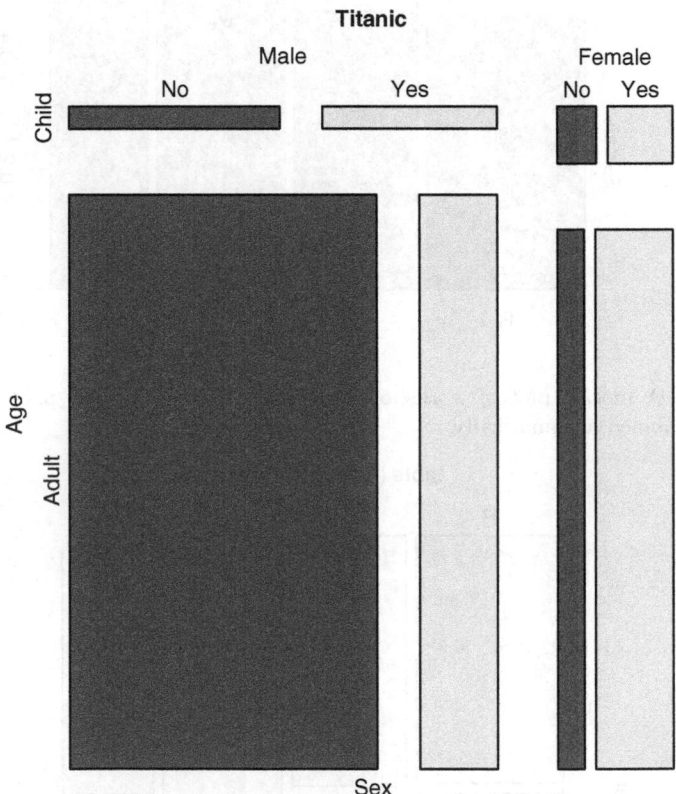

Fig. 15.10. A mosaic plot of Titanic survivors demonstrating the display of three factors at once.

15.1.3 Bar Plots of Means

The `table` function counted for us. Now let us use the `mean` function, along with the `tapply` function to get a similar table of means. To make it easier to read, we will store the table of means in myMeans and then plot it (Fig. 15.11).

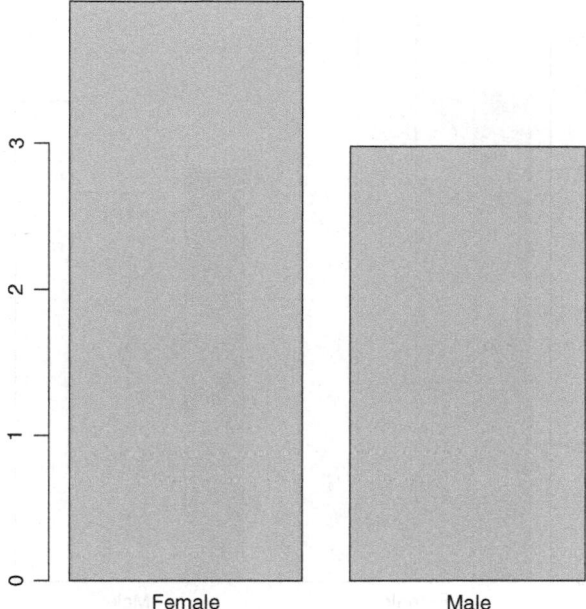

Fig. 15.11. A bar plot of means.

```
> myMeans <- tapply(q1, gender, mean, na.rm=TRUE)

> barplot(myMeans)
```

Adding workshop to the `tapply` function is easy, but you must combine gender and workshop into a list first, using the `list` function (Fig. 15.12).

```
> myMeans <- tapply(q1,
+    list(workshop,gender), mean,na.rm=TRUE)

> barplot(myMeans, beside=TRUE)
```

Many of the variations we used with bar plots of counts will work with means, of course. For example, the `horiz=TRUE` argument will flip any of the above examples on their sides.

15.2 Adding Titles, Labels, Colors, and Legends

So far our graphs have been fairly bland. Worse than that, without a legend, some of the above bar charts are essentially worthless. Let us now polish them up. Although we are using bar plots, these steps apply to many of R's traditional graphics functions (Fig. 15.13).

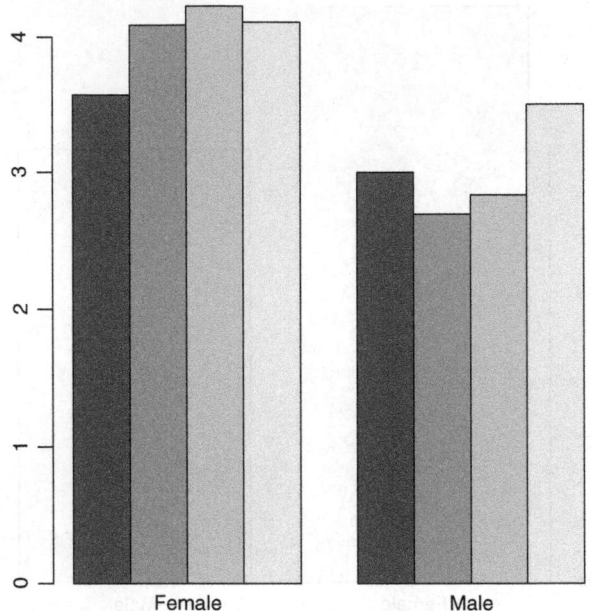

Fig. 15.12. A bar plot of q1 means by workshop (unlabeled) and gender.

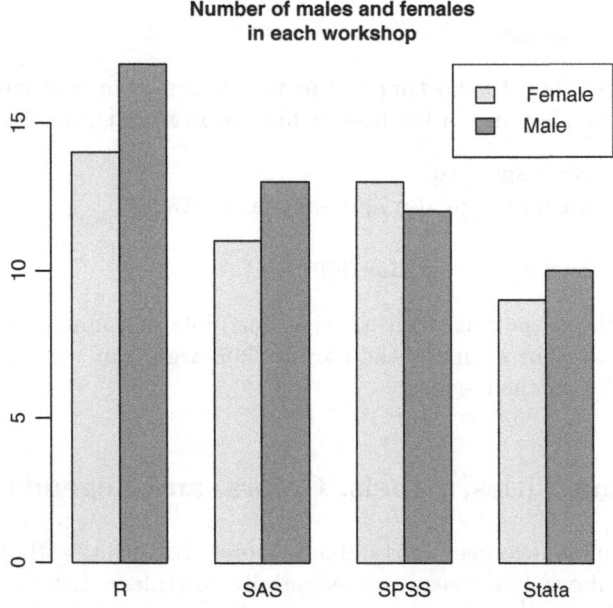

Fig. 15.13. A bar plot with a manually added title, legend, and shades of gray.

```
> barplot( table(gender,workshop),
+    beside=TRUE,
+    col=c("gray90","gray60"),
+    main="Number of males and females \nin each workshop" )

> legend( "topright",
+    c("Female","Male"),
+    fill=c("gray90","gray60") )
```

The `barplot` function call above has four arguments.

1. The `table(gender,workshop)` argument generates a two-way table of counts.
2. The `beside=TRUE` argument places the workshop bars side-by-side instead of stacking them on top of each other. That is better for perceiving the count per workshop. Leaving it off would result in a stacked bar chart that might be better for estimating relative total attendance of each workshop rather than absolute counts.
3. The `col=c("gray90","gray60")` argument supplies the *col*ors (well, shades of gray in this case) for the bars in order of the factor levels in gender. To get a complete list of colors, enter the function `colors()`.
4. The `main` argument lists the plot's title. The "**\n**" indicates where the title should skip new a *new* line. R uses this backslash character, "\," to introduce control characters. The "n" represents *new* line.

Until the `legend` function ran, the plot had no legend. It appeared after the fact.

The `legend` function call above has three arguments.

1. The first argument positions the legend itself. This can be the values "topleft," "topright," "bottomleft," "bottomright," "right," and "center". It can also be a pair of x, y values such as 10, 15. The 15 is a value of the y-axis, but the value of 10 for the x-axis was determined by the `barplot` function. You can query the settings with `par("usr")`, which will return the start and end of the x-axis followed by the same figures for the y-axis. Those figures for this graph are 0.56, 12.44, −0.17, 17.00. So we see that the x-axis goes from 0.56 to 12.44 and the y-axis goes from −0.17 to 17.00.
2. The `c("Female","Male")` argument supplies the value labels to print in the legend. It is up to you to match them to the values of the factor gender, so be careful!
3. The `fill=c("gray90","gray60")` argument supplies colors to match the `col` argument in the `barplot` function. Again, it is up to you to make these match the labels as well as the graph itself! The `ggplot2` package covered in the next chapter does this for you autotmatically.

This was a lot of work for a legend. R's traditional graphics trades off ease of use for power. We are only skimming the surface of R's traditional graphics flexibility.

15.3 Graphics *Par*ameters and Multiple Plots on a Page

R's traditional graphics make it very easy to place multiple graphs on a page. You could also use your word processor to create a table and insert graphs into the cells, but then you would have to do extra work to make them all of the proper size and position, especially if their axes should line up for comparison. You still have to specify the axes' ranges to ensure compatibility, but then R would size and position them properly. The built-in `lattice` package and the `ggplot2` package will also standardize the axes automatically.

Another problem with using word processors to place multiple graphs on a page is that text can shrink so small as to be illegible. Using R to create multiframe plots will solve these problems.

There are three different approaches to creating multiframe plots in R. We will discuss the approach that uses the `par` function. The name `par` is short for graphics *par*ameters. It is easy to use but is limited to equal-sized plots.

If you need to create more complex multiframe plots, see the help files for either the `layout` function or the `split.screen` function.

R also has some functions, such as `coplot` and `pairs`, that create multiframe plots themselves. Those plots cannot be one piece of an even larger multiframe plot. Even if R could do it, it would be quite a mess!

In traditional graphics, you use the `par` function to set or query graphic parameter settings. Entering simply `par()` will display all 71 parameters and how they are set. That is a lot, so we will use the `head` function to print just the top few parameters. Tables 15.1 through 15.4 show all of the graphics parameters and functions we use to embellish traditional plots.

```
> head( par() )

$xlog
 [1] FALSE

$ylog
 [1] FALSE

$adj
 [1] 0.5

$ann
 [1] TRUE

$ask
 [1] FALSE

$bg
 [1] "transparent"
```

We can see above that the xlog parameter is set to FALSE, meaning that the x-axis will not be scaled via the logarithm. The ask parameter is also FALSE, telling us that if R wants to display multiple graph pages, it will not pause to ask you to click your mouse (or Enter key) to continue. Entering the following will change that setting. However, if you are already running graphs one at a time, this setting can get irritating. Setting it back to FALSE will turn it off and plots will automatically replace one another again.

```
> par(ask=TRUE)
```

Notice that there is no verification of this for the moment. If we wish to query the setting of any particular parameter, we can enter it in quotes, as we do below.

```
> par( "mfrow" )
  [1] 1 1
```

The mfrow parameter sets how many rows and columns of graphs appear on one multiframe plot. The setting 1,1 means that only one graph will appear (one row and one column). Let us change that to 2,2 so we can see four graphs on a page. We will create four different bar charts of counts to see the impact of the argument, beside=TRUE (the default value is FALSE). The graphs will appear as we read words: left to right and top to bottom (Fig. 15.14).

```
> par( mfrow=c(2,2) ) #set to 2 rows, 2 columns of graphs.
>
> barplot( table(gender,workshop) ) #top left
> barplot( table(workshop,gender) ) #top right
> barplot( table(gender,workshop), beside=TRUE ) #bot left
> barplot( table(workshop,gender), beside=TRUE ) #bot right
>
> par( mfrow=c(1,1) ) #set back to 1 graph per page.
```

15.4 Pie Charts

As the R help file for the pie function says, "Pie charts are a very bad way of displaying information. The eye is good at judging linear measures and bad at judging relative areas. A bar chart or dot chart is a preferable way of displaying this type of data."

The pie function works much in the same way as the barplot function (Fig. 15.15).

```
> pie( table(workshop),
+    col=c("white","gray90","gray60","black" ),
+    main="Piechart of Workshop Attendance" )
```

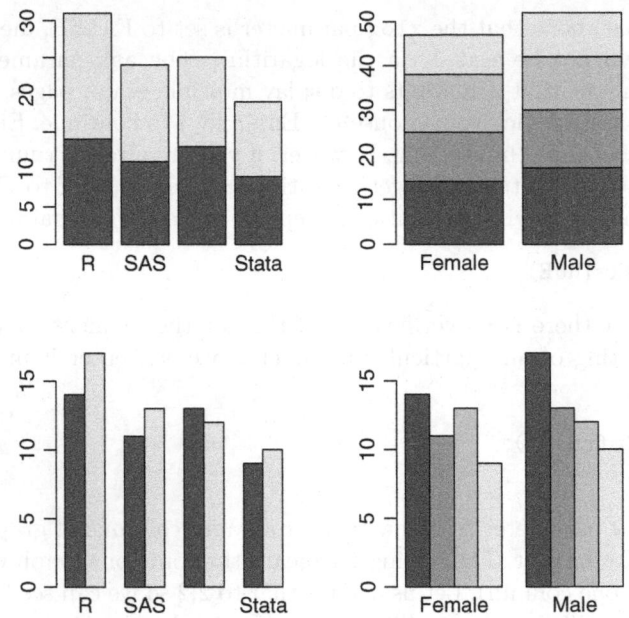

Fig. 15.14. Bar plots of counts by workshop and gender. The top two use the default argument, `beside=FALSE`; the bottom two specify `beside=TRUE`. The left two tabulated (`gender,workshop`); the right two tabulated (`workshop,gender`).

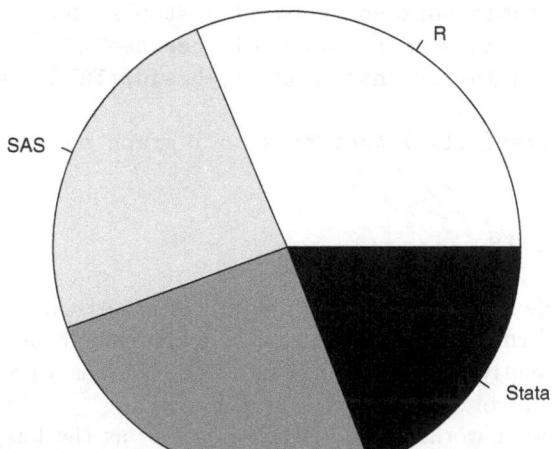

Fig. 15.15. A pie chart of workshop.

15.5 Dot Charts

William Cleveland popularized the dot chart in his book *Visualizing Data* [6]. Based on research that showed people excel at determining the length of a line, he reduced the bar chart to just dots on lines. R makes it very easy to do (Fig. 15.16). The arguments to the `dotchart` function are essentially the same as those for the `barplot` function. The dots in the dot chart do not show up well in the small image below, so I have added `cex=1.5` for character *ex*pansion.

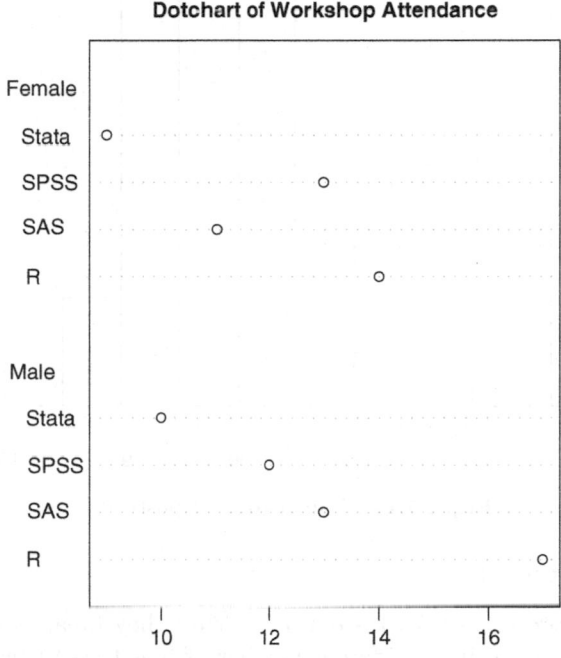

Fig. 15.16. A dot chart of workshop within gender.

```
> dotchart( table(workshop,gender),
+    main="Dotchart of Workshop Attendance",
+    cex=1.5)
```

15.6 Histograms

Many statistical methods make assumptions about the distribution of your data. As long as you have enough data, say 30 or more data points, histograms are a good way to examine those assumptions. We will start with basic histograms and then examine a few variations.

15.6.1 Basic Histograms

To get a histogram of our posttest score, all we need to do is enter a call to the hist function (Fig. 15.17).

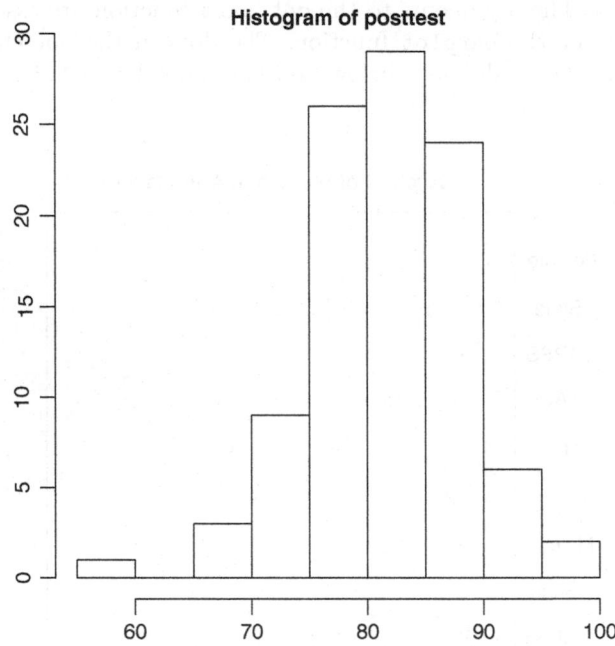

Fig. 15.17. A histogram of posttest.

```
> hist(posttest)
```

One of the problems with histograms is that they break continuous data into artificial bins. Trying a different number of bins to see how that changes the view of the distribution is a good idea.

In Fig. 15.18, we use the breaks=20 argument to get far more bars than we saw in the default plot. The argument probability=TRUE causes the y-axis to display probability instead of counts. That does not change the overall look of the histogram, but it does allow us to add a kernel density fit with a combination of the lines function and the density function.

```
> hist(posttest, breaks=20, probability=TRUE)
```

The lines function draws the smooth kernel density calculated by the call to the density function. You can vary the amount of smoothness in this function with the adjust argument. See the help file for details.

```
> lines( density(posttest) )
```

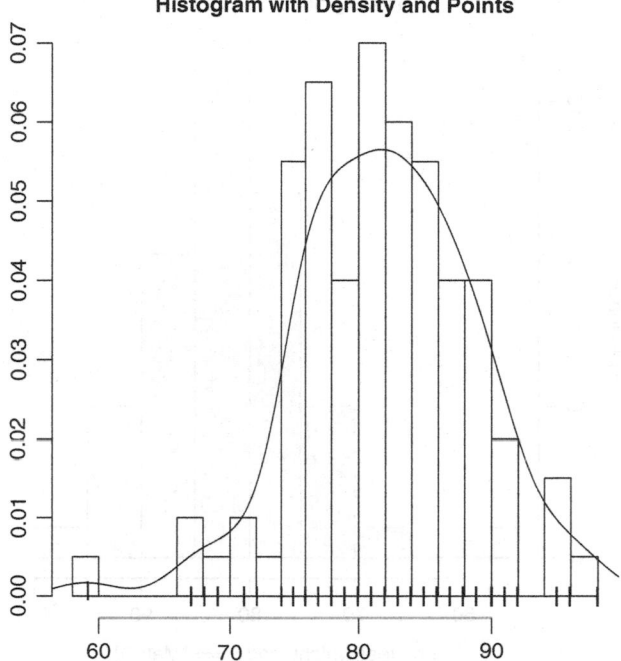

Fig. 15.18. A histogram of posttest with `breaks=20`, a kernel density curve and tick-marks for every data point on the x-axis.

Finally, we can add tick marks to the x-axis to show the exact data points. We can do that with the **points** function, which adds a series of x, y points anywhere on a plot. We already have the x values in our posttest variable. If we want ticks on the y-axis, we need a vector of zeros that is the same length as our posttest score. The **rep** function makes quick work of it by *rep*eating the value zero to match the length of the posttest variable.

```
> myZeros <- rep(0, length(posttest) )
```

```
> myZeros
 [1] 0 0 0 0 0 0 0 0 0 0 0 0 0 0 0 0 0 0 0 0 0 0 0 0 0 0 0 0 0
[30] 0 0 0 0 0 0 0 0 0 0 0 0 0 0 0 0 0 0 0 0 0 0 0 0 0 0 0 0 0
[59] 0 0 0 0 0 0 0 0 0 0 0 0 0 0 0 0 0 0 0 0 0 0 0 0 0 0 0 0 0
[88] 0 0 0 0 0 0 0 0 0 0 0 0 0
```

```
> points( posttest, myZeros, pch="|" )
```

Now let us get a histogram of just the males. Recall from Chapter 8, "Selecting Observations," that posttest[gender=="Male"] will make the selection we need. We will also add the argument `col=gray60` to give the bars a "color" of gray (Fig. 15.19).

```
> hist(posttest[ which(gender=="Male") ], col="gray60")
```

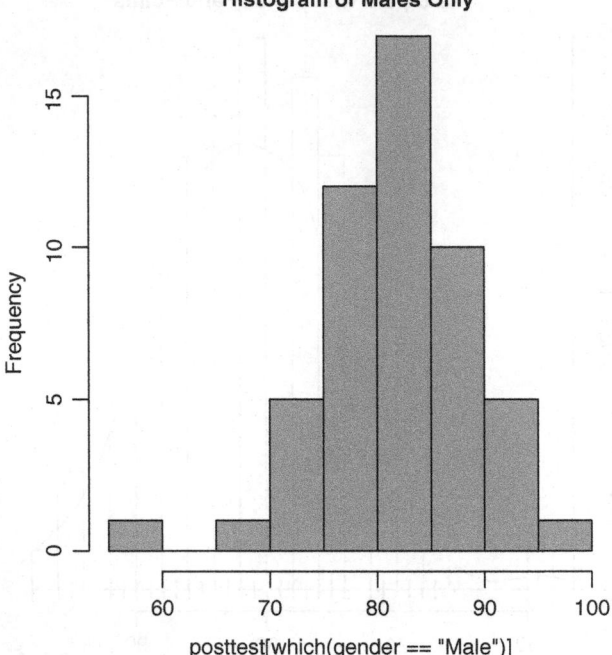

Fig. 15.19. A histogram of posttest for only the males.

15.6.2 Histograms Stacked

If we want to compare two plots more directly, we can put them onto a multiframe plot (Fig. 15.20) with the graphic parameter function

```
par( mfrow=c(2,1) )
```

To make them more comparable, we will ensure that they break the data into bars at the same spots using the breaks argument.

```
> par( mfrow=c(2,1) ) # multiframe plot, 2 rows, 1 column

> hist(posttest, col="gray90",
+    breaks=c(50,55,60,65,70,75,80,85,90,95,100) )

> hist(posttest[gender=="Male"], col="gray60",
+    breaks=c(50,55,60,65,70,75,80,85,90,95,100) )

> par( mfrow=c(1,1) ) # back to 1 graph per plot
```

I entered all of the break points to make it clear for beginners. Once you get more used to R, it will be much easier to specify *seq*uences of numbers using the seq function:

```
...breaks = seq(10, 100, by=50)
```

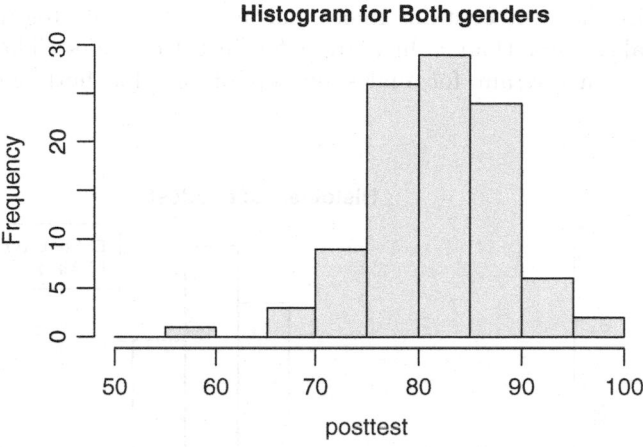

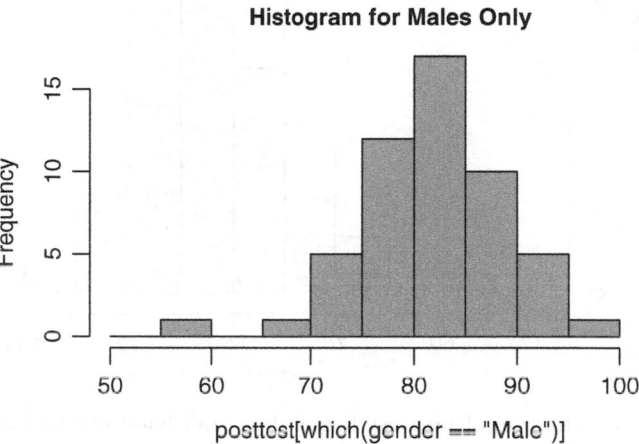

Fig. 15.20. Multiframe plot of posttest histograms for whole data set (top) and just the males (bottom).

See Chapter 12, "Generating Data" for more ways to generate values like this.

15.6.3 Histograms Overlaid

That looks nice, but we could get a bit fancier and plot the two graphs right on top of one another. The next few examples start slow and end up rather complicated compared to similar plots in Stata. In the next chapter, the same plot will be *much* simpler. However, this is an important example because it helps you learn the type of information held inside a graphics object.

Our entire data set contains males and females, so a histogram of both will have taller bars than a histogram for just the males. Therefore, we can overlay a histogram for males on top of one for both genders; see Fig. 15.21.

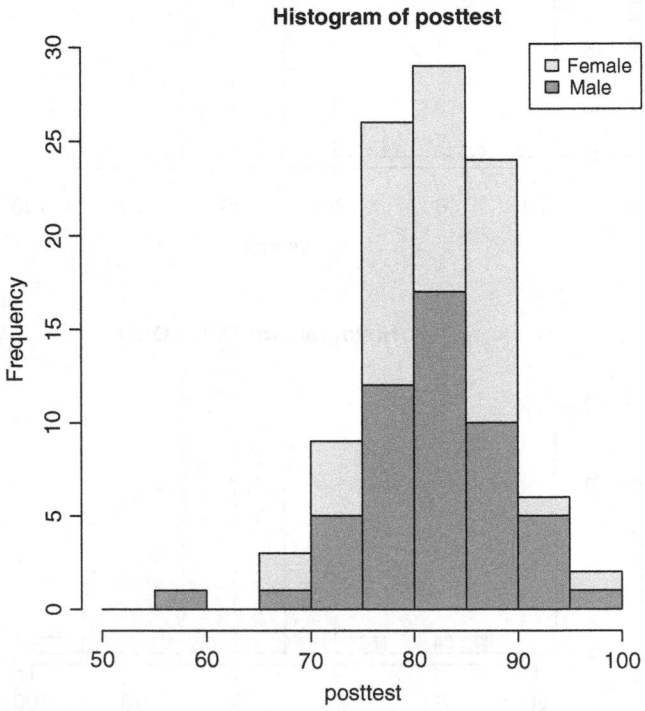

Fig. 15.21. A histogram of posttest for all data (tall bars) overlaid with just the males. The difference between the two represents the females.

The `add=TRUE` argument is what tells the `hist` function to add the second histogram on top of the first. Notice below that we also use the `seq` function to generate the numbers 50, 55,. . .,100 without having to write them all out as we did in the previous example.

```
> hist(posttest, col="gray90",
+   breaks=seq(from=50, to=100, by=5) )

> hist(posttest[gender=="Male"], col="gray60",
+   breaks=seq(from=50, to=100, by=5),
+   add=TRUE )

> legend( "topright", c("Female","Male"),
+   fill=c("gray90","gray60") )
```

This looks good, but we did have to manually decide what the breaks should be. In a more general-purpose program, we may want R to choose the break-points in the first plot and then apply them to the second automatically. We can do that by saving the first graph to an object called, say, myHistogram.

```
> myHistogram <- hist(posttest, col="gray90")
```

Now let us use the names function to see the names of its components.

```
> names(myHistogram)

[1] "breaks"      "counts"      "intensities" "density"
[5] "mids"        "xname"       "equidist"
```

One part of this object, myHistogram$breaks, stores the breakpoints that we will use in the second histogram. The graph of all of the data appears at this point and we can print the contents of myHistogram$breaks. Notice that R has decided that our manually selected breakpoint of 50 was not needed.

```
> myHistogram$breaks

[1]  55  60  65  70  75  80  85  90  95 100
```

Let us now do the histogram for males again, but this time with the argument,

```
breaks=myHistogram$breaks
```

so the break points for males will be the same as those automatically chosen for the whole sample (Fig. 15.22).

```
> hist(posttest[gender=="Male"], col='gray60',
+        add=TRUE, breaks=myHistogram$breaks)

> legend( "topright", c("Female","Male"),
+    fill=c("gray90","gray60") )
```

This is essentially the same as the previous graph, but the axis fits better by not extending all the way down to 50. Of course, we could have noticed that and fixed it manually if we had wanted. To see what else a histogram class object contains, simply enter its name. You see the breaks listed as its first element.

```
> myHistogram
$breaks
 [1]  55  60  65  70  75  80  85  90  95 100

$counts
 [1]  1  0  3  9 26 29 24  6  2
```

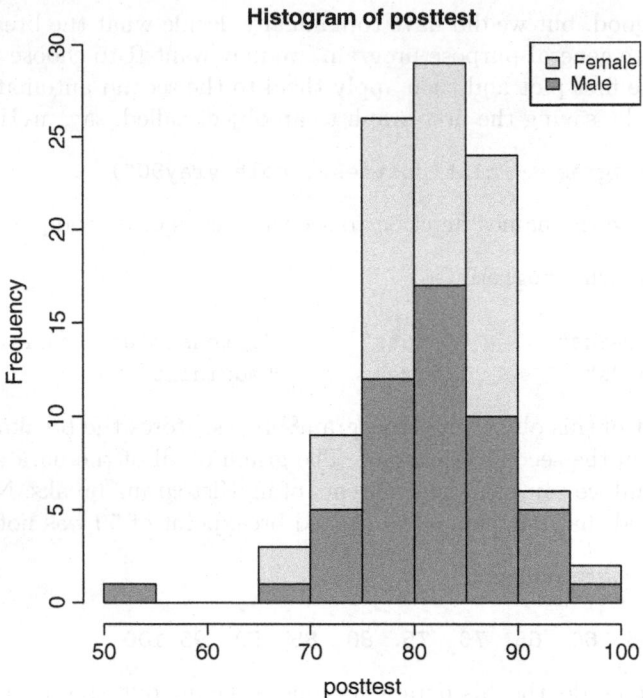

Fig. 15.22. Same histogram as in Fig. 15.21 but now bar breakpoints are chosen from the whole data set and then applied to males.

```
$intensities
 [1] 0.002 0.000 0.006 0.018 0.052 0.058 0.048 0.012 0.004

$density
 [1] 0.002 0.000 0.006 0.018 0.052 0.058 0.048 0.012 0.004

$mids
 [1] 57.5 62.5 67.5 72.5 77.5 82.5 87.5 92.5 97.5

$xname
 [1] "posttest"

$equidist
 [1] TRUE

attr(,"class")
 [1] "histogram"
```

Now that the plot is saved in myHistogram, we can display it any time with

```
plot(myHistogram)
```

You can change the plot object using standard R programming methods; you are not restricted to modifying it with the function that created it. That is a tricky way to work, but you can see how someone working to develop a new type of graph would revel in this extreme flexibility.

15.7 Normal QQ Plots

A normal QQ plot plots the quantiles of each data point against the quantiles that each point would get if the data were normally distributed. If these points fall on a straight line, they are likely to be from a normal distribution.

Histograms give you a nice view of a variable's distribution, but if you have fewer than 30 or so points, the resulting histogram is often impossible to interpret. Another problem with histograms is that they break the data into artificial bins, so unless you fiddle with bin size, you might miss an interesting pattern in your data. A QQ plot has neither of these limitations.

So why use histograms at all? Because they are easy to interpret. At a statistical meeting I attended, the speaker displayed a QQ plot and asked the audience, all statisticians, what the distribution looked like. It was clearly not normal and people offered quite an amusing array of responses! When the shape is not a straight line, it takes time to learn how the line's shape reflects the underlying distribution. To make matters worse, some software reverses the roles of the two axes! The plot shown in Fig. 15.23, created using the

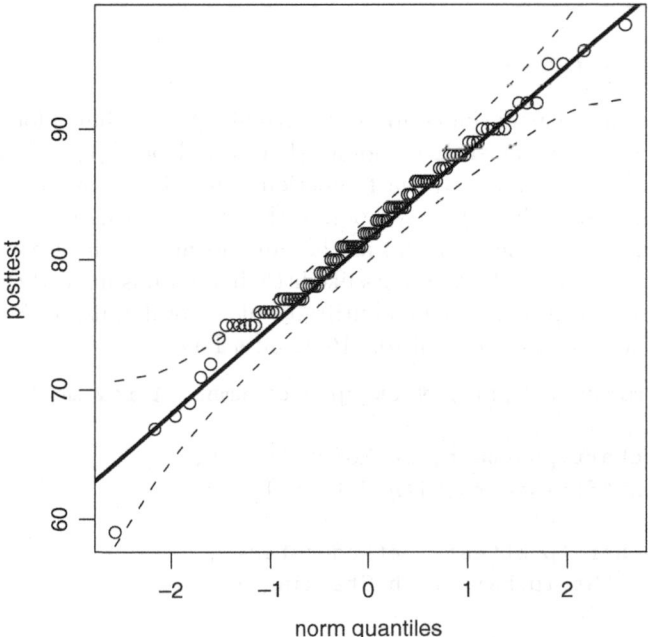

Fig. 15.23. A normal quantile plot of posttest using `qq.plot` from the `car` package.

qq.plot function from John Fox's car package, has the theoretical quantiles on the *x*-axis, like Stata.

```
> library("car")

> qq.plot(posttest,
+    labels=row.names(mydata100),
+    col="black" )

> detach("package:car")
```

The call to the qq.plot function above has three arguments.

1. The variable to plot.
2. labels=row.names(mydata100) allows you to interactively identify any point you wish and label it according by the values you request. Your cursor will become a cross-hair and when you click on (or near) a point, its label will appear. The escape key will end this interactive mode.
3. col="black" sets the color, which is red by default.

R also has a built-in function for QQ plots called qqnorm. However, it lacks confidence intervals. It also does not let you identify points without calling the identify function (graph not shown).

```
myQQ <- qqnorm(posttest)

identify(myQQ)
```

15.8 Strip Charts

Strip charts are scatter plots for one variable. Since they plot each data point, you might see clusters of points that would be lost in a box plot or error bar plot. The first stripchart function call below uses "jitter" or random noise added to help you see points that would otherwise be obscured by falling on top of other point(s) at the same location. The second one uses method="stack" to stack the points like little histograms instead (Fig. 15.24). Here we do both types in a single multiframe plot. For details, see Section 15.3, "Graphics Parameters and Multiple Plots on a Page."

```
> par( mfrow=c(2,1) ) #set up 2 columns, 1 row multiplot

> stripchart(posttest, method="jitter",
+    main="Stripchart with Jitter")

> stripchart(posttest, method="stack",
+    main="Stripchart with Stacking")

> par( mfrow=c(1,1) ) # restore to 1 plot
```

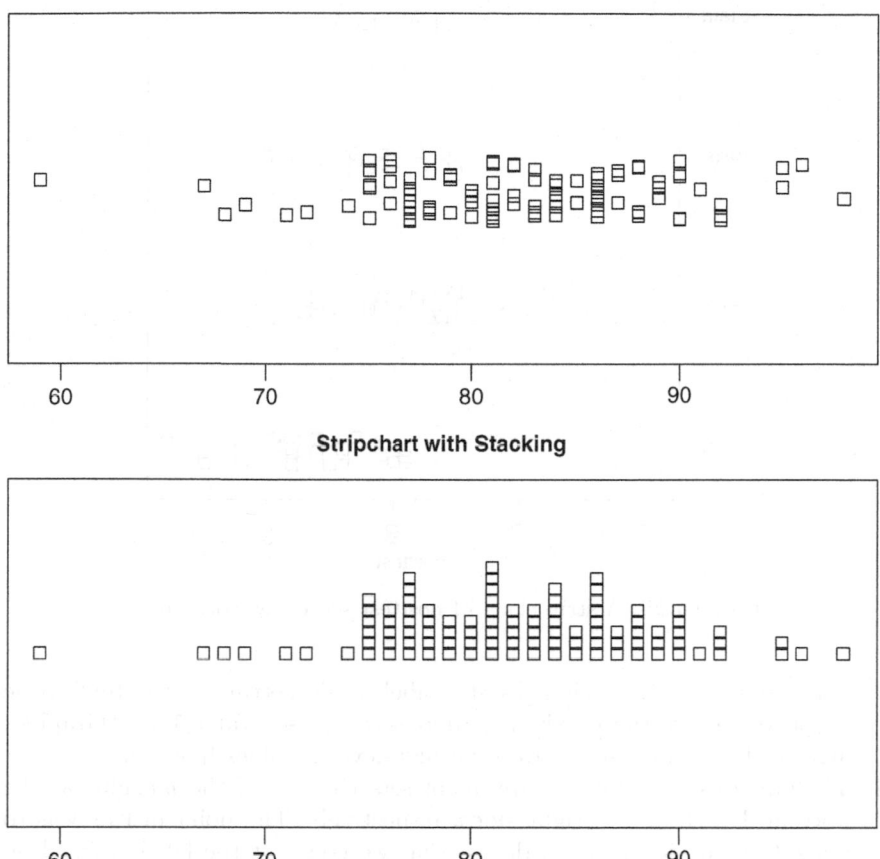

Fig. 15.24. Strip chart demonstrating the methods jitter and stack.

Let us now compare groups using strip charts (Fig. 15.25). Notice the use of the formula `posttest~workshop` to compare the workshop groups. You can reverse the order of those two variables to flip the scatter vertically, but you would lose the automated labels for the factor levels.

```
> par( las=2, mar=c(4,8,4,1)+0.1  )
```

```
> stripchart(posttest ~ workshop, method="jitter")
```

The `par` function here is optional. I use it just to angle the workshop value labels so that they are easier to read. Turned that way, they need more space on the left of the chart. The `par` function call above uses two arguments to accomplish this.

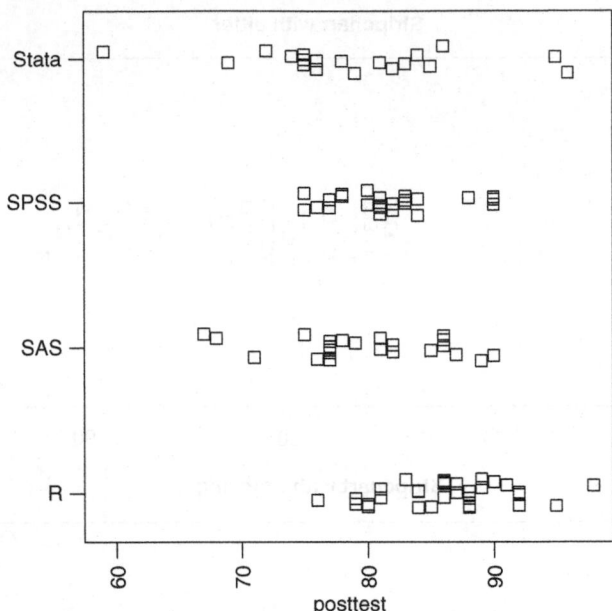

Fig. 15.25. A strip chart of posttest scores by workshop.

1. The `las=2` argument changes the *label angle setting* of the text to be perpendicular to the *y*-axis. For more settings, see Table 15.1, "Graphics arguments for use with traditional high-level graphics functions."
2. The `mar=c(4,8,4,1)0.1+` argument sets the size of the *margins* at the bottom, left, top, and right sides, respectively. The point of this was to make the left side much wider so that we could fit the labels turned on

Table 15.1. Graphics arguments for use with traditional high-level graphics functions.

main	Supplies the text to the *main* title.
	E.g. `plot(pretest,posttest,main="My Scatter plot")`
sub	Supplies the text to the *sub*-title.
	E.g. `plot(pretest,posttest...sub="My Scatter plot")`
xlab	An argument that supplies the *x*-axis *label* (variable labels from `Hmisc` package are ignored).
	E.g. `plot(pretest,posttest...xlab="Score Before Training")`
xlim	An argument that specifies the lower and upper *limits* of the *x*-axis.
	E.g. `plot(pretest, posttest, xlim=c(50,100) )`
ylab	An argument that supplies the *y*-axis *label* (variable labels from `Hmisc` package are ignored).
	E.g. `plot(pretest,posttest...ylab="Score After Training")`
ylim	An argument that specifies the lower and upper *limits* of the *y*-axis.
	E.g. `plot(pretest, posttest, ylim=c(50,100) )`

Table 15.2. Graphics *parameters* to set or query using only `par()`.

ask	`par(ask=TRUE)` causes R to prompt you before showing a new graphic. The default setting of FALSE causes it to automatically replace any existing plot with a new one. If you run a program in batch mode, you should set this to FALSE!
family	Sets font family for text. `par(family="sans")`, the default, requests Helvetica or Arial. `par(family="serif")` requests a serif font like Times Roman; `par(family="mono")` requests a monospaced font like Courier; `par(family="symbol")` requests math and greek Greek symbols.

mar	Sets *mar*gin size in number of lines. The default setting is
	 `par( mar=c(5,4,4,2)+0.1  )`
	 which sets number of margin lines in order (bottom, left, top, right). For graphs that lack labels, you may want to decrease the margins to eliminate superfluous white space. An example that sets label angle style to perpendicular and provides eight lines on the left side is
	 `par( las=2, mar=c(4,8,4,1)+0.1  )`

mfrow	Sets up a *multif*rame plot to contain several other plots. R will plot to them left to right, top to bottom. This example yields three rows of two plots. `par( mfrow=c(3,2)  )` This returns it to a single plot: `par( mfrow=c(1,1)  )`
mfcol	Sets up a *multif*rame plot like `mfrow`, but writes plots in *col*umns from top to bottom, left to right.
new	Setting `par(new=TRUE)` tells R that a new plot has already been started so that it will not erase what is there before adding to it.
par()	Will display all traditional graphics *parameters*.
ps	Sets the *p*oint *s*ize of text. For example, to select 12-point text: `par(ps=12)`
usr	Shows you the coordinates of a plot in the form x-start, x-stop, y-start, y-stop.
xlog	Setting `par(xlog=TRUE)`, requests a *log*arithm-transformed x-axis, including tick-marks.
ylog	Setting `par(ylog=TRUE)`, requests a *log*arithm-transformed y-axis, including tick-marks.

their sides. For details, see Table 15.2, "Graphics *parameters* to set or query using only `par()`."

The `stripchart` function call above contains two arguments.

1. The formula `posttest~workshop`, which asks for a strip chart of posttest for every value of workshop.
2. The `method="jitter"` argument that tells it to add random noise to help us see the points that would otherwise be plotted on top of others.

Table 15.3. Graphics parameters for both **par** and graphics functions.

adj	Sets justification of text with 0=left, 0.5=center, 1=right.
cex	Sets *character expansion* size of text as a multiplication factor. For example, **cex=1.5** would make all of the text in a plot 50% larger. You can control individual elements via the following:
	axis: **cex.axis**, axis labels: **cex.lab**, main title: **cex.main**,
	subtitles: **cex.sub**.
col	Sets *color* of bars, lines, and points. Enter **colors()** to see them all. You can control individual elements with the following:
	axis: **col.axis**, axis labels: **col.lab**, main titles: **col.main**,
	subtitles: **col.sub**.
	E.g. **barplot(table(gender), col=c("gray90","gray60"))**
font	Sets font for text elements. You can control individual elements with the following:
	axes: **font.axis**, labels: **font.lab**, main title: **font.main**,
	subtitles: **font.sub**.
	The levels are: 1=plain, 2=bold, 3=italic, 4=bold italic, 5=symbol.
	E.g. **plot(x,y...font.main=3,main="My Italic Title")**
las	Performs *label angle setting* in margins. Levels are the following:
	0=text parallel to its axis, 1=horizontal,
	2=text perpendicular to its axis, 3=vertical.
	E.g. **par(las=2)**
lty	The *line type* argument applies to functions that create lines such as the functions such as **abline** and **lines** as well as to the **par** and **legend** functions. The types of lines you can request are as follows:
	0=blank, 1=solid, 2=dashed, 3=dotted,
	4=dot-dash, 5=long dash, 6=two dashes.
	E.g. **lines(lowess(posttest ~ pretest), lty=3)**
lwd	Determines *line width*. The default value is 1 and the resulting width varies by graphics device.
	E.g. **lines(lowess(posttest ~ pretest), lwd=2)**
mtext	A function that adds *text* to the *m*argins of a plot. Its arguments are the line of text from 0 to N, the side of the margin (1=bottom, 2=left, 3=top, 4=right) and the "at" value, which is in terms of the axis scale itself. E.g. **mtext("line=2", side=2, line=2, at=65)**
pch	An argument to function that plot *point characters* like a scatter plot. "."=tiny dot, 1=circle, 2=triangle up, 3=+, 4=X, 5=diamond, 6=triangle pointing down. see **help(points)** for more.
	E.g. **plot(pretest,posttest,pch=2)**
srt	*S*ets *r*otation of *t*ext in plot region.
	E.g. text at 45°: **text(65,85,"My Tilted Text", srt=45)**

Table 15.4. Graphics functions to add elements to existing plots.

abline	A function that adds straight *line*(s) to an existing plot in the form $y=a+bx$. Example of intercept 0, slope 1: `abline(a=0, b=1, lty=5)` E.g. linear model line: `abline( lm(posttest ~ pretest), lty=1 )`
arrows	A function that draws an arrow with the arguments (from–*x*, from–*y*, to–*x*, to–*y*). The optional `length` argument sets the length of the arrowhead lines. E.g. `arrows(65,85,58.5,60.5, length=0.1)`
axis	A function that adds an axis to an existing plot. E.g. `axis(4)` adds it to the right side (1=bottom, 2=left, 3=top, 4=right).
box	A function that adds a box around an exsisting plot. E.g. `box()`
grid	A function that adds a set of vertical and horizontal lines to an exsisting plot. E.g. `grid()`
lines	A function that adds line(s) to an existing plot (need not be straight). E.g. lowess fit: `lines( lowess(posttest ~ pretest), lty=3 )`
text	A function that adds text to an existing plot. Its arguments are the *x*,*y* position of the plot, the text, and the position of the text. Its `pos` argument *pos*itions text relative to *x*,*y* values with 1=bottom, 2=left, 3=top, 4=right. E.g. `text (65,85,"Fit is linear", pos=3)`

15.9 Scatter Plots and Line Plots

Scatter plots are helpful in many ways. They show the nature of a relationship between two variables. Is it a line? Is it a curve? Is the variability in one variable the same at different levels of the other? Is there an outlier now visible that did not show up when checking minimum and maximum values one variable at a time? A scatter plot can answer all of these questions.

The `plot` function takes advantage of R's object orientation by being generic.; that is, it looks at the class of objects you provide it and takes the appropriate action. For example, when you give it two continuous variables, it does a scatter plot (Fig. 15.26).

```
> plot(pretest, posttest)
```

Note the "92" on the lower left point. That did not appear on the graph at first. We wanted to find which observation that was, so we used the `identify` function.

```
> identify(pretest,posttest)
```

```
[1] 92
```

The `identify` function lets label points by clicking on them. You list the *x* and *y* variables in your plot and optionally provide a `label=` argument to specify an ID variable, with the row names as the default. The function will

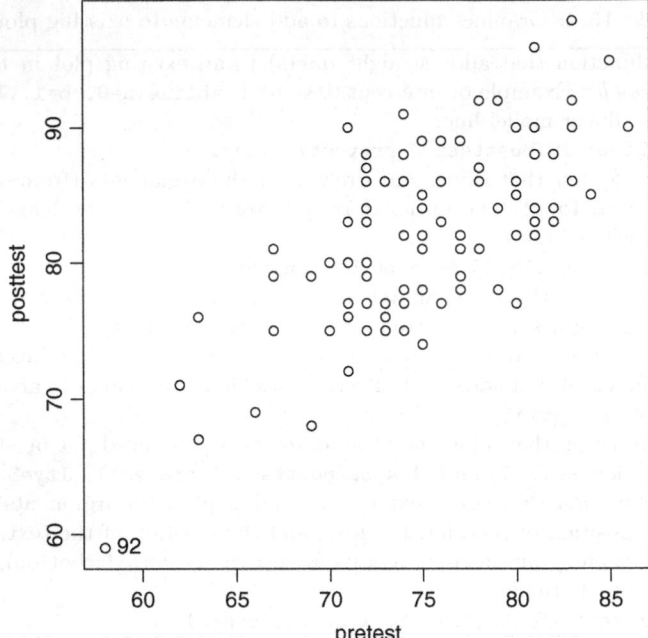

Fig. 15.26. A scatter plot of pretest and posttest. Observation 92 (lower left) was identified after the plot was created.

label the point you click on or near. Unfortunately, it does not let you draw a box around a set of points. You must click on each one, which can get a bit tedious. When finished, users can right-click and choose "stop" (or press the *Esc* key on Windows). It will then print out the values you chose. If you assigned the result to a vector as in

```
myPoints <- identify(pretest,posttest)
```

then that vector would contain all your selected points. You could then use logic like

```
summary( mydata100[!myPoints, ] )
```

(not myPoints) to exclude the selected points and see how it changes your analysis. Below, I use a logical selection to verify that it is indeed observation 92 that has the low score.

```
> mydata100[pretest<60, ]

      gender workshop q1 q2 q3 q4 pretest posttest
92      Male     Stata  3  4  4  4      58       59
```

Back to the scatter plot, you can specify the `type` argument to change how the points are displayed. The values use the letter "p" for points, the letter "l" for lines, "b" for both points and lines, and "h" for histogram-like lines that rise vertically from the x-axis. Connecting the points using either "l" or "b" makes sense only when the points are collected in a certain order, such as time series data. As you can see in Fig. 15.27, that is not the case with our data, so those appear as a jumbled nest of lines.

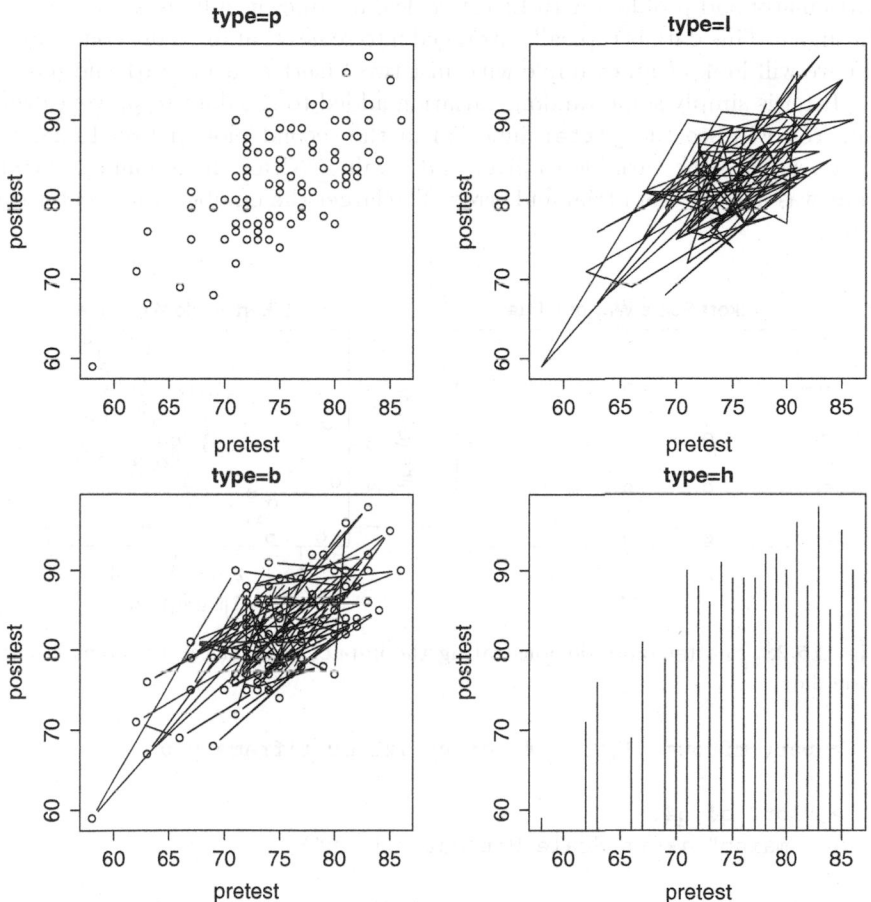

Fig. 15.27. Various scatter plots demonstrating the effect of the `type` argument.

```
> par( mfrow=c(2,2) ) # set up a 2x2 multiframe plot

> plot( pretest, posttest, type="p", main="type=p" )
> plot( pretest, posttest, type="l", main="type=l" )
> plot( pretest, posttest, type="b", main="type=b" )
```

```
> plot( pretest, posttest, type="h", main="type=h" )

> par( mfrow=c(1,1) ) # set parameter back to 1 plot
```

15.9.1 Scatter plots with Jitter

The more points you have in a scatter plot, the more likely you are to have them overlap, potentially hiding the true structure of the data. This is a particularly bad problem with Likert-scale data since it only uses the values 1 through 5. This data is typically averaged into scales that are more continuous, but we will look at an example with just two Likert measures: q1 and q4.

Jitter is simply some random variation added to the data to prevent overlap. You will see the `jitter` function in the second plot in Fig. 15.28. Its arguments are the variable to jitter and a value "3" for the amount of jitter. That was derived from trial and error. The larger the number, the greater the jitter.

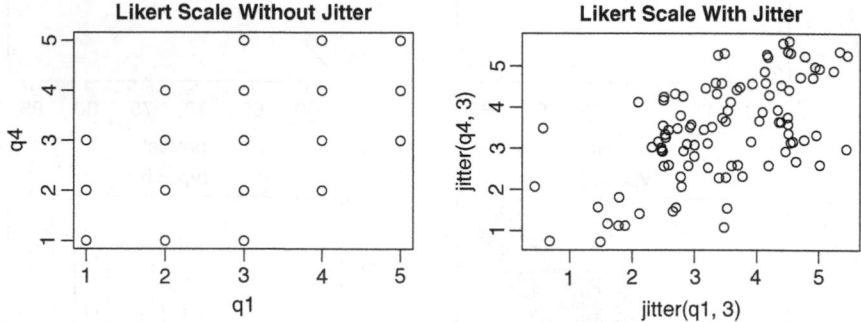

Fig. 15.28. Scatter plots demonstrating the impact of jitter on five-point Likert-scale data.

```
> par( mfrow=c(1,2) ) # set up 1x2 multiframe plot

> plot( q1,q4,
+   main="Likert Scale Without Jitter")

> plot( jitter(q1,3), jitter(q4,3),
+   main="Likert Scale With Jitter")

> par( mfrow=c(1,1) ) # reset to single plot
```

15.9.2 Scatter plots with Large Data Sets

The larger your data set, the more likely that it is some points will be hidden by others. That makes jitter, described in the previous subsection, particularly useful. It is also helpful to use the smallest *point ch*aracter with `pch="."`.

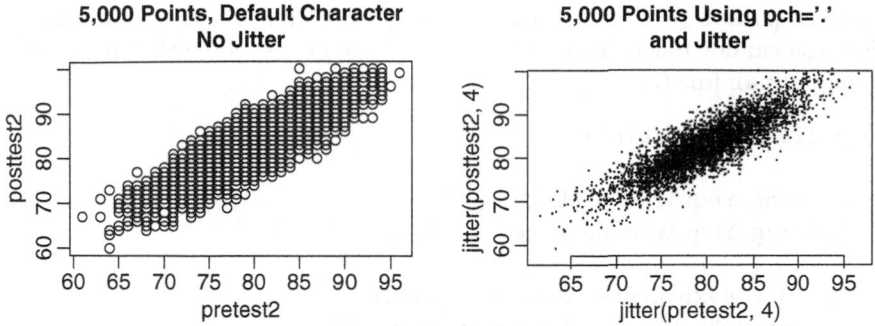

Fig. 15.29. Scatter plots showing how to handle large data sets. The plot on the left using default settings leaves many points obscured. The one on the right uses much smaller points and jitters them, allowing us to see more points.

The following is an example using 5,000 points (Fig. 15.29). The R code that generated pretest2 and posttest2 is included in the program at the end of this chapter.

```
> plot( jitter(pretest2,4), jitter(posttest2,4), pch=".",
+   main="5,000 Points Using pch='.' \nand Jitter")
```

Another way of plotting large amounts of data is a **hexbin** plot (Fig. 15.30). This is provided via the *hexbin* package, written by Dan Carr and ported by Nicholas Lewvin-Koh and Martin Maechler [4]. Note that **hexbin** uses the

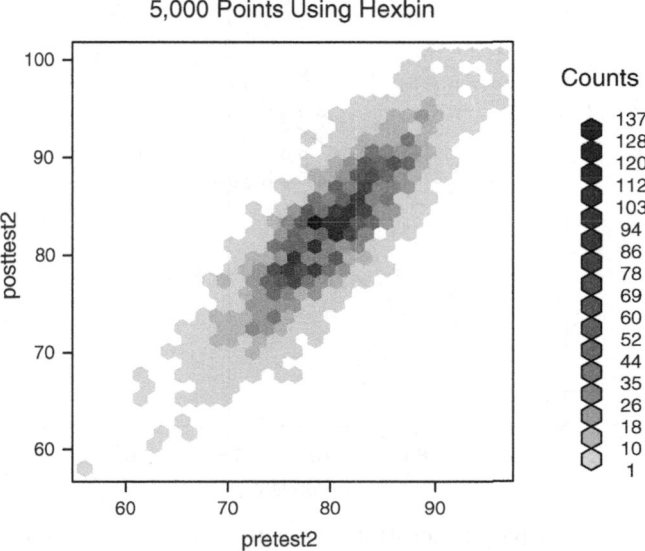

Fig. 15.30. A hexbin plot that divides large amounts of data into hexagonal bins to show structure in large data sets. Each bin can represent many original points.

lattice package, which in turn uses the **grid** graphics system. That means that you cannot put multiple graphs on a page nor set any other parameters using the **par** function.

```
> library("hexbin")

Loading required package: grid
Loading required package: lattice

> plot( hexbin(pretest2,posttest2),
+    main="5,000 Points Using Hexbin")

> detach("package:hexbin")
```

15.9.3 Scatter plots with Lines

You can add straight lines to your plots with the **abline** function. It has several different types of arguments. Let us start with a scatter plot with only points on it (Fig 15.31).

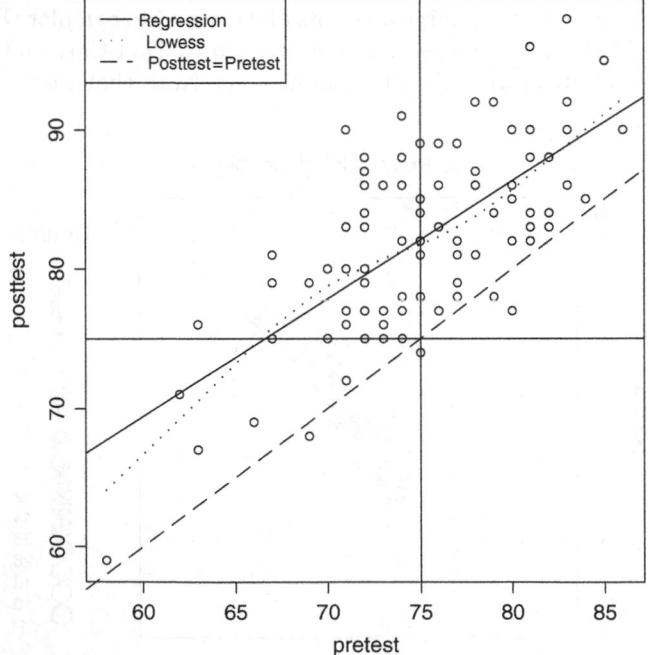

Fig. 15.31. A scatter plot demonstrating how to add various types of lines, as well as a legend and title.

```
> plot(posttest ~ pretest)
```

Now let us add a horizontal line and a vertical line at the value 75. You might do this if there were a cutoff below which students were not allowed to take the next workshop.

```
> abline( h=75, v=75 )
```

The `abline` function exists to add straight lines to the last plot you did, so there is no `add=TRUE` argument. Next, let us draw a diagonal line that has pretest equal to posttest. If the workshop training had no effect, the scatter would lie on this line. This line would have a y-intercept of 0 and a slope of 1. The `abline` function does formulas in the form $y = a + bx$, so we want to specify $a = 0$ and $b = 1$. We will also set the *line*type to dashed with `lty=5`.

```
> abline( a=0, b=1, lty=5 )
```

Next, let us add a regression fit using the `lm` function within `abline`. The `abline` function draws straight lines, so let us use the `lines` function along with the `lowess` function to draw smoothly fitting `lowess` curve. The `legend` function allows you to choose the order of the labels, so I have listed them as they appear from top to bottom in the upper left corner of the plot.

```
> abline( lm( posttest ~ pretest ),     lty=1 )

> lines( lowess( posttest ~ pretest ), lty=3 )

> legend( 60, 95,
+    c( "Regression", "Lowess", "Posttest=Pretest" ),
+    lty=c(1,3,5) )
```

15.9.4 Scatter plots with Linear Fit by Group

As we saw in the last subsection, it is easy to add regression lines to plots using R's traditional graphics. Let us now turn our attention to fitting a regression line separately for each group (Fig. 15.32). First, we will use the `plot` function to display the scatter, using the `pch` argument to set the *point* *ch*aracters based on gender. Gender is a factor, which cannot be used directly to set the point characters. Therefore, we are using the `as.numeric` function to convert it on the fly. That will cause it to use two symbols. If we used the `as.character` function instead, it would plot the actual characters M and F.

```
> plot(posttest~pretest,
+    pch=as.numeric(gender) )
```

Next, we simply use the `abline` function as we did earlier, but basing our regression on the males and females separately. For details about selecting observations based on group membership, see Chapter 8, "Selecting Observations."

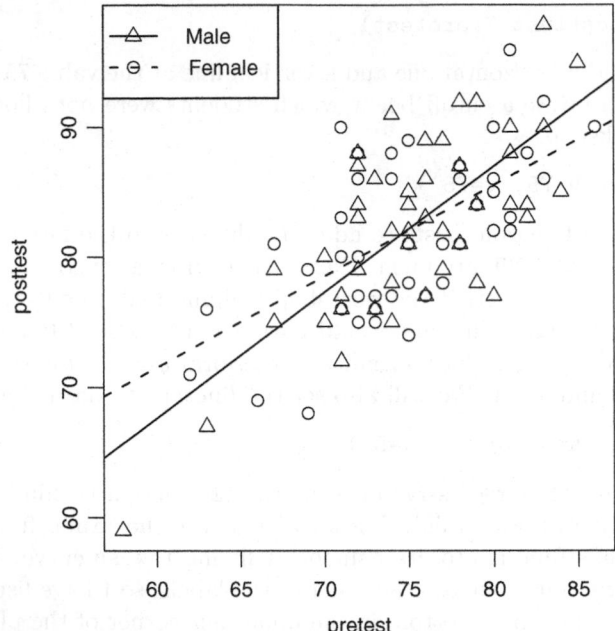

Fig. 15.32. A plot that displays different point symbols and regression lines for each gender.

```
> abline( lm( posttest[ which(gender=="Male") ]
+             ~ pretest[ which(gender=="Male") ] ),
+          lty=1 )

> abline( lm( posttest[ which(gender=="Female") ]
+             ~ pretest[ which(gender=="Female") ] ),
+          lty=2 )

> legend( "topleft", c("Male","Female"),
+          lty=c(1,2), pch=c(2,1) )
```

15.9.5 Scatter plots by Group or Level (Coplots)

Coplots are scatter plots conditioned on the levels of a third variable. For example, to get a scatter plot for each workshop is very easy. In Fig. 15.33, the box above the scatter plots indicates which plot is which. The bottom left is for R, the bottom right is for SAS, the top left is for SPSS, and the top right is for Stata. This is a rather odd layout for what could have been a simple 2 by 2 table of labels, but it makes more sense when the third variable is continuous. Both the lattice and ggplot2 packages do a better job of labeling such plots. The coplot function is easy to use. Simply specify a

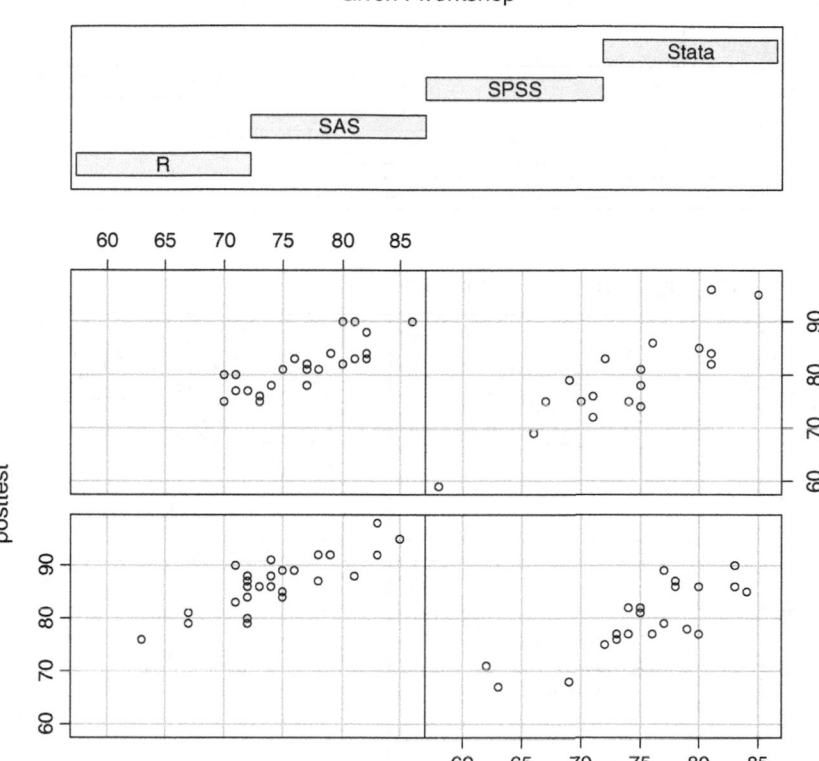

Fig. 15.33. A set of scatter plots for each workshop created using the `coplot` function. The bars in the top frame show which workshop each plot represents, from left to right, starting on the bottom row.

formula in the form **y˜x** and list your conditioning variable after a vertical bar, "|".

```
> coplot( posttest ~ pretest | workshop)
```

The next plot, Fig. 15.34, is conditioned on the levels of q1. Now the length of the bars and their overlap do an excellent job of showing the values of q1 that apply to each plot. The values of q1 in each plot overlap to prevent you from missing an important change that occurs at a single value of q1.

```
> coplot( posttest ~ pretest | q1)
```

The functions that modify plots apply to plots you create one at a time. That is true even when you build a multiframe plot one plot at a time. However, when you use a single R function that creates its own multiframe plot,

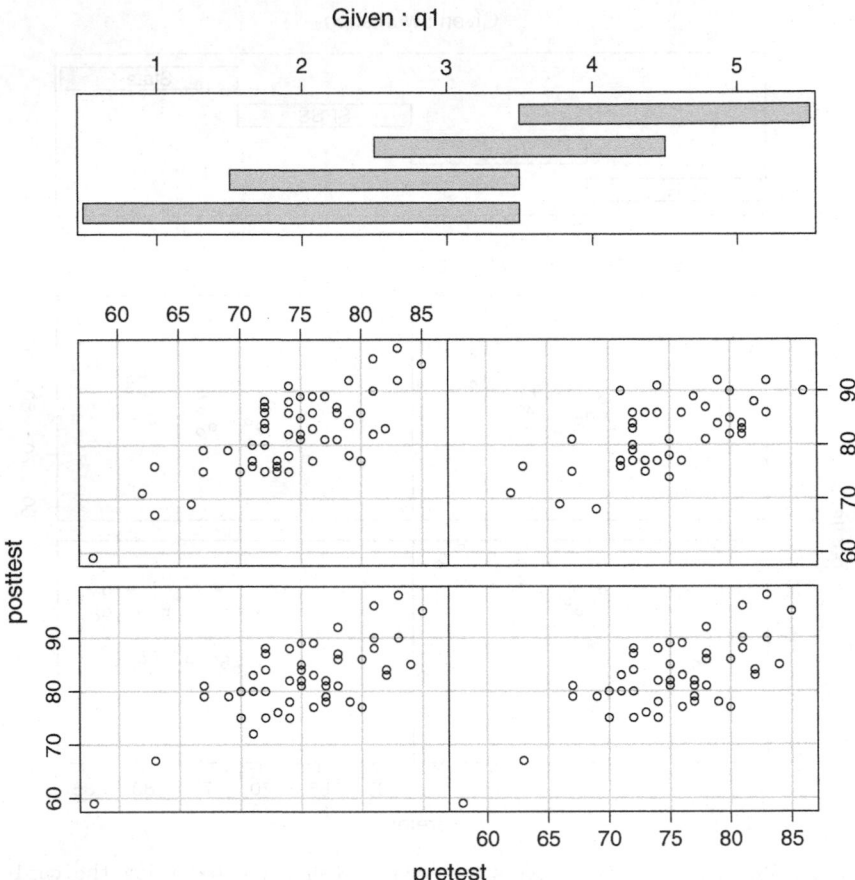

Fig. 15.34. A set of scatter plots for various levels of q1. The bars in the top frame show the values of q1 for each plot and how they overlap. Going left to right and from bottom to top, the values of q1 increase.

such as `coplot`, you can no longer use those functions. See the help file for ways to modify coplots.

15.9.6 Scatter plots with Confidence Ellipse

Confidence ellipses help visualize the strength of a correlation as well as provide a guide for identifying outliers. The `data.ellipse` function in John Fox's `car` package makes these quite easy to plot (Fig. 15.35). It works much like the `plot` function, with the first two arguments being your x and y variables, respectively. The `levels` argument lets you specify one confidence limit as shown below or you could specify a set in the usual way, for example:

```
levels=c(.25, .50, .75)
```

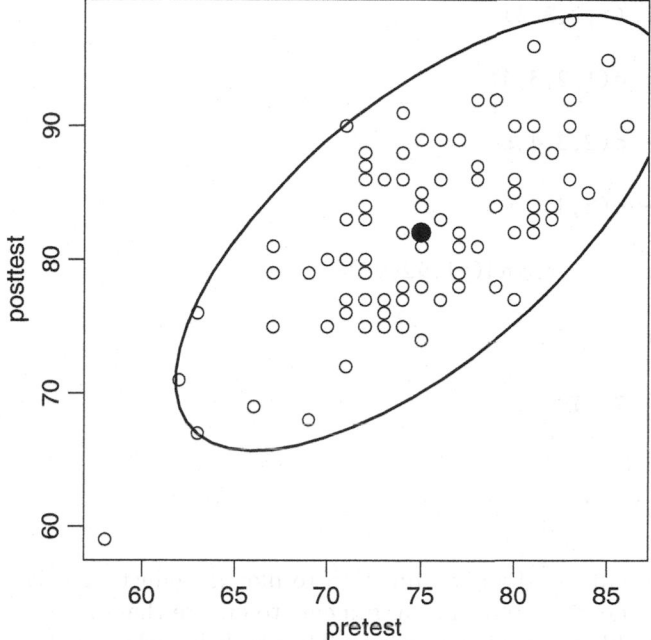

Fig. 15.35. A scatter plot with 95% confidence ellipse.

If you leave the `col="black"` argument off, it will display in its default color of red.

```
> library("car")

> data.ellipse(pretest, posttest,
+    levels=.95,
+    col="black")

> detach("package:car")
```

15.9.7 Scatter plots with Confidence and Prediction Intervals

As we saw previously, adding a regression line to a scatter plot is easy. However, adding confidence intervals is somewhat complicated. The **ggplot2** package, covered in the next chapter, makes getting a line and 95% confidence band about the line easy, but getting confidence limits about the predicted points is complicated even with it.

Let us start with a simple example. We will create a vector x and three vectors y1, y2, and y3. The three y's will represent a lower confidence limit, the prediction line, and the upper confidence limit, respectively.

```
> x <- c(1,2,3,4)

> y1 <- c(1,2,3,4)

> y2 <- c(2,3,4,5)

> y3 <- c(3,4,5,6)

> yMatrix <- cbind(y1,y2,y3)

> yMatrix

     y1 y2 y3
[1,]  1  2  3
[2,]  2  3  4
[3,]  3  4  5
[4,]  4  5  6
```

Now we will use the plot function to plot x against y2 (Fig. 15.36). We will specify the xlim and ylim arguments to ensure that the axes will be big enough to hold the other y variables. The result is rather dull! We have used

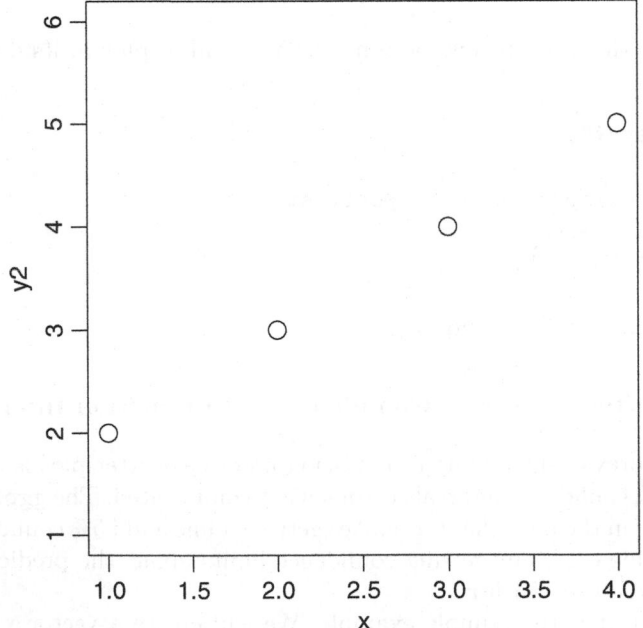

Fig. 15.36. A scatter plot of just four points on a straight line, a simple foundation to build on.

the cex=1.5 argument to do plot *character ex*pansion of 50% to make it easier to see in this small size.

```
> plot(x,y2, xlim=c(1,4), ylim=c(1,6), cex=1.5)
```

Next, we will use the `matlines` function (Fig. 15.37). It can plot a vector against every column of a matrix. We will use the `lty` argument to specify line types of dashed, solid, dashed for y1, y2, and y3, respectively. Finally, we will specify the line color as `col="black"` to prevent it from providing a different color for each line as it does by default.

```
> matlines( x, yMatrix, lty=c(2,1,2), col="black" )

> rm( x, y1, y2, y3, yMatrix)
```

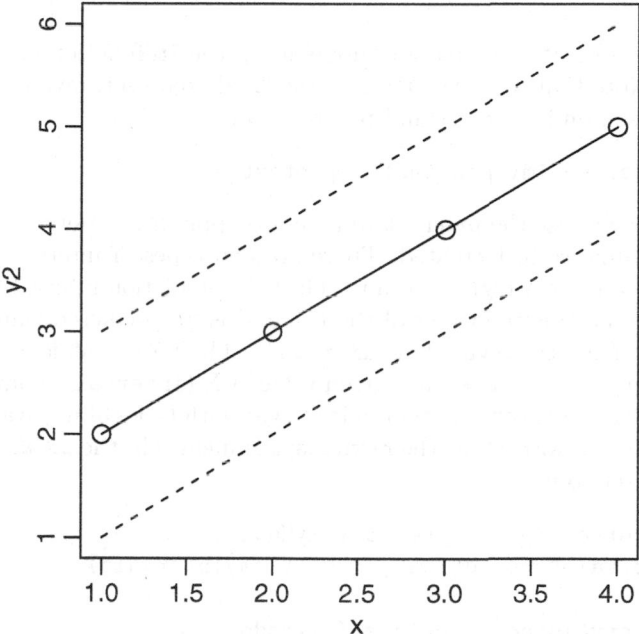

Fig. 15.37. A scatter plot that demonstrates the basic idea of a regression line with confidence intervals. With a more realistic example, the confidence bands would be curved.

This plot represents the essence of our goal. Now let us fill in the details. First, we need to create a new data frame that will hold a "well-designed" version of the pretest score. We want one that covers the range of possible values evenly. That will not be important for linear regression, since the spacing of points will not change the line, but we want to use a method that would work even if we were fitting a polynomial regression.

```
> myIntervals <-
  data.frame( pretest=seq(from=60, to=100, by=5) )

> myIntervals

  pretest
1      60
2      65
3      70
4      75
5      80
6      85
7      90
8      95
9     100
```

Now let us create a regression model using the lm function and store it in myModel. Note that we have attached the "real" data set, mydata100, so the model is based on its pretest and posttest scores.

```
> myModel <- lm( posttest ~ pretest )
```

Next, we will use the **predict** function to apply myModel to the myIntervals data frame we just created. There are two types of intervals you might wish to plot around a regression line. The 95% prediction interval (also called tolerance interval) is the wider of the two and is for predicted values of Y for new values of X (interval="prediction"). The 95% confidence interval is for the mean of the Y values at a given value of X (interval="confidence"). We will run the **predict** function twice to get both types of intervals and then look at the data. Notice that the **newdata** argument tells the **predict** function which data set to use.

```
> myIntervals$pp <- predict( myModel,
+  interval="prediction", newdata=myIntervals)

> myIntervals$pc <- predict( myModel,
+  interval="confidence", newdata=myIntervals)

> myIntervals
```

	pretest	pp.fit	pp.lwr	pp.upr	pc.fit	pc.lwr	pc.upr
1	60	69.401	59.330	79.472	69.401	66.497	72.305
2	65	73.629	63.768	83.491	73.629	71.566	75.693
3	70	77.857	68.124	87.591	77.857	76.532	79.183
4	75	82.085	72.394	91.776	82.085	81.121	83.050
5	80	86.313	76.579	96.048	86.313	84.980	87.646

6	85	90.541	80.678	100.405	90.541	88.468	92.615
7	90	94.770	84.696	104.843	94.770	91.855	97.684
8	95	98.998	88.636	109.359	98.998	95.207	102.788
9	100	103.226	92.507	113.945	103.226	98.545	107.906

Now we have all of the data we need. Look at the names pp.fit, pp.lwr, and pp.upr. They are the fit and lower/upper prediction confidence intervals. The three variables whose names begin with "pc" are the same variables for the line's narrower confidence interval. But why the funny names? Let us check the class of just "pp".

```
> class( myIntervals$pp )

 [1] "matrix"

> myIntervals$pp

       fit    lwr     upr
1  69.401 59.330  79.472
2  73.629 63.768  83.491
3  77.857 68.124  87.591
4  82.085 72.394  91.776
5  86.313 76.579  96.048
6  90.541 80.678 100.405
7  94.770 84.696 104.843
8  98.998 88.636 109.359
9 103.226 92.507 113.945
```

The predict function has added two matrices to the myIntervals data frame. Since the matlines function can plot all columns of a matrix at once, this is particularly helpful. Now let us use this information to complete our plot with both types of confidence intervals. The only argument that is new is setting the limits of the y-axis using the range function. I did that to ensure that the y-axis was wide enough to hold both the pretest scores and the wider prediction interval, pp. Finally, we see the plot in Fig. 15.38.

```
> plot( pretest, posttest,
+   ylim=range( myIntervals$pretest,
+     myIntervals$pp, na.rm=TRUE),
+     main="Regression Fit with Confidence Intervals" )

> matlines(myIntervals$pretest, myIntervals$pc,
+   lty=c(1,2,2), col="black" )

> matlines(myIntervals$pretest, myIntervals$pp,
+   lty=c(1,3,3), col="black" )
```

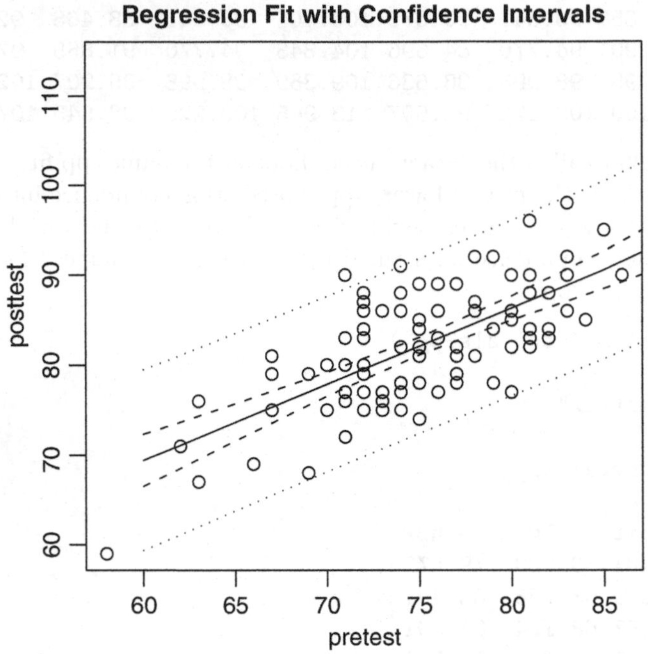

Regression Fit with Confidence Intervals

Fig. 15.38. Here we finally see the complete plot with both types of confidence intervals using our practice data set.

15.9.8 Plotting Labels Instead of Points

When you do not have too much data, it is often useful to plot labels instead of symbols (Fig. 15.39). If your label is a single character, you can do this using the pch argument. If you have a character variable, pch will accept it directly. In our case, gender is a factor, so we will use the as.character function to convert it on the fly.

```
> plot(pretest, posttest,
+    pch=as.character(gender) )
```

If you provide the pch function a longer label, it will plot only the first character. To see the whole label, you must first plot an empty graph with type="n", for *no* points, and then add to it with the text function. The text function works just like the plot function, but it plots labels instead of points. In Fig. 15.40, we are using the row.names function to provide labels. If we had wanted to plot the workshop value instead, we could have used label=as.character(workshop).

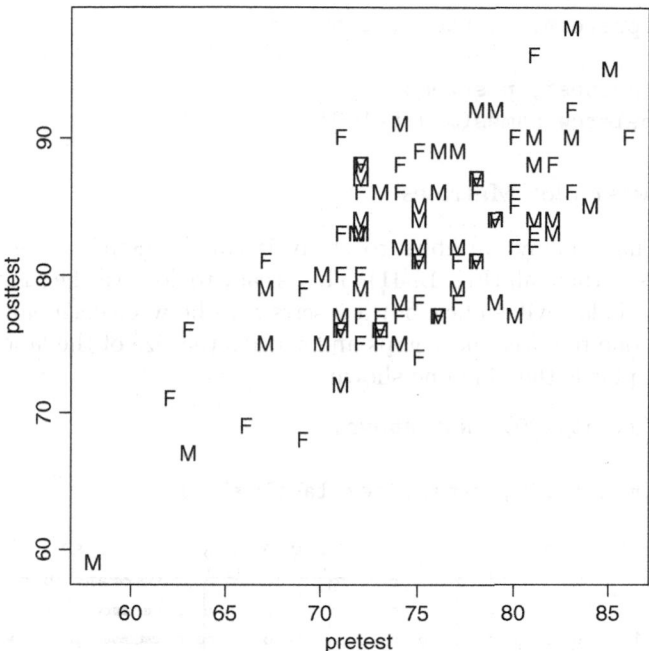

Fig. 15.39. A scatter plot using gender as its point symbol. This method only works with a single character.

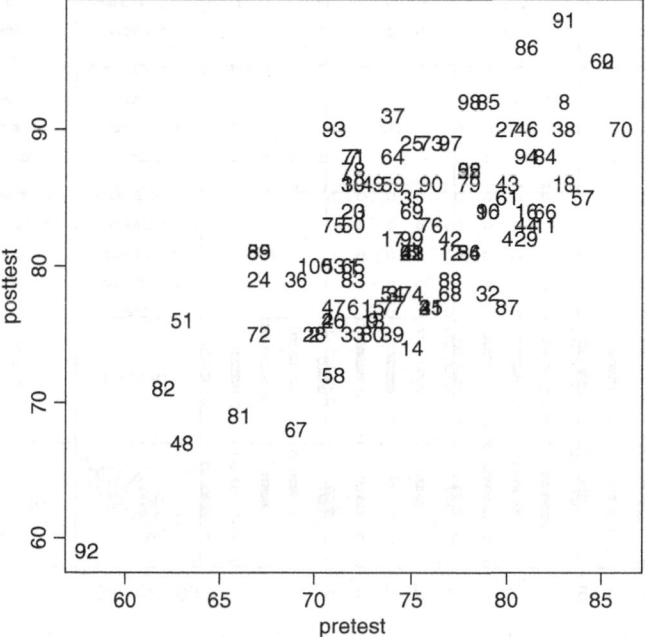

Fig. 15.40. A scatter plot with `row.names` as labels. This used the `text` function because it can handle labels longer than one character.

```
> plot(pretest, posttest, type="n" )

> text(pretest, posttest,
+   label=row.names(mydata100) )
```

15.9.9 Scatter plot Matrices

When you have many variables to study it can be helpful to get pairwise scatter plots of them all (Fig. 15.41). This is easy to do with the `plot` function. The first one below will suffice, but it inserts gaps between each pair of graphs. The second one removes those gaps and shrinks the size of the labels by 10%. The second plot is the only one shown.

```
> plot(mydata100) #Not shown.

> plot(mydata100, gap=0, cex.labels=0.9)
```

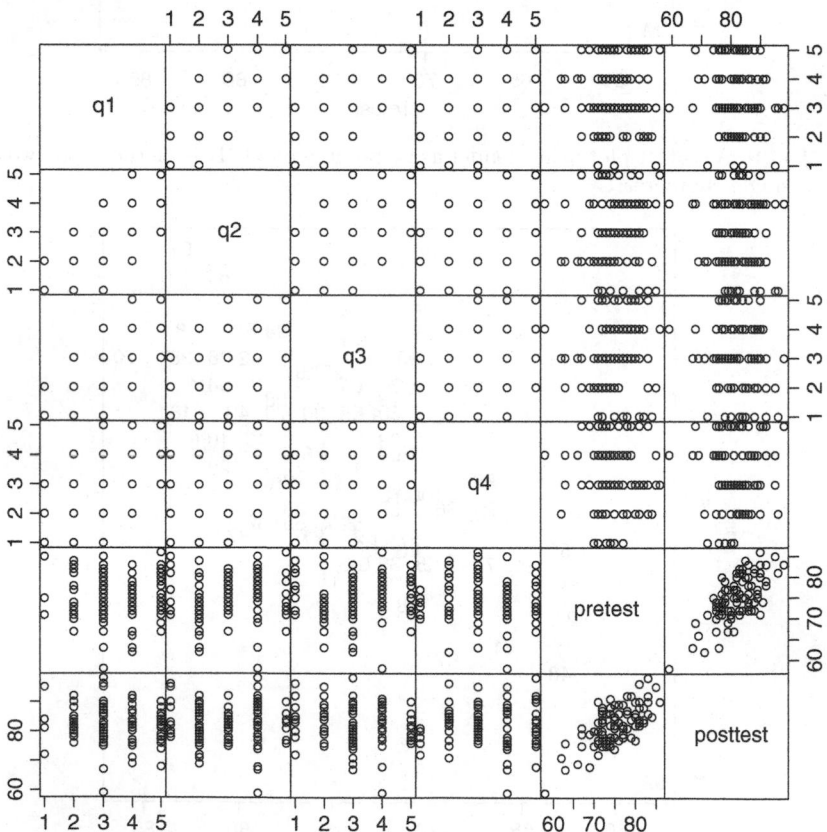

Fig. 15.41. A scatter plot matrix shows small plots for every combination of variables. This was created using the `plot` function.

You can use the entire data frame in this type of plot and it will convert factors to numeric and give you the following warning. The plots involving factors would appear as strip plots.

```
Warning message:
  In data.matrix(x) : class information lost
  from one or more columns
```

As with any generic function, you can see what other functions `plot` will call given different classes of data. The `methods` function will show you the following:

```
> methods(plot)
```

```
 [1] plot.acf*            plot.data.frame*  plot.Date*
 [4] plot.decomposed.ts*  plot.default      plot.dendrogram*
 [7] plot.density         plot.ecdf         plot.factor*
[10] plot.formula*        plot.hclust*      plot.histogram*
[13] plot.HoltWinters*    plot.isoreg*      plot.lm
[16] plot.medpolish*      plot.mlm          plot.POSIXct*
[19] plot.POSIXlt*        plot.ppr*         plot.prcomp*
[22] plot.princomp*       plot.profile.nls* plot.spec
[25] plot.spec.coherency  plot.spec.phase   plot.stepfun
[28] plot.stl*            plot.table*       plot.ts
[31] plot.tskernel*       plot.TukeyHSD
```

When you use the `plot` function on a data frame, it passes the data on to the `plot.data.frame` function. When you read the help file on that, you find that it then calls the `pairs` function! So to find out the options to use, you can finally enter `help(pairs)`. That will show you some interesting options, including adding histograms on the main diagonal and Pearson correlations on the upper right panels.

In the next example, I have added the `panel.smooth` values to draw lowess smoothing. Although I call the `pairs` function directly here, I could have used the `plot` function to achieve the same result. Since the `pairs` function is creating a multiframe plot by itself, you must use its own options to modify the plot. In this case, we cannot add a smoothed fit with the lines function; we must use `panel.smooth` instead (Fig. 15.42).

```
> pairs(mydata100[3:8], gap=0,
+    lower.panel=panel.smooth,
+    upper.panel=panel.smooth)
```

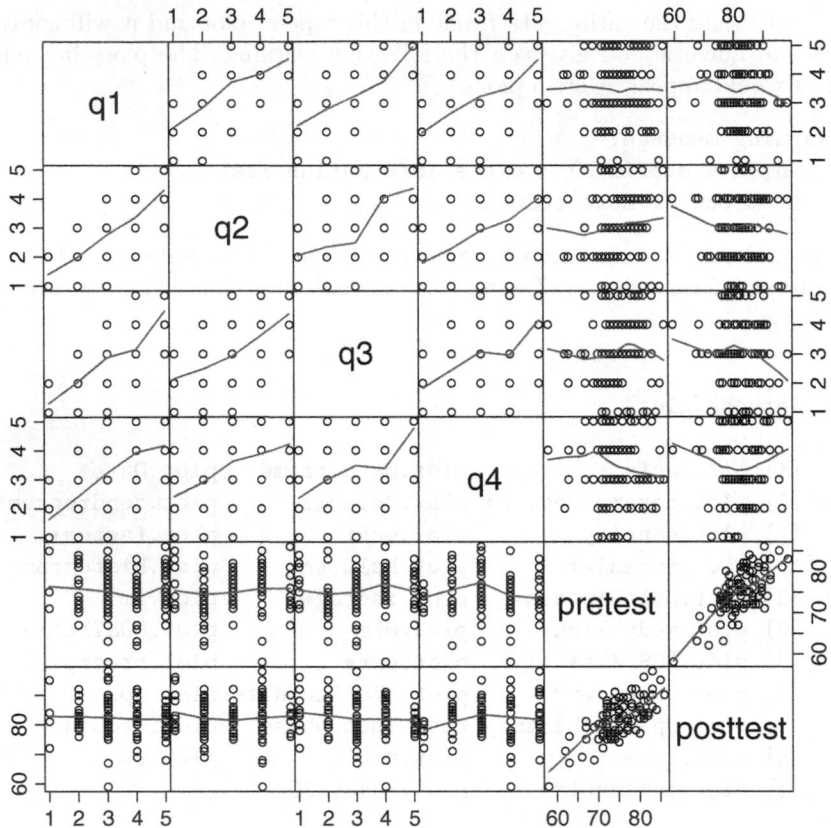

Fig. 15.42. A scatter plot matrix with smoothed fits from the `pairs` function.

15.10 Dual-Axes Plots

The usual plot has a y-axis on only the left side. However, to enhance readability you may wish to place it on the right as well. If you have the same y variable measured in two different units (Dollars & Euros, Fahrenheit & Celsius,...), you may wish a second axis in those units.

If you have two different y variables to plot, using a dual-axis plot is usually not a good idea [17]. Stacking two different plots in a multiframe plot is a better way to handle that situation. For examples of how to stack plots, see Section 15.3, "Graphics Parameters and Multiple Plots on a Page."

We will simply place the same axis on both sides, which can make it easier to read the y values of points near the right-hand side of the plot. We will plot the same graph, once without axes, then adding one on the right, and then the left.

First, we will need to add space in the margins, especially the right side, where the new axis will need labeling. That is done with the following function call, which changes the margins from their default values of (5,2,2,4)+0.1 to 5,5,4,5 as it applies to the bottom, left, top, and right sides, respectively:

```
> par( mar=c(5,5,4,5) )
```

Next, we will plot the points, but without the axes using the argument, axes=FALSE. We will also fix the limits of the x-axis with xlim=c(55,100). The limits of the y axis might be different of course, but we need to keep the x values in each overlaid plot in the exact same locations.

```
> plot( pretest, posttest, axes=FALSE, xlim=c(55,90),
+    main="Scatter plot with Dual Axes" )
```

The points and labels will appear now but without axes. The next call to the axis function asks R to place the current axis on the right side (side 4).

```
> axis(4)
```

Next, we can add text to the margin around that axis with the mtext function. It is placing its text, in a bold font (font=2) on line 3 of side 4 (the right). If this were a graph for publication rather than education, we would put the same label on both sides. Here I do different ones just to make it obvious which is which.

```
> mtext("Axis label on right size",
+    font=2, side=4, line=3)
```

Now comes the "secret sauce." If we were to use the plot function again, it would completely replace what we have done so far. But if we set the graphics parameter new=TRUE, it does not erase the screen, allowing us to complete our plot (Fig. 15.43).

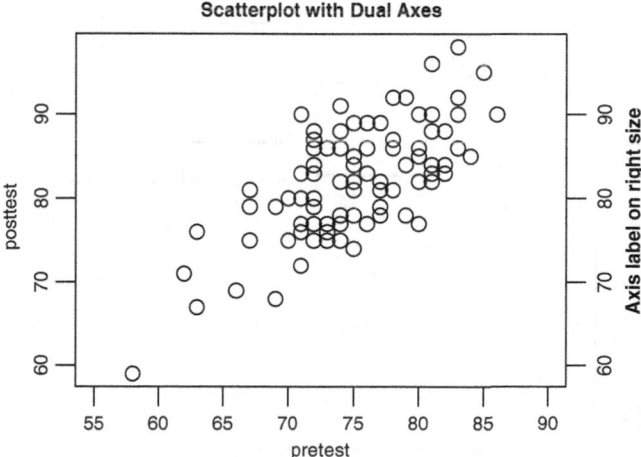

Fig. 15.43. A scatter plot demonstrating an additional axis on the right side.

```
> par( new=TRUE )
> plot( pretest, posttest, xlim=c(60,90) )
```

15.11 Box Plots

box plots put the middle 50% of the data in a box with a median line in the middle and lines, called "whiskers," extending to +/−1.5 times the height of the box (i.e., the 75th percentile minus the 25th). Points that lie outside the whiskers are considered outliers. You can create box plots using the plot function when the first variable you provide is a factor (Fig. 15.44).

```
> plot( workshop, posttest,
+    main="Box plot using plot function")
```

There are several variations we can do. First, let us use the mfrow argument of the par function to create a two by two multiframe plot.

```
> par( mfrow=c(2,2) )
```

Next, we will do a box plot of a single variable, posttest. It will appear in the upper left of Fig. 15.45. We will use the box plot function since it gives us more flexibility.

```
> boxplot(posttest)
```

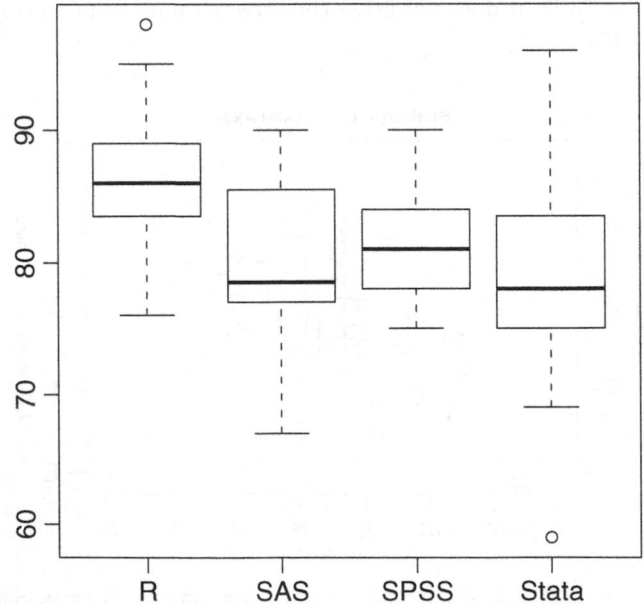

Fig. 15.44. A box plot of posttest scores for each workshop.

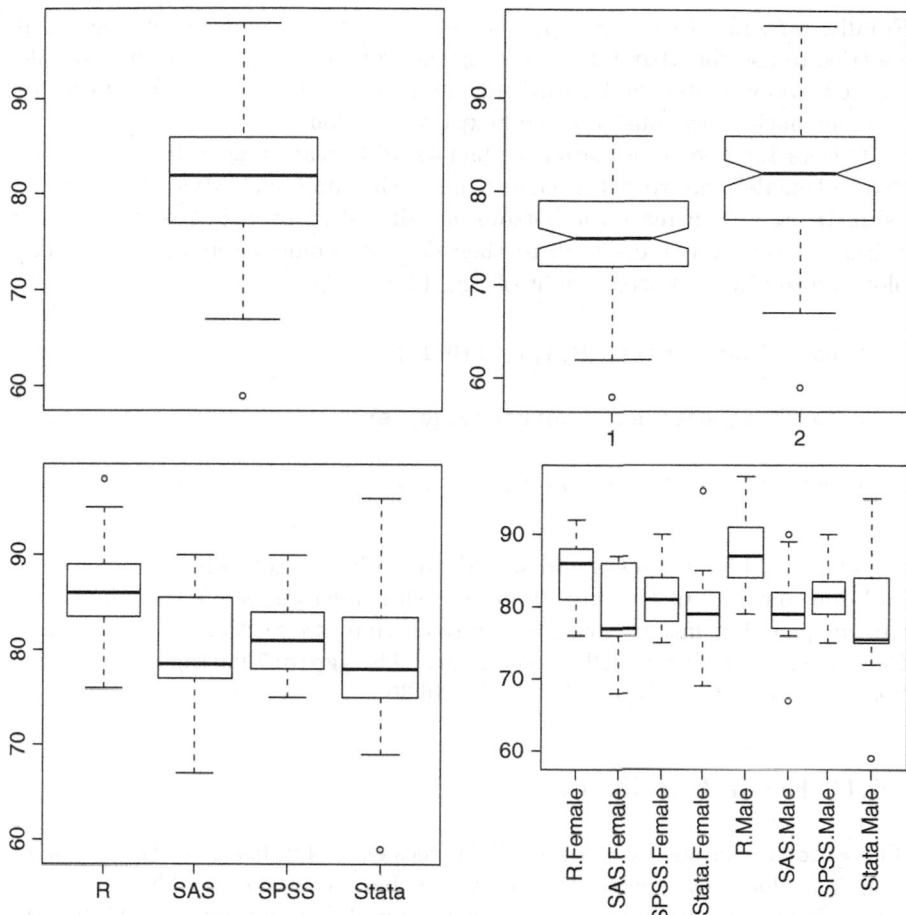

Fig. 15.45. Various box plots. The upper left is the posttest score. The upper right shows pretest and posttest, with notches indicating possible median differences. The lower left shows posttest scores for each workshop. The lower right shows posttest for the gender and workshop combinations as well as labels perpendicular to the *x*-axis.

Then we will put pretest and posttest side-by-side in the upper right of Fig. 15.45. The `notch` argument tells it to create notches such that when they do not overlap will provide "strong evidence" that the medians differ. It appears in the upper right.

```
> boxplot( pretest, posttest, notch=TRUE )
```

Next we will use a formula to get box plots for each workshop, side–by–side. It appears in the bottom left of Fig. 15.45.

```
> boxplot( posttest ~ workshop )
```

Finally, we will create a box plot for each workshop:gender combination. If
we tried to use the `plot` function using the workshop:gender syntax, it would
create two box plots: one for workshop and another for gender. To get one for
all combinations we must use the `boxplot` function.

Generating the combination of factors will create long value labels, like
"Stata.Female". So we will need to change the *label* axis *style* of the *x*-axis
using `las=2` and increase the bottom *mar*gin with `mar=c(8,4,4,2)0.1+`. We
will set those parameters back to their defaults immediately afterward. The
plot appears in the bottom right of Fig. 15.45.

```
> par( las=2, mar=c(8,4,4,2)+0.1 )

> boxplot(posttest ~ workshop:gender)

> par( las=0, mar=c(5,4,4,2)+0.1 )
```

This is a bit of a mess and would probably be more interpretable if we
had done one box plot of workshop for each gender and stack them in a multiframe plot. For instructions on how to do that, see Section 15.3, "Graphics
Parameters and Multiple Plots on a Page." The `ggplot2` package does a *much*
better version of this same plot in Fig. 16.36.

15.12 Error Bar Plots

The `gplots` package, by Gregory R. Warnes et al.[43], has a `plotmeans` function that plots means with 95% confidence bars around each. The confidence
intervals assume the data comes from a normal distribution (Fig. 15.46). Its
main argument is in the form `measure~group`.

```
> library("gplots")

> plotmeans( posttest ~ workshop,
+    main="Plotmeans from gplots Package")

> detach("package:gplots")
```

15.13 Interaction Plots

R has a built-in `interaction.plot` function that plots the means for a two-
way interaction (Fig. 15.47). For three-way or higher interactions, you can
use the `by` function to repeat the interaction plot for each level of the other
variables.

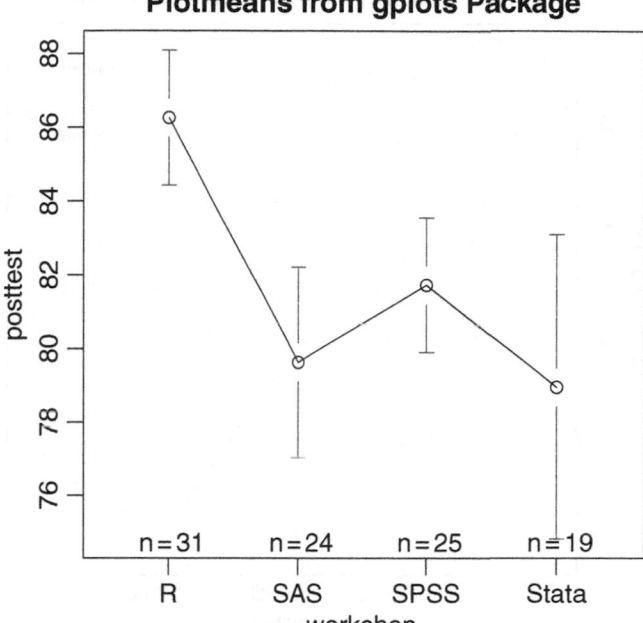

Fig. 15.46. An error bar plot showing the posttest mean for each workshop, along with 95% confidence intervals.

In Fig. 15.47, the males seem to be doing slightly better with R and the females with Stata. Since the plot does not display variability, we do not have any test of significance for this interpretation.

```
> interaction.plot( workshop, gender, posttest,
+    main="Means Using interaction.plot function")
```

15.14 Adding Equations and Symbols to Graphs

Any of the functions that add text to a graph, such as main, sub, xlab, and ylab, can display mathematical equations. For example, a well-known formula for multiple regression is

$$\hat{\beta} = (X^t X)^{-1} X^t Y$$

You can add this to any existing graph using the following call to the text function:

```
text(66, 88, "My Example Formula")
text(65, 85,
  expression( hat(beta) ==
  (X^t * X)^{-1} * X^t * Y) )
```

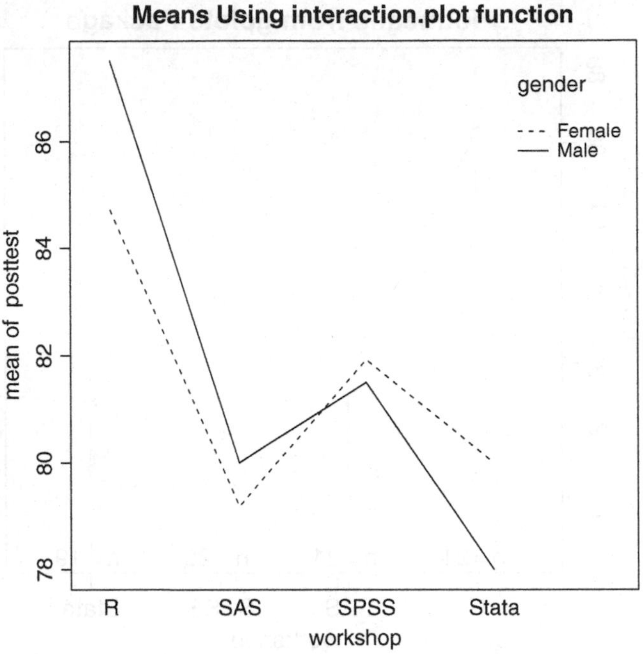

Means Using interaction.plot function

Fig. 15.47. An interaction plot of posttest means by the workshop and gender combinations.

The `text` function adds any text at the x,y position you specify—in this case, 66 and 88. So the use of it above adds "My Example Formula" to an existing graph at that position. In the second call to the `text` function, we also call the `expression` function. When used on any of the text annotation functions, the `expression` function tells R to interpret its arguments in a special way that allows it to display a wide variety of symbols. In this example, beta will cause the Greek letter β to appear. Two equal signs in a row (x==y) result in the display of one (x=y). Functions like `hat` and `bar` will cause those symbols to appear over their arguments. So `hat(beta)` will display a "^" symbol over the Greek letter beta. This example formula appears on the plot in Fig. 15.48. You can see several tables of symbols with `help(plotmath)`.

15.15 Summary of Graphics Elements and Parameters

As we have seen in the examples above, R's traditional graphics have a range of functions and arguments that you can use to embellish your plots.

Tables 15.1 through 15.4 summarize them.

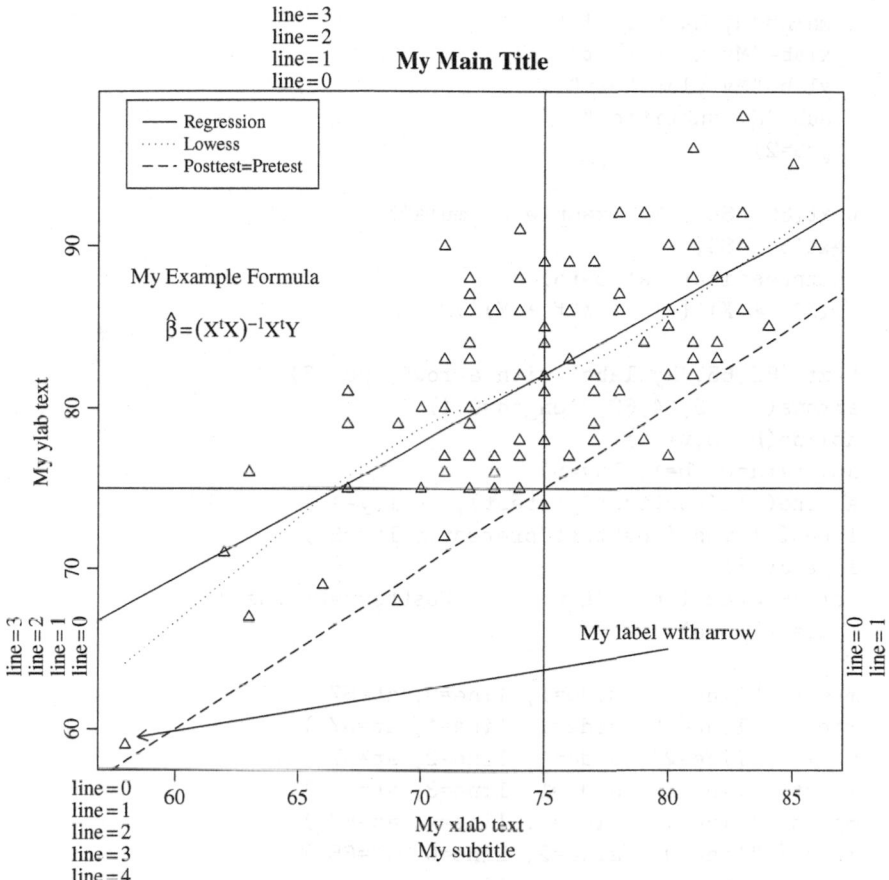

Fig. 15.48. A plot demonstrating many types of text and line annotations. The "line=n" labels around the margins display how the line numbers start at zero next to each axis and move outward as the line numbers increase.

15.16 Plot Demonstrating Many Modifications

Below is a program that creates a rather horrible looking plot (Fig. 15.48), but it does demonstrate many of the options you are likely to in need. The very repetitive `mtext` function calls that place labels all over the margins could be done with a loop, making it much more compact but less clear to beginners unfamiliar with loops.

```
par( mfrow=c(1,1) )
par(family="serif")
plot( pretest,posttest,
```

```
      main="My Main Title" ,
      xlab="My xlab text" ,
      ylab="My ylab text",
      sub="My subtitle ",
      pch=2)

  text(66, 88, "My Example Formula")
  text(65, 85,
     expression( hat(beta) ==
     (X^t * X)^{-1} * X^t * Y) )

  text (85,65,"My label with arrow", pos=3)
  arrows(85,65,64,62, length=0.1)
  abline(h=75,v=75)
  abline(a=0, b=1, lty=5)
  abline( lm(posttest~pretest),    lty=1 )
  lines( lowess(posttest~pretest), lty=3 )
  legend( 64, 99,
   c( "Regression", "Lowess", "Posttest=Pretest" ),
   lty=c(1,3,5) )

  mtext( "line=0", side=1, line=0, at=57 )
  mtext( "line=1", side=1, line=1, at=57 )
  mtext( "line=2", side=1, line=2, at=57 )
  mtext( "line=3", side=1, line=3, at=57 )
  mtext( "line=4", side=1, line=4, at=57 )
  mtext( "line=0", side=2, line=0, at=65 )
  mtext( "line=1", side=2, line=1, at=65 )
  mtext( "line=2", side=2, line=2, at=65 )
  mtext( "line=3", side=2, line=3, at=65 )
  mtext( "line=0", side=3, line=0, at=65 )
  mtext( "line=1", side=3, line=1, at=65 )
  mtext( "line=2", side=3, line=2, at=65 )
  mtext( "line=3", side=3, line=3, at=65 )
  mtext( "line=0", side=4, line=0, at=65 )
  mtext( "line=1", side=4, line=1, at=65 )
  mtext( "line=0", side=4, line=0, at=65 )
  mtext( "line=1", side=4, line=1, at=65 )
```

15.17 Example Program for Traditional Graphics

The Stata examples in this chapter are particularly sparse compared to those
for R. This is due to space constraints rather than due to lack of capability.

15.17.1 Stata Program for Traditional Graphics

```
* Filename: GraphicsTraditional.do

use c:\myRfolder\mydata100, clear

* Histogram of q1
histogram q1

* Bar chart of gender
graph bar (count) gender

* Bar chart of workshop and gender at their mean values
graph bar workshop gender

* Scatter plot of pretest and posttest
graph twoway scatter pretest postest

* Scatter plot matrix for all variables but gender
graph matrix workshop q1-q4
```

15.17.2 R Program for Traditional Graphics

```
# Filename: GraphicsTradtional.R

setwd("/myRfolder")
load(file="mydata100.Rdata")
attach(mydata100)
options(width=64)

# Request it to ask you to click for new graph.
par(ask=FALSE, mfrow=c(1,1) )

#---Barplots---

# Barplots of counts via table

barplot( c(60,40) )

barplot(q4)
table(q4)
barplot( table(q4) )

barplot( workshop )
```

```
barplot( table(workshop) )
barplot(gender)
barplot( table(gender) )

barplot( table(workshop), horiz=TRUE)

barplot( as.matrix( table(workshop) ),
  beside = FALSE)

# Grouped bar plots & mosaic plots

barplot( table(gender,workshop) )

plot( workshop,gender )

mosaicplot( table(workshop,gender) )

mosaicplot(~ Sex + Age + Survived,
  data = Titanic, color = TRUE)

barplot( table(gender,workshop), beside=TRUE )


# Barplots of means via tapply

myMeans <- tapply(q1, gender, mean, na.rm=TRUE)
barplot(myMeans)

myMeans <- tapply(q1, list(workshop,gender), mean,na.rm=TRUE)
barplot(myMeans, beside=TRUE)

#---Adding main title, color and legend---

barplot( table(gender,workshop),
  beside=TRUE,
  col=c("gray90","gray60"),
  main="Number of males and females \nin each workshop" )
legend( "topright",
  c("Female","Male"),
  fill=c("gray90","gray60") )

# A manually positioned legend at 10,15.
legend( 10,15,
  c("Female","Male"),
  fill=c("gray90","gray60") )
```

```
#---Mulitple Graphs on a Page---

par()
head( par() )

par( mar=c(3,3,3,1)+0.1 )
par( mfrow=c(2,2) )

barplot( table(gender,workshop) )
barplot( table(workshop,gender) )
barplot( table(gender,workshop), beside=TRUE )
barplot( table(workshop,gender), beside=TRUE )

par( mfrow=c(1,1) ) #Sets back to 1 plot per page.
par( mar=c(5,4,4,2)+0.1 )

#---Dotcharts---

dotchart( table(workshop,gender),
  main="Dotchart of Workshop Attendance",
  cex=1.5)

#---Piecharts---
pie( table(workshop),
  col=c("white","gray90","gray60","black" ),
  main="Piechart of Workshop Attendance" )

# ---Histograms---

hist(posttest)

# More bins plus density and ticks at values.
hist(posttest, breaks=20, probability=TRUE,
  main="Histogram with Density and Points")
lines( density(posttest) )
myZeros <- rep(0, each=length(posttest) )
myZeros
points( posttest, myZeros, pch="|" )

# Histogram of males only.
hist(posttest[gender=="Male"], col="gray60")

# Plotting above two on one page,
# matching breakpoints.
par(mfrow=c(2,1) )
```

```
hist(posttest, col="gray90",
  breaks=c(50,55,60,65,70,75,80,85,90,95,100) )
hist(posttest[gender=="Male"], col="gray60",
  breaks=c(50,55,60,65,70,75,80,85,90,95,100) )
par(mfrow=c(1,1) )

# Could have used either of these:
# breaks=seq(from=50, to=100, by=5) )
# breaks=seq(50,100,5) )

# Histograms overlaid

hist(posttest, col="gray90",
  breaks=seq(from=50, to=100, by=5) )
hist(posttest[gender=="Male"], col="gray60",
  breaks=seq(from=50, to=100, by=5),
  add=TRUE )
legend( "topright", c("Female","Male"),
  fill=c("gray90","gray60") )

# Same plot but extracting $breaks
# from previous graph.

myHistogram <- hist(posttest, col="gray90")
names(myHistogram)
myHistogram$breaks
myHistogram$xlim
hist(posttest[gender=="Male"], col='gray60',
    add=TRUE, breaks=myHistogram$breaks)
legend( "topright", c("Female","Male"),
  fill=c("gray90","gray60") )

# What else does myHistogram hold?
class(myHistogram)
myHistogram

#---Q-Q plots---

library("car")
qq.plot(posttest,
  labels=row.names(mydata100),
  col="black" )
detach("package:car")

myQQ <- qqnorm(posttest) #Not shown in text.
```

```
identify(myQQ)

#---Stripcharts---

par( mar=c(4,3,3,1)+0.1 )
par(mfrow=c(2,1) )
stripchart(posttest, method="jitter",
  main="Stripchart with Jitter")
stripchart(posttest, method="stack",
  main="Stripchart with Stacking")
par( mfrow=c(1,1) )
par( mar=c(5,4,4,2)+0.1 )

par( las=2, mar=c(4,8,4,1)+0.1  )
stripchart(posttest~workshop, method="jitter")
par( las=0, mar=c(5,4,4,2)+0.1 )

# --- Scatter plots ---

plot(pretest,posttest)

# Find low score interactively.
# Click 2nd mouse button to choose stop.
identify(pretest,posttest)

# Check it manually.
mydata100[pretest<60, ]

# Different types of plots.
par( mar=c(5,4,4,2)+0.1 )
par( mfrow=c(2,2) )
plot( pretest, posttest, type="p", main="type=p" )
plot( pretest, posttest, type="l", main="type=l" )
plot( pretest, posttest, type="b", main="type=b" )
plot( pretest, posttest, type="h", main="type=h" )
par( mfrow=c(1,1) )

# Scatter plots with Jitter

par( mar=c(5,4,4,2)+0.1 )
par( mfrow=c(1,2) )
plot( q1, q4,
  main="Likert Scale Without Jitter")
plot( jitter(q1,3), jitter(q4,3),
  main="Likert Scale With Jitter")
```

```
# Scatter plot of large data sets.

# Example with pch="." and jitter.
par(mfrow=c(1,2) )
pretest2   <- round( rnorm( n=5000, mean=80, sd=5) )
posttest2 <-
  round( pretest2 + rnorm( n=5000, mean=3, sd=3) )
pretest2[pretest2>100] <- 100
posttest2[posttest2>100] <- 100
plot( pretest2, posttest2,
  main="5,000 Points, Default Character \nNo Jitter")
plot( jitter(pretest2,4), jitter(posttest2,4), pch=".",
  main="5,000 Points Using pch='.' \nand Jitter")
par(mfrow=c(1,1) )

# Hexbins (resets mfrow automatically).
library("hexbin")
plot( hexbin(pretest2,posttest2),
  main="5,000 Points Using Hexbin")
detach("package:hexbin")

rm(pretest2,posttest2) # Cleaning up.

# Scatter plot with different lines added.
plot(posttest~pretest)
abline(h=75,v=75)
abline(a=0, b=1, lty=5)
abline( lm(posttest~pretest),   lty=1 )
lines( lowess(posttest~pretest), lty=3 )
legend( 60, 95,
  c( "Regression", "Lowess", "Posttest=Pretest" ),
  lty=c(1,3,5) )

# Scatter plot of q1 by q2 separately by gender.
plot(posttest~pretest,
  pch=as.numeric(gender) )

abline( lm( posttest[gender=="Male"]
          ~ pretest[gender=="Male"] ),
        lty=1 )

abline( lm( posttest[gender=="Female"]
          ~ pretest[gender=="Female"] ),
        lty=2 )
legend( "topleft", c("Male","Female"),
        lty=c(1,2), pch=c(2,1) )
```

```
# Coplots: conditioned scatter plots
coplot( posttest~pretest | workshop)
coplot( posttest~pretest | q1)

# Scatter plot plotting text labels.

plot(pretest, posttest,
  pch=as.character(gender) )

plot(pretest, posttest, type="n" )
text(pretest, posttest,
  label=row.names(mydata100) )

# Scatter plot matrix of whole data frame.
plot(mydata100[3:8]) #Not shown with text.

plot(mydata100[3:8], gap=0, cex.labels=0.9)

pairs(mydata100[3:8], gap=0,
  lower.panel=panel.smooth,
  upper.panel=panel.smooth)

# Dual axes
#Adds room for label on right margin.
par( mar=c(5,5,4,5) )
plot( pretest, posttest, axes=FALSE, xlim=c(55,90),
  main="Scatter plot with Dual Axes" )
axis(4)
mtext("Axis label on right size",
  font=2, side=4, line=3)
par(new=TRUE)
plot(pretest, posttest, xlim=c(55,90) )

# Scatter plot with Confidence Ellipse.
library("car")
data.ellipse(pretest, posttest,
  levels=.95,
  col="black")
detach("package:car")

# Confidence Intervals: A small example
x  <- c(1,2,3,4)
y1 <- c(1,2,3,4)
y2 <- c(2,3,4,5)
y3 <- c(3,4,5,6)
```

```
yMatrix <- cbind(y1,y2,y3)
yMatrix
plot( x, y2, xlim=c(1,4), ylim=c(1,6), cex=1.5 )
matlines( x, yMatrix, lty=c(2,1,2), col="black" )
rm( x, y1, y2, y3, yMatrix)

# Confidence Intervals: A realistic example
myIntervals <-
  data.frame(pretest=seq(from=60, to=100, by=5))
myIntervals
myModel <- lm( posttest~pretest )
myIntervals$pp <- predict( myModel,
  interval="prediction", newdata=myIntervals)
myIntervals$pc <- predict( myModel,
  interval="confidence", newdata=myIntervals)
myIntervals
class( myIntervals$pp )
myIntervals$pp
plot( pretest, posttest,
  ylim=range( myIntervals$pretest,
    myIntervals$pp, na.rm=TRUE),
  main="Regression Fit with Confidence Intervals" )
matlines(myIntervals$pretest, myIntervals$pc,
  lty=c(1,2,2), col="black" )
matlines(myIntervals$pretest, myIntervals$pp,
  lty=c(1,3,3), col="black" )

#---Box Plots---
plot(workshop, posttest,
  main="box plot using plot function")

par( mfrow=c(2,2) )
boxplot(posttest)
boxplot(pretest,posttest,notch=TRUE)
boxplot(posttest~workshop)
par( las=2, mar=c(8,4,4,2)+0.1 )
boxplot(posttest~workshop:gender)
par( las=1, mar=c(5,4,4,2)+0.1 )

#---Error bar plots---

library("gplots")
par( mfrow=c(1,1) )
plotmeans( posttest~workshop,
  main="Plotmeans from gplots Package")
detach("package:gplots")
```

```
interaction.plot( workshop, gender, posttest,
  main="Means Using interaction.plot function")

# ---Adding Labels---

# Many annotations at once.
par( mar=c(5,4,4,2)+0.1 )
par( mfrow=c(1,1) )
par(family="serif")
plot(pretest,posttest,
  main="My Main Title" ,
  xlab="My xlab text" ,
  ylab="My ylab text",
  sub="My subtitle ",
  pch=2)

text(66, 88, "My Example Formula")
text(65, 85,
  expression( hat(beta) ==
  (X^t * X)^{-1} * X^t * Y) )

text (85,65,"My label with arrow", pos=3)
arrows(85,65,64,62, length=0.1)
abline(h=75,v=75)
abline(a=0, b=1, lty=5)
abline( lm(posttest~pretest),    lty=1 )
lines( lowess(posttest~pretest), lty=3 )
legend( 64, 99,
 c( "Regression", "Lowess", "Posttest=Pretest" ),
 lty=c(1,3,5) )

mtext("line=0", side=1, line=0, at=57 )
mtext("line=1", side=1, line=1, at=57 )
mtext("line=2", side=1, line=2, at=57 )
mtext("line=3", side=1, line=3, at=57 )
mtext("line=4", side=1, line=4, at=57 )

mtext("line=0", side=2, line=0, at=65 )
mtext("line=1", side=2, line=1, at=65 )
mtext("line=2", side=2, line=2, at=65 )
mtext("line=3", side=2, line=3, at=65 )
mtext("line=0", side=3, line=0, at=65 )
mtext("line=1", side=3, line=1, at=65 )
mtext("line=2", side=3, line=2, at=65 )
mtext("line=3", side=3, line=3, at=65 )
```

```
mtext("line=0", side=4, line=0, at=65 )
mtext("line=1", side=4, line=1, at=65 )

#---Scatter plot with bells & whistles---
plot(pretest,posttest,pch=19,
  main="Scatter plot of Pretest and Postest",
  xlab="Test score before taking workshop",
  ylab="Test score after taking workshop" )
myModel <- lm(posttest~pretest)
abline(myModel)
arrows(60,82,65,71, length=0.1)
text(60,82,"Linear Fit", pos=3)
arrows(70,62,58.5,59, length=0.1)
text(70,62,"Double check this value", pos=4)
# Use locator() or:
# predict(myModel,data.frame(pretest=75) )
```

16

Graphics with ggplot2

16.1 Introduction

As we discussed in Chapter 14, "Graphics Overview," the ggplot2 package
is an implementation of Wilkinson's Grammar of Graphics (hence the "gg"
in its name). The last chapter focused on R's traditional graphics functions.
Many plots were easy, but other plots were a lot of work compared to Stata.
In particular, adding things like legends and confidence intervals were complicated.

The ggplot2 package makes many of those things easier, as you will now
see as we replicate many of the same graphs. The ggplot2 package has both a
shorter qplot function (also called quickplot) and a more powerful ggplot
function. We will use both so you can learn the difference and choose whichever
you prefer. Although less flexible overall, the built-in lattice package is also
capable of doing these examples.

While traditional graphics come with R, you will need to install the
ggplot2 package. For details, see Chapter 2, "Installing and Updating R."
Once installed, we need to load the package using the library function.

```
> library("ggplot2")

Loading required package: grid
Loading required package: reshape
Loading required package: proto
Loading required package: splines
Loading required package: MASS
Loading required package: RColorBrewer
Loading required package: colorspace
```

Notice that it requires the grid package. That is a completely different
graphics system than the traditional graphics system. That means that the
par function we used to set graphics parameters, like fonts, in the last chapter

R.A. Muenchen, J.M. Hilbe, *R for Stata Users*, Statistics
and Computing, DOI 10.1007/978-1-4419-1318-0_16,
© Springer Science+Business Media, LLC 2010

does not work with `ggplot2`, nor do any of the base functions that we have covered, including `abline`, `arrows`, `axis`, `box`, `grid`, `lines`, and `text`.

16.1.1 Overview `qplot` and `ggplot`

With the `ggplot2` package, you create your graphs by specifying the following elements:

- Aesthetics: The aesthetics map your data to the graph, telling it what role each variable will play. Some variables will map to an axis, and some will determine the color, shape, or size of a point in a scatter plot. Different groups might have differently shaped or colored points. The size or color of a point might reflect the magnitude of a third variable. Other variables might determine how to fill the bars of a bar chart with colors or patterns; so, for example, you can see the number of males and females within each bar.
- Geoms: Short for geometric objects, geoms determine the objects that will represent the data values. Possible geoms include bar, box plot, error bar, histogram, jitter, line, path, point, smooth, and text.
- Statistics: Statistics provide functions for features like adding regression lines to a scatter plot, or dividing a variable up into bins to form a histogram.
- Scales: These match your data to the aesthetic features—for example, in a legend that tells us that triangles represent males and circles represent females.
- Coordinate system: For most plots this is the usual rectangular Cartesian coordinate system. However, for pie charts it is the circular polar coordinate system.
- Facets: These describe how to repeat your plot for each subgroup, perhaps creating a separate scatter plot for males and females. A helpful feature with facets is that they standardize the axes on each plot, making comparisons across groups much easier.

The `qplot` function tries to simplify graph creation by (a) looking a lot like the traditional `plot` function and (b) allowing you to skip specifying as many of the items above as possible. As with the `plot` function, main arguments to the `qplot` function are the x and y variables. You can identify them with the argument name "x=" or "y=" or you can simply supply them in that order. Unlike the `plot` function, the `qplot` function has a `data` argument. That means you do not have to attach the data frame to use short variable names. (However, to minimize our code, our examples will assume the data is attached.)

Finally, as you would expect, elements are specified by an argument. For example, `geom="bar"`. A major difference between `plot` and `qplot` is that `qplot` will not automatically give you diagnostic plots for a model you have created. So it is much easier to get diagnostic plots using the `plot` function.

The `ggplot` function offers a complete implementation of the grammar of graphics. To do so, it gives up any resemblance to the `plot` function. It *requires* you to specify the data frame, since you can use different data frames in different layers of the graph. (The `qplot` function cannot.) Its options are specified by additional *functions* rather than the usual arguments. For example, rather than the `geom="bar"` format of `qplot`, they follow the form `+geom_bar(options)`. The form is quite consistent, so if you know there is a geom named "smooth," you can readily guess how to specify it in either `qplot` or `ggplot`.

The simplicity that `qplot` offers has another limitation. Since it cannot plot in layers, it occasionally needs help interpreting what you want it to do with legends. For example, you could do a scatter plot for which `size=q4`. This would cause the points to have five sizes, from small for people who did not like the workshop to large for those who did. The `qplot` function would generate the legend for you automatically. However, what happens when you just want to specify the size of all points with `size=4`? It generates a rather useless legend showing one of the points and telling you it represents "4." Whenever you want to tell `qplot` to *i*nhibit the *i*nterpretation of values, you nest them within the "`I()`" function: `size=I(4)`. As a mnemonic, think that I()=Inhibit unnecessary legends. The `ggplot` function does not need the `I` function since its level of control is fine enough to make your intentions obvious.

See Table 16.1 for a summary of the major differences between `qplot` and `ggplot`.

Although the `ggplot2` is based on *The Grammar of Graphics*, the package differs in several important ways from the syntax described in that book. It depends on R's ability to transform data, so you can use `log(x)` or any other function within `qplot` or `ggplot`. It also uses R's ability to reshape or aggregate data, so the `ggplot2` package does not include its own algebra for these steps. Also, `ggplot2` displays axes and legends automatically, so there is no "guide" function.

For a more detailed comparison, see *ggplot2: Elegant Graphics for Data Analysis* by Hadley Wickham [55].

Now let us look at some examples. When possible, each is done using both `qplot` and `ggplot`. You can decide which you prefer.

16.1.2 Missing Values

By default, the `ggplot2` package will display missing values. That would result in additional bars in bar charts and even entire additional plots when we repeat graphs for each level of a grouping variable. That might be fine in your initial analyses, but you are unlikely to want that in a plot for publication. We will use a version of our data set that has all missing values stripped out with

```
mydata100 <- na.omit(mydata100)
```

Table 16.1. Comparison of the `qplot` and `ggplot` functions.

	The `qplot` function	The `ggplot` function
Goal	Designed to be quick and as standard R as possible.	Designed as a full grammar of graphics system.
Aesthetics	Like most R functions: `qplot(x= , y= , fill= , color= , shape= ,...)`	You must specify the mapping between each graphical element, even x- and y-axes, and the variable(s): `ggplot(data= , aes(x= , y= , fill= , color= , shape= ,...) )`
ABline	`...geom="abline", intercept=a, slope=b)`	`+geom_abline( intercept=a, slope=b)`
Aspect ratio	Leave out for interactive adjustment. `+coord_equal(ratio=height/width)` `+coord_equal() is square`	Leave out for interactive adjustment. `+coord_equal(ratio=height/width)` `+coord_equal() is square`
Axis flipping	`+coord_flip()`	`+coord_flip()`
Axis labels	`...xlab("My Text")` Just like plot function.	`+scale_x_discrete("My Text")` `+scale_y_discrete("My Text")` `+scale_x_continuous("My Text")` `+scale_y_continuous("My Text")`
Axis logarithmic	`+scale_x_log10()` `+scale_x_log2()` `+scale_x_log()`	`+scale_x_log10()` `+scale_x_log2()` `+scale_x_log()`
Bars	`...geom="bar", position="stack" or dodge.`	`+geom_bar(position="stack") or dodge.`
Bar filling	`...posttest, fill=gender)`	`+aes( x=posttest, fill=gender )`
Data	Optional data= argument as with most R functions.	You must specify data= argument. `ggplot(data=mydata, aes(...`
Facets	`...,facets=gender ~ .)`	`+ facet_grid( gender ~ . )`
Greyscale	`+scale_fill_grey(start=0, end=1)` Change values to control grey.	`+scale_fill_grey(start=0, end=1)` Change values to control grey.
Histogram	`...geom="histogram", binwidth=1)`	`+geom_bar(binwidth=1)`
Density	`...geom="density")`	`+geom_density()`
Jitter	`..position=position_jitter()` Lessen jitter with e.g., (width=.02).	`+geom_jitter(position=position_jitter()` Lessen jitter with e.g., (width=.02).
Legend inhibit	Use I() function, e.g., `...geom="point", size=I(4) )`	Precise control makes I() function unnecessary.
Line	`...geom="line"`	`+geom_line()`
Line vertical	`...geom="vline", intercept=?)`	`+geom_vline(intercept=?)`
Line horiz.	`...geom="hline", intercept=?)`	`+geom_hline(intercept=?)`
Pie (polar)	`+coord_polar(theta="y")`	`+coord_polar(theta="y")`
Points	`...geom="point")` That is the default for two variables.	`+geom_point(size=2)` There is no default geom for ggplot. The default size is 2.
QQ plot	`...stat="qq")`	`+stat_qq()`
Smooth	`...geom="smooth", method="lm")` Lowess is default method.	`+geom_smooth(method="lm")` Lowess is default method.
Smooth w/o Confidence	`...geom="smooth", method="lm", se=FALSE)`	`+geom_smooth(method="lm", se=FALSE)`
Titles	`...main="My Title")` Just like plot function.	`+opts(title="My Title" )`

See Section 10.5, "Missing Values" for other ways to address missing values.

16.1.3 Typographic Conventions

Throughout this book we have displayed R's prompt characters only when input was followed by output. The prompt characters helped us discriminate between the two. Each of our function calls will result in a graph, so there is no chance of confusing input with output. Therefore, we will dispense with the prompt characters for the remainder of this chapter. This will make the code much cleaner to read because our examples of the `ggplot` function often end in a "+" sign. That is something you type. Since R prompts you with "+" at the beginning of a continued line, that looks a bit confusing at first.

16.2 Bar Plots

Let us do a simple bar chart of counts for our workshop variable (Fig. 16.1). Both of the following function calls will do it.

The `qplot` approach to Fig. 16.1 is

```
> attach(mydata100) # Assumed for all qplot examples

> qplot(workshop)
```

The `ggplot` approach to to Fig. 16.1 is

```
> ggplot(mydata100, aes(workshop) ) +
+    geom_bar()
```

Bars are the default geom when you give `qplot` only one factor, so we only need a single argument, workshop.

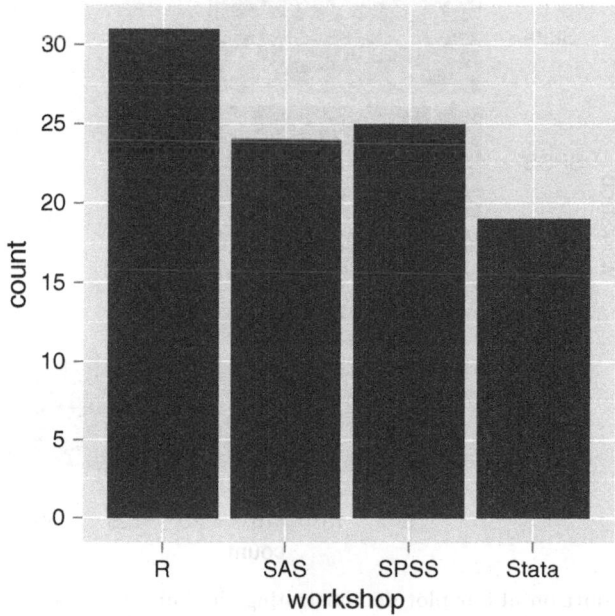

Fig. 16.1. A bar plot of workshop attendance.

The `ggplot` function call above requires three arguments:

1. Unlike most other R functions, it requires that you specify the data frame. As we will see later, that is because `ggplot` can plot multiple layers, and each layer can use a different data frame.
2. The `aes` function defines the *aes*thetic role that workshop will play. It maps workshop to the *x*-axis. We could have named the argument as in `aes(x=workshop)`. The first two parameters to the `aes` function are x and y, in that order. To simplify the code, we will not bother listing their names.
3. The `geom_bar` function tells it that the geometric object, or geom, needed is a bar. Therefore, a bar chart will result. This function call is tied to the first one through the "+" sign.

We did that the same plot using traditional graphics `bar plot` function, but that required us to summarize the data using `table(workshop)`. The `ggplot2` package is more like Stata in this regard; it does that type of summarization for you.

If we want to change to a horizontal bar chart (Fig. 16.2), all we need to do is flip the coordinates. In the following examples, it is clear that we simply added the `cord_flip` function to the end of both `qplot` and `ggplot`. There is no argument to `qplot` like `coord="flip"`.

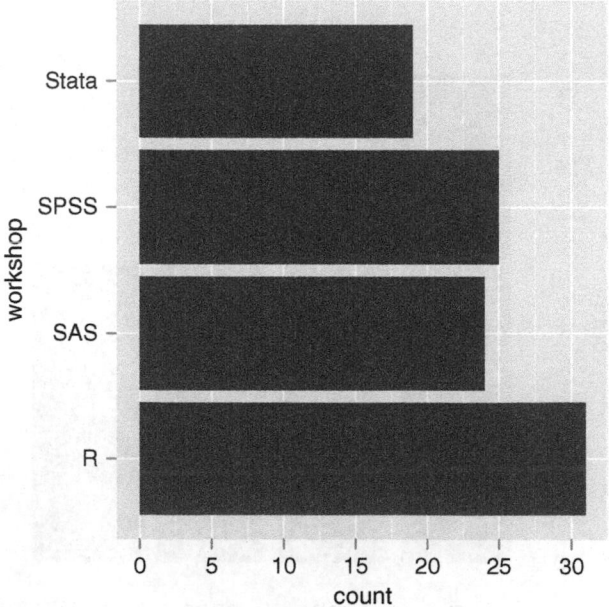

Fig. 16.2. A horizontal bar plot demonstrating the impact of the `coord_flip` function.

This brings up an interesting point. Both methods create the exact same graphics object. Even if there is a `qplot` equivalent, you can always add a `ggplot` function call to a `qplot` function call.

The `qplot` approach to Fig. 16.2 is

```
qplot(workshop) + coord_flip()
```

The `ggplot` approach to Fig. 16.2 is

```
ggplot(mydata100, aes(workshop) ) +
  geom_bar() + coord_flip()
```

You can create the usual types of grouped bar plots. Let us start with a simple stacked one (Fig. 16.3). You can use either function below. They contain two new arguments. Although we are requesting only a single bar, we must still supply a variable for the x-axis. The function call `factor("")` provides the variable we need, and it is simply an unnamed factor whose value is empty. We use the `factor` function to keep it from labeling the x-axis from 0 to 1, which it would do if the variable were continuous. The `fill=workshop` aesthetic argument tells the function to fill the bars with the number of students who took each workshop.

With `qplot`, we are clearing labels on the x-axis with `xlab=""`. Otherwise, the word "factor" would occur there from our `factor("")` statement.

The equivalent way to label `ggplot` is to use the `scale_x_discrete` function, also providing an empty label for the x-axis. Finally, the

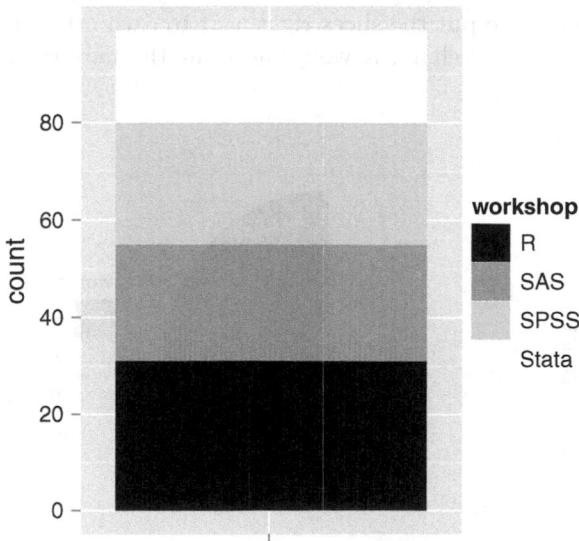

Fig. 16.3. A stacked bar plot of workshop attendance.

`scale_fill_grey` function tells each function to use shades of grey. You can leave this out, of course, and both functions will choose the same nice color scheme. The start and end values tell the function to go all the way to black and white, respectively. If you use just `scale_fill_grey()`, it will use four shades of grey.

The qplot approach to Fig. 16.3 is

```
qplot(factor(""), fill=workshop,
  geom="bar", xlab="") +
  scale_fill_grey(start=0, end=1)
```

The ggplot approach to Fig. 16.3 is

```
ggplot(mydata100,
  aes(factor(""), fill=workshop) ) +
  geom_bar() +
  scale_x_discrete("") +
  scale_fill_grey(start=0, end=1)
```

16.2.1 Pie Charts

One interesting aspect to the grammar of graphics concept is that a pie chart (Fig. 16.4) is just a single stacked bar chart (Fig. 16.3), drawn in polar coordinates. So we can use the same function calls that we used for the bar chart in the previous section, but convert to polar afterward using the `coord_polar` function.

This is a plot that only **ggplot** can do correctly. The `geom_bar(width=1)` function call tells it to put the slices right next to each other. If you included that on a standard bar chart, it would also put the bars right next to each other.

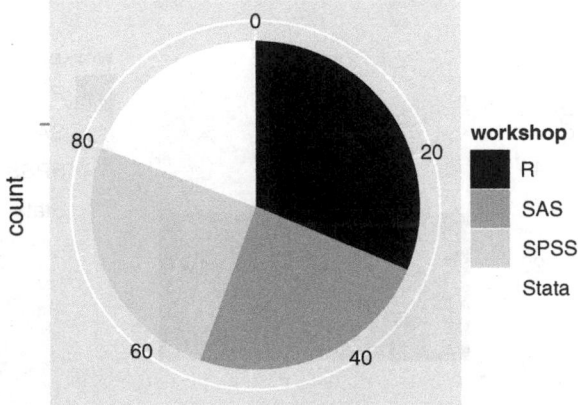

Fig. 16.4. A pie chart of workshop attendance.

```
ggplot(mydata100,
  aes( factor(""), fill=workshop ) ) +
  geom_bar( width=1 ) +
  scale_x_discrete("") +
  coord_polar(theta="y") +
  scale_fill_grey(start=0, end=1)
```

That is a lot of code for a simple pie chart! In the previous chapter, we created this graph with a simple

```
pie( table(workshop) )
```

So traditional graphics are the better approach in some cases. However, as we will see in the coming sections, the ggplot2 package is the easiest to use for most things.

16.2.2 Bar Charts for Groups

Let us now look at repeating bar charts for levels of a factor, like gender. This requires having factors named for both the x argument and the fill argument. By default, the position argument stacks the fill groups—in this case, the workshops. That graph is displayed in the upper left frame of Fig. 16.5.

The qplot approach to Fig. 16.5, upper left is

```
qplot(gender, geom="bar",
  fill=workshop, position="stack") +
  scale_fill_grey(start=0, end=1)
```

The ggplot apprach to Fig. 16.5, upper left is

```
ggplot(mydata100, aes(gender, fill=workshop) ) +
  geom_bar(position="stack") +
  scale_fill_grey( start=0, end=1 )
```

Changing either of the above examples to:
    position="fill"
makes every bar fill the y-axis, displaying the proportion in each group rather than the number. That type of graph is called a *spine plot* and it is displayed in the upper right of Fig. 16.5.

Finally, if you set
position="dodge" the filled segments appear beside one another, "dodging" each other. That takes more room on the x-axis, so it appears across the whole bottom row of Fig. 16.5.

We will discuss how to convey similar information using multiframe plots in Section 16.15, "Multiple Plots on a Page."

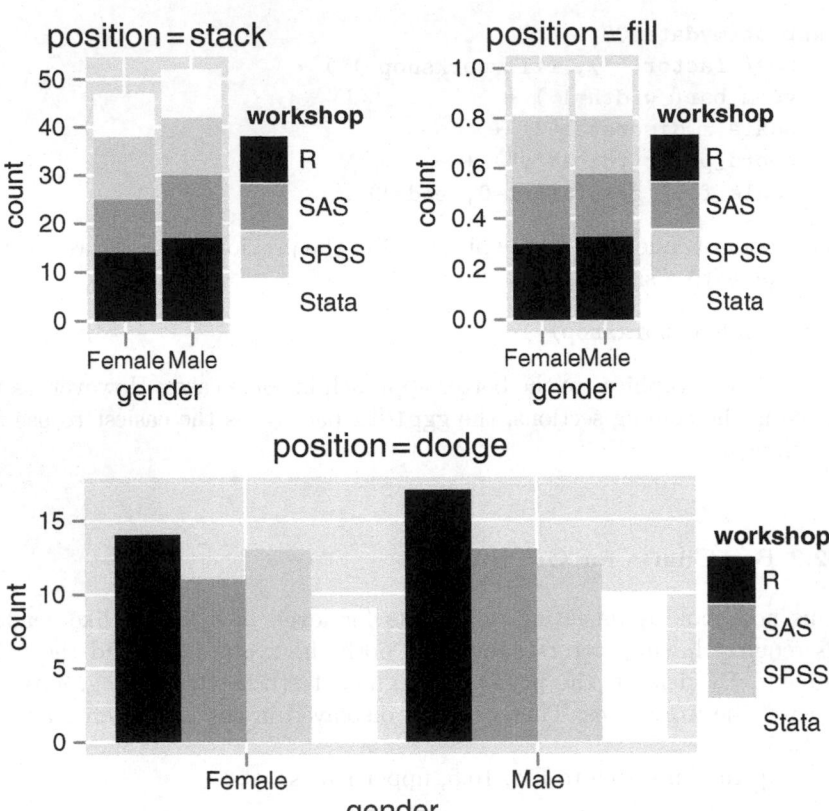

Fig. 16.5. A multiframe plot showing the impact of the various position settings.

16.3 Plots by Group or Level

One of the nicest features of the ggplot2 package is its ability to easily plot groups within a single plot (Fig. 16.6). To fully appreciate all of the work it is doing for us, let us first consider how to do this with traditional graphics functions.

1. We would set up a multiframe plot, say for males and females.
2. Then we might create a bar chart on workshop, selecting
   which(gender=="Female").
3. Then we would repeat the step above, selecting the males.
4. We probably want to standardize the axes to better enable comparisons and do the plots again.
5. We would add a legend, making sure to manually match any color or symbol differences across the plots.
6. Finally, we would turn off the multiframe plot settings to get back to one plot-per-page.

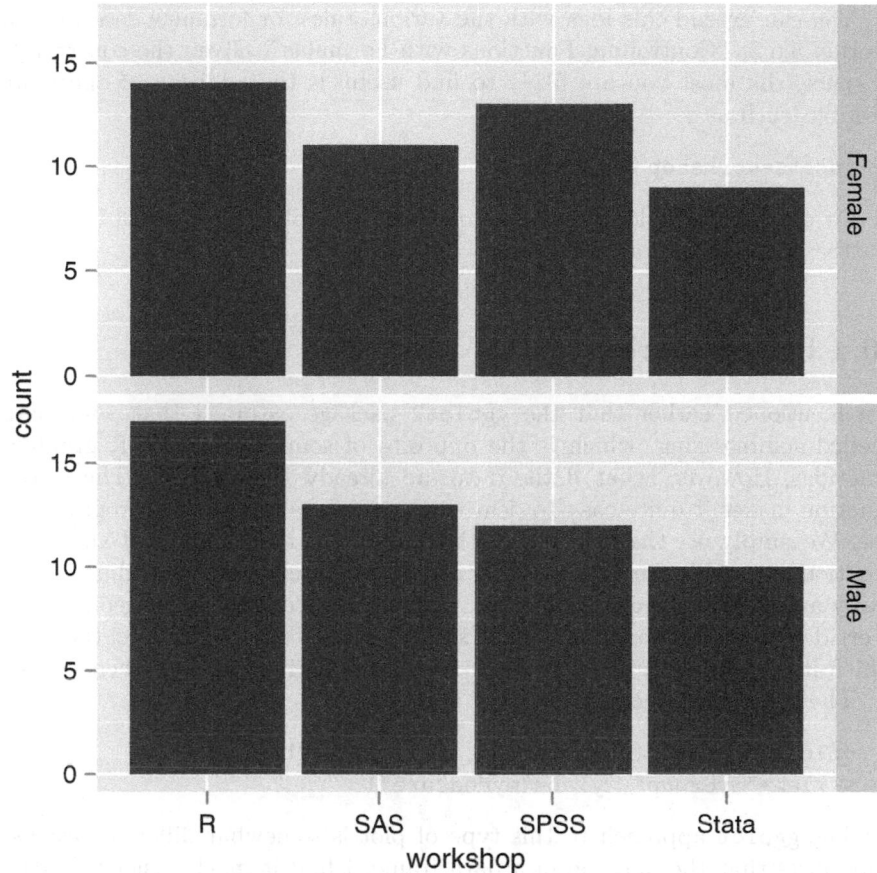

Fig. 16.6. A bar plot of workshop attendance with facets for the genders.

Thank goodness the `ggplot2` package can perform the equivalent of those tedious steps using either of the following simple function calls:

The `qplot` approach to Fig. 16.6 is

```
qplot(workshop, facets=gender ~ . )
```

The `ggplot` approach to Fig. 16.6 is

```
ggplot(mydata100, aes(workshop) ) +
  geom_bar() + facet_grid( gender ~ . )
```

The new feature is the `facets` argument in `qplot` and the `facet_grid` function in `ggplot`. The formula it uses is in the form "rows~columns". In this case, we have "gender~." so we will get rows of plots for each gender and no columns. The "." represents "1" row or column. If we instead did ".~gender", we would have one row and two columns of plots side-by-side.

You can extend this idea with the various rules for formulas described in Section 5.6.2, "Controlling Functions with Formulas." Given the constraints of space, the most you are likely to find useful is the addition of one more variable, such as

```
facets=workshop ~ gender
```

In our current example, that leaves us nothing to plot, but we will look at a scatter plot example of that later.

16.4 Presummarized Data

We mentioned earlier that the `ggplot2` package assumed that your data needed summarizing, which is the opposite of some traditional R graphics functions. However, what if the data are already summarized? The `qplot` function makes it quite easy to deal with, as you can see in the program below. We simply use the `factor` function to provide the x argument and the c function to provide the data for the y argument. Since we are providing both x and y arguments, the `qplot` function will provide a default point geom, so we override that with `geom="bar"`. The `xlab` and `ylab` arguments *lab*el the axes, which it would otherwise label with the `factor` and c functions themselves.

The `qplot` approach to Fig. 16.7 is

```
qplot( factor(c(1,2)), c(40, 60), geom="bar",
  xlab="myGroup", ylab="myMeasure")
```

The `ggplot` approach to this type of plot is somewhat different because it requires that the data be in a data frame. I find it much easier to create a temporary data frame containing the summary data. Trying to nest a data frame creation within the `ggplot` function will work, but you end up with so many parentheses that it can be a challenge getting it to work. The example program at the end of this chapter contains that example as well.

The following is the more complicated `ggplot` approach to Fig. 16.7. We are displaying R's prompts here to differentiate input from output.

```
> myTemp <- data.frame(
+   myGroup=factor( c(1,2) ),
+   myMeasure=c(40, 60)
+ )

> myTemp

  myGroup myMeasure
1       1        40
2       2        60
```

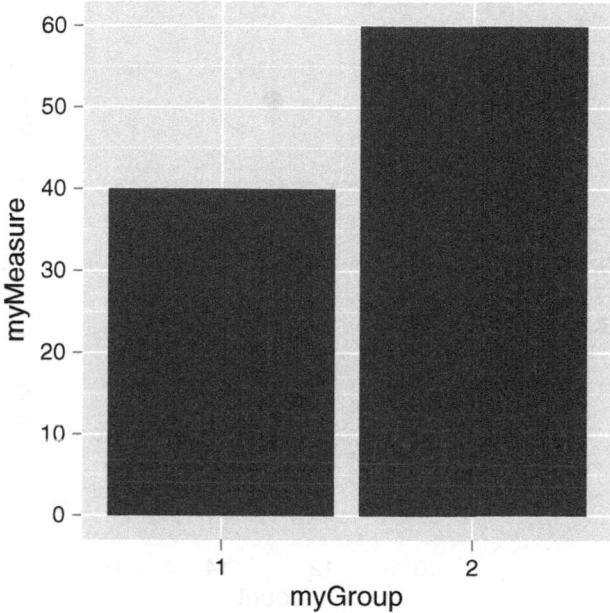

Fig. 16.7. A bar plot of presummarized data.

```
> ggplot(data=myTemp, aes(myX, myY) ) +
+    geom_bar()

> rm(myTemp) #Cleaning up.
```

16.5 Dot Charts

Dot charts are bar charts reduced to just points on lines, so you can take any of the above bar chart examples and turn them into dot charts (Fig. 16.8).

Dot charts are particularly good at packing in a lot of information on a single plot, so let us look at the counts for the attendance in each workshop, for both males and females. This example demonstrates how very different qplot and ggplot can be. It also shows how flexible ggplot is and that it is sometimes much easier to understand than qplot.

First, let us look at how qplot does it. The variable workshop is in the x position, so this is the same as saying x=workshop. If you look at the plot, workshop is on the y-axis. However, qplot requires an x variable, so we cannot simply say y=workshop and not specify an x variable. Next, it specifies geom="point" and sets the size of the points to I(4), which is much larger than in a standard scatter plot. Remember that the I() function around the

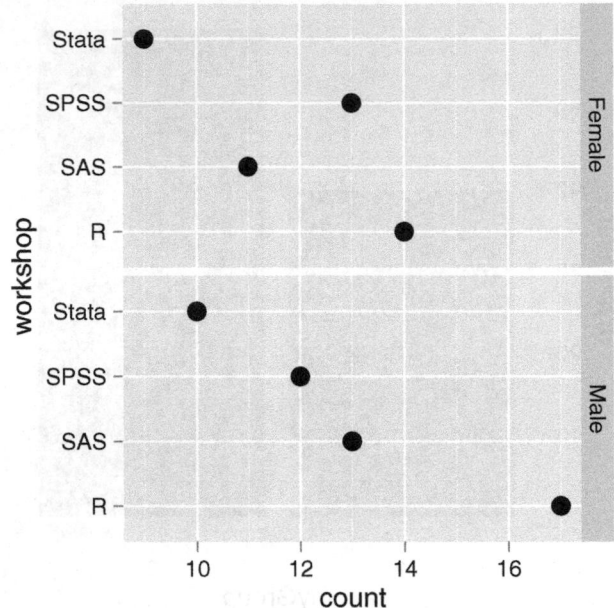

Fig. 16.8. A dot chart of workshop attendance with facets for the genders.

4 *i*nhibits *i*nterpretation, which in this case means that it stops `qplot` from displaying a legend showing which point size represents a "4." In this example, that is useless information. You can try various size values to see how it looks. The `stat="bin"` argument tells it to combine all of the values that it finds for each level of workshop as a histogram might do. So it ends up counting the number of observations in each combination of workshop and gender. The `facets` argument tells it to create a row for each gender. The `coord_flip` function rotates it in the direction we desire.

The `qplot` approach to Fig. 16.8 is

```
qplot(workshop, geom="point", size=I(4),
  stat="bin", facets=gender~.) +
  coord_flip()
```

Now let us see how `ggplot` does the same plot. The `aes` function supplies the *x*-axis variable and the *y*-axis variable uses the special "`..count..`" computed variable. That variable is also used by `qplot`, but it is the default y variable. The `geom_point` function adds points, bins them, and sets their size. The `coord_flip` function then reverses the axes. Finally, the `facet_grid` function specifies the same formula used earlier in `qplot`. Notice here that we did not need the `I()` function, as `ggplot` "knows" that the legend is not needed. If we were adjusting the point sizes based on a third variable, we would have to specify the variable as an additional aesthetic. The syntax to `ggplot` is verbose, but more precise.

```
ggplot(mydata100,
    aes(workshop, ..count..) ) +
    geom_point(stat="bin", size=4) + coord_flip()+
    facet_grid( gender~. )
```

16.6 Adding Titles and Labels

Sprucing up your graphs with titles and labels is easy to do (Fig. 16.9). The `qplot` function adds them exactly like the traditional graphics functions do. You supply the main title with the `main` argument, and the x and y labels with `xlab` and `ylab`, respectively. There is no subtitle argument. As with all labels in R, the characters "\n" causes it to go to a new line, so "\nWorkshops" below will put just the word "Workshops" at the beginning of a new line.

The `qplot` approach to Fig.16.9 is

```
qplot(workshop, geom="bar",
    main="Workshop Attendance",
    xlab="Statistics Package \nWorkshops")
```

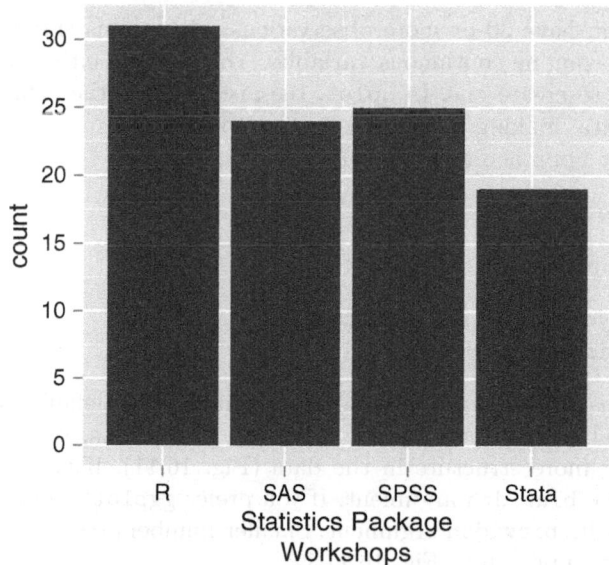

Fig. 16.9. A bar plot demonstrating titles and x-axis labels.

The `ggplot` approach to Fig.16.9 is

```
ggplot(mydata100, aes(workshop, ..count..) ) +
  geom_bar() +
  opts( title="Workshop Attendance" ) +
  scale_x_discrete("Statistics Package \nWorkshops")
```

Adding titles and labels in `ggplot` is slightly more verbose. The `opts` function sets various *opt*ions, one of which is `title`. The axis labels are attributes of the axes themselves. They are controlled by the functions, `scale_x_discrete`, `scale_y_discrete`, and for continuous axes, they are controlled by the functions, `scale_x_continuous`, `scale_y_continuous`, which are clearly named according to their function. We find it odd that you use different functions for labeling axes if they are discrete or continuous, but it is one of the trade-offs you make when getting all of the flexibility that `ggplot` offers.

16.7 Histograms and Density Plots

Many statistical methods make assumptions about the distribution of your data, or at least of your model residuals. Histograms and density plots are two effective plots to help you assess the distributions of your data.

16.7.1 Histograms

As long as you have 30 or more observations, histograms (Fig. 16.10) are a good way to examine continuous variables. You can use either of the following examples to create one. In `qplot`, the histogram is the default geom for continuous data, making it particulary easy to perform.

The `qplot` approach to Fig. 16.10 is

```
qplot(posttest)
```

The `ggplot` approach to Fig. 16.10 is

```
ggplot(mydata100, aes(posttest) ) +
  geom_histogram()
```

Both functions will print the number of bins it uses by default (30) to the R console (not shown). If you narrow the width of the bins, you will get more bars, showing more structure in the data (Fig. 16.11). If you prefer `qplot`, simply add the `binwidth` argument. If you prefer `ggplot`, add the `geom_bar` function with its `binwidth` argument. Smaller numbers result in more bars.

The `qplot` approach to Fig. 16.11 is

```
qplot(posttest, geom="histogram", binwidth=0.5)
```

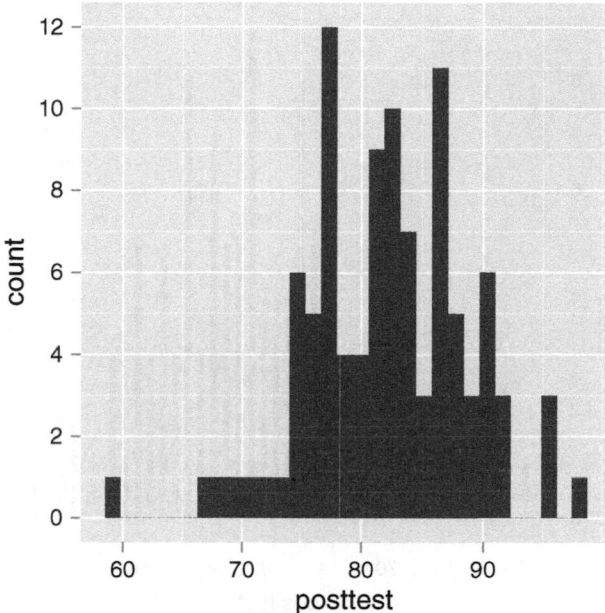

Fig. 16.10. A histogram of posttest.

The **ggplot** approach to Fig. 16.11 is

```
ggplot(mydata100, aes(posttest) ) +
  geom_bar( binwidth=0.5 )
```

16.7.2 Density Plots

If you prefer to see a density curve, just change the **geom** argument or function to **density** (Fig. 16.12).

The qplot approach to Fig. 16.12 is

```
qplot(posttest, geom="density" )
```

The **ggplot** approach to Fig. 16.12 is

```
ggplot(mydata100, aes(posttest) ) +
  geom_density()
```

16.7.3 Histograms with Density Overlaid

Overlaying the density on the histogram, as in Fig. 16.13, is only slightly more complicated. The variable that qplot or ggplot computes in the background

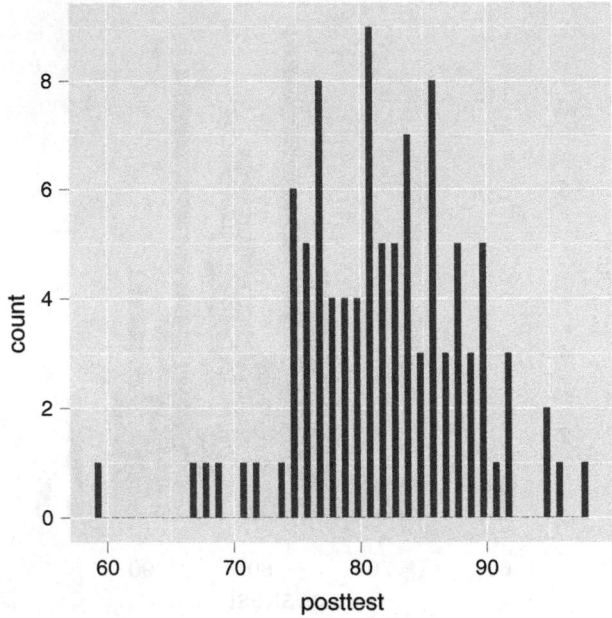

Fig. 16.11. A histogram of posttest with smaller bin widths.

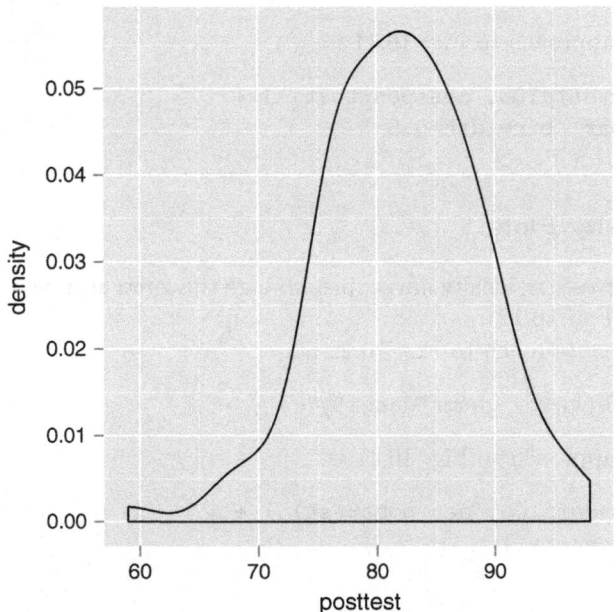

Fig. 16.12. A density plot of posttest.

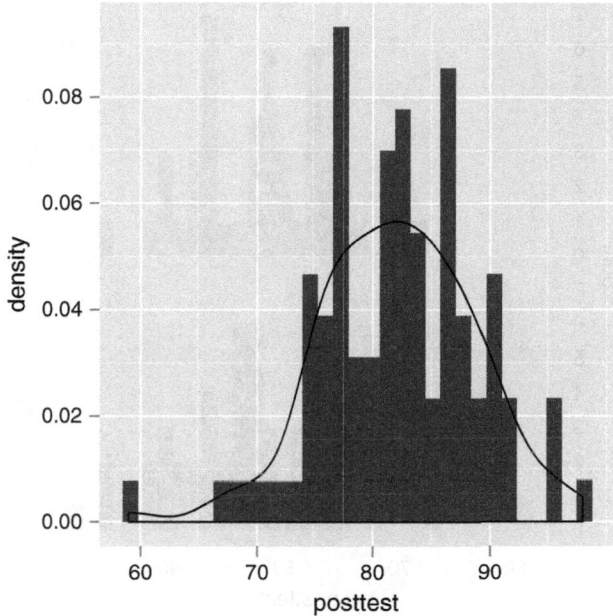

Fig. 16.13. A density plot overlaid on a histogram.

for the y-axis is named ".`.density.`.". To ask for both a histogram and the density, you must explicitly list `..density..` as the y variable. Then for `qplot`, you provide both `histogram` and `density` to the `geom` argument by combining them into a character vector using the `c` function.

For `ggplot`, you simply call both functions.

The `qplot` approach to Fig. 16.13 is

```
qplot(posttest, ..density..,
  geom=c( "histogram", "density" ) )
```

The `ggplot` approach to Fig. 16.13 is

```
ggplot(mydata100, aes(posttest, ..density..)) +
  geom_histogram() + geom_density()
```

16.7.4 Histograms for Groups, Stacked

What if we want to compare the histograms for males and females (Fig. 16.14)? Using base graphics, we had to set up a multiframe plot and learn how to control breakpoints for the bars so that they would be comparable. Using `ggplot2`, the facet feature makes the job trivial.

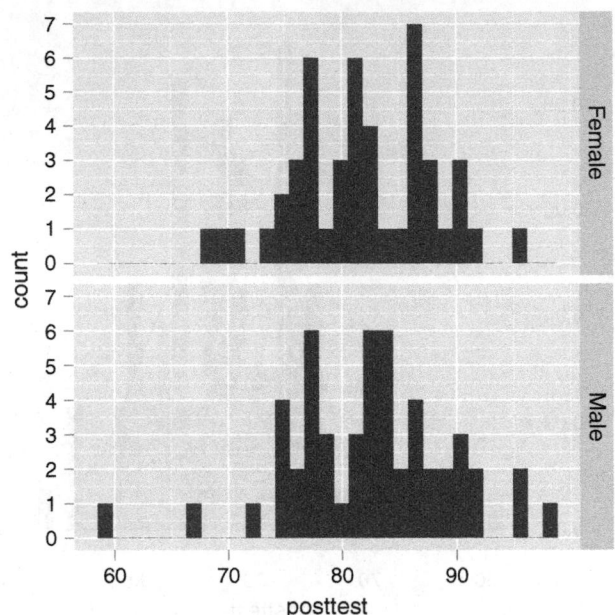

Fig. 16.14. Histograms of posttest with facets for the genders.

The `qplot` approach to Fig. 16.14 is

```
qplot(posttest, facets=gender~.)
```

The `ggplot` approach to Fig. 16.14 is

```
ggplot(mydata100, aes(posttest) ) +
  geom_histogram() + facet_grid( gender ~ . )
```

16.7.5 Histograms for Groups, Overlaid

We can also compare males and females by filling the bars by gender as in Fig. 16.15. As earlier, if you leave off the `scale_fill_grey` function, the bars will come out in two colors rather than black and white.

The `qplot` approach to Fig. 16.15 is

```
qplot( posttest, fill=gender ) +
  scale_fill_grey(start = 0, end = 1)
```

The `ggplot` approach to Fig. 16.15 is

```
ggplot(mydata100, aes(posttest, fill=gender) ) +
  geom_bar() + scale_fill_grey( start=0, end=1 )
```

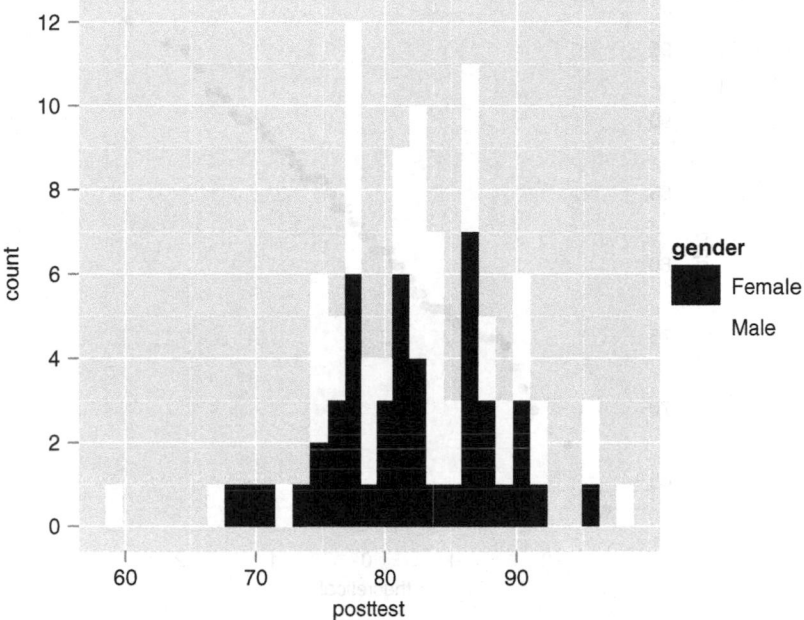

Fig. 16.15. A histogram with bars filled by gender.

16.8 Normal QQ Plots

We defined what a QQ plot is the previous chapter on traditional graphics. Creating them in the **ggplot2** package is straightforward (Fig. 16.16). If you prefer the **qplot** function, supply the **stat="qq"** argument. In ggplot, the similar **stat_qq** function will do the trick.

The qplot approach to Fig. 16.16 is

```
qplot( posttest, stat="qq" )
```

The ggplot approach to Fig. 16.16 is

```
ggplot( mydata100, aes(posttest) ) +
  stat_qq()
```

16.9 Strip Plots

Strip plots are scatter plots of single continuous variables, or a continuous variable displayed at each level of a factor like workshop. As with the single stacked bar chart, the case of a single strip plot still requires a variable on the x-axis (Fig. 16.17). As you see below, factor("") will suffice. The variable to actually plot is the y argument. Reversing the x and y variables will turn the

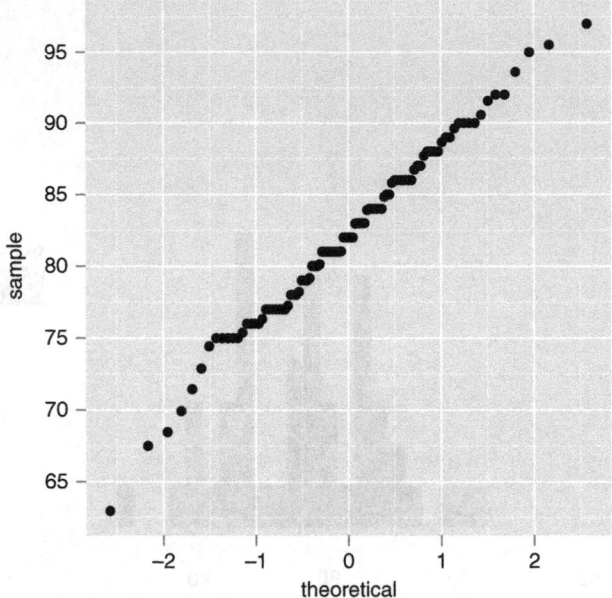

Fig. 16.16. A normal quantile–quantile plot of posttest.

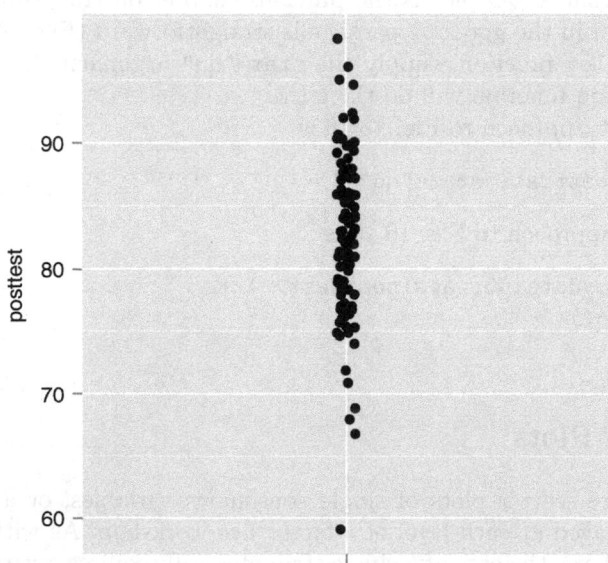

Fig. 16.17. A strip chart done using the `jitter` geom.

plot on its side, the default way the traditional graphics function, `stripchart`, does it. We prefer the vertical approach, as it matches the style of box plots and error bar plots when you use them to compare groups. The `geom="jitter"` adds some noise to separate points that would otherwise obscure other points by plotting on top of them. Finally, the `xlab=""` and `scale_x_discrete("")` labels erase what would have been a meaningless label about `factor("")` for `qplot` and `ggplot`, respectively.

This `qplot` approach does a strip plot with wider jitter than Fig 16.17:

```
qplot( factor(""), posttest, geom="jitter", xlab="")
```

This `ggplot` approach does a strip plot with wider jitter than Fig. 16.17:

```
ggplot(mydata100, aes(factor(""), posttest) ) +
  geom_jitter() +
  scale_x_discrete("")
```

The above two examples use an amount of jitter that is best for large data sets. For smaller data sets, it is best to limit the amount of jitter to separate the groups into clear strips of points. Unfortunately, this complicates the syntax.

The qplot function controls jitter width with the `position` argument, setting `position_jitter` with `width=scalefactor`.

The ggplot approach places that same parameter within its `geom_jitter` function call.

The qplot approach to Fig. 16.17 is

```
qplot( factor(""), posttest, data = mydata100, xlab="",
  position=position_jitter(width=.02))
```

The ggplot approach to Fig. 16.17 is

```
ggplot(mydata100, aes(factor(""), posttest) ) +
  geom_jitter(position=position_jitter(width=.02)) +
  scale_x_discrete("")
```

Placing a factor like workshop on the x-axis will result in a strip chart for each level of the factor (Fig. 16.18).

This qplot approach does a grouped strip plot with wider jitter than Fig 16.18, but its code is simpler:

```
> qplot(workshop, posttest, geom="jitter")
```

This ggplot approach does a grouped strip plot with wider jitter than Fig 16.18, but with simpler code:

```
> ggplot(mydata100, aes(workshop, posttest ) ) +
+   geom_jitter()
```

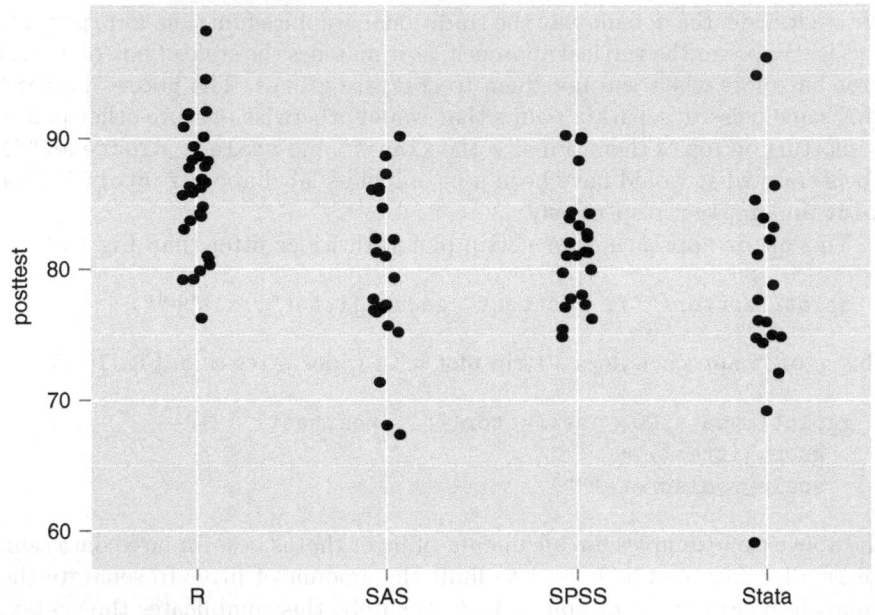

Fig. 16.18. A strip chart with facets for the workshops.

Limiting the amount of jitter for a grouped strip plot uses exactly the same parameters we used for a single strip plot.

The `qplot` approach to Fig. 16.18 is

```
qplot(workshop, posttest, data = mydata100, xlab="",
  position=position_jitter(width=.08))
```

The `ggplot` approach to Fig. 16.18 is

```
ggplot(mydata100, aes(workshop, posttest) ) +
  geom_jitter(position=position_jitter(width=.08)) +
  scale_x_discrete("")
```

16.10 Scatter Plots and Line Plots

The simplest scatter plot hardly takes any effort in `qplot`. Just list x and y variables in that order. You could add the `geom="point"` argument, but it is the default when you list two variables.

The `ggplot` function is slightly more complicated. Since it has no default geometric object to display, we must specify `geom_point()`.

The `qplot` approach to Fig. 16.19, upper left, is

```
qplot(pretest, posttest)
```

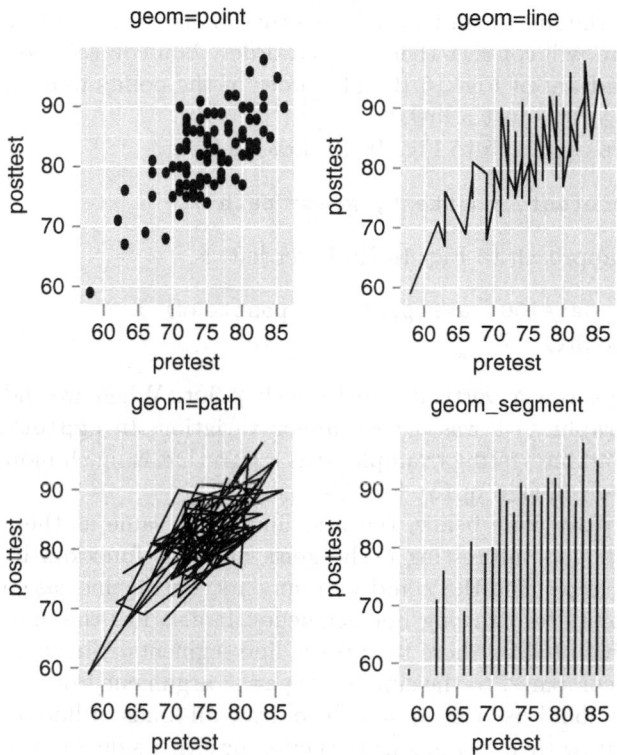

Fig. 16.19. A multiframe plot demonstrating various styles of scatter plots and line plots. The top two and the bottom left show different geoms. The bottom right is done a very different way, by drawing line segments from each point to the x-axis.

The `ggplot` approach to Fig. 16.19, upper left, is

```
ggplot(mydata100, aes(pretest, posttest) ) +
  geom_point()
```

We can connect the points using the line geom, as you see below. However, the result is different from what you get in traditional R graphics. The line connects the points in the order that they appear on the x-axis. That almost makes our data appear as a time series, when it is not.

The `qplot` approach to Fig. 16.19, upper right, is

```
qplot( pretest, posttest, geom="line")
```

The `qplot` approach to Fig. 16.19, upper right, is

```
ggplot(mydata100, aes(pretest, posttest) ) +
  geom_line()
```

Although the line geom ignored the order of the points in the data frame, the path geom will connect them in that order. You can see the result in the lower left quadrant of Fig. 16.19. The order of the points in our data set has no meaning, so it is just a mess!

The `qplot` approach to Fig. 16.19, lower left, is

```
qplot( pretest, posttest, geom="path")
```

The `ggplot` approach to Fig. 16.19, lower left, is

```
ggplot(mydata100, aes(pretest, posttest) ) +
  geom_path()
```

Now let us run a vertical line to each point. When we did that using traditional graphics, it was a very minor variation. In `ggplot2`, it is quite different but an interesting example. It is a plot that is much more clear using `ggplot`, so we will skip `qplot` for this one.

In the `ggplot` code below, the first line is the same as the above examples. Where it gets interesting is the `geom_segment` function. It has its own `aes` function, repeating the x and y arguments, but in this case, they are the beginning points for drawing line segments! It also has the arguments `xend` and `yend`, which tell it where to end the line segments. This may look overly complicated compared to the simple `"type=h"` argument from the `plot` function, but you could use this approach to draw all kinds of line segments. You could easily draw them coming from the top or either side, or even among sets of points. The `"type=h"` approach is a one trick pony. With that approach, adding features to a function leads to a very large number of options, and the developer is still unlikely to think of all of the interesting variations in advance.

The following is the code, and the resulting plot is in the lower right panel of Fig. 16.19.

```
ggplot(mydata100, aes(pretest, posttest) ) +
  geom_segment( aes(  pretest, posttest,
                    xend=pretest, yend=58) )
```

16.10.1 Scatter Plots with Jitter

We discussed the benefits of jitter in the previous chapter. To get a nonjittered plot of q1 and q4, we will just use `qplot` (Fig. 16.20, left).

```
qplot(q1,q4)
```

To add jitter, below are both the `qplot` and `gglot` approaches (Fig. 16.20, right). Note that the `geom="point"` argument is the default in `qplot` when two variables are used. Since that default is not shown, the fact that the `position` argument applies to it is not obvious. That relationship is clearer in the `ggplot`

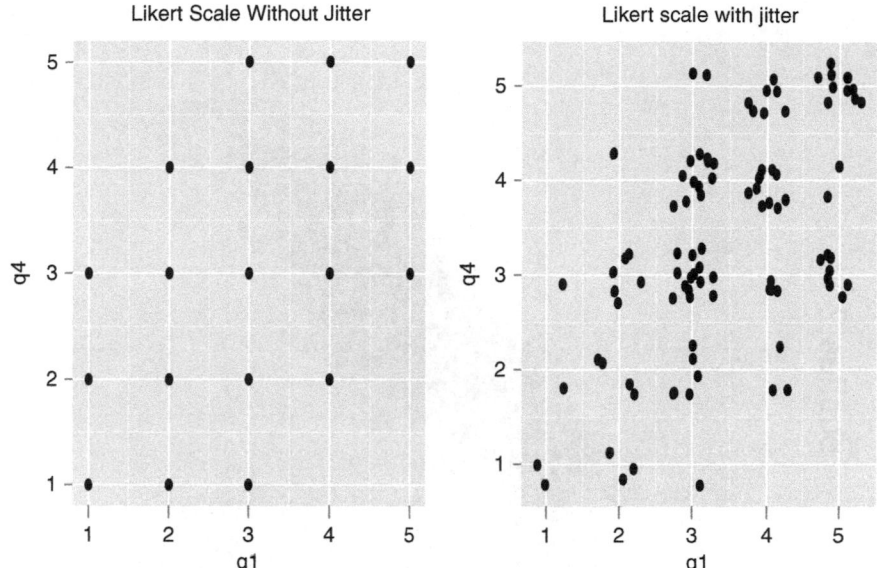

Fig. 16.20. A multiframe plot showing the impact of jitter on five-point Likert–scale data. The plot on the left is not jittered, so many points are obscured. The plot on the right is jittered, randomly moving points out from behind one another.

code, where the `position` argument is clearly part of the `geom_point` function. You can try various amounts of jitter to see which provides the best view of your data.

The `qplot` approach to Fig. 16.20, right, is

```
qplot(q1, q4, position=position_jitter(width=.3,height=.3))
```

The `ggplot` approach to Fig. 16.20, right, is

```
ggplot(mydata100, aes(x=q1, y=q2) ) +
  geom_point(position=position_jitter(width=.3,height=.3))
```

16.10.2 Scatter Plots for Large Data Sets

When plotting large data sets, points often obscure one another. The `ggplot2` package offers several ways to deal with this problem, including decreasing point size, adding jitter and/or transparency, displaying density contours, and replacing sets of points with hexagonal bins.

Scatter Plots with Jitter and Transparency

By adjusting the amount of jitter and the amount of transparency, you can find a good combination that lets you see through points into the heart of a dense scatter plot (Fig. 16.21).

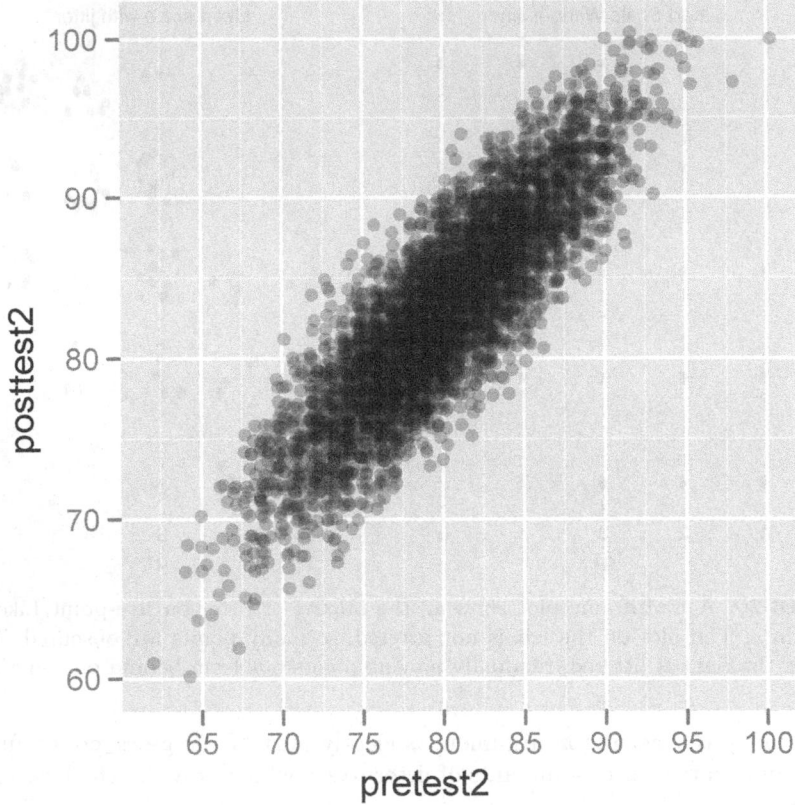

Fig. 16.21. A scatter plot demonstrating how transparency allows you to see many points at once.

Unfortunately, transparency is not yet supported in Windows metafiles. So if you are a Windows user, choose "Copy as bitmap" when cutting and pasting graphs into your word processor. For a higher-resolution image, route your graph to a file using the `png` function. For an example, see Section 14.6, "Graphics Devices." You can also use the `ggsave` function, which is part of the `ggplot2` package. For details, see Section 16.16, "Saving `ggplot2` Graphs to a File."

To get 5,000 points to work with, we generated them with the following:

```
pretest2  <- round( rnorm(n=5000,mean=80,sd=5) )

posttest2 <- round( pretest2 + rnorm(n=5000,mean=3,sd=3) )

pretest2[pretest2>100] <- 100

posttest2[posttest2>100] <- 100

temp=data.frame(pretest2,posttest2)
```

Now let us plot this data. This builds on our previous plots that used jitter and size. In computer terminology, controlling transparency is called *alpha compositing*. The qplot function makes this easy with a simple alpha argument. You can try various levels of transparency until you get the result you desire.

The size and alpha arguments could be set as variables. In which case, they would vary the point size or transparency to reflect the levels of the assigned variables. That would require a legend to help us interpret the plot. However, when you want to set them equal to fixed values, you can nest the numbers using the I() function. The I() function *i*nhibits the *i*nterpretation of its arguments. Without the I() function, the qplot function would print a legend saying that "size=2" and "alpha=0.15," which in our case is fairly useless information.

The ggplot function controls transparency with the colour argument to the geom_jitter function. That lets you control color and amount of transparency in the same option.

The qplot approach to Fig. 16.21 is

```
qplot(pretest2, posttest2, data=temp,
  geom="jitter", size=I(2), alpha=I(0.15),
  position=position_jitter(width=2) )
```

The ggplot approach to Fig. 16.21 is

```
ggplot(temp, aes(pretest2, posttest2),
  size=2, position = position_jitter(x=2,y=2) ) +
  geom_jitter(colour=alpha("black",0.15) )
```

Scatter Plots with Density Contours

A different approach to study a dense scatter plot is to draw density contours on top of the data (Fig. 16.22). With this approach, it is often better not to jitter the data, so that you can more clearly see the contours. You can do this with the density2d geom in qplot or the geom_density function in ggplot. The size=I(1) argument below reduces the point size to make it easier to see many points at once. As before, the I() function simply suppressed a superfluous legend.

The qplot approach to Fig. 16.22 is

```
qplot(pretest2, posttest2, data=temp,
  geom=c("point","density2d"), size = I(1) )
```

The ggplot approach to Fig. 16.22 is

```
ggplot(temp, aes( pretest2, posttest2) ) +
  geom_point( size=1 ) + geom_density_2d()
```

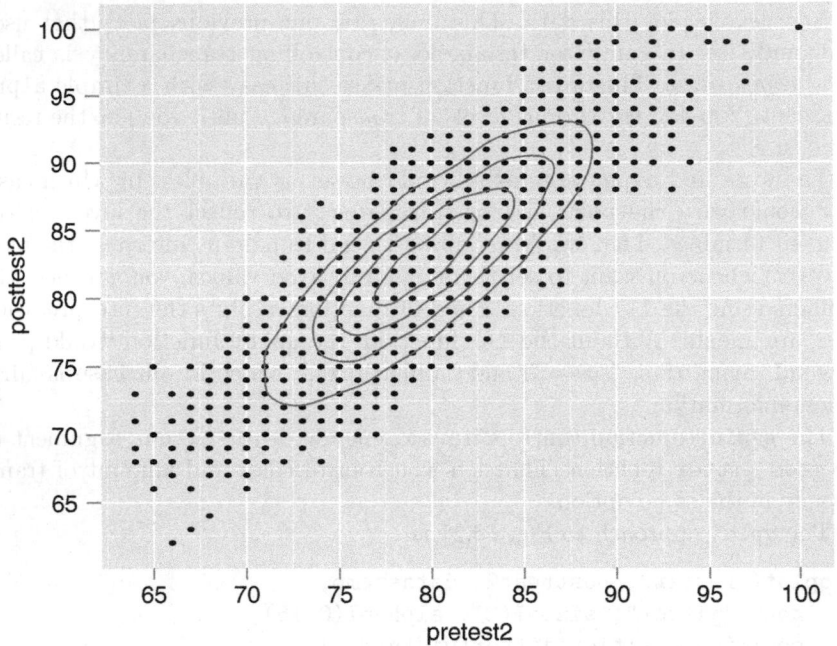

Fig. 16.22. This scatter plot shows an alternate way to see the structure in a large data set. These points are small, but not jittered, making more space for us to see the density contour lines.

16.10.3 Hexbin Plots

Another approach to plotting large data sets is to divide the plot surface into a set of hexagons and shade each hexagon to represent the number of points that fall within it; see Fig. 16.23. In that way, you can scale millions of points down into tens of bins.

In `qplot`, we can use the `hex` geom. In `ggplot`, we use the equivalent `geom_hex` function. Both use the `bins` argument to set the number of hexagonal bins you want. The default is 30; we use it here only so that you can see how to change it. As with histograms, increasing the number of bins may reveal more structure within the data.

The following function call uses `qplot` to create a color version of Fig. 16.23:

```
qplot(pretest2, posttest2, geom="hex", bins=30)
```

The following code uses `ggplot` to create the actual greyscale version of Fig. 16.23. The `scale_fill_continuous` function allows us to shade the plot using levels of grey. You can change the `low="grey80"` argument to other values to get the range of grey you prefer. Of course, you could add this function call to the above `qplot` call to get it to be grey instead of color.

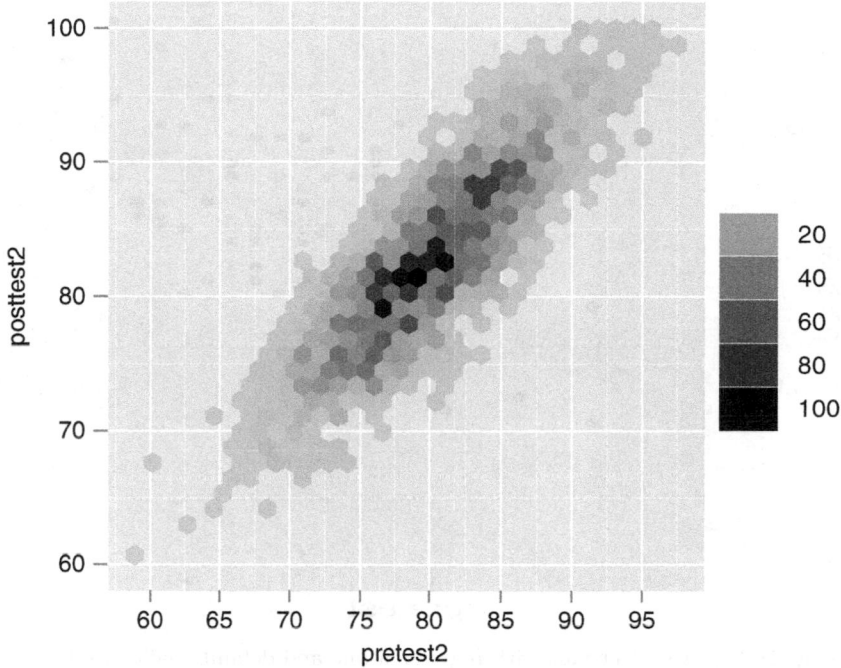

Fig. 16.23. A hexbin plot of pretest and posttest.

```
ggplot(temp, aes(pretest2, posttest2))   +
  geom_hex( bins=30 ) +
  scale_fill_continuous(
    low = "grey80", high = "black")
```

16.10.4 Scatter Plots with Fit Lines

While the traditional graphics `plot` function took quite a lot of extra effort to add confidence lines around a regression fit (Fig. 15.38), the `ggplot2` package makes that automatic. Unfortunately, the transparency used to create the confidence band is not supported when you cut and paste the image as a metafile in Windows. The image in Fig. 16.24 is a slightly lower resolution 600-dpi bitmap.

To get a regression line in `qplot`, simply specify `geom="smooth"`. However, that alone will replace the default of `geom="point"`, so if you want both, you need to specify `geom=c("point","smooth")`.

In `ggplot`, you use both the `geom_point` and `geom_smooth` functions. The default smoothing method is a lowess function, so if you prefer a linear model, include the `method=lm` argument.

The `qplot` approach to Fig. 16.24 is

```
qplot(pretest, posttest,
  geom=c("point","smooth"), method=lm )
```

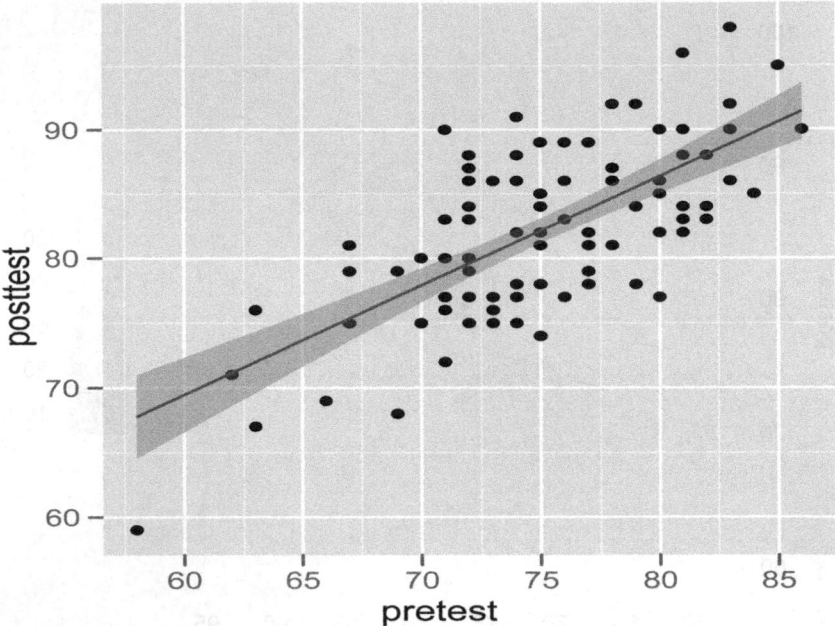

Fig. 16.24. A scatter plot with regression line and default confidence band.

The `ggplot` approach to Fig. 16.24 is

```
ggplot(mydata100, aes(pretest, posttest) ) +
  geom_point() + geom_smooth(method=lm)
```

Since the confidence bands appear by default, we have to set the `se` argument (standard error) to `FALSE` to turn it off.

The `qplot` approach to Fig. 16.25 is

```
qplot(pretest, posttest,
  geom=c("point","smooth"), method=lm, se=FALSE )
```

The `ggplot` approach to Fig. 16.25 is

```
ggplot(mydata100, aes(pretest, posttest) ) +
  geom_point() + geom_smooth(method=lm, se=FALSE)
```

16.10.5 Scatter Plots with Reference Lines

To place an arbitrary straight line on a plot, use the `abline` geom in `qplot`. You specify your slope and intercept using clearly named arguments. Here we are using intercept=0 and slope=1 since this is the line where posttest=pretest. If the students did not learn anything in the workshops,

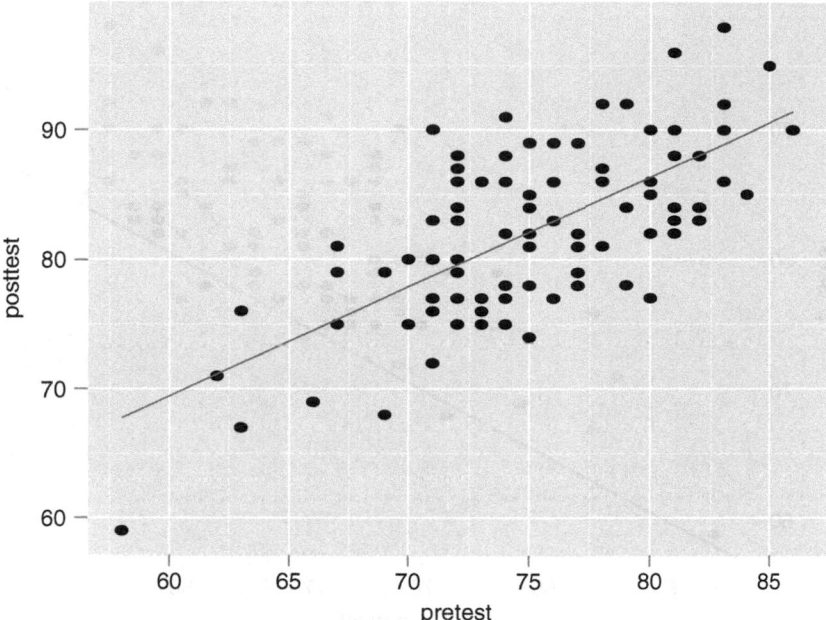

Fig. 16.25. A scatter plot with regression line with default confidence band removed.

the data would fall on this line (assuming a reliable test). The ggplot function adds the abline function with arguments for intercept and slope.

The qplot approach to Fig. 16.26 is

```
qplot(pretest, posttest,
  geom=c("point","abline"),
  intercept=0, slope=1 )
```

The ggplot approach to Fig. 16.26 is

```
ggplot(mydata100, aes(pretest, posttest) ) +
  geom_point()+ geom_abline( intercept=0, slope=1 )
```

Vertical or horizontal reference lines can help emphasize points or cutoffs. For example, if our students are required to get a score greater than 75 before moving on, we might want to display those cutoffs on our plot (Fig. 16.27).

In qplot, we can do this with the xintercept and yintercept arguments. In ggplot, the functions are named geom_vline and geom_hline, each with an intercept argument.

The qplot approach to Fig. 16.27 is

```
qplot(pretest, posttest,
  geom=c("point", "vline", "hline"),
  xintercept=75, yintercept=75)
```

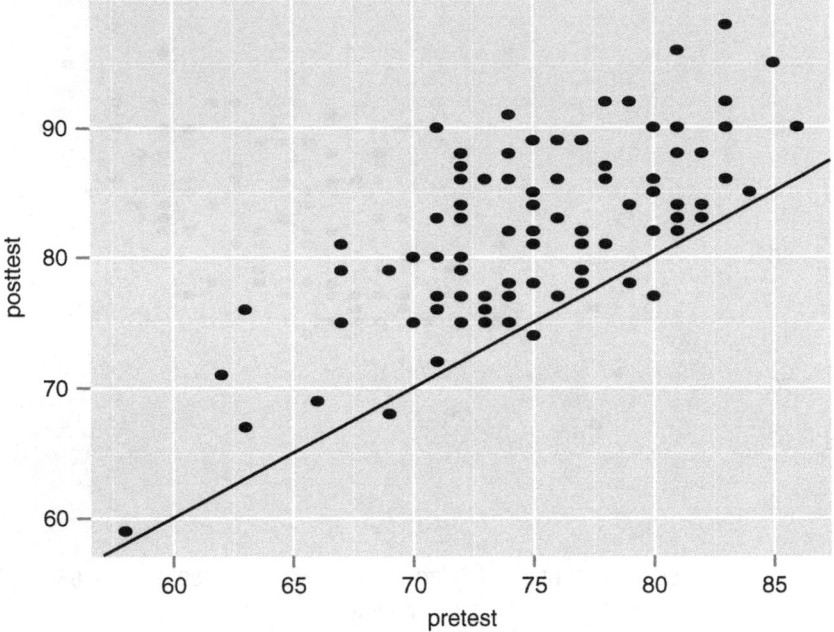

Fig. 16.26. A scatter plot with a line added where pretest=posttest. Most of the points lie above this line, showing that students did learn.

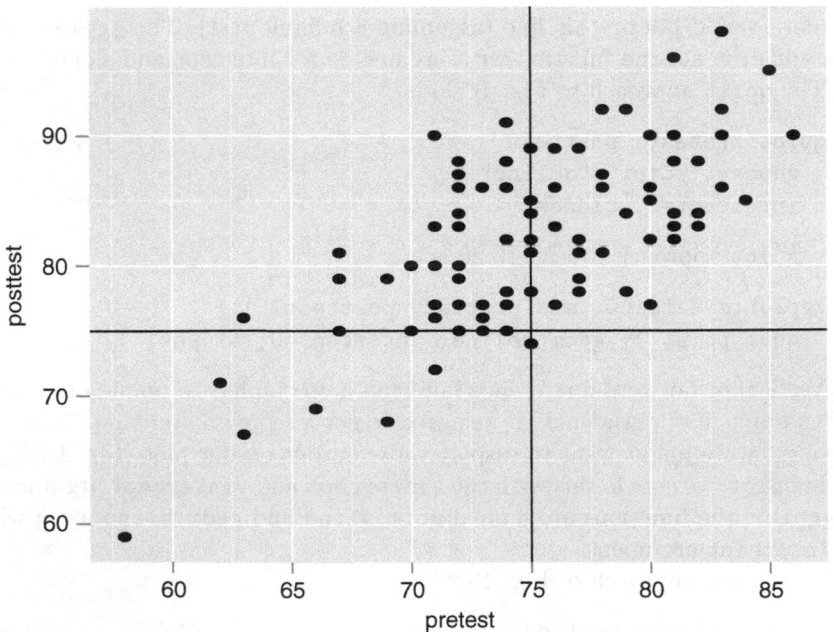

Fig. 16.27. A scatter plot with vertical and horizontal reference lines.

The `ggplot` approach to Fig. 16.27 is

```
ggplot(mydata100, aes(pretest, posttest)) +
   geom_point() +
   geom_vline( xintercept=75 ) +
   geom_hline( yintercept=75 )
```

To add a series of reference lines, we need to use the `geom_vline` or `geom_hline` functions (Fig. 16.28). The `qplot` example does not do much with qplot itself since it cannot create multiple reference lines. So for both examples, we use the identical `geom_vline` function. It includes the `seq` function to generate the *seq*uence of numbers we needed. Without it we could have used `intercept=c(70,72,74,76,78,80)`. In this case, we did not save much effort, but if we wanted to add dozens of lines, the `seq` function would be much easier.

The `qplot` approach to Fig. 16.28 is

```
qplot(pretest, posttest, type="point") +
   geom_vline( intercept=seq(from=70,to=80,by=2) )
```

The `ggplot` approach to Fig. 16.28 is

```
ggplot(mydata100, aes(pretest, posttest)) +
   geom_point() +
   geom_vline( xintercept=seq(from=70,to=80,by=2) )
```

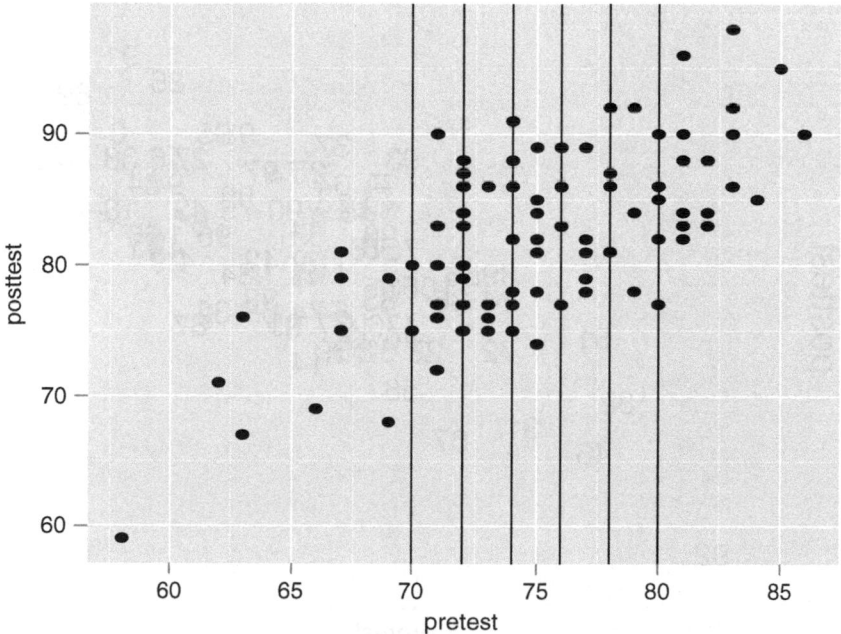

Fig. 16.28. A scatter plot with multiple vertical reference lines.

16.10.6 Scatter Plots with Labels Instead of Points

If you do not have much data or you are only interested in points around the edges, you can plot labels instead of plots symbols (Fig. 16.29). The labels can be identifiers such as ID numbers, people's names or row names, or they could be values of other variables of interest to add a third dimension to the plot.

You do this using the `geom="text"` argument in `qplot` or the `geom_text` function in `ggplot`. In either case, the `label` argument points to the values to use. Recall that in R, `row.names(mydata)` gives you the stored row names, even if these are just the sequential characters, "1," "2," and so on. We will store them in a variable named `mydata$id` and then use it with the `label` argument. The reason we do not use the form `label=row.names(mydata100)` is that the `ggplot2` package puts all of the variables it uses into a separate temporary data frame before running.

The `qplot` approach to Fig. 16.29 is

```
mydata100$id <- row.names(mydata100)
qplot(pretest, posttest, geom="text",
  label=mydata100$id )
```

The `ggplot` approach to Fig. 16.29 is

```
ggplot(mydata100, aes(pretest, posttest,
  label=mydata100$id ) ) + geom_text()
```

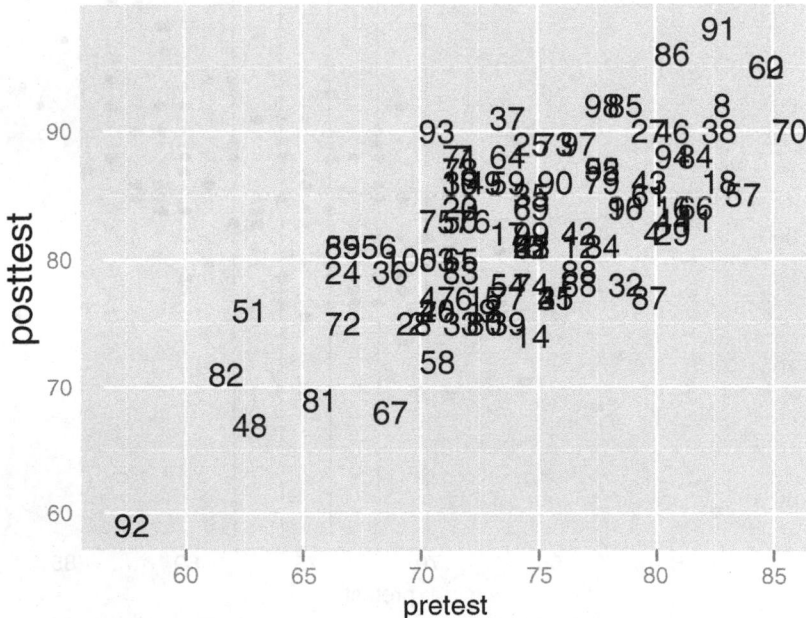

Fig. 16.29. A scatter plot with ID numbers plotted instead of points.

16.10.7 Changing Plot Symbols

You can use different plot symbols to represent levels of any third variable. Factor values, such as those representing group membership, can be displayed by different plot symbols (shapes) and/or colors. You could use a continuous third variable to shade the colors of each point or to vary the size of each point. The ggplot2 package makes quick work of any of these options. Let us consider a plot of pretest versus posttest that uses different points for males and females (Fig. 16.30).

The qplot function can do this using the shape argument.

The ggplot function must bring a new variable into the geom_point function. Recall that aesthetics map variables into their roles, so we will nest aes(shape=gender) within the call to geom_point.

You can also set color and size by substituting either of those arguments for shape.

The qplot approach to Fig. 16.30 is

```
qplot(pretest, posttest, shape=gender)
```

The ggplot approach to Fig. 16.30 is

```
ggplot(mydata100, aes(pretest, posttest) ) +
   geom_point( aes(shape=gender) )
```

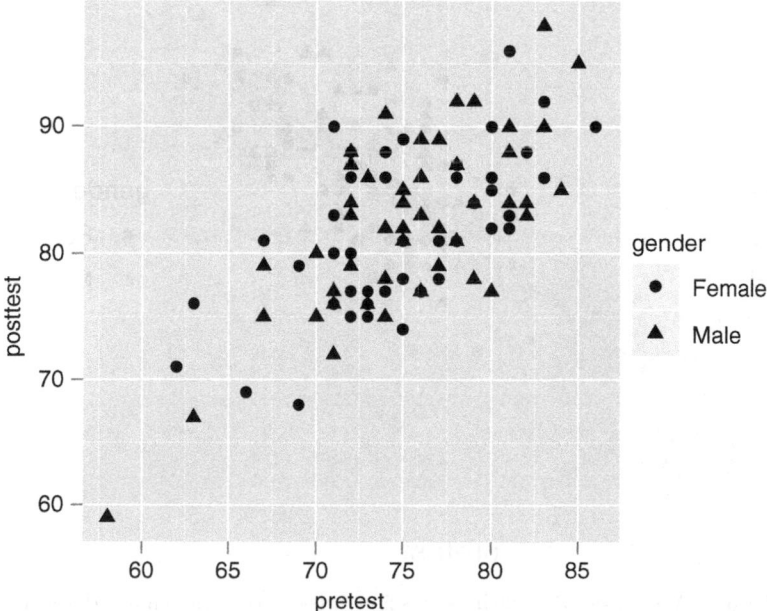

Fig. 16.30. A scatter plot with point shape determined by gender.

16.10.8 Scatter Plot with Linear Fits by Group

We have seen that the `smooth` geom adds a lowess or regression line and that `shape` can include group membership. If we do both of these in the same plot, we can get separate lines for each group as shown in Fig. 16.31.

The `qplot` approach to Fig. 16.31 is

```
qplot(pretest, posttest, geom=c("smooth","point"),
  method="lm", shape=gender)
```

The `ggplot` approach to Fig. 16.31 is

```
ggplot(mydata100,
  aes(x = pretest, y=posttest, shape=gender) ) +
  geom_smooth( method="lm" ) + geom_point()
```

16.10.9 Scatter Plots Faceted for Groups

Another way to compare groups on scatter with or without lines of fit is through facets (Fig. 16.32). As we have seen several times before, simply adding the `facets` argument to the `qplot` function allows you to specify `rows~columns` of categorical variables. So `facets=workshop~gender` is

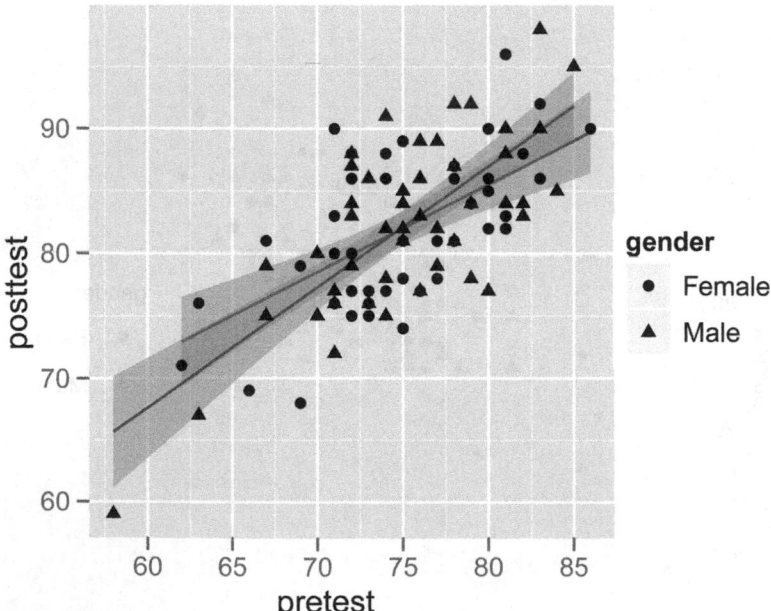

Fig. 16.31. A scatter plot with regression lines and point shape determined by gender.

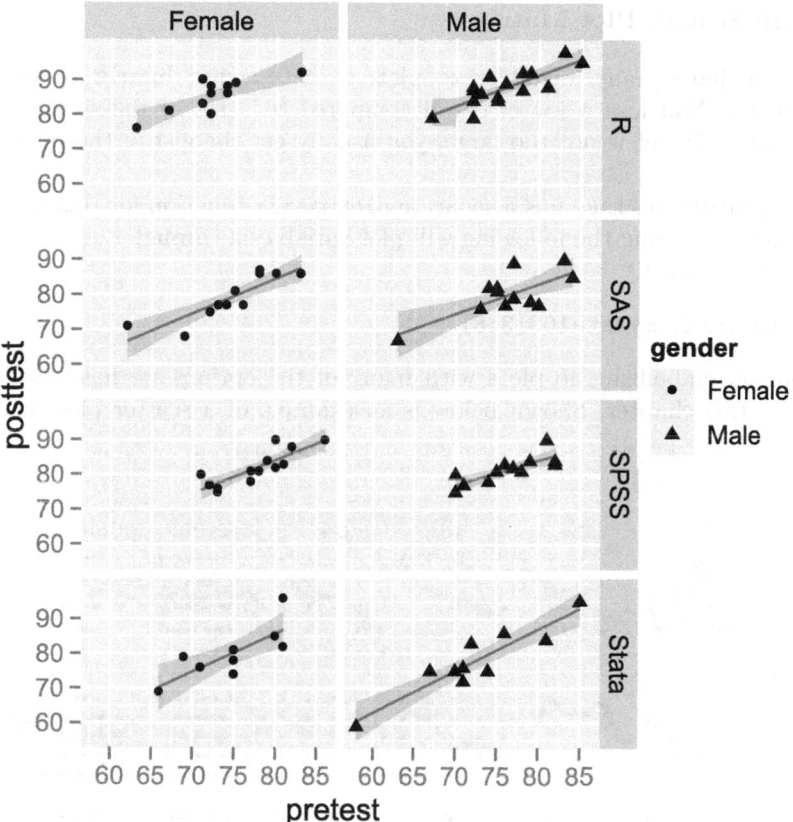

Fig. 16.32. A scatter plot with facets showing linear fits for each workshop and gender combination.

requesting a grid of plots for each workshop:gender combination, with workshop determining the rows and gender determining the columns.

The ggplot function works similarly, using the facet_grid function to do the same. If you have a continuous variable to condition on, you can use the chop function from the ggplot2 package or the cut function that is built into R to break the variable into groups.

The qplot approach to Fig. 16.32 is

```
qplot(pretest, posttest, geom=c("smooth","point"),
  method="lm", shape=gender, facets=workshop ~ gender)
```

The ggplot approach to Fig. 16.32 is

```
ggplot(mydata100, aes( pretest, posttest) ) +
  geom_smooth( method="lm" ) + geom_point() +
  facet_grid( workshop ~ gender )
```

16.10.10 Scatter Plot Matrix

When you have many variables to plot, a scatter plot matrix is helpful (Fig. 16.33). You lose a lot of detail compared to a set of full-sized plots, but if your data set is not too large, you usually get the gist of the relationships.

The `ggplot2` package has a separate `plotmatrix` function for this type of plot. Simply entering the following will plot variables 3 through 8 against one another (not shown):

```
plotmatrix( mydata100[3:8] )
```

You can embellish the plots with many of the options we have covered earlier in this chapter. Shown below is an example of a scatter plot matrix

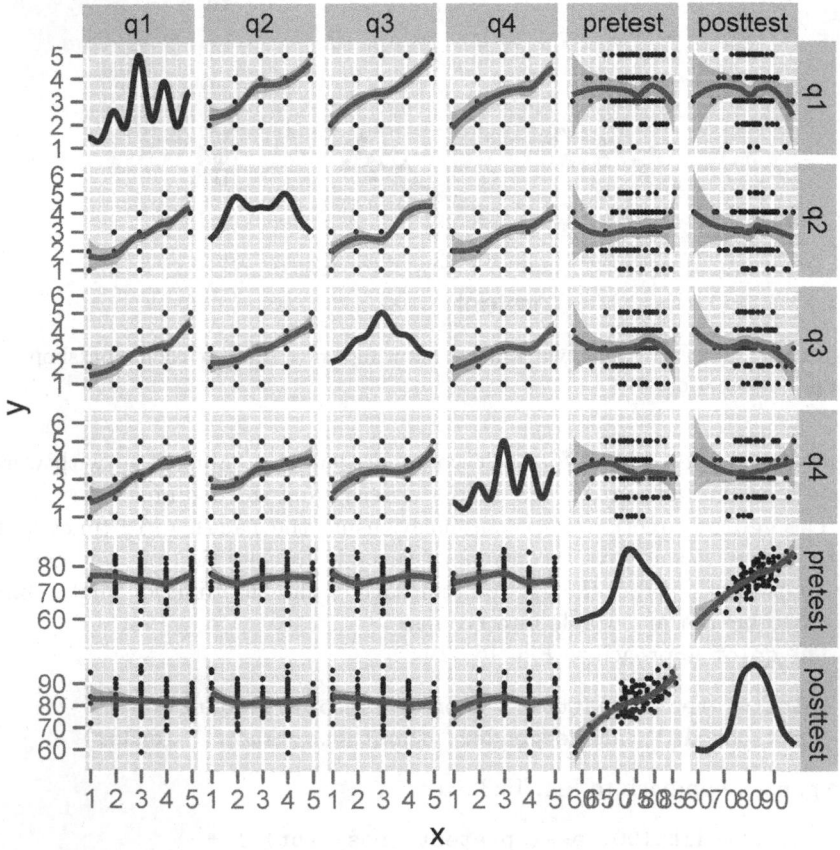

Fig. 16.33. A scatter plot matrix with lowess curve fits on the off-diagonal plots, and density plots on the diagonals.

(Fig. 16.33) with smoothed lowess fits for the entire data set (i.e., not by group). The density plots on the diagonals appear by default.

```
plotmatrix( mydata100[3:8] ) +
  geom_smooth()
```

The lowess fit generated some warnings but that is not a problem. It said, "There were 50 or more warnings (use warnings() to see the first 50)."

The next example gets fancier by assigning a different symbol shape and linear fits per group (plot not shown.)

```
plotmatrix( mydata100[3:8],
  aes( shape=gender ) ) +
  geom_smooth(method=lm)
```

16.11 Box Plots

We discussed what box plots are in the Chapter "Traditional Graphics," Section 15.11. We can recreate all those examples using the ggplot2 package, except for the "notches" to indicate possible group differences, shown in the upper right of Fig. 15.45

The simplest type of box plot is for a single variable (Fig. 16.34). The qplot function uses the simple form of factor("") to act as its x-axis value.

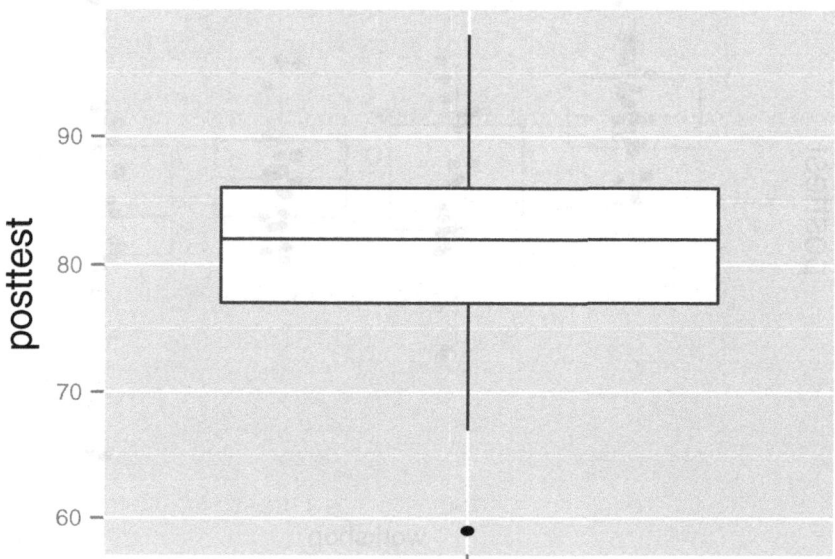

Fig. 16.34. A box plot of posttest.

The y value is the variable to plot: in this case, posttest. The geom of `boxplot` specifies the main display type. The `xlab=""` argument blanks out the label on the x-axis, which would have been a meaningless "`factor("")`".

The equivalent `ggplot` approach is almost identical with its ever-present `aes` arguments for x and y and the `geom_boxplot` function to draw the box. The `scale_x_discrete` function simply blanks out the x-axis label.

The `qplot` approach to Fig. 16.34 is

```
qplot(factor(""), posttest,
  geom="boxplot", xlab="")
```

The `ggplot` approach to Fig. 16.34 is

```
ggplot(mydata100,
  aes(factor(""), posttest) ) +
  geom_boxplot() +
  scale_x_discrete("")
```

Adding a grouping variable like workshop makes box plots much more informative (Fig. 16.35, ignore the overlaid strip plot points for now). These are the same function calls as above but with the x variable specified as workshop. We will skip showing this one in favor of the next.

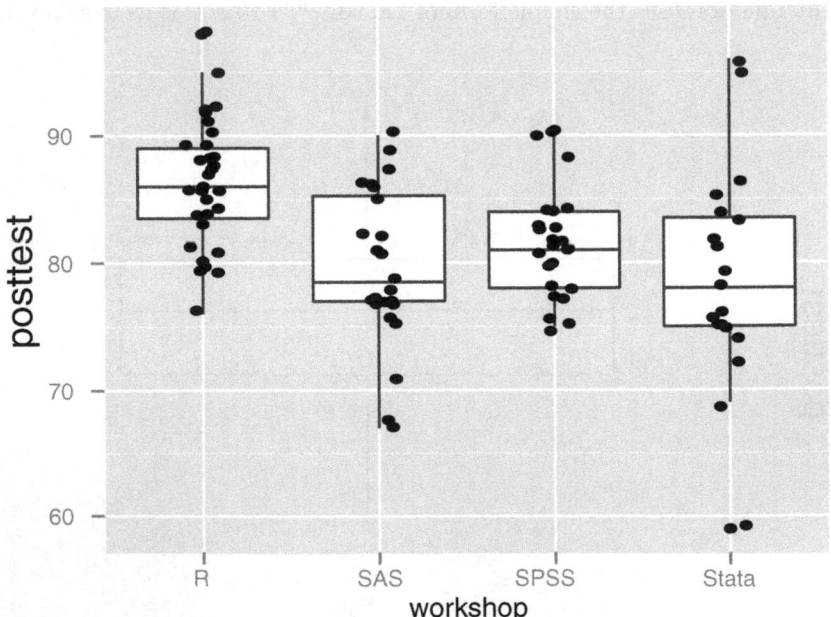

Fig. 16.35. A box plot comparing workshop groups on posttest, with jittered points on top.

The qplot approach to box plots (figure not shown) is

```
qplot(workshop, posttest, geom="boxplot" )
```

The ggplot approach to box plots (figure not shown) is

```
ggplot(mydata100,
  aes( workshop, posttest) ) +
  geom_boxplot()
```

Now we will do the same plot but with an added jittered strip plot on top of it (Fig. 16.35). This way we get the box plot information about the median and quartiles plus we get to see any interesting structure in the points that would otherwise have been lost. As you can see, the qplot now has jitter added to its geom argument, and ggplot has an additional geom_jitter function. Unfortunately, the amount of jitter that both functions provide by default is optimized for a much larger data set. So these next two sets of code do the plot shown in Fig. 16.35, but with much more jitter.

The qplot approach to Fig. 16.35 with more jitter added is

```
qplot(workshop, posttest,
  geom=c("boxplot","jitter") )
```

The ggplot approach to Fig. 16.35 with more jitter added is

```
ggplot(mydata100,
  aes(workshop, posttest )) +
  geom_boxplot() + geom_jitter()
```

The following is the exact code that created Fig. 16.35. The qplot function does not have enough control to request both the box plot and jitter while adjusting the amount of jitter.

```
ggplot(mydata100,
  aes(workshop, posttest )) +
  geom_boxplot() +
  geom_jitter(position=position_jitter(width=.1))
```

To add another grouping variable, you only need to only add the fill argument to either qplot or ggplot. Compare the resulting Fig. 16.36 to the result we obtained from traditional graphics, in the lower right panel of Fig. 15.45. The ggplot2 version is superior in many ways. The genders are easier to compare for a given workshop, because they are now grouped side-by-side. The shading makes it easy to focus on one gender at a time to see how they changed across the levels of workshop. The labels are easier to read and did not require the custom sizing that we did earlier to make room for the labels. The ggplot2 package usually does a better job with complex plots and makes quick work of them too.

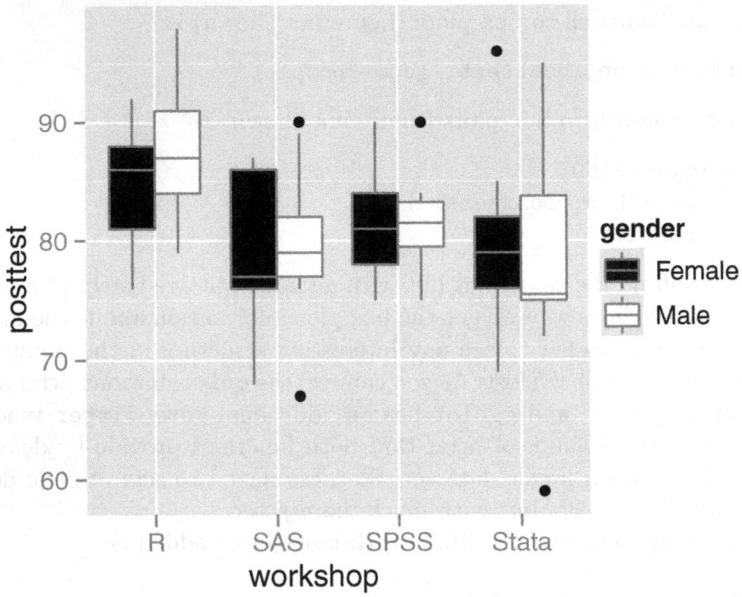

Fig. 16.36. A box plot comparing workshop and gender groups on posttest.

The qplot approach to Fig. 16.36 is

```
qplot(workshop, posttest,
  geom="boxplot", fill=gender ) +
  scale_fill_grey( start=0, end=1 )
```

The ggplot approach to Fig. 16.36 is

```
ggplot(mydata100,
  aes(workshop, posttest) ) +
  geom_boxplot( aes(fill=gender), colour="black") +
  scale_fill_grey( start=0, end=1 )
```

16.12 Error Bar Plots

Plotting means and 95% confidence intervals, as in Fig. 16.37, is a task that stretches what qplot was designed to do. As you can see from the two examples below, there is very little typing saved by using qplot over ggplot. In both cases, we are adding a jittered strip plot of points, as we did earlier in the section on strip plots (Section 16.9). Notice that we had to use the as.numeric function for our x variable: workshop. Since workshop is a factor, the software would not connect the means across the levels of x. Workshop

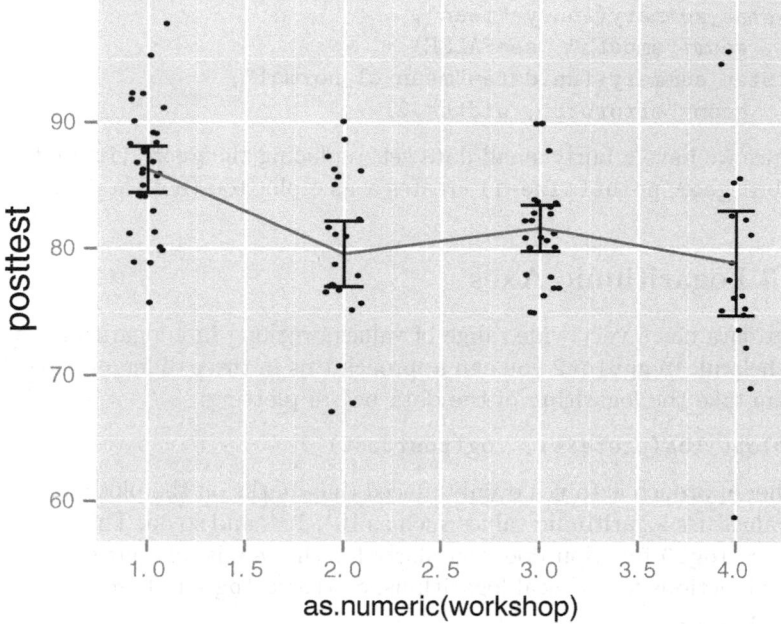

Fig. 16.37. An error bar plot with lines running through the means, with default axis labels.

is not a continuous variable, so that makes sense! Still, connecting the means with a line is a common approach, one that facilitates the study of higher level-interactions.

The key function for this plot is stat_summary, which we use twice. First, we use the argument fun.y="mean" to calculate the group means. We also use the geom="smooth" argument to connect them with a line. Next, we use fun.data="mean_cl_normal" to calculate confidence limits for the means based on a normal distribution and display them with the errorbar geom. You can try various values for the width argument until you are satisfied with the error bar widths.

```
qplot( as.numeric(workshop), posttest) +
  geom_jitter(position=position_jitter(width=.1))  +
  stat_summary(fun.y="mean",
    geom="smooth", se=FALSE) +
  stat_summary(fun.data="mean_cl_normal",
    geom="errorbar", width=.2)

ggplot(mydata100,
  aes( as.numeric(workshop), posttest ) ) +
  geom_jitter(size=1,
    position=position_jitter(width=.1) )  +
```

```
stat_summary(fun.y="mean",
  geom="smooth", se=FALSE) +
stat_summary(fun.data="mean_cl_normal",
  geom="errorbar", width=.2)
```

Since we have a fairly small data set, replacing the geom_jitter function with just geom_point(size=1) creates a nice plot too (not shown).

16.13 Logarithmic Axes

If your data has a very wide range of values, working in a logarithmic scale is often helpful. In ggplot2 you can approach this in three different ways. First, you can take the logarithm of the data before plotting:

```
qplot( log(pretest), log(posttest) )
```

Another approach is to use evenly placed tick-marks on the plot but have the axis values use logarithmic values such as 10^1, 10^2, and so on. This is what the scale_x_log10 function does (similarly for the y-axis, of course). There are similar functions for natural logarithms, scale_x_log and base 2 logarithms, scale_x_log2:

```
qplot(pretest, posttest, data=mydata100) +
  scale_x_log10() + scale_y_log10()
```

Finally, you can have the tick marks spaced unevenly and use values on your original scale. The coord_trans function does that. Its arguments for the various bases of logarithms are log10, log, and log2.

```
qplot(pretest, posttest, data=mydata100) +
  coord_trans("log10", "log10")
```

With our data set, the range of values is so small that this last plot will not noticeably change the axes. Therefore, we do not show it.

16.14 Aspect Ratio

Changing the aspect ratio of a graph can be far more important than you might first think. Research has shown that when most of the lines or scatter on a plot are angled at 45°, people make more accurate comparisons to those parts that are not [6].

Unless you specify an aspect ratio for your graph, qplot and ggplot will match the dimensions of your output window and allow you to change those dimensions using your mouse, as you would for any other window.

If you are routing your output to a file however, it is helpful to be able to set it using code. You set the aspect ratio using the coord_equal function. If you leave it empty, as in coord_equal(), it will make the x- and y-axes of equal lengths. If you specify this while working interactively, you can stillreshape your window, but the graph will remain square. Specifying a ratio parameter follows the form "height/width." For a mnemonic, think of how R specifies [rows,columns]. The following example would result in a graph that is four times wider than it is high (not shown):

```
qplot(pretest, posttest) + coord_equal(ratio=1/4)
```

16.15 Multiple Plots on a Page

In the previous chapter on traditional graphics, we discussed how to put multiple plots on a page. However, ggplot2 uses the grid graphics system, so that method does not work. We saw the multiframe plot in Fig. 16.38 in the section on bar plots. Let us now look at how it was constructed. We will skip the bar plot details here and focus on how we combined them.

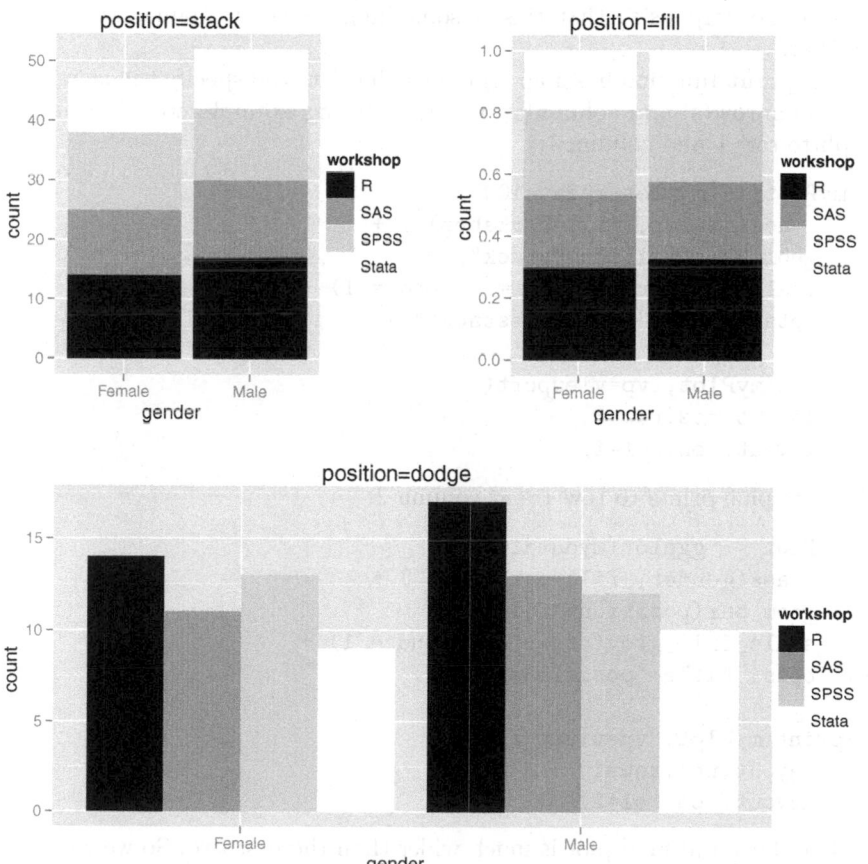

Fig. 16.38. A multiframe plot showing the impact of the various position settings.

We first clear the page with the `grid.newpage` function. This is an important step as otherwise plots printed using the following methods will appear on top of others.

```
grid.newpage()
```

Next, we use the `pushViewport` function to define the various frames called *viewports* in the grid graphics system. The `grid.layout` argument uses R's common format of (rows, columns). The following example sets up a two by two grid for us to use:

```
pushViewport( viewport(layout=grid.layout(2,2) ) )
```

In traditional graphics, you would now just do the graphs in order and they would find their place. However, in the grid system, we must save the plot to an object and then use the `print` function to print it into the viewport we desire. The object name of "p" is commonly used as an object name for the plot. Since there are many ways to add to this object, it is helpful to keep it short. To emphasize that this is something we get to name, we will use "myPlot."

The `print` function has a `vp` argument that lets you specify the *viewport's* position in row(s) and column(s). In the following example, we will print the graph to row 1 and column 1:

```
myPlot <- ggplot(mydata100,
    aes(gender, fill=workshop) ) +
  geom_bar(position="stack") +
  scale_fill_grey(start = 0, end = 1) +
  opts( title="position=stack " )

print(myPlot, vp=viewport(
  layout.pos.row=1,
  layout.pos.col=1) )
```

The next plot prints to row 1 and column 2.

```
myPlot <- ggplot(mydata100,
    aes(gender, fill=workshop) ) +
  geom_bar(position="fill") +
  scale_fill_grey(start = 0, end = 1) +
  opts( title="position=fill" )

print(myPlot, vp=viewport(
  layout.pos.row=1,
  layout.pos.col=2) )
```

The third and final plot is much wider than the first two. So we will print it to row 2 in both columns 1 and 2. Since we did not set the aspect ratio explicitly, the graph will resize to fit the double-wide viewport.

```
myPlot <- ggplot(mydata100,
    aes(gender, fill=workshop) ) +
  geom_bar(position="dodge")  +
  scale_fill_grey(start = 0, end = 1) +
  opts( title="position=dodge" )

print(myPlot, vp=viewport(
  layout.pos.row=2,
  layout.pos.col=1:2) )
```

The next time you print a plot without specifying a viewport, the screen resets back to its previous full-window display. The code for the other multi-frame plots is in the example program in Section 16.19.

16.16 Saving ggplot2 Graphs to a File

In Section 14.6, "Graphics Devices," we discussed various ways to save plots in files. Those methods work with the ggplot2 package, and in fact they are the only way to save a multiframe plot to a file.

However, the ggplot2 package has its own function that is optimized for saving single plots to a file. To save the last graph you created, with either qplot or ggplot, use the ggsave function. It will choose the proper graphics device from the file extension.

For example, the following function call will save the last graph created in an encapsulated postscript file:

```
> ggsave("mygraph.eps")
```

```
Saving 4.00" x 3.50" image
```

It will choose the width and height from your computer monitor and will report back those dimensions. If you did not get it right, you can change those dimensions and rerun the function. Alternately, you can specify the width and height arguments in inches or, for bitmapped formats like Portable Network Graphics (png), in dots-per-inch. See help(ggsave) for additional options.

16.17 An Example Specifying All Defaults

Now that you have seen some examples of both qplot and ggplot, let us take a brief look at the full power of ggplot by revisiting the scatter plot with a regression line (Fig. 16.39). We will first review both sets of code, exactly as described in Section 16.10.4.

First, done with qplot, it is quite easy and it feels similar to the traditional graphics plot function:

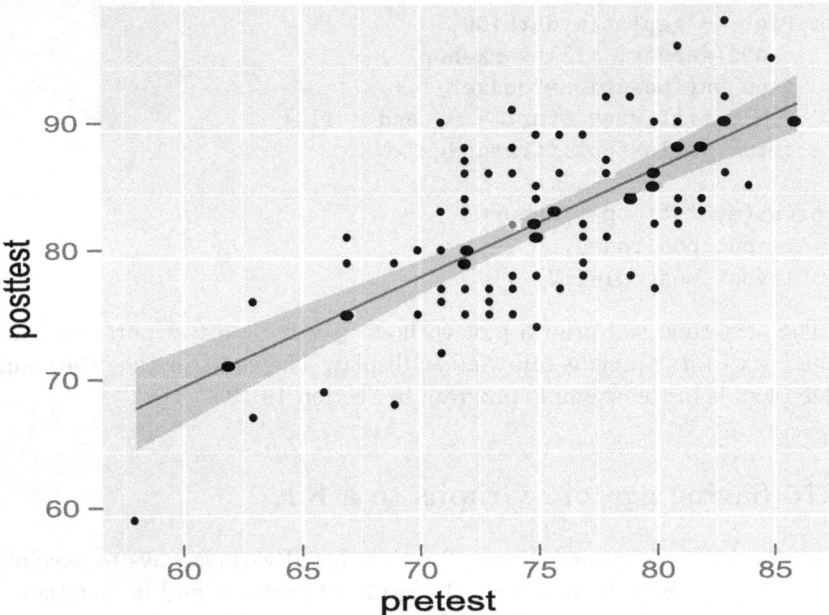

Fig. 16.39. This same scatter plot results from several types of programs shown in the text.

```
qplot(pretest, posttest,
  geom=c("point","smooth"), method="lm" )
```

Next, let us do it using `ggplot` with as many default settings as possible. It is not too much more typing, and it brings us into the grammar of graphics world. We see the new concepts of aesthetic mapping of variables and geometric objects, or geoms:

```
ggplot(mydata100, aes(pretest, posttest) ) +
  geom_point() +
  geom_smooth(method="lm")
```

Finally, here it is again in `ggplot` but with no default settings. We see that the plot is actually two layers: one with points and another with the smooth line. Each layer can use different data frames, variables, geometric objects, statistics, and so on. If you need graphics flexibility, `ggplot2` is the package for you!

```
ggplot() +
layer(
  data=mydata100,
  mapping=aes(pretest, posttest),
  geom="point",
```

```
    stat="identity"
  ) +
  layer(
    data=mydata100,
    mapping=aes(pretest, posttest),
    geom="smooth",
    stat="smooth",
    method="lm"
  ) +
  coord_cartesian()
```

16.18 Summary of Graphic Elements and Parameters

We have seen many ways to modify plots in the ggplot2 package. The ggopt function is another way. You can set the parameters of all future graphs in the current session with the following function call. See help(ggopt) function for many more parameters.

```
ggopt(
  background.fill = "black",
  background.color ="white",
  axis.colour = "black"  #default axis fonts are grey.
  )
```

The opts function is useful for modifying settings for a single plot. For example, when colors, shapes, or labels make a legend superfluous, you can suppress it with

```
+ opts(legend.position="none")
```

See help(opts) for more examples.

The plots created with both qplot and ggplot make copious use of color. Since our examples did not really need color we supressed it with

```
...+ scale_fill_grey(start=0,end=1)
```

An alternate way of doing this the theme_set function. To use levels of grey, use:

```
theme_set( theme_grey() )
```

To limit colors to black and white, use:

```
theme_set( theme_bw() )
```

To return to the default colors, use:

```
theme_set()
```

Enter help(theme_set) for details.

16.19 Example Programs for ggplot2

Stata does not offer the grammar of graphics model. See previous the chapter for Stata graphics examples.

This program brings together the examples discussed in this chapter and a few variations that were not.

```
# Filename: GraphicsGG.R

setwd("/myRfolder")
load(file="mydata100.Rdata")
detach(mydata100) #In case I'm running repeatedly.

# Get rid of missing values for facets
mydata100 <- na.omit(mydata100)
attach(mydata100)
library(ggplot2)

# ---Barplots---

# Barplot - Vertical

qplot(workshop)

ggplot(mydata100, aes( workshop ) ) +
  geom_bar()

# Can also follow this form:
ggplot( mydata100 ) +
  aes( x=workshop ) +
  geom_bar()

# Barplot - Horizontal

qplot(workshop) + coord_flip()

ggplot(mydata100, aes( workshop ) ) +
  geom_bar() + coord_flip()

# Barplot - Single Bar Stacked

qplot(factor(""), fill=workshop,
  geom="bar", xlab="") +
  scale_fill_grey(start=0, end=1)
```

```
ggplot(mydata100,
  aes(factor(""), fill=workshop) ) +
  geom_bar() +
  scale_x_discrete("") +
  scale_fill_grey(start=0, end=1)

# Pie charts, same as stacked bar
  but polar coordinates

qplot( factor(""), fill=workshop,
  geom="bar", xlab="") +
  coord_polar(theta="y") +
  scale_fill_grey(start=0, end=1)

ggplot(mydata100,
  aes( factor(""), fill=workshop ) ) +
  geom_bar( width=1 ) +
  scale_x_discrete("") +
  coord_polar(theta="y") +
  scale_fill_grey(start=0, end=1)

# Barplots - Grouped
#   position=stack, fill, dodge,
#   for qplot, then ggplot

qplot(gender, geom="bar",
    fill=workshop, position="stack") +
  scale_fill_grey(start = 0, end = 1)

qplot(gender, geom="bar",
    fill=workshop, position="fill")  +
  scale_fill_grey(start = 0, end = 1)

qplot(gender, geom="bar",
    fill=workshop, position="dodge") +
  scale_fill_grey(start = 0, end = 1)

ggplot(mydata100, aes(gender, fill=workshop) ) +
  geom_bar(position="stack") +
  scale_fill_grey(start = 0, end = 1)

ggplot(mydata100, aes(gender, fill=workshop) ) +
  geom_bar(position="fill") +
  scale_fill_grey(start = 0, end = 1)
```

```
ggplot(mydata100, aes(gender, fill=workshop ) ) +
  geom_bar(position="dodge") +
  scale_fill_grey(start = 0, end = 1)


# Barplots - Faceted

qplot(workshop, facets=gender~.)

ggplot(mydata100, aes(workshop) ) +
  geom_bar() + facet_grid( gender~. )


# Barplots - Presummarized data

qplot( factor(c(1,2)), c(40, 60), geom="bar",
  xlab="myGroup", ylab="myMeasure")

myTemp <- data.frame(
  myGroup=factor( c(1,2) ),
  myMeasure=c(40, 60)
)
myTemp

ggplot(data=myTemp, aes(myGroup, myMeasure) ) +
  geom_bar()


# ---Dotcharts---

qplot(workshop, geom="point", size=I(4),
  stat="bin", facets=gender~.) +
 coord_flip()

ggplot(mydata100) +
   aes(x=workshop, y=..count.. ) +
   geom_point(stat="bin", size=4) + coord_flip()+
   facet_grid( gender~. )


# ---Adding Titles and Labels---

qplot(workshop, geom="bar",
  main="Workshop Attendance",
  xlab="Statistics Package \nWorkshops")
```

```
ggplot(mydata100) +
  aes(workshop, ..count..) +
  geom_bar() +
  opts( title="Workshop Attendance" ) +
  scale_x_discrete("Statistics Package \nWorkshops")

# Example not in book: labels of continuous scales.
ggplot(mydata100) +
  aes(pretest,posttest ) +
  geom_point() +
  scale_x_continuous("Test Score Before Training") +
  scale_y_continuous("Test Score After Training")  +
  opts( title="The Relationship is Linear" )

# ---Histograms and Density Plots---

# Simle Histogram
qplot(posttest)

ggplot(mydata100) +
  aes(posttest)    +
  geom_histogram()

# Histogram with more bars.
qplot(posttest, geom="histogram", binwidth=0.5)

ggplot(mydata100) +
  aes(posttest)    +
  geom_histogram( binwidth=0.5 )

# Density plot
qplot(posttest, geom="density")

ggplot(mydata100) +
  aes(posttest)    +
  geom_density()

# Histogram with Density

qplot(data=mydata100,posttest, ..density..,
  geom=c("histogram","density") )

ggplot(mydata100, aes(posttest, ..density.. ) ) +
  geom_histogram() + geom_density()
```

```
# Histogram - Separate plots by group

qplot(posttest, geom="histogram", facets=gender~.)
qplot(posttest, facets=gender~.)

ggplot(mydata100, aes(posttest) ) +
  geom_histogram() + facet_grid( gender~. )

# Histograms - Overlaid

qplot( posttest, fill=gender ) +
  scale_fill_grey(start = 0, end = 1)

ggplot(mydata100, aes(posttest, fill=gender) ) +
  geom_bar() +
  scale_fill_grey(start = 0, end = 1)


# ---QQ plots---

qplot(sample=posttest, stat="qq")

ggplot( mydata100, aes(sample=posttest) ) +
  stat_qq()


# ---Strip plots---

# With too much jitter for our small data set:

qplot( factor(""), posttest, geom="jitter", xlab="")

ggplot(mydata100, aes(factor(""), posttest) ) +
  geom_jitter() +
  scale_x_discrete("")


# Strip plot by group.
qplot(workshop, posttest, geom="jitter")

ggplot(mydata100, aes(workshop, posttest) ) +
  geom_jitter()

# Again, with limited jitter that fits our data better.
```

```
qplot( factor(""), posttest, xlab="",
  position=position_jitter(width=.02))

ggplot(mydata100, aes(factor(""), posttest) ) +
  geom_jitter(position=position_jitter(width=.02)) +
  scale_x_discrete("")


# Strip plot by group.
# Note that I am increasing the jitter width from
# .02 to .08 because there is only one fourth the
# room for each graph.

qplot(workshop, posttest, data = mydata100, xlab="",
  position=position_jitter(width=.08))

ggplot(mydata100, aes(workshop, posttest) ) +
  geom_jitter(position=position_jitter(width=.08)) +
  scale_x_discrete("")


# ---Scatter Plots---

# Simple scatter plot

qplot(pretest, posttest)
qplot(pretest, posttest, geom="point")

ggplot(mydata100, aes(pretest, posttest)) +
  geom_point()

# Scatter plot connecting points sorted on x.
qplot( pretest, posttest, geom="line")

ggplot(mydata100, aes(pretest, posttest) ) +
  geom_line()

# Scatter plot connecting points in data set order.

qplot( pretest, posttest, geom="path")

ggplot(mydata100, aes(pretest, posttest) ) +
  geom_path()
```

```
# Scatter plot with skinny histogram-like bars to X axis.

qplot(pretest,posttest,
  xend=pretest, yend=50,
  geom="segment")

ggplot(mydata100, aes(pretest, posttest) ) +
  geom_segment( aes(  pretest, posttest,
                   xend=pretest, yend=50) )


# Scatter plot with jitter
qplot(q1, q4) #First without

# Now with jitter.
qplot(q1, q4, position=
  position_jitter(width=.3,height=.3))

ggplot(mydata100, aes(x=q1, y=q2) ) +
 geom_point(position=
   position_jitter(width=.3,height=.3))


# Scatter plot on large data sets

pretest2   <-
  round( rnorm( n=5000, mean=80, sd=5) )
posttest2  <-
  round( pretest2 + rnorm( n=5000, mean=3, sd=3) )
pretest2[pretest2>100] <- 100
posttest2[posttest2>100] <- 100
temp=data.frame(pretest2,posttest2)


# Small, jittered, transparent points.

qplot(pretest2, posttest2, data = temp,
  size = I(1), colour = I(alpha("black", 0.15)),
  geom = "jitter")


# Or in the next version of ggplot2:

qplot(pretest2, posttest2, data = temp,
  size = I(1), alpha = I(0.15),
  geom = "jitter")


ggplot(temp, aes(pretest2, posttest2),
```

```
      size=2, position = position_jitter(x=2,y=2) ) +
      geom_jitter(colour=alpha("black",0.15) )

ggplot(temp, aes(pretest2, posttest2)+
 geom_point(colour=alpha("black",0.15),
   position=position_jitter(width=.3,height=.3)) )

# Hexbin plots

qplot(pretest2, posttest2, geom="hex", bins=30)

ggplot(temp, aes(pretest2, posttest2))  +
  geom_hex( bins=30 )


# This works too:

ggplot(temp, aes(pretest2, posttest2))  +
  stat_binhex(bins = 30)


# Using density contours and small points.

qplot(pretest2, posttest2, data=temp,
  geom=c("point","density2d"), size = I(1) )


# geom_density_2d was renamed geom_density2d

ggplot(temp, aes( x=pretest2, y=posttest2) ) +
 geom_point( size=1 ) + geom_density2d()

rm(pretest2,posttest2,temp)

# Scatter plot with regression line,
  95% confidence intervals.

qplot(pretest, posttest,
  geom=c("point","smooth"), method=lm )

ggplot(mydata100, aes(pretest, posttest) ) +
  geom_point() + geom_smooth(method=lm)

# Scatter plot with regression line
  but NO confidence intervals.
```

```
qplot(pretest, posttest,
  geom=c("point","smooth"),
  method=lm, se=FALSE )

ggplot(mydata100, aes(pretest, posttest) ) +
  geom_point() +
  geom_smooth(method=lm, se=FALSE)

# Scatter with x=y line

qplot(pretest, posttest,
  geom=c("point","abline"),
  intercept=0, slope=1 )

ggplot(mydata100, aes(pretest, posttest) ) +
  geom_point()+
  geom_abline(intercept=0, slope=1)

# Scatter with vertical or horizontal lines

# When the book was written, qplot required the
# values to be equal. Now it does not using
# xintercept and yintercept.

qplot(pretest, posttest,
 geom=c("point", "vline", "hline"),
 xintercept=75, yintercept=75)

ggplot(mydata100, aes(pretest, posttest)) +
  geom_point() +
  geom_vline( xintercept=75 ) +
  geom_hline( yintercept=75 )


# Scatter plot with a set of vertical lines

qplot(pretest, posttest, type="point") +
  geom_vline( xintercept=seq(from=70,to=80,by=2) )

ggplot(mydata100, aes(pretest, posttest)) +
  geom_point() +
  geom_vline( xintercept=seq(from=70,to=80,by=2) )

# Scatter plotting text labels
```

```
qplot(pretest, posttest, geom="text",
  label=rownames(mydata100) )

ggplot(mydata100,
  aes(pretest, posttest,
  label=rownames(mydata100) ) ) +
  geom_text()

# Scatter plot with different
  point shapes for each group.

qplot(pretest, posttest, shape=gender)

ggplot(mydata100, aes(pretest, posttest) ) +
  geom_point( aes(shape=gender ) )

# Scatter plot with regressions fit for each group.

qplot(pretest, posttest,
  geom=c("smooth","point"),
  method="lm", shape=gender)

ggplot(mydata100,
  aes(pretest, posttest, shape=gender) ) +
  geom_smooth( method="lm" ) + geom_point()

# Scatter plot faceted for groups

qplot(pretest, posttest,
  geom=c("smooth", "point"),
  method="lm", shape=gender,
  facets=workshop~gender)

ggplot(mydata100,
  aes(pretest, posttest, shape=gender) ) +
  geom_smooth( method="lm" ) + geom_point() +
  facet_grid( workshop~gender )

# Scatter plot matrix

plotmatrix( mydata100[3:8] )

# Small points & lowess fit.
plotmatrix( mydata100[3:8], aes( size=1 ) ) +
```

```
      geom_smooth() +
      opts(legend.position="none")

# Shape and gender fits.
plotmatrix( mydata100[3:8],
   aes( shape=gender ) ) +
   geom_smooth(method=lm)

# ---Box Plots---

# box plot of one variable

qplot(factor(""), posttest,
   geom="boxplot", xlab="")

ggplot(mydata100,
   aes(factor(""), posttest) ) +
   geom_boxplot() +
   scale_x_discrete("")

# Box plot by group

qplot(workshop, posttest, geom="boxplot" )

ggplot(mydata100,
   aes(workshop, posttest) ) +
   geom_boxplot()

# Box plot by group with jitter

# First, with default jitter,
# that is too much for our small data set

qplot(workshop, posttest,
   geom=c("boxplot","jitter") )

ggplot(mydata100,
   aes(workshop, posttest )) +
   geom_boxplot() + geom_jitter()

# Again, with a smaller amount of jitter.

ggplot(mydata100,
  aes(workshop, posttest )) +
  geom_boxplot() +
```

```
  geom_jitter(position=
    position_jitter(width=.1))

# Box plot for two-way interaction.

qplot(workshop, posttest,
  geom="boxplot", fill=gender ) +
  scale_fill_grey(start = 0, end = 1)

ggplot(mydata100,
  aes(workshop, posttest) ) +
  geom_boxplot( aes(fill=gender),
    colour="grey50") +
  scale_fill_grey(start = 0, end = 1)

# Error bar plot

# This is the code for qplot.

qplot( as.numeric(workshop), posttest) +
  geom_jitter(position=
    position_jitter(width=.1))  +
  stat_summary(fun.y="mean",
    geom="smooth", se=FALSE) +
  stat_summary(fun.data="mean_cl_normal",
    geom="errorbar", width=.2)

# This is the code for ggplot.

ggplot(mydata100,
  aes( as.numeric(workshop), posttest ) ) +
  geom_jitter(size=1,
    position=position_jitter(width=.1) )  +
  stat_summary(fun.y="mean",
    geom="smooth", se=FALSE) +
  stat_summary(fun.data="mean_cl_normal",
    geom="errorbar", width=.2)

# This does away with the jitter and looks nice.

ggplot(mydata100,
  aes( as.numeric(workshop), posttest ) ) +
  geom_point(size=1)   +
  stat_summary(fun.y="mean",
    geom="smooth", se=FALSE) +
```

```
    stat_summary(fun.data="mean_cl_normal",
      geom="errorbar", width=.2)

# This uses large points for the means.

ggplot(mydata100,
  aes( workshop, posttest ) ) +
  geom_point(size=1) +
  stat_summary(fun.y="mean",
    geom="point", size=3) +
  stat_summary(fun.data="mean_cl_normal",
    geom="errorbar", width=.2)

# ---Logarithmic Axes---

# Change the variables

qplot( log(pretest), log(posttest) )

ggplot(mydata100,
  aes( log(pretest), log(posttest) ) ) +
  geom_point()

# Change axis labels

qplot(pretest, posttest, log="xy")

ggplot(mydata100,
    aes( x=pretest, y=posttest) ) +
  geom_point() +
  scale_x_log10() +
  scale_y_log10()

# Change axis scaling

# Tickmarks remain uniformly spaced,
# because scale of our data is too limited.

qplot(pretest, posttest, data=mydata100)  +
  coord_trans(x="log10", y="log10")

ggplot(mydata100,
    aes( x=pretest, y=posttest) ) +
  geom_point() +
  coord_trans(x="log10", y="log10")
```

```
# ---Aspect Ratio---

# This forces x and y to be equal.
qplot(pretest, posttest) + coord_equal()

# This sets aspect ratio to height/width.
qplot(pretest, posttest) +
  coord_equal(ratio=1/4)

#---Multiframe Plots: Bar Chart Example---

# Clears the page, otherwise new plots
# will appear on top of old.

grid.newpage()

# Sets up a 2 by 2 grid to plot into.
pushViewport(
  viewport( layout=grid.layout(2,2) )
)

# Bar Chart dodged in row 1, column 1.
myPlot <- ggplot(mydata100,
    aes(gender, fill=workshop) ) +
  geom_bar(position="stack") +
  scale_fill_grey(start = 0, end = 1) +
  opts( title="position=stack " )
print(myPlot, vp=viewport(
  layout.pos.row=1,
  layout.pos.col=1) )

# Bar Chart stacked, in row 1, column 2.
myPlot <- ggplot(mydata100,
    aes(gender, fill=workshop) ) +
  geom_bar(position="fill") +
  scale_fill_grey(start = 0, end = 1) +
  opts( title="position=fill" )
print(myPlot, vp=viewport(
  layout.pos.row=1,
  layout.pos.col=2) )

# Bar Chart dodged, given frames,
# in row 2, columns 1 and 2.
myPlot <- ggplot(mydata100,
```

```
    aes(gender, fill=workshop) ) +
  geom_bar(position="dodge")  +
  scale_fill_grey(start = 0, end = 1) +
  opts( title="position=dodge" )
print(myPlot, vp=viewport(
  layout.pos.row=2,
  layout.pos.col=1:2) )


dev.off()

#---Multiframe Scatter Plots---

# Clears the page, otherwise new plots
  will appear on top of old.
grid.newpage()

# Sets up a 2 by 2 grid to plot into.
pushViewport(
  viewport( layout=grid.layout(2,2) )
)

# Scatter plot of points
myPlot <- qplot(pretest, posttest,
  main="geom=point")
print(myPlot, vp=viewport(
  layout.pos.row=1,
  layout.pos.col=1) )

myPlot <- qplot( pretest, posttest,
         geom="line", main="geom=line" )
print(myPlot, vp=viewport(
  layout.pos.row=1,
  layout.pos.col=2) )

myPlot <- qplot( pretest, posttest,
         geom="path", main="geom=path" )
print(myPlot, vp=viewport(
  layout.pos.row=2,
  layout.pos.col=1) )

myPlot <- ggplot( mydata100,
  aes(pretest, posttest) ) +
  geom_segment( aes(x=pretest, y=posttest,
                    xend=pretest, yend=58) ) +
  opts( title="geom_segment" )
```

```
print(myPlot,
  vp=viewport(
    layout.pos.row=2,
    layout.pos.col=2 )
)


# ---Multiframe Scatter Plot for Jitter---

grid.newpage()

pushViewport(
  viewport( layout=grid.layout(1,2) )
)

# Scatter plot without
myPlot <- qplot( q1, q4,
        main="Likert Scale Without Jitter")
print(myPlot, vp=viewport(
  layout.pos.row=1,
  layout.pos.col=1) )

myPlot <- qplot(q1, q4,
    position=position_jitter(
      width=.3,height=.3),
    main="Likert scale with jitter")

print(myPlot,
  vp=viewport( layout.pos.row=1,
               layout.pos.col=2 )
)


# ---Detailed Comparison of qplot and ggplot---

qplot(pretest, posttest,
  geom=c("point","smooth"), method="lm" )

# Or ggplot with default settings:

ggplot(mydata100, aes(x=pretest, y=posttest) ) +
  geom_point() +
  geom_smooth(method="lm")
```

```
# Or with all of the defaults displayed:
ggplot() +
layer(
  data=mydata100,
  mapping=aes(x=pretest, y=posttest),
  geom="point",
  stat="identity"
) +
layer(
  data=mydata100,
  mapping=aes(x=pretest, y=posttest),
  geom="smooth",
  stat="smooth",
  method="lm"
) +
coord_cartesian()
```

17

Statistics

This chapter demonstrates some basic statistical methods. Since this book is aimed at people who already know Stata, we assume you are already familiar with most of these methods. We briefly list each example test's goal and assumptions and how to get R to perform them. For more statistical coverage see Dalgaard's *Introductory Statistics with R* [9], or Venable and Ripley's much more advanced *Modern Applied Statistics with S* [51]. For a comprehensive text that shows Stata and R code being used for the same analysis, see Hilbe's *Logistic Regression Models*, [21]. As usual, Stata code duplicating the R examples used throughout the text is found at the end of the chapter.

The examples in this chapter will use the mydata100 data set described in Section 14.7. When using functions from the Hmisc package, we use mydata100L (L for labeled) that adds the variable labels described in Section 11.2.1.

To get things to fit well on these pages, we have set

```
options(linesize=64)
```

You can use that if you want your output to match perfectly, but that is not necessary.

17.1 Scientific Notation

While Stata tends to print its small probability values as 0.000, R often uses scientific notation. An example is $7.447e - 5$ which means 7.447×10^{-5} or 0.00007447. When the number after the "e" is negative, you move the decimal place that many places to the left.

You may also see p-values of just "0." That value is controlled by the digits option, which is set to be seven significant digits by default. If you wanted to increase the number of digits to 10, you could do so with the following function call:

R.A. Muenchen, J.M. Hilbe, *R for Stata Users*, Statistics
and Computing, DOI 10.1007/978-1-4419-1318-0_17,
© Springer Science+Business Media, LLC 2010

```
options(digits=10)
```

Stata has a similar option, "%1.0f," but it applies only to the *p*-values that the user creates or abstracts from the return codes.

In both packages, setting the number of digits affects only their display. The full precision of *p*-values is always available when the numbers are stored.

Supplying a positive number to R's *scientific penalty* option, `scipen`, biases the printing away from scientific notation and more toward fixed notation. A negative number does the reverse. So if you want to completely block scientific notation, you can do so with the following function call:

```
options(scipen=999)
```

17.2 Descriptive Statistics

In Stata, you get frequencies from the **tabulate** command and means, standard deviations, and the like from the **summarize** command.

R also has functions that handle categorical and continuous variables together or separately. Let us start with functions that are most like Stata, and then move on to functions that are more unique in style to R.

17.2.1 The Hmisc describe Function

Frank Harrell's **Hmisc** package [14] offers a wide selection of functions that have more comprehensive output than the standard R functions. One of these is the **describe** function, which we use below. It is similar to the **summary** function we have used throughout this book. Before using the **describe** function, you must install **Hmisc**. See Chapter 2, "Installing and Updating R." Then you must load it with either the *Packages> Load Packages* menu item or the function call:

```
library("Hmisc")
```

You can select variables in many ways. See Chapter 7, "Selecting Variables" for details. One of the nicest features of the **describe** function is that it provides frequencies on nonfactors as well as factors, so long as they do not have too many values.

```
> describe(mydata100L)

mydata100L

 8 Variables      100  Observations
------------------------------------------------------------
gender
```

```
      n missing  unique
     99       1      2
Female (47, 47%), Male (52, 53%)
```

```
workshop
      n missing  unique
     99       1      4
R (31, 31%), Stata (24, 24%), SPSS (25, 25%), SAS (19, 19%)
```
----
q1 : The instructor was well prepared.
```
      n missing  unique   Mean
    100       0      5   3.45
            1  2  3  4  5
Frequency 4 14 36 25 21
%         4 14 36 25 21
```
----
q2 : The instructor communicated well.
```
      n missing  unique   Mean
    100       0      5   3.06
            1  2  3  4  5
Frequency 10 28 21 28 13
%         10 28 21 28 13
```
----
q3 : The course materials were helpful.
```
      n missing  unique   Mean
     99       1      5   3.081
            1  2  3  4  5
Frequency 10 20 34 22 13
%         10 20 34 22 13
```
----
q4 : Overall, I found this workshop useful.
```
      n missing  unique   Mean
    100       0      5   3.4
            1  2  3  4  5
Frequency 6 14 34 26 20
%         6 14 34 26 20
```
----
pretest
```
  n missing  unique    Mean     .05     .10     .25     .50
100       0      23   74.97   66.95   69.00   72.00   75.00
 .75     .90     .95
79.00   82.00   83.00
```

lowest : 58 62 63 66 67, highest: 82 83 84 85 86

```
------------------------------------------------------------
posttest

   n missing  unique    Mean     .05     .10     .25     .50
100       0      28    82.06   71.95   75.00   77.00   82.00
 .75     .90     .95
86.00   90.00   92.00


lowest : 59 67 68 69 71, highest: 91 92 95 96 98
------------------------------------------------------------
```

Unlike Stata, the `describe` function does not provide percents that include missing values. Of course, in Stata, you must provide the "miss" option to the `describe` command in order to have the count and frequency of missing values displayed, but they are able to be displayed nonetheless. In R, you can change this limitation by setting the `exclude.missing` argument to FALSE. The `describe` function will automatically provide a table of frequencies whenever a variable has no more than 20 unique values. Beyond that, it will print the five largest and five smallest values, just like the `summarize, detail` command in Stata.

Notice that the survey questions themselves appear in the R output. That is because this version of the data frame was prepared as described in Section 11.2, "Variable Labels," using the `Hmisc` package's approach. For the remainder of this chapter, we use the unlabeled version, mydata100, so that those labels will not cause problems with functions that do not recognize them.

17.2.2 The summary Function

R's built-in function for univariate statistics is `summary`. We have used the `summary` function extensively throughout this book, but we repeat its output here for comparison.

```
> summary(mydata100)

    gender      workshop          q1              q2
  Female:47   R     :31   Min.    :1.00   Min.    :1.00
  Male   :52   Stata:24   1st Qu.:3.00   1st Qu.:2.00
  NA's  : 1   SPSS :25   Median :3.00   Median :3.00
              SAS   :19   Mean    :3.45   Mean    :3.06
              NA's  : 1   3rd Qu.:4.00   3rd Qu.:4.00
                          Max.    :5.00   Max.    :5.00


        q3              q4            pretest
  Min.   :1.000   Min.    :1.0   Min.    :58.00
```

```
1st Qu.:2.000    1st Qu.:3.0    1st Qu.:72.00
Median :3.000    Median :3.0    Median :75.00
Mean   :3.081    Mean   :3.4    Mean   :74.97
3rd Qu.:4.000    3rd Qu.:4.0    3rd Qu.:79.00
Max.   :5.000    Max.   :5.0    Max.   :86.00
NA's   :1.000

       posttest
Min.    :59.00
1st Qu.:77.00
Median :82.00
Mean   :82.06
3rd Qu.:86.00
Max.   :98.00
```

As you can see, it is much sparser, lacking percents for factors, frequencies and percents for numeric variables (even if they have a small number of values), number of nonmissing values, and so on. However, it is much more compact. The numbers labeled "1st Qu." and "3rd Qu." are the first and third quartiles, or the 25th and 75th percentiles, respectively.

The summary function works with a much wider range of objects, as we will soon see. The describe function works only with data frames, vectors, matrices, or formulas. For data frames, choose whichever of these two functions that meets your needs.

17.2.3 The table Function and Its Relatives

Now let us review R's built-in functions for frequencies and proportions. We have covered those in earlier sections also, but we repeat them here for ease of comparison and elaboration.

R's built-in function for frequency counts provide output that is much sparser than those of the describe function:

```
> table(workshop)

workshop
    R   Stata  SPSS SAS
   31     24    25   19

> table(gender)

gender
Female    Male
    47      52
```

The above output is quite minimal, displaying only the frequencies. This sparcity makes it very easy to use this output as input to other functions such as `barplot`; see Chapter 15, "TraditionalGraphics," for examples.

We can get proportions by using the `prop.table` function.

```
> prop.table( table(workshop) )
```

```
workshop

        R       Stata      SPSS      SAS
0.3131313 0.2424242 0.2525253 0.1919192
```

```
> prop.table( table(gender) )
```

```
gender

   Female      Male
0.4747475 0.5252525
```

You can round off the proportions using the `round` function. The only arguments you need are the object to round and the number of decimals you would like to keep.

```
> round( prop.table( table(gender) ), 2 )
```

```
gender

Female   Male
  0.47   0.53
```

Converting that to percents is, of course, just a matter of multiplying by 100. If you multiply before rounding, you will not even need to specify the number of decimals to keep, since the default is to round to whole numbers.

```
> round( 100* ( prop.table( table(gender) ) ) )
```

```
gender

Female   Male
    47     53
```

When examining test scores, it is often helpful to get cumulative proportions. R does this by adding the `cumsum` function that *cumulatively sums* a variable. Here we apply it to the output of the `prop.table` function to sum its proportions.

```
> cumsum( prop.table( table(posttest) ) )
```

59	67	68	69	71	72	74	75	76	77	78
0.01	0.02	0.03	0.04	0.05	0.06	0.07	0.13	0.18	0.26	0.31
79	80	81	82	83	84	85	86	87	88	89
0.35	0.39	0.48	0.53	0.58	0.65	0.68	0.76	0.79	0.84	0.87
90	91	92	95	96	98					
0.92	0.93	0.96	0.98	0.99	1.00					

We can see that 0.92 of the students received a score of 90 or lower. This is information we would get from the Stata `tabulate` command. We can even make R do the vertical display that Stata would use. To do so, we write a short function to put the table into a data frame and then add the proportions and cumulative proportions to the data frame:

```
myTable <- function(X)
  {
  myDF <- data.frame( table(Score) )
  myDF$Prop <- prop.table( myDF$Freq )
  myDF$CumProp <-  cumsum( myDF$Prop )
  myDF
  }
```

Now when we call our new function, we get the vertical layout with which we are familiar (middle removed to save space):

```
> myTable(Score)

   Score Freq  Prop CumProp
1      70   39 0.039   0.039
2      71   36 0.036   0.075
3      72   40 0.040   0.115
...
24     93   40 0.040   0.916
25     94   41 0.041   0.957
26     95   43 0.043   1.000
```

A word of caution about the `table` function. Unlike the `summary` function, if you use it on a whole data frame, it will not give you all one-way frequency tables. Instead, it will cross-tabulate all of the variables at once. You can use it on a surprising number of factors at once. When you convert its output to a data frame, you have a concise list of counts for all possible combinations. For an example, see Section 10.11.4, "Tabular Aggregation."

17.2.4 The mean Function and Its Relatives

R's built-in functions offers similarly sparse output for univariate statistics. To get just the means of variables q1 through posttest (variables 3 through 8), we can use

```
> sapply( mydata100[3:8], mean,  na.rm=TRUE)

      q1       q2       q3        q4  pretest posttest
  3.4500   3.0600   3.0808    3.4000  74.9700  82.0600
```

Similarly, for the standard deviations:

```
> sapply( mydata100[3:8], sd,    na.rm=TRUE)

      q1       q2       q3        q4  pretest posttest
  1.0952   1.2212   1.1665    1.1371   5.2962   6.5902
```

You can also substitute the `var` function for variance or the `median` function for that statistic. You can apply several of these functions at once by combining them into your own single function. For an example of that, see "Writing Your Own Functions (Macros)," (Section 5.8). For details about the `sapply` function, see Section 10.2, "Procedures or Functions? The `Apply` Function Decides."

17.3 Cross-Tabulation

You can compare groups on categorical measures with the chi-squared test; for example, testing to see if males and females attended the various workshops in the same proportions. In Stata, you would use the `tabulate` command.

Assumptions:

- No more than 20% of the cells in your cross-tabulation have counts fewer than 5. If you have sparse tables, the exact `fisher.test` function is more appropriate.
- Observations are independent. For example, if you measured the same subjects repeatedly, it would be important to take that into account in a more complex model.
- The variables are not the same thing measured at two times. If that is the case, the `mcnemar.test` function may be what you need.

17.3.1 The `CrossTable` Function

To get output most like that from Stata, we will first use the functions from Gregory Warnes' `gmodels` package [42]. Then we will cover the cross-tabulation functions that are built into R. Note that we use the `format=SAS` argument to produce output that is closest to Stata. It is the default, however, so you need not type it. There is no specific `format=Stata` argument.

```
> library("gmodels")

> CrossTable(workshop, gender,
```

```
+    chisq=TRUE, format="SAS")

    Cell Contents
|-------------------------|
|                       N |
| Chi-square contribution |
|           N / Row Total |
|           N / Col Total |
|         N / Table Total |
|-------------------------|
Total Observations in Table:  99
             | gender
   workshop  |   Female |       Male | Row Total |
-------------|----------|------------|-----------|
          R  |      14  |        17  |       31  |
             |   0.035  |     0.032  |           |
             |   0.452  |     0.548  |    0.313  |
             |   0.298  |     0.327  |           |
             |   0.141  |     0.172  |           |
-------------|----------|------------|-----------|
       Stata |      11  |        13  |       24  |
             |   0.014  |     0.012  |           |
             |   0.458  |     0.542  |    0.242  |
             |   0.234  |     0.250  |           |
             |   0.111  |     0.131  |           |
-------------|----------|------------|-----------|
        SPSS |      13  |        12  |       25  |
             |   0.108  |     0.097  |           |
             |   0.520  |     0.480  |    0.253  |
             |   0.277  |     0.231  |           |
             |   0.131  |     0.121  |           |
-------------|----------|------------|-----------|
         SAS |       9  |        10  |       19  |
             |   0.000  |     0.000  |           |
             |   0.474  |     0.526  |    0.192  |
             |   0.191  |     0.192  |           |
             |   0.091  |     0.101  |           |
-------------|----------|------------|-----------|
Column Total |      47  |        52  |       99  |
             |   0.475  |     0.525  |           |
-------------|----------|------------|-----------|
Statistics for All Table Factors
Pearson's Chi-squared test
-----------------------------------------------------
Chi^2 =  0.2978553     d.f. =  3     p =  0.9604313
```

The `CrossTable` function call above has three arguments.

1. The variable that determines the table rows.
2. The variable that determines the table columns.
3. The `chisq=TRUE` argument tells R to perform that test. As with Stata, if you leave this argument out, it will perform the cross-tabulation, but not the chi-squared test. Of course, in Stata you need only type "chi" to obtain the Chi-squares test and "exact" to obtain the Fisher's exact test.

17.3.2 The `tables` and `chisq.test` Functions

R also has built-in functions to do cross-tabulation and the chi-squared test. As usual, the built-in functions present sparse results. We will first use the `table` function. To simplify the coding and to demonstrate a new type of data structure, we will save the table and name it myWG for workshop and gender:

```
> myWG <- table(workshop, gender)
```

Printing myWG will show us that it contains the form of counts to which Stata users are accustomed.

```
> myWG

         gender

workshop Female Male
   R         14   17
   Stata     11   13
   SPSS      13   12
   SAS        9   10
```

You may recall from our discussion of factors that you can create factor levels (and their labels) that do not exist in your data. That will help if you were to enter more data later that is likely to contain those values or if you were to merge your data frame with others that have a full set of values. However, when performing a cross-tabulation, the levels with zero values will become part of the table. These empty cells will affect the resulting chi-squared statistic which will drastically change its value. To get rid of the unused levels, append [,drop=TRUE] to the variable reference—for example,

```
myWG <- table( workshop[ ,drop=TRUE], gender)
```

Some R functions work better with this type of data in a data frame. You probably associate this style of tabular data with output from the Stata `tabulate` command. The `as.data.frame` function can provide it.

```
> myWGdata <- as.data.frame(myWG)

> myWGdata

  workshop gender Freq
1        R Female   14
2    Stata Female   11
3     SPSS Female   13
4      SAS Female    9
5        R   Male   17
6    Stata   Male   13
7     SPSS   Male   12
8      SAS   Male   10
```

The functions we discuss now work well on table objects, so we will use myWG. We can use the chisq.test function to perform the chi-squared test:

```
> chisq.test(myWG)

        Pearson's Chi-squared test

data:  myWG
X-squared = 0.2979, df = 3, p-value = 0.9604
```

The table function does not calculate any percents or proportions. To get row or column proportions, we can use the prop.table function. The arguments in the example below are the table and the margin to analyze where 1=row and 2=column. So this will calculate row proportions.

```
> prop.table(myWG, 1)

        gender

workshop Female    Male
    R    0.45161 0.54839
    Stata 0.45833 0.54167
    SPSS  0.52000 0.48000
    SAS   0.47368 0.52632
```

Similarly, changing the 1 to 2 requests column proportions:

```
> prop.table(myWG, 2)

        gender

workshop Female    Male
    R    0.29787 0.32692
```

```
Stata 0.23404 0.25000
SPSS  0.27660 0.23077
SAS   0.19149 0.19231
```

If you do not provide the `margin` argument, the function will calculate total proportions.

```
> prop.table(myWG)

        gender

workshop Female    Male
   R       0.14141 0.17172
   Stata   0.11111 0.13131
   SPSS    0.13131 0.12121
   SAS     0.09091 0.10101
```

The `round` function will round off unneeded digits by telling it how many decimal places you want—in this case, 2. These are the row proportions.

```
> round( prop.table(myWG, 1), 2 )

        gender

workshop Female Male
   R       0.45 0.55
   Stata   0.46 0.54
   SPSS    0.52 0.48
   SAS     0.47 0.53
```

To convert proportions to percents, multiply by 100 and round off. If you want to round to the nearest whole percent, multiply by 100 before rounding off. That way you do not even have to tell the `round` function how many decimal places to keep as its default is to round off to whole numbers.

```
> round( 100* ( prop.table(myWG, 1) ) )

        gender

workshop Female Male
   R         45   55
   Stata     46   54
   SPSS      52   48
   SAS       47   53
```

If you wish to add marginal totals, the `addmargins` function will do so. It works much like the `prop.table` function, in that its second argument is a 1 to add a row with totals or 2 to add a column.

```
> addmargins(myWG, 1)
```

```
         gender

workshop Female Male
   R         14   17
   Stata     11   13
   SPSS      13   12
   SAS        9   10
   Sum       47   52
```

If you do not specify a preference for row or column totals, you will get both:

```
> addmargins(myWG)
```

```
         gender

workshop Female Male Sum
   R         14   17  31
   Stata     11   13  24
   SPSS      13   12  25
   SAS        9   10  19
   Sum       47   52  99
```

17.4 Correlation

Correlations measure the strength of linear association between two continuous variables. Stata calculates them with the correlate command for both parametric and nonparametric correlations. For pairwise, correlations Stata uses the pwcorr command.

R has both built-in functions and some in add-on packages.

Assumptions:

1. Scatter plots of the variables shows essentially a straight line. The function plot(x,y) would do the scatter plots. If you have a curve, transformations such as square roots or logarithms often help.
2. The spread in the data is the same at low, medium, and high values. Transformations often help with this assumption also.
3. For a Pearson correlation, the data should be at least interval level and normally distributed. As discussed in Chapter 15, "Traditional Graphics," hist(myvar) or qqnorm(myvar) is a quick way to examine the data. If your data are not normally distributed or are just ordinal measures (e.g., low, medium, high), you can use the nonparametric Spearman or the (less popular) Kendall correlation.

The `Hmisc` package has a good function for doing correlations. We will use it first and then cover the functions that are built into R. Before using the `Hmisc` package, you must install it. See Chapter 2, "Installing and Updating R." Then you must load it with either the *Packages> Load Packages* menu item or the function call:

```
library("Hmisc")
```

To correlate two variables, simply use their names as arguments to the `rcorr` function.

```
> rcorr(q1,q4)

        x     y
x    1.00  0.58
y    0.58  1.00

n= 100

P
    x  y
x      0
y   0
```

The first piece of output is the Pearson correlation of 0.58. That is a strong positive relationship, at least for the social sciences. The more a student likes the instructor (q1), the more he or she likes the workshop overall (q4).

Next, it reports the number of valid observations: 100. Since the `rcorr` function uses pairwise deletion of missing values by default, each correlation is done on the maximum number of cases.

Finally, it reports the p-value of 0. So we can reject the null hypothesis that the correlation is zero, a significant result. When the p-value gets very small, it prints just 0 but the full accuracy is available if you save the output (example below).

To get correlations on a set of variables, you must first put them into a matrix. That is easily done with the `cbind` function, which binds the columns. Below, we place the survey questions into a matrix called myQs and then use it as the first argument for to `rcorr` function. We also specify the type of correlation as Pearson. That is the default, so we are just doing it here for educational purposes. Note that although Pearson in a proper noun, as an argument it does *not* begin with a capital "P."

```
> myQs <- cbind(q1,q2,q3,q4)

> rcorr( myQs, type="pearson" )

       q1    q2    q3    q4
```

```
q1 1.00 0.67 0.69 0.58
q2 0.67 1.00 0.60 0.49
q3 0.69 0.60 1.00 0.47
q4 0.58 0.49 0.47 1.00


n
      q1  q2 q3  q4
q1 100 100 99 100
q2 100 100 99 100
q3  99  99 99  99
q4 100 100 99 100


P
   q1 q2 q3 q4
q1     0  0  0
q2 0      0  0
q3 0  0      0
q4 0  0  0
```

You can change that value to "spearman" to get correlations on variables that are not normally distributed or are only ordinal in scale (e.g., low, medium, high):

```
> rcorr(myQs, type="spearman")

      q1    q2    q3    q4
q1 1.00 0.67 0.67 0.55
q2 0.67 1.00 0.61 0.49
q3 0.67 0.61 1.00 0.43
q4 0.55 0.49 0.43 1.00


n
      q1  q2 q3  q4
q1 100 100 99 100
q2 100 100 99 100
q3  99  99 99  99
q4 100 100 99 100

P
   q1 q2 q3 q4
q1     0  0  0
q2 0      0  0
q3 0  0      0
q4 0  0  0
```

If you want to see the very small *p*-values, you can save the the output to a list object like myCorrs. We will use the **names** function to see what components it contains:

```
> myCorrs <- rcorr(myQs, type="pearson")

> names(myCorrs)

[1] "r" "n" "P"
```

Notice that the correlations are stored in a component named "r," even though that name did not appear in our output above. The **print** function determines how output prints, and when we installed the **Hmisc** package, it provided the methods for the **print** function to use on its objects. The method that printed the output from **rcorr** included the instruction to not to print the "r," as it is obvious what the correlations are.

We can guess that the "P" object contains the *p*-values, so let us print just myCorrs$P. By changing the **options** function's **digits** argument to various values (7 is the default), you can adjust the precision of the output. As you can see, all of the *p*-values are so tiny that it is not worth the effort. Getting at *p*-values like this can be helpful when you want to do something like adjusting them for the affects of multiple testing. You could also set **options(scipen=999)** to block scientific notation, but we do not show this as the numbers are **very** small.

```
> options(digits=7)

> myCorrs$P

              q1           q2           q3           q4
q1            NA 3.597123e-14 1.554312e-15 3.646581e-10
q2 3.597123e-14           NA 3.602896e-11 2.040895e-07
q3 1.554312e-15 3.602896e-11           NA 7.624040e-07
q4 3.646581e-10 2.040895e-07 7.624040e-07           NA
```

17.4.1 The cor Function

Now let us take a look at R's built-in functions for calculating correlations. As usual, they provide more sparse output.

```
> cor( data.frame(q1, q2, q3, q4),
+    method="pearson", use="pairwise")

            q1        q2        q3        q4
q1 1.0000000 0.6668711 0.6948419 0.5758860
q2 0.6668711 1.0000000 0.6040746 0.4917447
```

```
q3 0.6948419 0.6040746 1.0000000 0.4730732
q4 0.5758860 0.4917447 0.4730732 1.0000000
```

The `cor` function call above uses three arguments.

1. The variables to correlate. This can be a vector, matrix, or data frame. If it is a vector, then the next argument must be another vector with which to correlate. You can label them `x=` and `y=` or just put them in the first two positions.
2. The `method` argument can be pearson, spearman, or kendall for those types of correlations. Be careful not to capitalize these names when used with arguments in R.
3. The `use` argument determines how the function will deal with missing data. The value `pairwise.complete`, abbreviated `pairwise` above, uses as much data as possible. That is the default approach in Stata. The value `complete.obs` is the Stata equivalent of listwise deletion of missing values. This tosses out cases that have any missing values for the variables analyzed. If each variable has just a few missing values, but each are missing on different cases, you can lose a very large percent of your data with this option. However, it does ensure that every correlation is done on the exact same cases. That can be important if you plan to use the correlation matrix in additional computations. As usual, by default R provides no results if it finds missing values. That is the `use=all.obs` setting. So if you omit the `use` argument and have missing values, `cor` will print only an error message telling you that it has found missing values.

Unlike the `Hmisc` package's `rcorr` function, the built-in `cor` function provides only a correlation matrix. Another built-in function, `cor.test`, provides comprehensive output but only for two variables at a time.

```
> cor.test(q1, q2, use="pairwise")

        Pearson's product-moment correlation

data:  q1 and q2

t = 8.8593, df = 98, p-value = 3.597e-14

alternative hypothesis: true correlation is not equal to 0
95 percent confidence interval:

 0.5413638 0.7633070

sample estimates:
      cor
0.6668711
```

Stata users will recognize this function as similar to the `pwcorr` command.

17.5 Linear Regression

Linear regression models the linear association between one continuous dependent variable and a set of continuous independent or predictor variables. Stata performs linear regression with `regress` command, among others.

Assumptions:

- Each scatter plot of the dependent variable with each independent variable forms essentially a straight line. The function `plot(x,y)` would do the scatter plots. If you have a curve, transformations such as square roots or logarithms often help straighten it out.
- The spread in the data is the same at low, medium, and high values. This is called homoscedasticity. Transformations often help with this requirement also.
- The model residuals (difference between the predicted values and the actual values) are normally distributed. We will use the `plot` function to generate a normal QQ plot to test this assumption.
- The model residuals are independent. If they contain a relationship, such as the same subjects measured through time or classes of subjects sharing the same teacher, you would want to use a more complex model to take that into account.

When performing a single type of analysis in Stata, you generally type the appropriate statistical command together with its options on the command line. It is nearly always possible to duplicate what is typed on the command line by using the menu system. In addition, most statistical commands have postestimation commands, which may be unique to a particular primary command. Residuals, linear predictors, fitted values, and so forth are typically requested by means of postestimation commands. However, if a researcher simply wants the basic output for a given statistical command (e.g. `regress`), then typing the command, the related variables, any selection criteria, and associated options as a single line of code is all that is needed. The statistical results are immediately displayed on the screen, or they can be referred to a "log" file, or they can be executed quietly without being displayed on screen.

Let us look at a simple example in R. First, we will use the `lm` function to do a *linear model* predicting the values of q4 from the survey questions. Although this type of data is viewed as ordinal scale by many, social scientists often view it as interval level. With a more realistic data set, we would be working with a scale for each measure that consisted of the means of several questions, resulting in far more than just five values.

```
> lm(q4 ~ q1+q2+q3, data=mydata100)
```

```
Call:

lm(formula = q4 ~ q1 + q2 + q3, data = mydata100)

Coefficients:

(Intercept)            q1            q2            q3
    1.20940       0.41134       0.15791       0.09372
```

We see that the results provide only the coefficients to the linear regression model. So the model is as follows:

$$Predictedq4 = 1.20940 + 0.41134 \times q1 + 0.15791 \times q2 + 0.09372 \times q3$$

The other results that Stata would provide, such as R-squared or tests of significance, are not displayed. Now we will run the model again and save its results in an object called myModel.

```
> myModel <- lm(q4 ~ q1 + q2 + q3, data=mydata100)
```

This time, no printed results appear. We can see the contents of myModel by entering its name just like any other R object.

```
> myModel
```

```
Call:

lm(formula = q4 ~ q1 + q2 + q3, data = mydata100)

Coefficients:

(Intercept)            q1            q2            q3
    1.20940       0.41134       0.15791       0.09372
```

The above results are exactly the same as we saw initially. So what type of object is myModel? The mode and class functions can tell us.

```
> mode(myModel)
```

```
[1] "list"
```

```
> class(myModel)
```

```
[1] "lm"
```

So we see the lm function saved our model as a list with a class of lm. Now that we have the model stored, we can apply a series of *extractor functions*— which work like Stata's postestimation commands— to get much more information.

Each of these functions will see the class of lm and will apply the methods that it has available for that class of object. We have used the summary function previously. With our data frame object, mydata100, the summary function "knew" to get frequency counts on factors and other measures, like means, on continuous variables. The following is what it will do with lm objects:

```
> summary(myModel)

Call:

lm(formula = q4 ~ q1 + q2 + q3, data = mydata100)

Residuals:

Overall, I found this workshop useful.
    Min      1Q  Median      3Q     Max
-1.9467 -0.6418  0.1175  0.5960  2.0533

Coefficients:

             Estimate Std. Error t value Pr(>|t|)
(Intercept)  1.20940    0.31787   3.805 0.000251 ***
q1           0.41134    0.13170   3.123 0.002370 **
q2           0.15791    0.10690   1.477 0.142942
q3           0.09372    0.11617   0.807 0.421838

---
Signif. codes: 0 '***'0.001 '**'0.01 '*'0.05 '.'0.1
Residual standard error: 0.9308 on 95 degrees of freedom
  (1 observation deleted due to missingness)

Multiple R-squared: 0.3561,   Adjusted R-squared: 0.3358

F-statistic: 17.51 on 3 and 95 DF,  p-value: 3.944e-09
```

That is much the same output we would get from Stata.

From the perspective of this table it might appear that neither q2 nor q3 is adding significantly to the model. However, the next table will provide a different perspective. The very small p-value of $3.944e - 09$ or 0.000000003944 is quite a bit smaller than 0.05, so we would reject the hypothesis that the overall model is worthless. The significant p-value of 0.002370 for q1 makes it the only significant predictor, given the other variables in the model. We will test that below.

You can ask for an analysis of variance (ANOVA) table with the anova function.

```
> anova(myModel)

Analysis of Variance Table
Response: q4

          Df Sum Sq Mean Sq F value    Pr(>F)
q1         1 42.306  42.306 48.8278 3.824e-10 ***
q2         1  2.657   2.657  3.0661   0.08317 .
q3         1  0.564   0.564  0.6508   0.42184
Residuals 95 82.312   0.866
---
```

Signif. codes: 0 '***'0.001 '**'0.01 '*'0.05 '.'0.1

These tests are what Stata would call sequential or Type I tests. So the first test is for q1 by itself. The second is for q2, given that q1 is already in the model. The third is for q3, given that q1 and q2 are already in the model. Changing the order of the variables in the lm function would change these results. From this perspective, q1 is even more significant.

17.5.1 Plotting Diagnostics

The plot function also has methods for lm class objects. The single call to the plot function below was sufficient to generate all four of the plots shown in Fig. 17.1

```
> plot(myModel)
```

The Residuals vs. Fitted plot shown in Fig. 17.1 (upper left), shows the fitted values plotted against the model residuals. If the residuals follow any particular pattern, such as a diagonal line, there may be other predictors not yet in the model that could improve it. The fairly flat lowess line looks good.

The Normal Q-Q Plot in Fig. 17.1 (upper right), shows the quantiles of the standardized residuals plotted against the quantiles you would expect if the data were normally distributed. Since these fall mostly on the straight line, the assumption of normally distributed residuals is met.

The Scale-Location plot in Fig. 17.1 (lower left), shows the square root of the absolute standardized residuals plotted against the fitted, or predicted, values. Since the lowess line that fits this is fairly flat, it indicates that the spread in the predictions is roughly the same across the prediction line, meeting the assumption of homoscedasticity.

Finally, the Residuals vs. Leverage plot in Fig. 17.1 (lower right), shows a measure of the influence of each point on the overall equation against the standardized residuals. Since no points stand out far from the pack, we can assume that there are no outliers having undue influence on the fit of the model.

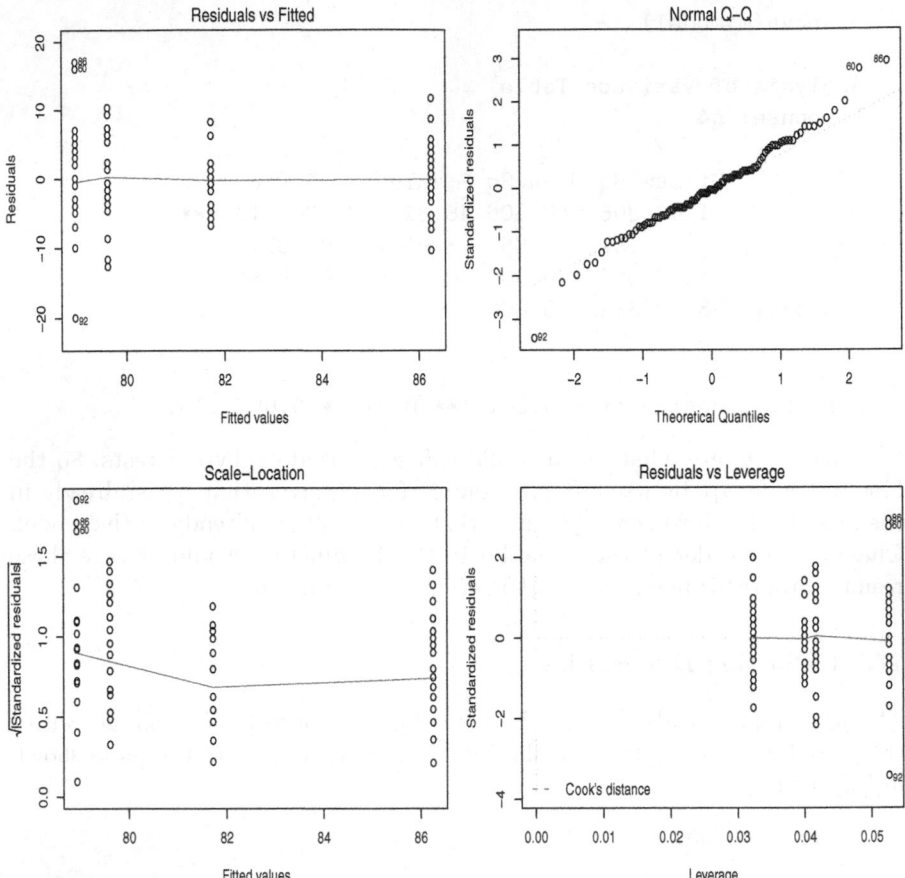

Fig. 17.1. Linear regression diagnostic plots generated automatically by the `plot` function.

17.5.2 Comparing Models

To do a stepwise model selection, first create the full model and save it, and then apply one of the functions: `step`, `add1`, `drop1`, or, from Venable and Ripley's `MASS` package, `stepAIC`. `MASS` is named after their book *Modern Applied Statistics with S* [51]. Keep in mind that if you start with a large number of variables, stepwise methods make your *p*-values essentially worthless. If you can choose a model on part of your data and see that it still works on the remainder, then the *p*-values obtained from the remainder data should be valid.

The `anova` function can also compare two models, as long as one is a subset of the other. So to see if q2 and q3 combined added significantly to a model over q1, we created the two models and then compared them. One catch with this scenario is that with missing values present, the two models will be calculated on different sample sizes and R will not be able to compare them. It will warn you, "models were not all fitted to the same size of data set." To deal with this problem, we will use the `na.omit` function discussed in Section 10.5, to remove the missing values first.

```
> myNoMissing <- na.omit(
+    mydata100[ , c("q1","q2","q3","q4") ] )

> myFullModel    <- lm( q4 ~ q1+q2+q3, data=myNoMissing)

> myReducedModel <- lm( q4 ~ q1,       data=myNoMissing)

> anova( myReducedModel, myFullModel)

Analysis of Variance Table

Model 1: q4 ~ q1
Model 2: q4 ~ q1 + q2 + q3

  Res.Df    RSS Df Sum of Sq      F Pr(>F)
1     97 85.532
2     95 82.312  2     3.220 1.8585 0.1615
```

The p-value of 0.1615 tells us that variables q2 and q3 combined did not add significantly to the model that had only q1. When you compare two models using the **anova** function, you should list the reduced model first.

17.5.3 Making Predictions with New Data

You can apply a saved model to a new set of data using the `predict` function. Of course, the new data set must have the same variables, with the same names and the same types. Under those conditions, you can apply myModel to myNewData using

```
myPredictions <- predict(myModel, myNewData)
```

Because the variables must have the *exact* same names, it is very important not to use the $ format in names. The following two statements perform what is statistically the same model, but the one using mydata100$q4 will only work on future data frames named "mydata100"!

```
myModel <- lm( mydata100$q4 ~ mydata$q1 ) #Bad
myModel <- lm(q4 ~ q1, data=mydata100) #Good
```

17.6 t-Test: Independent Groups

A t-test for independent groups compares two groups at a time on the mean of a continuous measure. Stata uses the `ttest` command for this purpose.

The assumptions for t-tests are as follows:

- The measure is interval-level continuous data. If the data are only ordinal (e.g., low-medium-high), consider the Wilcoxon rank sum test, also known as the Mann-Whitney test.
- The measures are normally distributed. You can examine that with `hist(myVar)` or `qqnorm(myvar)` as shown in Chapter 15, "Traditional Graphics." If they are not, consider the Mann-Whitney-Wilcoxon test. For details, see Section 17.9.
- The observations are independent. For example, if you measured the same subjects repeatedly, it would be important to take that into account in a more complex model.
- The distributions should have roughly the same variance. See Section 17.7, for details.

You can perform t-tests in R using the `t.test` function.

```
> t.test( q1 ~ gender, data=mydata100)

        Welch Two Sample t-test

data:  q1 by gender

t = 5.0578, df = 96.938, p-value = 2.008e-06

alternative hypothesis:
true difference in means is not equal to 0

95 percent confidence interval:
 0.6063427 1.3895656

sample estimates:

mean in group Female   mean in group Male
            3.978723               2.980769
```

The `t.test` function call above has two arguments, the formula and the data frame to use.

The formula `q4~gender` is in the form dependent~independent. For details, see Section 5.6.2, "Controlling Functions with Formulas."

Instead of a formula, you can specify two variables to compare such as `t.test(x,y)` and they can be selected using any of R's many variable selection approaches. The **data** argument specifies the data frame to use only in the case of a formula. So you might think that this form works:

```
t.test( q4[which(gender=='m') ],
        q4[which(gender=='f') ], data=mydata100)
```

However, unless the data is attached, it does not! You would have to enter **attach(mydata100)** before the function call above would work. Alternatively, with an unattached data frame, you could leave off the **data** argument and use the form

```
with(mydata100,
  t.test( q4[ which(gender=='m') ],
          q4[ which(gender=='f') ] ) )
)
```

or, you might prefer to use the **subset** function

```
t.test(
  subset(mydata100, gender=="m", select=q4),
  subset(mydata100, gender=="f", select=q4)
)
```

For more details see Chapter 9, "Selecting Variables and Observations."

The results show that the mean for the females is 3.96 and for the males is 2.98. The p-value of $2.748e - 06$, or 0.000002748, is much smaller than 0.05, so we would reject the hypothesis that those means are the same.

Unlike Stata, R does not provide a test for homogeneity of variance and two t-test calculations for equal and unequal variances. Instead, it provides only the unequal variance test by default. The additional argument, **var.equal=TRUE** will ask it to perform the other test. See Section 17.7, for that topic.

17.7 Equality of Variance

Stata offers tests for equality (homogeneity) of variance in its t-test and analysis of variance procedures. R, in keeping with its minimalist perspective, offers such tests in separate functions.

The Levene test for equality of variance is the most popular. John Fox's car package [12] contains the **levene.test** function.

```
> library("car")

> levene.test(posttest, gender)

Levene's Test for Homogeneity of Variance
```

```
         Df F value Pr(>F)
group  1  0.4308 0.5131
       97
```

The `levene.test` function has only two arguments of the form (var, group). Its null hypothesis is that your groups have equal variances. If its *p*-value is smaller than 0.05, you reject that hypothesis. So in the above case, we would accept the hypothesis that the variances are equal.

Other tests for comparing variances are R's built-in `var.test` and `bartlett.test` functions.

17.8 t-Test: Paired or Repeated Measures

The goal of a paired t-test is to compare the mean of two correlated measures. These are often the same measure taken on the same subjects at two different times. Stata uses the same procedures for paired t-tests as for independent samples t-tests. R does too.

The paired t-test's assumptions are:

- The two measures are interval-level continuous data. If the data are only ordinal (e.g., low-medium-high) consider the Wilcoxon signed-rank test. For details see Section 17.10.
- The differences between the measures are normally distributed. You can examine that with `hist(posttest-pretest)` or `qqnorm(posttest-pretest)` as shown in the chapters on graphics. If they are not, consider the Wilcoxon signed-rank test. For details see Section 17.10.
- Other than the obvious pairing, observations are independent. For example, if siblings were also in your data set, it would be important to take that into account in a more complex model.

You can perform the paired t-tests in R using the `t.test` function. This example assumes the data frame is attached.

```
> t.test(posttest, pretest, paired=TRUE)

        Paired t-test

data:  posttest and pretest
t = 14.4597, df = 99, p-value < 2.2e-16

alternative hypothesis:
  true difference in means is not equal to 0
```

```
95 percent confidence interval:
 6.11708 8.06292
```

```
sample estimates:
mean of the differences
              7.09
```

The t.test function call above has three main arguments.

1. The first variable to compare.
2. The second test variable to compare. The function will subtract this from the first to get the mean difference. If these two were reversed, the p-value would be the same, however the mean difference would be negative -7.09 and the confidence interval would be around that.
3. The paired=TRUE argument tells it that the two variables are correlated rather than independent. It is extremely important that you set this option for a paired test! If you forget this, it will perform an independent-groups t-test instead.

The results show that the mean difference of 7.09 is statistically significant with a p-value of $2.2e - 16$ or 0.00000000000000022. So we would reject the hypothesis that the means are the same.

17.9 Wilcoxon Mann-Whitney Rank Sum Test: Independent Groups

The Wilcoxon rank sum test, also known as the Mann-Whitney U test, compares two groups on the mean rank of a dependent variable that is at least ordinal (e.g., low, medium, high).

In Stata this test is executed using the ranksum command.

The Wilcoxon-Mann-Whitney test's assumptions are as follows:

- The distributions in the two groups must be the same, other than a shift in location; that is, the distributions should have the same variance and skewness. Examining a histogram is a good idea if you have at least 30 subjects. A box plot is also helpful regardless of the number of subjects in each group.
- Observations are independent. For example, if you measured the same subjects repeatedly, it would be important to take that into account in a more complex model.

The wilcox.test function works very much like the t.test function.

```
> wilcox.test( q1~gender, data=mydata100 )

        Wilcoxon rank sum test with continuity correction
```

```
data:  q1 by gender

W = 1841.5, p-value = 6.666e-06

alternative hypothesis: true location shift is not equal to 0
```

The `wilcox.test` function call above has two main arguments.

1. The formula `q4~gender` is in the form dependent~independent. For details, see Section 5.6.2, "Controlling Functions with Formulas." Instead of a formula, you can specify two variables to compare, such as `wilcox.test` `(x,y)`, and they can be selected using any of R's many variable selection approaches. See the examples in the Section 17.6.
2. The `data` argument specifies the data frame to use, if (and only if) you are using a formula.

The p-value of $6.666e - 06$ or 0.000006666 is less than 0.05, so we would reject the hypothesis that the males and females have the same distribution on the q4 variable. The median is the more popular measure of location to report on for a nonparametric test, and we can apply that function to calculate them using the `aggregate` function. Recall that `aggregate` requires its group argument be a list or data frame.

```
> aggregate( q1, data.frame(gender),
+    median, na.rm=TRUE)

  gender x

1 Female 4
2   Male 3
```

We see that the median of the females is 4 and the males is 3.

17.10 Wilcoxon Signed-Rank Test: Paired Groups

The goal of a Wilcoxon signed-rank test is to compare the mean rank of two correlated measures that are at least ordinal (e.g., low, medium, high) in scale. These are often the same measure taken on the same subjects at two different times.

In Stata you can perform this test by creating a difference score and then running that though the `signrank` command.

The assumptions of the Wilcoxon signed-rank test are as follows:

- The distribution of the difference between the two measures has a symmetric distribution.

- Other than the obvious pairing, the observations are independent. For example, if your data also contained siblings, you would want a more complex model to make the most of that information.

This test works very much like the `t.test` function with the `paired` argument.

```
> wilcox.test(posttest, pretest, paired=TRUE)

        Wilcoxon signed rank test with continuity correction

data:  posttest and pretest

V = 5005, p-value < 2.2e-16

alternative hypothesis: true location shift is not equal to 0
```

The `wilcox.test` function call above has three main arguments.

1. The first variable to compare.
2. The second variable to compare. The function will subtract this from the first and then convert the difference to ranks.
3. The `paired=TRUE` argument tells it that the variables are correlated. Be careful, as without this argument, it will perform the Wilcoxon rank sum test for independent groups. That is a completely different test and it would be inappropriate for correlated data.

The p-value of $2.2e-16$ is less than 0.05, so we would reject the hypothesis that the location difference is zero. As Dalgaard [9] pointed out, with a sample size of 6 or fewer, it is impossible to achieve a significant result with this test.

The median is the more popular measure of location to report for a nonparametric test and we can calculate them with the `median` function.

```
> median(pretest)

[1] 75

> median(posttest)

[1] 82
```

17.11 Analysis of Variance

An analysis of variance (ANOVA or AOV) tests for group differences on the mean of a continuous variable divided up by one or more categorical factors.

Stata has two commands that performs this analysis: oneway and anova. Which you choose depends on the extent of the analysis you need. You can use anova for repeated measures analysis as well as for the analysis of covariance. The oneway command is primarily used for a one-way ANOVA as well as for multiple comparison tests.

The assumptions of R's ANOVA are as follows:

- The measure is interval-level continuous data. If the data are only ordinal (e.g., low-medium-high), consider the Kruskal-Wallis test for a single factor (i.e., one-way ANOVA).
- The measure is normally distributed. You can examine that assumption with hist(myVar) or qqnorm(myvar), as shown in the chapters on graphics. If they are not, consider the Kruskal-Wallis test.
- The observations are independent. For example, if each group contains subjects that were measured repeatedly over time or who are correlated (e.g., same family), you would want a more complex model to make the most of that information.
- The variance of the measure is the same in each group.

We can get the group means using the aggregate function.

```
> aggregate( posttest,
+    data.frame(workshop),
+    mean, na.rm=TRUE)

  workshop      x
1        R 86.258
2    Stata 79.625
3     SPSS 81.720
4      SAS 78.947
```

Similarly, we can get variances by applying the var function.

```
> aggregate( posttest,
+    data.frame(workshop),
+    var, na.rm=TRUE)

  workshop      x
1        R 24.998
2    Stata 37.549
3     SPSS 19.543
4      SAS 73.608
```

You can see the variance for the Stata group is quite a bit higher than the rest. Levene's test will provide a test of significance for that.

```
> levene.test(posttest, workshop)

Levene's Test for Homogeneity of Variance

      Df F value  Pr(>F)
group  3    2.51 0.06337 .
      95


---
Signif. codes:  0 '***'0.001 '**'0.01 '*'0.05 '.'0.1
```

The Levene test's null hypothesis is that the variances do not differ. Since it calculated a p-value of 0.06337, we can conclude that the differences in variance are not significant.

The aov function calculates the *analysis of variance*.

```
> myModel <- aov( posttest ~ workshop, data=mydata100 )
```

The aov function call above has two arguments.

1. The formula posttest~workshop is in the form dependent~independent. The independent variable must be a factor. See Section 5.6.2, "Controlling Functions with Formulas," for details about models with more factors, interactions, nesting, and so forth.
2. The data argument specifies the data frame to use for the formula. If you do not supply this argument, you can use any other valid form of variable specification that tells it in which data frame your variables are stored (e.g., mydata$posttest~mydata$workshop).

We can see some results by printing myModel.

```
> myModel

Call:
   aov(formula = posttest ~ workshop, data = mydata100)

Terms:
                 workshop Residuals
Sum of Squares    875.442  3407.548
Deg. of Freedom         3        95
Residual standard error: 5.989067

Estimated effects may be unbalanced
1 observation deleted due to missingness
```

Of course, the summary function has methods for ANOVA models; it prints the same result.

```
> anova(myModel)

Analysis of Variance Table

Response: posttest
          Df Sum Sq Mean Sq F value    Pr(>F)
workshop   3  875.4   291.8  8.1356 7.062e-05 ***
Residuals 95 3407.5    35.9

---
Signif. codes:  0 '***' 0.001 '**' 0.01 '*' 0.05 '.' 0.1
```

Given the p-value of $7.062e - 05$ or 0.00007062, we would reject the hypothesis that the means are all the same. However, which ones differ? The pairwise.t.test function provides all possible tests and corrects them for multiple testing using the Holm method by default. In our case, we are doing six t-tests, so the best (smallest) p-value is multiplied by 6, the next best by 5, and so on. This is also called a sequential Bonferroni correction.

```
> pairwise.t.test(posttest, workshop)
        Pairwise comparisons using t tests with pooled SD

data:  posttest and workshop

      R       Stata   SPSS
Stata 0.00048 -       -
SPSS  0.02346 0.44791 -
SAS   0.00038 0.71335 0.39468

P value adjustment method: holm
```

We see that the posttest scores are significantly different for R compared to the other three. The mean scores for the other workshops do not differ significantly among themselves.

An alternate comparison approach is to use Tukey's HSD test. The TukeyHSD function call below uses only two arguments: the model and the factor whose means you would like to compare.

```
> TukeyHSD(myModel, "workshop")

  Tukey multiple comparisons of means
    95% family-wise confidence level

Fit: aov(formula = posttest ~ workshop, data = mydata100)

$workshop
```

	diff	lwr	upr	p adj
Stata-R	-6.63306	-10.8914	-2.37472	0.00055
SPSS-R	-4.53806	-8.7481	-0.32799	0.02943
SAS-R	-7.31070	-11.8739	-2.74745	0.00036
SPSS-Stata	2.09500	-2.3808	6.57078	0.61321
SAS-Stata	-0.67763	-5.4871	4.13185	0.98281
SAS-SPSS	-2.77263	-7.5394	1.99416	0.42904

The "diff" column provides mean differences. The "lwr" and "upr" columns provide lower and upper 95% confidence bounds, respectively. Finally, the "p adj" column provides the p-values adjusted for the number of comparisons made. The conclusion is the same: the R group's posttest score differs significantly from the others, but the others do not differ significantly among themselves.

We can graph these results using the `plot` function (Fig. 17.2).

```
> plot( TukeyHSD(myModel, "workshop") )
```

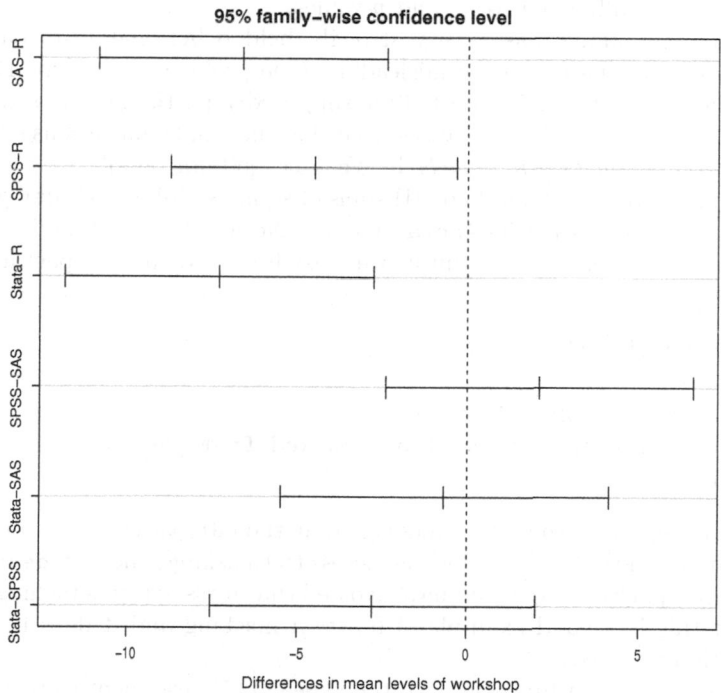

Fig. 17.2. A plot of the Tukey HSD test results showing the R group differing from the other three workshops.

The `plot` function also provides appropriate diagnostic plots (not shown). These are the same plots shown and discussed in Section 17.5, "Linear Regression."

```
> plot(myModel)
```

You can perform much more complex ANOVA models in R, but they are beyond the scope of this book. A good book on ANOVA is Pinheiro and Bates' *Mixed Effects Models in S and S-Plus* [37].

17.12 Sums of Squares

In analysis of variance, Stata provides partial (Type III) sums of squares and F-tests by default. Stata also provides sequential sums of squares and F-tests as an option. R provides sequential ones in its built-in functions. For one-way ANOVAs or for two-way or higher ANOVAS with equal cell sizes, there is no difference between sequential and partial tests. However, in two-way or higher models that have unequal cell counts (unbalanced models), these two sums of squares lead to different F-tests and *p*-values.

The R community has a very strongly held belief that tests based on partial sums of squares can be misleading. One problem with Type III tests is that they test the main effect after supposedly partialing out significant interactions. In many circumstances, that does not make much sense. See the paper, *Exegeses on Linear Models*, by Venables [50] for details.

If you are sure you want Type III sums of squares, John Fox's `car` package will calculate them using its `Anova` function. Notice that the function begins with a capital letter "A"! To run it, we must first load the `car` package from the library.

```
> library("car")
```

```
Attaching package: 'car'
  The following object(s) are masked from package:Hmisc :
    recode
```

You can see from the above message that the `car` package also contains a `recode` function that is now blocking access to (masking) the `recode` function in the `Hmisc` package. We could have avoided that message by detaching `Hmisc` first, but this is a good example of function masking and it does not affect the function we need.

We use the `Anova` function with the `type="III"` argument to request the sums of squares you need. Since our model is a one-way ANOVA, the results are identical to those from the lowercase `anova` function that is built-in to R, except that the *p*-values are expressed in scientific notation and the intercept, the grand mean in this case, is tested.

```
> Anova(myModel, type="III")

Anova Table (Type III tests)

Response: posttest

            Sum Sq Df   F value     Pr(>F)
(Intercept) 230654  1 6430.4706 < 2.2e-16 ***
workshop       875  3    8.1356 7.062e-05 ***
Residuals     3408 95


---
Signif. codes:  0 '***' 0.001 '**' 0.01 '*' 0.05 '.' 0.1
```

To get reasonable Type III tests when doing more complex ANOVA models, it is important to set the contrasts option. The function call

```
options( contrasts=c("contr.sum", "contr.poly") )
```

is an example of this. See an R book devoted to analysis of variance for details.

17.13 The Kruskal–Wallis Test

The nonparametric equivalent to a one-way analysis of variance is the Kruskal-Wallis test. The Kruskal-Wallis test compares groups on the mean rank of a variable that is at least ordinal (e.g., low, medium, high). Stata offers it as the **kwallis** command.

Its assumptions are as follows:

- The distributions in the groups must be the same, other than a shift in location. This is often misinterpreted to mean that the distributions do not matter at all. That is not the case. They do not need to be normally distributed, but they do need to generally look alike. Otherwise the test can produce a significant result if, for example, the distributions are skewed in opposite directions but are centered in roughly the same place.
- The distributions should have roughly the same variance. Since the test requires no particular distribution, there is no single test for this assumption. Box plots are a good way to examine this assumption.
- The observations are independent. For example, if each group contains subjects that were measured repeatedly over time or who are correlated (e.g., same family), you would want a more complex model to make the most of that information.

The following is an example that uses the nonparametric **kruskal.test** function to compare the different workshops on the means of the q4 variable:

```
> kruskal.test(posttest~workshop)

        Kruskal-Wallis rank sum test

data:  posttest by workshop

Kruskal-Wallis chi-squared=21.4448, df=3, p-value=8.51e-05
```

The kruskal.test function call above has two arguments.

1. The formula posttest~workshop is in the form dependent~independent. For details, see Section 5.6.2.
2. The data argument specifies the data frame to use for the formula. If you do not supply this argument, you can use any other valid form of variable specification that tells it in which data frame your variables are stored (e.g., mydata$postest~mydata$workshop).

The p-value of $8.51e - 05$ or 0.0000851 is smaller than the typical cutoff of 0.05, so you would reject the hypothesis that the groups do not differ. The next question would be, "which of the groups differ?" The pairwise.wilcox.test function answers that question. The only arguments we use below are the measure and the factor, respectively.

```
> pairwise.wilcox.test(posttest, workshop)

        Pairwise comparisons using Wilcoxon rank sum test

data:  posttest and workshop

      R       Stata   SPSS
Stata 0.0012 -       -
SPSS  0.0061 0.4801  -
SAS   0.0023 0.5079  0.4033

P value adjustment method: holm

Warning messages:

1: In wilcox.test.default(xi, xj, ...) :
    cannot compute exact p-value with ties
```

So we see that R workshop group differs significantly from the other three and that the other three do not differ among themselves. The median is the more popular measure to report with a nonparametric test. We can use the aggregate function to apply the median function.

```
> aggregate( posttest,
```

```
+    data.frame(workshop),
+    median, na.rm=TRUE)

   workshop    x
1         R 86.0
2     Stata 78.5
3      SPSS 81.0
4       SAS 78.0
```

17.14 Example Programs for Statistical Tests

The R examples require installing the car, Gmodels and Hmisc packages. See details in Chapter 2, "Installing and Updating R."

17.14.1 Stata Program for Statistical Tests

```
* Filename: Statistics.do

* ---Various Statistics Commands---
use c:\myRfolder\mydata100, clear
* Show variable obs number, mean, sd, min, max for q1-q4
summ q*

* Same, with percentiles, variance, skew, kurtosis...
summ q*, detail

* Display statistics to use in other commands
return list

* Tabluation of gender and workshop,
* showing percentages of column and rows,
* and a fisher exact Chi2 test.
tab gender workshop, row col exact

* Create dummy or indicator variables
* q1_1, q1_2, q1_3, and q1_4 are created
tab q1, gen(q1_)

* Table of means, sd, min, and max values for q1-q4.
tabstat q1-q4, by(gender) stat(mean sd min max)

* meanq1 through meanq4 created with mean values of q1-q4
forvalues i = 1/4 {
egen meanq'i' = mean(q'i')
}
```

```
* Correlations
corr q1 q4
corr q*

* Pairwise correlations, with *=sign at 0.05
pwcorr q*, star(.05)

* Linear regression of q4 on q1-q3
regress q4 q1-q3

* ANOVA table of above regression
regress q4 q1-q3, notab

* plot of leverage on normalized residuals
lvr2plot

* -----group comparisons--------

* T-test male vs female
ttest q1, by(gender) unpair unequ

* Paired tttest of pretest and posttest
ttest pretest = posttest

* Levene test for equality of variance
robvar posttest, by(gender)

* Two-sample variance-comparison test
sdtest posttest = gender

* ANOVA oF posttest on workshop
anova posttest workshop

* -----Non-parametric versions of above

* Wilcoxon signed-rank test or pretest and posttest
signtest pretest = posttest

* Kruskal-Wallis equality-of-populations rank test
kwallis posttest, by(workshop)

* Wilcoxon matched pairs test of posttest and workshop
signrank posttest = workshop
```

```
* Two-sample Wilcoxon rank-sum (Mann-Whitney) test
ranksum posttest, by(gender)

* Pearson chi-squared test of the equality of medians
median posttest, by(gender)

* Fisher's exact test of the equality of the medians
median posttest, by(gender) exact
```

17.14.2 R Program for Statistical Tests

```
# Filename: Statistics.R

setwd("/myRfolder")
load("mydata100.Rdata")
attach(mydata100)
options(linesize=64)

head(mydata100)

# --- Frequencies & Univariate Statistics ---

# The easy way using the Hmisc package.
library("Hmisc")
describe(mydata100)

# R's build in function.
summary(mydata100)

# The flexible way using built-in functions.

table(workshop)
table(gender)

# Proportions of valid values.
prop.table( table(workshop) )
prop.table( table(gender) )

# Rounding off proportions.
round( prop.table( table(gender) ), 2 )

# Converting proportions to percents.
round( 100* ( prop.table( table(gender) ) ) )
```

```
# Cumulative proportions.
cumsum( prop.table( table(posttest) ) )

# A Function to Mimic Stata Cum Proportions

# My original function, Score now called "x"
myTable <- function(X)
 {
  myDF <- data.frame( table(Score) )
  myDF$Prop <- prop.table( myDF$Freq )
  myDF$CumProp <-  cumsum( myDF$Prop )
  myDF
 }
myTable(Score)

# Frequencies & Univariate
summary(mydata100)

# Means & Std Deviations
options(width=64)
sapply( mydata100[3:8], mean,  na.rm=TRUE)
sapply( mydata100[3:8], sd,     na.rm=TRUE)

# --- Crosstabulations---

# The easy way, using the gmodels package.
library("gmodels")
CrossTable(workshop, gender,
  chisq=TRUE, format="SAS")

# The flexible way using built in functions.

# Counts

myWG <- table(workshop, gender)
myWG      # Crosstabulation format.
myWGdata <- as.data.frame(myWG)
myWGdata # Summary or Aggregation format.

chisq.test(myWG)

# Row proportions.
prop.table(myWG, 1)
```

```
# Column proportions.
prop.table(myWG, 2)


# Total proportions.
prop.table(myWG)


# Rounding off proportions.
round( prop.table(myWG, 1), 2 )


# Row percents.
round( 100* ( prop.table(myWG, 1) ) )


# Adding Row and Column Totals.

addmargins(myWG, 1)
addmargins(myWG, 2)
addmargins(myWG)


# ---Correlation & Linear Regression---

# The rcorr function from the Hmisc package

library("Hmisc")

rcorr(q1,q4)

myQs <- cbind(q1, q2, q3, q4)
rcorr(myQs, type="pearson")


# See just the P values.
options(digits=7)
myCorrs <- rcorr(myQs, type="pearson")
myCorrs$P


# See P values without scientific notation.
options(scipen=999) #Block scientific notation.
myCorrs$P
options(scipen=0) # Restore scientific notation.


# Spearman correlations using the Hmisc rcorr function.
rcorr( cbind(q1,q2,q3,q4), type="spearman" )


# The built-in cor function.
cor( data.frame(q1, q2, q3, q4),
  method="pearson", use="pairwise")
```

```
# The built-in cor.test function
cor.test(q1, q2, use="pairwise")

# Linear regression.
lm( q4 ~ q1 + q2 + q3, data=mydata100)

myModel <- lm( q4 ~ q1 + q2 + q3, data=mydata100 )
myModel
summary(myModel)
anova(myModel) #Same as summary result.

# Set graphics parameters for 4 plots (optional).
par( mfrow=c(2,2), mar=c(5,4,2,1)+0.1 )

plot(myModel)

# Set graphics parameters back to default settings.
par( mfrow=c(1,1), mar=c(5,4,4,2)+0.1 )

# Repeat the diagnostic plots and route them
# to a file.
postscript("LinearRegDiagnostics.eps")
par( mfrow=c(2,2), mar=c(5,4,2,1)+0.1 )
plot(myModel)
dev.off()
par( mfrow=c(1,1), mar=c(5,4,4,2)+0.1 )

myNoMissing <-
  na.omit(mydata100[ , c("q1","q2","q3","q4") ] )
myFullModel    <- lm( q4 ~ q1 + q2 + q3, data=myNoMissing)
myReducedModel <- lm( q4 ~ q1,        data=myNoMissing)
anova( myReducedModel, myFullModel)


#---Group Comparisons---

# Independent samples t-test.
t.test( q1 ~ gender, data=mydata100)

t.test( q1[gender=='Male'], q1[gender=='Female'] )

# Paired samples t-test.
t.test(posttest, pretest, paired=TRUE)
```

```
# Equality of variance.
library("car")
levene.test(posttest, gender)

var.test(posttest~gender)

# Wilcoxon/Mann-Whitney test.
wilcox.test( q1 ~ gender, data=mydata100)
# Same test specified differently.
wilcox.test( q1[gender=='Male'],
             q1[gender=='Female'] )
aggregate( q1, data.frame(gender),
  median, na.rm=TRUE)

# Wilcoxon signed rank test.
wilcox.test( posttest, pretest, paired=TRUE)
median(pretest)
median(posttest)

# Analysis of Variance (ANOVA).
aggregate( posttest,
  data.frame(workshop),
  mean, na.rm=TRUE)

aggregate( posttest,
  data.frame(workshop),
  var, na.rm=TRUE)

library("car")
levene.test(posttest, workshop)

myModel <- aov(posttest~workshop,
  data=mydata100)
myModel

anova(myModel)
summary(myModel) #same as anova result.

# type III sums of squares
library("car")
Anova(myModel, type="III")

pairwise.t.test(posttest, workshop)

TukeyHSD(myModel, "workshop")
```

```
plot( TukeyHSD(myModel, "workshop") )
# Repeat TukeyHSD plot and route to a file.
postscript("TukeyHSD.eps")
plot( TukeyHSD(myModel, "workshop") )
dev.off()

# Set graphics parameters for 4 plots (optional).
par( mfrow=c(2,2), mar=c(5,4,2,1)+0.1 )
plot(myModel)
# Set graphics parameters back to default settings.
par( mfrow=c(1,1), mar=c(5,4,4,2)+0.1 )

#Nonparametric oneway ANOVA using
# the Kruskal-Wallis test.
kruskal.test(posttest~workshop)

pairwise.wilcox.test(posttest, workshop)

aggregate( posttest,
  data.frame(workshop),
  median, na.rm=TRUE)
```

18

Conclusion

As we have seen, R has many features in common with Stata. Both share rich programming environments optimized for extensibility, functions open for you to see and modify, and flourishing ecosystems of extensions written by their devoted users.

R also has features that Stata lacks, such as a much wider selection of user-written functions, its rich collection of data structures, functions that optimize their output automatically for different data structures, and a flexibility that extends all the way to the core of the system. You can change *anything* about it you like.

R's extreme flexibility may seem daunting to learn at first. However, its many thousands of add-on packages and its free price make it well worth the effort.

This book has covered how R compares to Stata and how you can do the very same things in each. However, what we have not covered literally fills many volumes. We hope this will start you on a long and successful journey with R.

We also hope to improve this book as time goes on, so if there are changes you would like to see in the next edition, please drop us a line at muenchen.bob@gmail.com or jhilbe@aol.com. Negative comments are often the most useful, so do not worry about being critical.

Have fun working with R!

R.A. Muenchen, J.M. Hilbe, *R for Stata Users*, Statistics and Computing, DOI 10.1007/978-1-4419-1318-0_18, © Springer Science+Business Media, LLC 2010

A

Glossary of R jargon

Below is a selection of common R terms defined first using Stata jargon (or plain English when possible) and then more formally using R jargon. Some definitions in Stata jargon are quite loose given the fact that they have no direct analog of some R terms. Definitions in R terms are often quoted (with permission) or paraphrased from *S Poetry* by Patrick Burns [3].

Apply
> The process of having a command work on variables or observations. Determines whether a procedure will act as a typical command or as a function instead. Also the name of a function that controls that process. More formally, the process of targeting a function on rows or columns. Also a function that does that.

Argument
> The options that control what the commands do and the arguments that control what functions do. Confusing because in R, functions do what both commands and functions do in Stata. More formally, input(s) to a function that control it. Includes data to analyze.

Array
> A matrix with more than two dimensions. All variables must be only one type (e.g., all numeric or all character). More formally, a vector with a dim attribute. The dim controls the number and size of dimensions.

Assignment function
> Assigns values like the equal sign in Stata. The two-key sequence, "<-", that places data or results of procedures or transformations into a variable or data set. More formally, the two-key sequence, "<-", that gives names to objects.

Atomic object
> A variable whose values are all of one type, such as all numeric or all character. More formally, an object whose components are all of one mode. Modes allowed are numeric, character, logical, or complex.

R.A. Muenchen, J.M. Hilbe, *R for Stata Users*, Statistics and Computing, DOI 10.1007/978-1-4419-1318-0,

Attach

The process of adding a data set or add-on module to your path. Attaching a data set appears to copy the variables into an area that lets you use them by a simple component name like "gender" rather than by using the $ format name like "mydata$gender." Done using the `attach` function. More formally, the process of adding a database to your search list. Also a function that does this.

Attributes

Traits of a data set like its variable names and labels. More formally, traits of objects such as names, class, or dim.

Class

An attribute of a variable or data set that a command used to change its options automatically. More formally, the class attribute of an object determines which method of a generic function is used when the object is an argument in the function call.

Component

Like one data set stored in a zipped set of data sets. More formally, an item in a list. The length of a list is the number of components it has.

CRAN

The Comprehensive R Archive Network at `http://cran.r-project.org/`. An Internet archive like the Statistical Software Components (SSC) Archive. Consists of a set of sites around the world called mirrors that provide R and its add-on packages for you to download and install.

Data frame

A data set. More formally, a set of vectors bound together in a list. They can be different modes or classes (e.g., numeric and character), but they must have equal length.

Database

One data set or a set of them, or an add-on module. More formally, an item on the search list or something that might be. Can be an R data file or a package.

Dim

A variable whose values are the number of rows and columns in a data set. It is stored in the data set itself. Also, a procedure that prints or sets these values. More formally, the attribute that describes the *dim*ensions of an array. Also, the function that retrieves or changes that attribute.

Element

A specific value for a variable. More formally, an item in a vector.

Extractor function

A postestimation command. More formally, a function that has methods that apply to modeling objects.

Factor

A categorical variable and its value labels. Value labels may be nothing more than "1," "2,"..., if not assigned explicitly. More formally, the type of object that represents a categorical variable. It stores its labels in its levels attribute.

Function

A command and/or a function. When you apply it down through cases, it is just like a Stata command. However, you can also apply it across rows like a Stata function. More formally, an R program that is stored as an object.

Generic function

A command or function that has different default options or arguments set depending on the type of data you give it. More formally, a function whose behavior is determined by the class of one or more of its arguments. The class of the relevant argument(s) determines which method the generic function will use.

Index

The order number of a variable in a data set or the subscript of a value in a variable. In our practice data set gender is the second variable, so its index is 2. Gender is `mydata[ ,2]`. The first index selects rows, the second selects columns. If empty, it refers to all rows/columns. More formally, the number of the component in a list or data frame, or of an element in a vector.

Install

You install packages just like ado files, just once per version of R. However, you must load it from the library every time you start R. More formally, adding a package into your library.

Label

A procedure that creates variable labels. Also, a parameter that sets value labels using the `factor` or `ordered` commands. More formally, a function from the `Hmisc` package that creates variable labels. Also an argument that sets factor labels using the `factor` or `ordered` functions.

Length

The number of observations/cases in a variable, including missing values, or the number of variables in a data set. More formally, a measure of objects. For vectors, it is the number of its elements (including NAs). For lists or data frames, it is the number of its components.

Levels

The values that a categorical variable can have. Actually stored as a part of the variable itself in what appears to be a very short character variable (even when the values themselves are numbers). More formally, an attribute to a factor object that is a character vector of the values the factor can have. Also an argument to the `factor` and `ordered` functions that can set the levels.

Library

Where a given version of R stores its base packages and the add-on modules you have installed. Also a procedure that loads a package from the library into working memory. You must do that in every R session before using a package. More formally, a directory containing R packages that is set up so that the library function can attach it. Also a function that attaches a package from the library onto your search list.

List

Like a zipped collection of data sets that you can analyze easily without unzipping. More formally, a set of objects of any class. Can contain vectors, data frames, matrices and even other lists.

Load

Bringing a data set (or collection of data sets) from disk to memory. You must do this before you can use data in R. Also the command that performs that task, like the Stata **use** command. More formally, bringing an R data file into your workspace. Also the function that performs that task.

Matrix

A data set that must contain only one type of variable, e.g. all numeric or character. More formally, a two-dimensional array; that is, a vector with a dim attribute of length 2.

Method

The analyses and/or graphs that a procedure will perform by default, that is different for different types of variables. The default settings for some commands depend on the scale of the variables you provide. E.g. summary(temperature) provides mean temperature, summary(gender) counts males & females. More formally, a function that provides the calculation of a generic function for a specific class of object.

Mode

A variable's type such as numeric or character. More formally, a fundamental property of an object. Can be numeric, character, logical or complex.

Modeling function

A command that performs estimation. More formally, a function that tests association or group differences and usually accepts a formula (e.g. y~x) and a **data=** argument.

Modeling objects

A model created by a modeling function.

NA

A missing value. Stands for *N*ot *A*vailable. See also NaN.

Names

Variable names. They are stored in a character variable that is a part of a data set or variable. Since R can use an index number instead, names are optional. Also a procedure that extracts or changes variable names. More formally, an attribute of many objects that labels the elements or components of the object. Also the function that retrieves or sets this attribute.

NaN

A missing value. Stands for *N*ot a *N*umber. Something that is undefined mathematically such as zero divided by zero.

NULL

An object you can use to drop variables or values. E.g. mydata$x ¡- NULL drops the variable x from the data set mydata. More formally, NULL has a zero length and no particular mode. Assigning it to an object deletes it.

Numeric

A variable that contains only numbers. More formally, the atomic mode that represents real numbers. This contains storage modes double, single and integer.

Object

A data set, a variable or even the equivalent of a Stata command). More formally, almost everything in R. If it has a mode, it is an object. Includes data frames, vectors, matrices, arrays, lists and functions.

Object Oriented Programming

A style of software in which the output of a procedure depends on the type of data you provide it. R has an object orientation, Stata added it in version 11.

Option

A statement that sets general parameters, such as the width of each line of output. More formally, settings that control some aspect of your R session, such as the width of each line of output. Also a function that queries or changes the settings.

Package

A set of ado-files, and related files, such as help, for each bundled together. Like the packages at the SSC. May come with R or be written by its users. More formally, a collection of functions and, optionally, data objects.

R

A language and environment for statistical computing and graphics. An implementation of the S language.

R-PLUS

A commercial version of R. It includes a graphical user interface, context-sensitive editor and other features.

Replacement

A way to replace values. More formally, when you use subscripts on the left side of an assignment to change the values in an object. E.g. setting 9 to missing: x[x==9]   <-   NA

S

The language from which R evolved. R can run many S programs, but S cannot use R packages.

S3, S4

Used in the R help files to refer to different versions of S. The differences between them are of importance mainly to advanced programmers.

Script

The equivalent of a do file. An R program.

Search list

Somewhat like an operating system search path for R objects. More formally, the collection of databases that R will search, in order, for objects.

S-PLUS

The commercial version of S. Mostly compatible with R but will not run R packages. It includes graphical user interface and can analyze "big data" that is larger than your computer's main memory.

Subscript

Choosing variables or values by the order in which they appear or by their name. More formally, the extraction or replacement of an object using its index or name in square [brackets].

Vector

A variable. It can exist on its own in memory or it can be part of a data set. More formally, a set of values that have the same mode, i.e. an atomic object.

Workspace

A temporary work area in which all R computation happens. Data that exists there will vanish if not saved to your hard drive before quitting R. More formally, the area of your computer's main memory where R does all its work. Data must be loaded into it from files, and packages must be loaded into it from the library, before you can use either.

B

Comparison of Stata commands and R functions

With over 3,000 add-on packages, many containing multiple procedures, R can do almost everything that Stata can do and quite a bit more. People are releasing new packages at a rapid pace and R can give you the latest count with the following program.

The first function sets the repositories for R to search. A dialog box will prompt you so you can select them all. Next, the `available.packages` function searches the Internet repositories for the packages that are currently available, and stores their names in myPackageNames. Finally, the `unique` function counts the number of unique package names.

```
> setRepositories()
       (select all of the repositories it offers)
> myPackageNames <- available.packages()
> length(unique( rownames(myPackageNames) ))

[1] 3175
```

So at the time of publication, there were 3,175 add-on packages.

The table below focuses only on a small but important subset of areas. Much more detailed information about R packages is available organized in Task Views at http://cran.r-project.org/web/views/index.html. Another site to search by task is at http://biostat.mc.vanderbilt.edu/s/finder/finder.html. Detailed information about most R packages is available at http://www.r-project.org/, choose CRAN, then choose a mirror, then choose Packages.

Table B.1. Comparison of Stata commands and functions to R functions.

Stata command or function	R function (or package name)
* comment	# comment
append	rbind.fill (reshape); rbind
anova; oneway	aov
bitest	binom.test
ci	confint
clear	rm(list=ls())
correlate	cor, corr.test, corr (Hmisc)
describe	attributes; str; ls.str; contents (Hmisc)
drop	mydata["varname"]<-NULL
edit	fix; edit
findit	help.search
help	help.start
help <topic>	help(<topic>) or ?<topic>
include	source
glm	glm
graph	plot; qplot (Hmisc); ggplot (Hmisc)
infile; infix	read.table; read.csv; read.FWF
keep	Select the variables using any technique.
kwallis	kruskal.test
label values	factor; ordered
label variables	label (Hmisc)
list	print; head; tail;
logistic	glm(...family=binomial)
mean	mean
merge	merge
nbreg	glm.nb()
ologit	polr
outsheet	write.table
poisson	glm(...family=poisson)
predict	predict
qnorm	qqnorm
recode	recode (car)
rename	rename (reshape); names
regress	lm
reshape	reshape; melt/cast (reshape)
save	save; save.image
set	options
search	help.search
ssc	install.packages
signrank	wilcox.test
sort	order
sum	sum
summarize	summary
tab <x>, gen()	factor, ordered
table	CrossTable (gmodels); table
tabulate	table
tabstat	tapply; by; aggregate
ttest	t.test
type	file.show
update	update.packages
use	load
xtgee	gee

C

Automating Your R Setup

Stata has the *profile.do* file lets you automatically set options. R has a similar file called .Rprofile. This file is stored in your initial working directory, which you can locate with the `getwd()` function.

We will look at some useful things to automate in an .Rprofile.

C.1 Setting Options

In your .Rprofile, you can set options just as you would in R. I usually set my console width to 64 so the output fits training examples better. I also ask for five significant digits and tell it to mark significant results with stars. The latter is the default, but since many people prefer to turn that feature off, I included it. You would turn them off with a setting of FALSE.

```
options(width=64, digits=5, show.signif.stars=TRUE)
```

Enter `help(options)` for a comprehensive list of parameters that you can set using the `options` function.

Setting the random number seed is a good idea if you want to generate numbers that are random but repeatable. That is handy for training examples in which you would like every student to see the same result. Here I set it to the number 1234.

```
set.seed(1234)
```

The `setwd` function sets the working directory, the place that all of your files will go if you do not specify a path.

```
setwd("/myRfolder")
```

Since I included the "/" in the working directory path, it will go to the root level of my hard drive. That works in most operating systems. Note that it must be a forward slash, even in Windows, which usually uses backward slashes in filenames. If you leave the slash off completely, it will set it to be a folder within your normal working directory.

C.2 Creating Objects

We also like to define the set of packages that we install whenever we upgrade to a new version of R. With these stored in myPackages, I can install them all with a single function call. For details, see Chapter 2, "Installing and Updating R." This is the list of some of the packages used in this book.

```
myPackages <- c("car","hexbin","ggplot2",
  "gmodels","gplots", "Hmisc",
  "reshape","Rcmdr","prettyR")
```

C.3 Loading Packages

You can have R load load your favorite packages automatically too. This is particularly helpful when setting up a computer to run R with a graphical user interface like R Commander. Loading packages at startup does have some disadvantages though. It slows down your startup time, takes up memory in your workspace, and can create conflicts when different packages have functions with the same name. Therefore, you do not want to load too many this way.

Loading packages at startup requires the use of the `local` function. The `getOption` function gets the names of the original packages to load and stores them in a character vector I named myOriginal. I then created a second character vector, myAutoLoads, containing the names of the packages I want to add to the list. I then combined them into one character vector, myBoth. Finally, I used the `options` function to change the default packages to the combined list of both the original list and my chosen packages:

```
local({
    myOriginal <- getOption("defaultPackages")

    # edit next line to be your list of favorites.
    myAutoLoads <- c("Hmisc","ggplot2")

    myBoth <- c(myOriginal,myAutoLoads)

    options(defaultPackages = myBoth)
})
```

C.4 Running Functions

If you want R to run any functions automatically, you create your own single functions that do the required steps. To have R run a function before all others, name it ".First." To have it run the function after all others, name it ".Last." Notice that utility functions require a prefix of "utils::" or R will not find them while it is starting up. The timestamp function is one of those. It returns the time and date. The cat function prints messages. Its name comes from the UNIX command "cat". It is short for *catenate* (a synonym for concatenate). In essence, we will use it to concatenate the timestamp to your console output.

```
.First <- function()
  {
    cat("\n                Welcome to R!\n")
    utils::timestamp()
    cat("\n")
  }
```

You can also have R run any functions before exiting the package. I have it turn off my graphics device drivers with the graphics.off function to ensure that no files are left open.

I like to have it save my command history in case I later decide I should have saved some of the commands to a script file. Below I print a farewell message and then save the history to a file named myLatest.Rhistory.

```
.Last <- function()
  {
    graphics.off() #turns off graphics devices just in case.
    cat("\n\n  myCumulative.Rhistory has been saved." )
    cat("\n\n  Goodbye!\n\n")
    utils::savehistory(file="myCumulative.Rhistory")
  }
```

WARNING: Since the .First and .Last functions begin with a period, they are invisible to the ls function by default. The function call

```
ls(all.names=TRUE)
```

will show them to you. Since they are functions, if you save a workspace that contains them, they will continue to operate whenever you load that workspace, even if you delete the .Rprofile! This can make it *very* difficult to debug a problem until you realize what is happening. As usual, you can display them by typing their names and run them by adding empty parentheses to them:

```
.First()
```

If you need to delete them from the workspace, rm will do it with no added arguments:

```
rm(.First,.Last)
```

C.5 Example .Rprofile

The following is the .Rprofile with all of the above function calls combined.
You do not have to type this in; it is included in the book's programs and
data files at http://r4stats.com.

```
#      Startup Settings
# Place any R commands below.

options(width=64, digits=5, show.signif.stars=TRUE)
set.seed(1234)
setwd("/myRfolder")
myPackages <- c("car","hexbin","ggplot2",
  "gmodels","gplots", "Hmisc",
  "reshape","ggplot2","Rcmdr")
utils::loadhistory(file = "myCumulative.Rhistory")

# Load packages automatically below.

 local({
   myOriginal <- getOption("defaultPackages")

   # Edit next line to include your favorites.
   myAutoLoads <- c("Hmisc","ggplot2")
   myBoth <- c(myOriginal,myAutoLoads)
   options(defaultPackages = myBoth)
 })

# Things put here are done first.
.First <- function()
  {
    cat("\n                 Welcome to R!\n")
    utils::timestamp()
    cat("\n")
  }

# Things put here are done last.
.Last <- function()
  {
    graphics.off()
    cat("\n\n  myCumulative.Rhistory has been saved." )
    cat("\n\n  Goodbye!\n\n")
    utils::savehistory(file="myCumulative.Rhistory")
  }
```

D

Example Simulation

The following examples are fully working program files. When run, they each create the same synthetic logistic regression data set consisting of 50,000 observations and a response or dependent variable with two normally distributed continuous predictors, x1 and x2. The values assigned to the predictors and intercept are

x1 = 0.75 x2 = −1.25 intercept or constant = 3

The binary response, or dependent variable, is created using a binomial random number generator, based on the linear predictor, xb, which is created from the randomly generated data.

Once the data has been created, it is estimated using the GLM functions of the two software applications. For details, see Joseph Hilbe's article, Creation of Synthetic Discrete Response Regression Models [22].

D.1 Stata Example Simulation

```
* Filename: GenerateLogit.do

clear
set obs 50000
set seed 13579
gen x1 = invnorm(runiform())
gen x2 = invnorm(runiform())
gen xb = 2 + 0.75*x1 - 1.25*x2
gen exb = 1/(1+exp(-xb))
gen by = rbinomial(1, exb)
glm by x1 x2, nolog fam(bin 1)
```

D.2 R Example Simulation

```
# Filename: GenerateLogit.R

library(MASS)
x1 <- runif(50000)
x2 <- runif(50000)
xb <- 2 + .75*x1 - 1.25*x2
exb <- 1/(1+exp(-xb))
by <- rbinom(50000, size = 1, prob =exp)

lry <- glm(by ~ x1 + x2, family=binomial(link="logit"))
summary(lry)
```

References

[1] Carlos Alzola and Jr. Frank E. Harrell. *An Introduction to S and the Hmisc and Design Libraries.* Available from http://biostat.mc.vanderbilt.edu/RS/sintro.pdf, 2006.

[2] Richard A. Becker, Allan R. Wilks, Ray Brownrigg, and Thomas P Minka. *maps: Draw Geographical Maps.* Available from http://cran.r-project.org, 2009. R package version 2.1-0.

[3] Burns. *S poetry.* Available from http://www.burns-stat.com/pages/spoetry.html, 1998.

[4] Dan Carr, ported by Nicholas Lewin-Koh, and Martin Maechler. *hexbin: Hexagonal Binning Routines.* Available from http://cran.r-project.org, 2008.

[5] John M. Chambers. *Software for Data Analysis: Programming with R.* Springer, 2008.

[6] W. S. Cleveland. *Visualizing Data.* Hobart Press, 1993.

[7] R core members, Saikat DebRoy, Roger Bivand, et al. *foreign: Read Data Stored by Minitab, S, SAS, SPSS, Stata, Systat, dBase, ...* Available from http://cran.r-project.org, 2009. R package version 0.8-33.

[8] David B. Dahl. *xtable: Export tables to LaTeX or HTML.* Available from http://cran.r-project.org, 2009. R package version 1.5-5.

[9] Peter Dalgaard. *Introductory Statistics with R (Statistics and Computing).* Springer, 2008.

[10] Martin Elff. *memisc: Tools for Management of Survey Data, Graphics, Programming, Statistics, and Simulation.* Available from http://cran.r-project.org, 2009. R package version 0.95-22.

[11] The R Foundation for Statistical Computing. R: Regulatory compliance and validation issues a guidance document for the use of r in regulated clinical trial environments, 2008. Available from http://www.r-project.org/doc/R-FDA.pdf.

[12] John Fox. *car: Companion to Applied Regression.* Available from http://cran.r-project.org, 2009. R package version 1.2-12.

514   References

[13] John Fox and with contributions from many others. *Rcmdr: R Commander.* Available from http://CRAN.R-project.org, 2009. R package version 1.4-7.

[14] Jr. Frank E. Harrell and with contributions from many other users. *Hmisc: Harrell Miscellaneous.*
Available from http://cran.r-project.org, 2008. R package version 3.5-2.

[15] Michael Friendly. *Visualizing Categorical Data: Data, Stories, and Pictures.* SAS Publishing, 2000.

[16] Robert C. Gentleman, Vincent J. Carey, Douglas M. Bates, Ben Bolstad, Marcel Dettling, Sandrine Dudoit, Byron Ellis, Laurent Gautier, Yongchao Ge, Jeff Gentry, Kurt Hornik, Torsten Hothorn, Wolfgang Huber, Stefano Iacus, Rafael Irizarry, Friedrich Leisch, Cheng Li, Martin Maechler, Anthony J. Rossini, Gunther Sawitzki, Colin Smith, Gordon Smyth, Luke Tierney, Jean Y. H. Yang, and Jianhua Zhang. Bioconductor: Open software development for computational biology and bioinformatics. *Genome Biology,* 5:R80, 2004.

[17] Kenneth W. Haemer. Double scales are dangerous. *The American Statistician,* 2(3):24, 1948.

[18] James W. Hardin and Joseph Hilbe. *Generalized Linear Models and Extensions.* Stata Press, 2001.

[19] James W. Hardin and Joseph Hilbe. *Generalized Estimating Equations.* Chapman & Hall/CRC, 2003.

[20] Markus Helbig and Simon Urbanek. *JGR—Java Gui for R.*
Available from http://www.rosuda.org/JGR, 2009. R package version 1.6-3.

[21] Joeseph Hilbe. *Logistic Regression Models.* Chapman & Hall/CRC Press, 2009.

[22] Joeseph Hilbe. *Creation of Synthetic Discrete Response Regression Models.* Stata Journal, 2010. forthcoming.

[23] Joseph Hilbe. *Negative Binomial Regression.* Cambridge University Press, 2007.

[24] Roger Koenker. *quantreg: Quantile Regression.*
Available from http://cran.r-project.org, 2009. R package version 4.38.

[25] Ulrich Kohler and Frauke Kreuter. *Data Analysis using Stata, 2nd ed.* Stata Press books. Stata Press, 2009.

[26] Max Kuhn and Steve Weaston. *odfWeave: Sweave processing of Open Document Format (ODF) files.*
Available from http://cran.r-project.org, 2009.

[27] Duncan Temple Lang, Debby Swayne, Hadley Wickham, and Michael Lawrence. *rggobi: Interface between R and GGobi.*
Available from http://www.ggobi.org/rggobi, 2008. R package version 2.1.10.

[28] Eric Lecoutre. The R2HTML package. *R News,* 3(3):33–36, 2003.
Available from http://cran.r-project.org.

[29] Friedrich Leisch. Sweave: Dynamic generation of statistical reports using literate data analysis. In Wolfgang Härdle and Bernd Rönz, editors, *Compstat 2002 — Proceedings in Computational Statistics*, pages 575–580. Physica Verlag, 2002.

[30] Jim Lemon and Philippe Grosjean. *prettyR: Pretty descriptive stats*. Available from http://cran.r-project.org, 2009.

[31] Thomas Lumley. *biglm: Bounded Memory Linear and Generalized Linear Models*. Available from http://CRAN.R-project.org, 2009. R package version 0.7.

[32] David Meyer, Achim Zeileis, and Kurt Hornik. *vcd: Visualizing Categorical Data*. Available from http://www.jstatsoft.org/v17/i03/, 2009. R package version 1.2-3.

[33] Michael N. Mitchell. *A Visual Guide to Stata Graphics, 2nd ed.* Stata Press, 2008.

[34] Robert A. Muenchen. *R for SAS and SPSS Users*. Springer, 2008.

[35] Paul Murrell. *R Graphics*. Chapman & Hall/CRC, 2005.

[36] Roger B. Newson. Rsource: Stata module to run r from inside stata using an r source file, 2008. Available from http://ideas.repec.org/c/boc/bocode/s456847.html.

[37] Jose C. Pinheiro and Douglas M. Bates. *Mixed Effects Models in S and S-Plus*. Springer, 2002.

[38] R Development Core Team. *R: A Language and Environment for Statistical Computing*. Available from http://www.R-project.org, 2008.

[39] R Development Core Team. *R Data Import/Export*. Available from http://www.R-project.org, 2008.

[40] Deepayan Sarkar. *Lattice Multivariate Data Visualization with R*. Springer, 2007.

[41] Deepayan Sarkar. *lattice: Lattice Graphics*. Available from http://CRAN.R-project.org, 2009. R package version 0.17-22.

[42] Gregory R. Warnes. Includes R source code and/or documentation contributed by Ben Bolker, Thomas Lumley, , and Randall C Johnson. *gmodels: Various R Programming Tools for Model Fitting*. Available from http://CRAN.R-project.org, 2009. R package version 2.15.0.

[43] Gregory R. Warnes. Includes R source code and/or documentation contributed by (in alphabetical order) Ben Bolker, Lodewijk Bonebakker, Robert Gentleman, Wolfgang Huber Andy Liaw, Thomas Lumley, Martin Maechler, Arni Magnusson, Steffen Moeller, Marc Schwartz, and Bill Venables. *gplots: Various R Programming Tools for Plotting Data*. Available from http://CRAN.R-project.org, 2009. R package version 2.7.1.

[44] Phil Spector. *Data Manipulation with R (Use R)*. Springer, 2008.

[45] StataCorp. *Base Reference Manual*. Stata Press, 2009.

[46] StataCorp. *Data-Management Reference Manual*. Stata Press, 2009.

[47] Deborah F. Swayne, Duncan Temple Lang, Andreas Buja, and Dianne Cook. GGobi: Evolving from XGobi into an extensible framework for interactive data visualization. *Computational Statistics & Data Analysis*, 43:423–444, 2003.

[48] Duncan Temple Lang. The omegahat environment: New possibilities for statistical computing. *Journal of Computational and Graphical Statistics*, 9(3), 2000.

[49] S. Urbanek and M Theus. High interaction graphics for r, 2003. Available from http://rosuda.org/iPlots/iplots.html.

[50] W. N. Venables. Exegeses on linear models, 1998. Available from http://www.stats.ox.ac.uk/pub/MASS3/Exegeses.pdf.

[51] W. N. Venables and B. D. Ripley. *Modern Applied Statistics with S, 4th ed.* Springer, 2002.

[52] W. N. Venables, B. D. Ripley, and the R Core Development Team. *An Introduction to R*. Springer, 2007.

[53] Hadley Wickham. Reshaping data with the reshape package. *Journal of Statistical Software*, 21(12), 2007.

[54] Hadley Wickham. *ggplot2: An Implementation of the Grammar of Graphics*. Available from http://cran.r-project.org, 2008. R package version 0.8.1.

[55] Hadley Wickham. *ggplot2: Elegant Graphics for Data Analysis*. Springer, 2009.

[56] Leland Wilkinson, Graham Wills, Graham Wills, and Anonymous. *The Grammar of Graphics*. Springer, 2005.

[57] Graham Williams. *rattle: A Graphical User Interface for Data Mining in R Using GTK*. Available from http://rattle.togaware.com, 2008. R package version 2.3.128.

Index

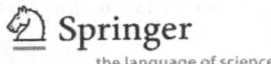
☑ Springer

the language of science

springer.com

R for SAS and SPSS Users

Robert A. Muenchen

Content: Introduction. The five main parts of SAS and SPSS.- Programming conventions.- Typographic conventions.- Installing & updating R.- Running R.- Help and documentation.- Programming language basics.- Data Acquisition.- Selecting Variables - Var, Variables.- Selecting observations - where, if select if, filter.- Selecting both variables and observations.- Converting data structures.- Data management.- Recoding variables. Value labels or formats (& measurement level).- Variable labels.- Generating data.- How R stores data.- Managing your files and workspace.- Graphics overview. - Traditional graphics.- The ggplot2 package.- Statistics.- Summary.- Conclusion.- Appendix A.- Appendix B.- Appendix C.- Bibliography.

2009. XVII, 470 p. Hardcover
Statistics and Computing
ISBN: 978-0-387-09417-5

A Modern Approach to Regression with R

Simon J. Sheather

Content: Introduction.- Simple linear regression.- Diagnostics and transformations for simple linear regression.- Weighted least squares.- Diagnostics and transformations for multiple linear regression.- Variable selection.- Logistic regression.- Serially correlated errors.- Mixed models.- Appendix: Nonparametric smoothing.

2009.XIV, 393 p. Hardcover
2010. Springer Texts in Statistics
ISBN: 978-0-387-09607-0

Data Manipulation with R

Phil Spector

This book presents a wide array of methods applicable for reading data into R, and efficiently manipulating that data. In addition to the built-in functions, a number of readily available packages from CRAN (the Comprehensive R Archive Network) are also covered.

Content: Data in R.- Reading and writing data.- R and databases.- Dates.- Factors.- Subscripting.- Character manipulation.- Data aggregation.- Reshaping data.- Index.

2008. X, 154 p. Softcover
Use R
ISBN: 978-0-387-74730-9

Easy Ways to Order ▶   Call: Toll-Free 1-800-SPRINGER • E-mail: orders-ny@springer.com • Write: Springer, Dept. S8113, PO Box 2485, Secaucus, NJ 07096-2485 • Visit: Your local scientific bookstore or urge your librarian to order.